T0228876

Mobile Agents

Mobile Agents

Basic Concepts, Mobility Models, and the Tracy Toolkit

Peter Braun

Swinburne University of Technology, Victoria, Australia

Wilhelm Rossak

Friedrich Schiller University, Jena, Thuringia, Germany

ELSEVIER

MORGAN KAUFMANN PUBLISHERS

AMSTERDAM • BOSTON • HEIDELBERG • LONDON • NEW YORK • OXFORD
PARIS • SAN DIEGO • SAN FRANCISCO • SINGAPORE • SYDNEY • TOKYO

HEIDELBERG

MORGAN KAUFMANN PUBLISHERS IS AN IMPRINT OF ELSEVIER

Copublished by Morgan Kaufmann Publishers and dpunkt.verlag

Morgan Kaufmann Publishers		**dpunkt.verlag**	
Senior Editor	Tim Cox	Senior Editor	Christa Preisendanz
Publishing Services Manager	Simon Crump		
Assistant Editor	Richard Camp		
Cover Design	Gregory Smith Graphic Design		
Cover Image	Paper, scissors, rock cover image © Digital Vision		
Composition	Cepha Imaging Pvt. Ltd.		
Technical Illustration	Dartmouth Publishing, Inc.		
Copyeditor	Graphic World Inc.		
Proofreader	Graphic World Inc.		
Indexer	Graphic World Inc.		
Interior Printer	The Maple-Vail Book Manufacturing Group		
Cover Printer	Phoenix Color		

Morgan Kaufmann Publishers is an imprint of Elsevier.
500 Sansome Street, Suite 400, San Francisco, CA 94111

This book is printed on acid-free paper.
Available in Germany, Austria, and Switzerland from
dpunkt.verlag
Ringstraße 19B
69115 Heidelberg, Germany
http://www.dpunkt.de

© 2005 by Elsevier Inc. (USA) and dpunkt.verlag (Germany)

Designations used by companies to distinguish their products are often claimed as trademarks or registered trademarks. In all instances in which Morgan Kaufmann Publishers is aware of a claim, the product names appear in initial capital or all capital letters. Readers, however, should contact the appropriate companies for more complete information regarding trademarks and registration.

No part of this publication may be reproduced, stored in a retrieval system, or transmitted in any form or by any means—electronic, mechanical, photocopying, scanning, or otherwise—without prior written permission of the publisher.

Permissions may be sought directly from Elsevier's Science & Technology Rights Department in Oxford, UK: phone: (+44) 1865 843830, fax: (+44) 1865 853333, e-mail: *permissions@ elsevier.com.uk*. You may also complete your request on-line via the Elsevier homepage (*http://elsevier.com*) by selecting "Customer Support" and then "Obtaining Permissions."

Library of Congress Cataloging-in-Publication Data
Application submitted

MK ISBN: 1-55860-817-6
dpunkt ISBN: 3-89864-298-4

For information on all Morgan Kaufmann publications,
visit our Web site at *www.mkp.com* or *www.books.elsevier.com*

Printed and bound by CPI Group (UK) Ltd, Croydon, CR0 4YY

Transferred to digital print 2012

Dedicated to Ines, my soul and my life.
Willi

For my parents.
Peter

Preface

The Internet, as we know it and use it today, is a huge repository of information about almost any possible topic. However, the full power of available technologies has not yet been exhausted, and new technologies are integrated into the World Wide Web on a daily basis. The focus of these technologies and new features moves more and more toward the easy use of all the resources provided by the Internet, while the question of simply providing relatively unstructured information will be of less importance in the future. Thus, we expect the World Wide Web to evolve dramatically in the future, improving accessibility, flexibility, and automation most of all.

Currently, the two most used applications on the World Wide Web are search engines and online shops. Search engines are supposed to help you navigate through the sheer mass of unstructured information. However, in most cases they fall short of that goal because they cannot manage the information overload in any suitable manner, especially for the professional usage of the Internet's resources. Most online shops still act more or less like electronic catalogs, being a simple copy of what was delivered in plain paper to our doorsteps for years. They lack the necessary support of customer management and target a fairly conservative client-server type of network, failing to acknowledge the advent of new and mobile communication platforms.

The new buzzwords for the Internet community in the future must and will be *automation* and *mobility*. Ubiquitous computing will be the standard, and products will be ordered and consumed "on demand," that is, when and where the need is triggered. This means that the typical customer is no longer prepared to wait until a fat client with a high-bandwidth connection is available. Small devices that can be carried around without effort will have to do, while we expect, of course, to stay connected to the Internet at all times. Placing an order will not be time-consuming matter of navigating an endless number of nodes but rather will be a specification of what we want. The rest will be left to our trusted, and hopefully personalized, software that will take care of business in a highly autonomous and professional fashion.

Imagine yourself, for example, instructing your mobile phone to go shopping on the Internet: A piece of software will search for product information, compare prices, hunt down bargains, and, finally, buy the desired good with electronic cash—all without keeping your phone online for the next 3 hours and ruining your eyes with a tiny display. In addition, we expect our software to act in a proactive fashion, that is, to be intelligent enough to interpret our needs beyond the level of basic keyword matching. Mobility will be the key issue not only for the hardware platform but also for the software agent that actually performs the task at hand. The agent should travel to visit the distributed information sources and perform the proactive filtering right at the source instead of downloading massive amounts of possibly irrelevant data to its master's home platform.

Assume that you want to organize a business trip while you are driving home in your car. Wouldn't it be helpful if you could instruct your laptop software, in a short break, to negotiate a fitting flight, reserve a rental car, book a hotel, coordinate the date with your business partner, and buy the tickets for your favorite opera (as you are in town anyway)? The software has, of course, learned that you prefer to drive a Mercedes rather than a Volkswagen and will act accordingly—a fact that is automatically ignored should you work for a university. The job will be done faster and more efficiently than any human could do it, all while you are driving home safely. Your laptop will act as the starting platform only and go offline, thus avoiding the need to squeeze possibly relevant data through a low-bandwidth connection. The agent goes to the data and works in an asynchronous mode. The results, already checked and filtered for relevance, can then be delivered to a new destination, for example, the workstation at your office. There they can checked by you the next morning, in a situation that fits your time frame and needs.

How will we enable, support, design, and program these new types of applications? What is the technology that will serve as the infrastructure for these new features? We want to go further than basic capability; we want a well-structured and scalable technology based on solid engineering principles. Thus, we accept arguments that a number of technologies might be able to solve the tasks involved in our scenario, but we believe strongly that only one technology has the potential to do it right. As you might have already guessed reading the title of this book, we believe that *mobile agents* will be the technology to enable this next generation of Web-based software systems. So what are mobile agents?

Mobile agents are small software entities that can act as your autonomous representative. They can travel through the World Wide Web, or any other network, in order to translate your specification—the "what"—into a possible solution (e.g., tickets for the opera or 50 tons of crude oil for your refinery). They take care of how that solution is found (i.e., they will do the browsing, comparing, and negotiating). In more technical terms, mobile agents have the capacity to work in an asynchronous and autonomous mode, as long as the basic infrastructure they need is available. This infrastructure is basically a network of execution platforms and will be discussed at length in this book.

Using mobile agents means that you, as the owner of such an agent, do not have to stay glued to your workstation to get the job done; your mobile agent will do it faster and most likely more completely, giving you a free hand to do the really important things in life (which means, of course, to do your job even better).

The most important characteristic of mobile agents is that they will be able to visit the nodes of the network directly and are not limited to down-loading information to a fixed platform. Imagine them as a very sophisticated search engine that works on demand and is able to go where the information is, not only adding improved flexibility to the search process but also saving bandwidth, avoiding network latency, and reacting more quickly to a dynamic network environment. This makes the whole concept extremely flexible and supports very naturally the need for automation and mobility. Agents are fast, are smart if necessary, and will accept very small platforms and fairly simple interfaces to start their task. Later on, while migrating through the Web, they will simply use the available local computing power of the Web (i.e., that of hosting servers and other nodes).

Well, this sounds crazy, doesn't it? Mobile agents are indeed a fascinating topic. However, although most of the techniques necessary to implement theses applications are readily available, probably only a few people have ever used mobile agents for industrial-strength applications. The reasons for this are that, despite almost 10 years of research all over the world, only a few systems exist that support the related concepts sufficiently, and some problem areas (e.g., security questions) are still in discussion.

Thus, the intention of our book is twofold. On one hand, we want to introduce you to this fascinating topic and survey the current state-of-the-art technology in a wide area of mobile agent–related research. As fans of the technology, we will present the far reaching possibilities this new technology offers, especially for the future of advanced distributed (information) systems. In doing this, we hope to encourage practitioners to use this technology and to compare it with alternatives. We are sure that the evaluation will be quite favorable for mobile agent systems.

However, we also want to pinpoint the limits and shortcomings of the currently available mobile agent technology. This should help you mitigate risks and make an educated decision about whether mobile agents are the right solution for your problem. Through this discussion, we hope to provide the mobile agent community with links and ideas for future improvements.

This book is the first attempt we are aware of to provide a common introduction to the technology of mobile agents. Earlier books about this topic typically have dealt with specific mobile agent toolkits and/or introduced mostly the programming perspective of mobile agents without discussing the technological infrastructure.

The most valuable and complete book we know of is *Programming and Deploying Java Mobile Agents with Aglets*, by **?**. It introduces the Aglets mobile agent toolkit developed by IBM. After a short presentation of software agents and mobile agents, the more technical advantages of mobile agents are explained. The rest of this book serves as a very good introduction into programming the Aglets systems. Another good book is *Mobile Agents: Explanations and Examples*, by **?**, but it is rather outdated by now. Their book focuses on programming aspects of four mobile mobile agent toolkits (Telescript, Ara, AgentTCL, and Aglets). Two of them are no longer available products or ongoing projects. Aglets is now an open-source project (see *aglets.sourceforge.net* for more information), and AgentTCL, now named *D'Agents*, is an ongoing project at Dartmouth College (see *www.agent.cs.dartmouth.edu* for more information). This book also introduces briefly the technology on which the whole mobile agent paradigm is based and touches on the problems that come along with the mobility of agents.

Of course, some good books about specialized topics in the area of mobile agent systems do exist, for example, discussing security or agent communication. These books complement the more general focus of our presentation nicely. We provide links to them in Part II of our book, where we present the technological framework for mobile agents and refer to the individual related topics.

Who Should Read This Book?

Our book is designed to be useful for different audiences. First, it can be used as an introduction to the wide field of mobile agent technology, for researchers, students, and practitioners alike. It can help to get the big picture and to understand trade-offs and capabilities. Second, it can be used by researchers who work in a particular subdomain and want to get an overview of related ongoing research and topics. Finally, it can be used to get some detailed hands-on experience in programming mobile agents within a working environment that has reached industrial strength. We have set up a Web site from which our Tracy mobile agent toolkit can be downloaded.

We assume that you have some basic understanding of object-oriented programming languages in general, and specifically of the Java programming language. Java has been for some years now the *de facto* standard programming language for mobile agents. We will introduce and explain techniques such as object serialization, dynamic downloading, and reflection, where necessary, but we will not provide a Java beginner's course.

Contents

The following outline shows the structure of our book. We recommend that you read it first to determine the sequence of chapters that suits your needs best.

Part I: Motivation for and Introduction to Mobile Agents This part provides a brief introduction to mobile software agents. We encourage the use of mobile agents by drawing a picture of the requirements of future distributed systems and comparing mobile agents to some other techniques currently used on the Internet.

Part II: Mobile Agents—Concepts, Functions, and Possible Problems This part of our book is intended to establish a firm understanding of mobile agents as a technology. We abstract from specific toolkits and establish a common framework of basic concepts, functions, and features. We also address problems common to most mobile agent systems and characterize the current state-of-the-art technology.

Part III: The Kalong Mobility Model This part contains a detailed specification of our new mobility model, Kalong, and the underlying network protocol, SATP. A reference implementation as independent software component is presented.

Part IV: The Tracy Mobile Agent Toolkit In the last part of this book, we will show how to actually work with a mobile agent toolkit, called Tracy, which we developed. We will also present architecture and implementation details, using Tracy as a test bed and example.

Acknowledgments

First, our thanks go to all the members of the Tracy research team for the many years of devoted work they invested into the project and their constant belief in a new and still little-known technology. It is sometimes not easy to be asked for the hundredth time what this is all about and whether you really believe that it is a good idea to specialize in this research domain. You did the right thing, guys! We would like to include a short list of names of the most important team members.

Thanks to Christian Erfurth for his work on the first version of Tracy and on letting agents communicate. Thanks to Jan Eismann for his work on the domain manager concept and for never-ending discussions on the architecture of mobile agent toolkits, which led to the idea for the second version of Tracy and the new plugin-oriented software architecture.

Many thanks to Sven Geisenhainer for his unfatiguing work on Tracy2. Sven was mainly involved in the development of the kernel and did a great job with developing some of the main plugins, in particular the command line user interface. Thanks to Volkmar Schau for his initial work in implementing the new Tracy architecture and thanks to Ingo Müller for this work on the application level of mobile agents by designing an electronic marketplace on top of Tracy.

Many thanks to Christian Fensch and Steffen Schlötzer for their work on ByCAl, a Java Application Programming Interface (API) to analyze Java byte code; Steffen Kern for his work on migration optimization techniques; and Tino Schlegel for designing and implementing Tiffany, the Web-based graphical user interface, and for developing a whole test suite for Tracy. Thanks to Matthias Heunecke for implementing the pipeline concept in the migration plugin. Thanks to Carsten Panzner for implementing some of the security enhancements. Finally, thanks to Arndt Döhler for interesting discussions about possible improvements of Tracy with regard to Web services and Grid computing.

Beyond the core Tracy team, we would also like to thank Bill Buchanan, Ulrich Pinsdorf, and Corinna Flues. Their feedback and support, as well as their always-constructive criticism, helped us to keep going and to strive for the better solution, even if the easier one might have been good enough for internal purposes. You helped us take a big step toward a framework in which theory and practice coexist in a healthy balance. Finally, many thanks to Tim Cox and Richard Camp at Morgan Kaufmann and Sarah Hager at Graphic World for all of their assistance and advice, which has been a real help to us.

Peter Braun   Willi Rossak
Melbourne, Australia   Jena, Germany

How to Contact Us

We have verified all information and tested all examples presented in this book to the best of our ability, but you might find a mistake or an omission, or you might just have suggestions for future editions. Please contact us by writing an e mail to

braun@mobile-agents.org   or   *rossak@mobile-agents.org.*

We have a Web page for this book, where you can find all source code examples and where we will list known errors and frequently asked questions. You will also find links to all projects and persons mentioned in this book. You can access this page at:

www.mobile-agents.org.

At this Web site, you can also download the latest version of the Tracy mobile agent toolkit, in an evaluation version, for free.

About the Authors

Peter Braun is a postdoctoral research fellow at the Center for Intelligent and Multi-Agent Systems in the Faculty of Information and Communication Technology at Swinburne University of Technology, Melbourne, Australia. He received an M.S. and a Ph.D. in computer science from Friedrich Schiller University of Jena, Germany. His research interests include mobile agents, especially agent migration protocols, and Grid services.

Willi Rossak is a professor of Software and Systems Engineering at Friedrich Schiller University Jena, Germany. He received his diploma and Ph.D. in computer science from the Vienna University of Technology, Austria. He specializes in the modeling and development of distributed dynamic systems with a focus on the upstream tasks of the software life cycle and has published more than sixty research papers on a wide variety of topics in software and systems engineering.

Contents

Part II
Mobile Agents—Concepts, Functions, and Possible Problems

Part III

The Kalong Mobility Model—Specification and Implementation

Part IV
The Tracy Mobile Agent Toolkit

Part I

Motivation for and Introduction to Mobile Agents

Chapter 1

Designing Innovative Distributed Systems

Until some years ago, the term *distributed system* was mainly used to describe a network of several computer systems with separated memory that are connected to each other by a dedicated network. The computers used in such a distributed system are almost homogeneous, which means that they have the same type of processor and the same type of operating system. The network is more or less static: Computers are only rarely switched off, network connections between hosts are always reliable and provide constant bandwidths, each computer has a fixed IP address, and network packet routing is done via local switches. This type of network is still typical for most applications.

Currently, we see rapidly evolving network and computer technologies. The Internet as a *network of networks* with heterogeneous computers has become widely accepted as a very important medium for any kind of information exchange. The number of people and companies providing services on the Internet increases continuously and is even surpassed by the number of Internet users. Many different types of services are offered on the Internet, first of all electronic mail and electronic file exchange. Without any doubt, the most successful Internet service is the World Wide Web. Whereas in the beginning the Web was only a medium to publish your data on your Web site, we now see novel applications in the Web that involve a growing amount of computation, dynamics, and interdependencies.

Most of these applications are part of the electronic commerce domain, for example, online shops or electronic marketplaces. However, they are still built using a traditional design technique called client-server, in which a single powerful computer system (server) holds data to be shared over the network and less powerful computer systems (clients) access the server using a network. In Internet applications the server not only holds data but also executes application code in the form of Java servlets or some other kind of server-based language. In this paradigm the client is responsible only for the graphical user interface, which is, in Internet applications, some kind of Web interface using HTML pages.

We believe that what we know as a distributed system has to be expanded. Again, the Web can be considered a predecessor of these future distributed systems, as we notice an exponential growth of services available on the Internet already. In the future we will see hundreds of millions of people getting online by different means, using hundreds of millions of services on the Internet. Only in the network's core, the portion that remains stable for most of the time it exists, will connections be of copper or fiber; on the edges of the network, wireless connections based on new standards such as Bluetooth, WLAN, and UMTS will become popular. Bandwidth in the center of the network will increase dramatically in the future, and it will cover upcoming demands for the transmission of large amounts of data as needed, for example, in video streaming. On the outskirts of the network, however, available bandwidth will not increase as quickly as in the center. People still use, and perhaps will continue to use, Internet connections via ISDN or xDSL. Therefore, the bandwidth gap between backbone and end-user connection will increase. Because backbone connections are frequently renewed compared with the local bandwidths, this trend will continue in the future.

Two major trends can already be seen entering the mainstream of interest. *Pervasive computing* means that everything might become a node in a distributed system. As computers become smaller and smaller, they can be found not only on desks but also in cars to regulate speed control, on wrists to show the time and control pulse, and in refrigerators to monitor the temperature.

In the future, even more devices and appliances will be equipped with small computers, for example, your coffee machine might be able to *learn* that you always have two cups of coffee at 6:30 AM and make them for you, an intelligent light switch could recognize you coming into a room and switch on the light the way you prefer it, or intelligent cloth might monitor your vital functions and notify you (or your doctor) in case of any serious event. These computer systems are characterized by limited resources, especially in regard to memory and processing power.

Moreover, all these tiny computer systems will be able to communicate to each other using spontaneous *ad hoc* networks: Your refrigerator will inform your personal digital assistant (PDA) to ask for fresh groceries; your PDA will order them in the supermarket, should you be there anyway to pick up other items, or will contact your preferred market via a remote message (or better, an agent that will be able to negotiate the best price and quality) should you run out of time; finally, your refrigerator will be notified that the groceries were delivered, perhaps by the PDA of the delivery service. Your T-shirt will set up a meeting with your physician if your heart rate and blood pressure go through the roof too often, or it might cut the chips and the donuts from your shopping list, even though your refrigerator wanted to order them for you. All these transactions will have to use, at least partially, wireless networks, and they will be characterized by small bandwidth and low reliability. (Thus, if you are lucky, your chips will never be successfully cut from the list, but it could also mean that your doctor appointment was never set up!)

The second trend we want to mention here is *nomadic computing*, which means that users move from place to place while working, logging into the system from very different computer systems (e.g., first from a system in the office over the company-wide LAN, later from home over an ISDN dial-up connection). Nevertheless, users want to see nearly the same working environment, the same applications, and, above all, the same data. In addition, nomadic users demand a seamless integration of different devices, making it possible to change the working environment from a desktop computer to a PDA in a few seconds.

All these new trends require new network-centric programming techniques that are based on a true peer-to-peer principle. The client-server design pattern, successfully used for distributed systems in LANs, is not able to face all the challenges of future distributed systems described previously and is, in its basic concept, still a centralized paradigm.

As we mentioned, many technologies have the potential to solve some of the new problems encountered, such as proxy-based concepts. However, most of them are just variations of the centralized approach or invoke, by definition, network centered penalties. Thus, they will, as we see it, not be able to manage the task at hand and lack the elegance and natural fit necessary to survive in a dynamic and fully distributed world of networked information sources.

Because something is possible does not mean that it is appropriate for the task at hand; we usually do not program large applications on the level of assembler code anymore, even though we could. Today we use object-oriented methods and languages, because they come much closer to the concepts and needs of our customers and our own, relatively high, level of thinking during systems development. In a similar fashion you could look at mobile code as a paradigm that inherently accepts distribution and networking as a basic concept and, thus, fits our new network-centric projects well, giving us the chance to reach a new level of abstraction and quality. This argument, above all technical details and discussions, is what drives our belief in the mobile agent approach.

Mobile agents are a special type of mobile code. *Mobile code* is a technique in which code is transferred from the computer system that stores the code files to the computer system that will execute the code. A well-known example of mobile code is Java applets, which are small programs available in a portable and interpretable byte code format. Applets are transferred from a Web server to a Web browser in order to be executed as part of an HTML page.

A mobile agent is a program that can migrate from a starting host to many other hosts in a network of heterogeneous computer systems and fulfill a task specified by its owner. It works autonomously and communicates with other agents and host systems. During the self-initiated migration, the agent carries all its code and data, and in some systems it also carries some kind of execution state.

One difference between Java applets and mobile agents is the fact that mobile agents initiate the migration process, whereas the migration of Java applets is initiated from other software components (e.g., the Web browser). Another difference is that Java applets migrate only from a server to a client and do not leave the client to migrate to another client or back to the server. An applet's lifetime is bound to the lifetime of the Web page it is part of and dies when the browser terminates or another Web page is requested. In contrast to this, mobile agents usually migrate more than once. Think of a mobile agent that travels to several hosts to collect prices for a desired product.

As a consequence, the software components we design will have to be as dynamic and mobile as the end users and the networks. They will have to be proactive and act in a very autonomous fashion, or even better "intelligently." The concept of software agents emerges from these demands.

Chapter 2

From Client-Server to Mobile Agents

We start our exploration of mobile agents at the origin of the notion *agent*, and we compare the already widespread term of *intelligent agents* to our understanding of *mobile agents*. When looking at the history of mobile agents we will learn that this research topic has its roots in distributed computing rather than in artificial intelligence.

After reading this chapter, you will have a basic understanding of the most important technical terms and will have a general idea of the main advantages of mobile agents compared with other, more traditional paradigms to design distributed systems, such as client-server.

Contents

2.1 A First Look at Mobile Agents

In this section we try to converge on the idea of mobile agents from two sides. First, we discuss *software agents* as a concept developed in the area of artificial intelligence in the mid-1970s. People from artificial intelligence disciplines define software agents as having some mandatory features, which do not include *mobility*. Sometimes, it is mentioned that there might arise some benefits from using mobile agents in the future; otherwise it is claimed that agent mobility is a pretty useless feature. This view can be best described by the statement that mobile agents are a *solution in search of a problem.*[1]

Second, we try to define mobile agents from the viewpoint of software engineering and distributed systems. We will see that *mobile agents* in our understanding do not have much to do with artificial intelligence but are to be considered another design paradigm for a special type of distributed systems. From this viewpoint, emphasis lies on research of the *consequences* of the mobility of code, and it is these consequences that we focus on in this book.

Naturally, both research communities can benefit from each other. Some work has already been done to add intelligent agents with mobility as a common feature, and recently people have begun to work to make mobile agents more intelligent, for example, to help them plan their itineraries. Hopefully, both branches of research will join each other eventually.

2.1.1 The Artificial Intelligence Point of View

Let's start with the notion of *software agents.* The word *agent* derives from the Latin word for actor, meaning a person who acts on behalf of another. In different languages the notion *agent* is used with different meanings. In English-speaking countries, for example, the word agent is often used in a more general context, whereas in German-speaking countries an agent mostly works for the secret service. Usually, a *real estate agent* is employed to aid in renting or buying a house, and a *travel agent* is visited to aid in planning a vacation. In physical science, an agent can be an active substance that causes a reaction. Other sciences also use the term *agent.* For example, in legal sciences an *agent provocateur* is a person hired to incite suspected persons to commit some illegal action that will make them liable for punishment.

In computer science, the term *agent* has been used since the mid-1970s. It was introduced to the area of artificial intelligence. Most authors refer to a paper written by Hewitt [1977] as origin of the term *agent.* According to Foner [1997], the first reference can be traced back to Vannevar Bush and Douglas Engelbart in the late 1950s and early 1960s.

---

1. Stated by John Ousterhout during an interview that is published online [IEEE IC-Online, 1997].

Nowadays, the term *agent* has (unfortunately) become a buzzword to signal innovative system characteristics. For example, some electronic mail clients are called *mail agents*, although they do nothing aside from the usual task of delivering and collecting emails from your mailbox.

A software agent is a software entity that continuously performs tasks given by a user within a particular restricted environment. The involved software entity can be a computer program, a software component, or, in the meaning of object-oriented programming languages, just a simple object. However, true software agents must be seen as an extension of the more general concept of objects or software components. Whereas software objects are passive, agents are active.

The definition of what exactly constitutes a software agent has been intensely debated in the research community for several years. Although this debate continues, there is a common understanding that a software entity must exhibit certain minimal features to qualify as an agent:

Autonomy Agents operate and behave according to a self-made plan that is generated in accordance with the user-given task. Agents do not need every step of this plan stipulated by their owner in advance, and they do not ask their owner for confirmation of every step.

Social behavior Agents are able to communicate with other agents or human beings by means of an agent communication language. Communication can be restricted to pure exchange of information or can include sophisticated protocols for negotiation, for example, when trading the price for a good or joining an auction. A separate branch of research deals with the problem of multiple agents working together on a single task in so-called multi-agent systems. In this case, benevolent behavior is necessary for a successful undertaking.

Reactivity Agents perceive their environment by some kind of sensors and are able to react to identified events.

Proactivity Not only do agents react to stimuli from their environment, but they are also able to take initiative and actively plan. B. Le Du explains this with the following metaphor: *"The difference between an automaton and an agent is somewhat like the difference between a dog and a butler. If you send your dog to buy a copy of the New York Times every morning, it will come back with its mouth empty if the news stand happens to have run out of this specific newspaper one day. In contrast, the butler will probably take the initiative and buy a copy of the*

Washington Post, since he knows, that sometimes you read it instead." [Bradshaw, 1996, p. 16]

The interested reader is referred to some books that serve as comprehensive introductions to all fields of intelligent software agent research and from which more information about these topics can be gleaned and also more definitions for software agents found. *Software Agents,* edited by Bradshaw [1996], contains a collection of papers concerning the areas of agent-supported user interfaces, agents for learning and intelligent assistance, and a summary of agent communication, collaboration, and mobility. Second, *Agent Technology Handbook,* by Chorafas [1997] also gives an introduction to many agent-related topics. In addition, the book contains several links to real-world projects. It describes possible application areas for software agents. A part of it is dedicated to application areas in business, for example, information filtering agents. *Readings in Agents,* edited by Huhns and Singh [1997], contains articles concerning a wide area of software agent topics, especially including a chapter in which possible agent-based applications are described. Finally, we would like to mention two books which focus on multi-agent systems. The first is *Multi-agent Systems. Introduction to Distributed Artificial Intelligence* by Jacques Ferber [1999]. It is a wonderful introduction to multi-agent systems and distributed artificial intelligence, and covers topics like cooperation, organization, and communication between agents. The second is *Multiagent Systems: A Modern Approach to Distributed Artificial Intelligence,* edited by Gerhard Weiss [2000]. This book provides a comprehensive introduction multi-agent systems. Many important topics, from distributed problem solving and searching algorithms for agents, to learning in multi-agent systems, are covered. Good overview papers for software agents, from the point of view of artificial intelligence, are given by Wooldridge and Jennings [1995a,b]. Another paper that can serve as an introduction to the wider field of software agents is the presentation of Green et al. [1997]. The authors provide a good overview of the various areas of agent research, and they already mention the concept of mobile agents.

We can now try to add *mobility* to our definitions of software agents:

Mobile software agents are computer programs that act as representatives in the global network of computer systems. The agent knows its owner, knows his or her preferences, and learns by communicating with its owner. The user can delegate tasks to the agent, which is able to search the network efficiently by moving to the service or information provider. Mobile agents support nomadic users because the agent can work asynchronously while the user is offline. Finally, the agent reports results of its work to the user through different communication channels such as electronic mails, Web sites, pagers, or mobile phones.

In this definition, many of the characteristics of software agents that we described earlier can be found. A mobile agent acts on behalf of a user; it knows its user and gets to know him or her better over time. It has social behavior because it is able to communicate with the user, services, or even other agents. It works proactively, because it can, for example, contact its owner by many means of communication. The additional property of mobility can be seen as a very straightforward extension, at least from a human point of view, as it goes well with our natural understanding of how to search for information in a distributed environment.

2.1.2 The Distributed Systems Point of View

In contrast to the more end-user–oriented definition for mobile agents given in the last section, in which mobility was just a nice-to-have feature, we start here with a definition that draws more attention on the technical aspects of agent mobility.

Mobile agents refer to self-contained and identifiable computer programs, bundled with their code, data, and execution state, that can move within a heterogeneous network of computer systems. They can suspend their execution on an arbitrary point and transport themselves to another computer system. During this *migration* the agent is transmitted completely, that is, as a set of code, data, and execution state. At the destination computer system, an agent's execution is resumed at exactly the point where it was suspended before.

There is nothing left in this definition from the characteristics of a software agent. We simply talk about computer programs or processes in the meaning of operating systems that are able to freeze themselves, move to other computer systems, and resume execution there. This more technical definition can be seen as a complement of the user-driven definition, simply targeting a lower level of abstraction.

In this case, mobile agents are seen from the viewpoint of software engineering and distributed systems. They can be considered an additional design paradigm in the area of distributed programming and a useful supplement of traditional techniques such as the client-server architecture.

Traditional Techniques for Distributed Computing

In this section we summarize three very important design paradigms used for the development of today's distributed systems. In this short discussion we restrict ourselves to approaches regarding distribution of functions in contrast to distribution of data. In the first group of approaches, we focus on client-server–based design paradigms as an example, where all code components are immobile, and introduce two early approaches of paradigms based on the idea of mobile code. We do not consider implementation and language details in this section; we describe only the architecture of systems based on these paradigms. In this overview, we are not interested in approaches to distribute data, as, for example, distributed database systems or peer-to-peer file sharing.[2]

In particular, we use the following definitions.[3] A *site* represents the notion of location in a distributed system, for example, a single computer as part of a network. A site hosts *resources*, which are any kind of immovable files, databases, or any external devices. A site also hosts and executes *code*, for example, by using a *virtual machine* or simply a microprocessor. We assume virtual machines to be immobile too,[4] although moving processes is possible in distributed operating systems. The code contains the know-how to perform a specific computation. Note that a computation can be successful only if code and necessary resources are located at the same site. Finally, we have *interactions* between code, resources, and virtual machines on the same or on different sites.

---

2. We are aware of the fact that we disregard some aspects of peer-to-peer systems when we restrict ourselves to file-sharing approaches. The peer-to-peer network architecture is built on the idea of having almost identical computer systems with regard to capabilities and responsibilities. This type of architecture must obviously be seen in contrast to client-server built systems, in which we have a clear separation of both capabilities and responsibility between client and server. In a peer-to-peer network, each user publishes resources (e.g., files, computing power) that are going to be shared with other users directly, without management of some central server. However, peer-to-peer systems neither imply nor prohibit code mobility as we will describe it. Compare, for example, Seti@home [Anderson, 2001] as a project where clients offer their computing power, or Napster [Shirky, 2001] and Freenet [Langley, 2001] as file-sharing approaches. None of these projects makes use of code mobility. For a comprehensive introduction into the ideas of peer-to-peer systems, we refer to the book by Oram [2001].

3. For the following, we were inspired by Vigna [1998, p. 36] and Picco [1998, p. 38].

4. Vigna and Picco define a *computational component* as "active executors capable to carry out a computation," which are allowed to migrate to other sites, whereas in our approach *virtual machines* are immobile.

In the following, we write S_A for a site with name A, R_A^M for a resource with name M at S_A, C^N for code with name N, C_A^N for code with name N at S_A, and M_A^N for a virtual machine executing code C_A^N at site S_A.

Client-Server Paradigm

Client-server is the most common paradigm of distributed computing at present. In this paradigm (Fig. 2.1(a)), there is code C^S executed by a virtual

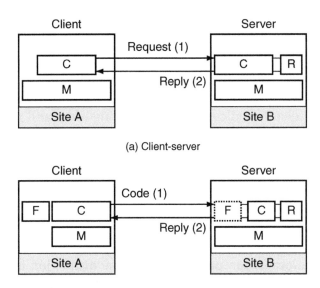

(a) Client-server

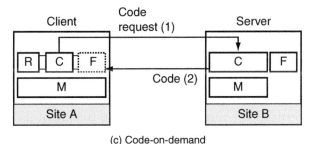

(b) Remote-evaluation: Code fragment F, which is not executed at site A, is sent to site B and executed there. Dashed lines indicate that a component is dynamically loaded at site B

(c) Code-on-demand

Figure 2.1 Examples for traditional design paradigms. M stands for a virtual machine, R for a resource, C for a code component, and F for a code fragment. Lines between components indicate interactions; numbers indicate the order. No numbers are needed for a simple request/reply interaction.

machine M_B^S (server) offering a set of services (e.g., access to resources R_B^x) at S_B and code C^C executed by virtual machine M_A^C (client) that needs these services to accomplish its task. Therefore, it sends a request to the server using an interaction in which it asks for execution of a specific service, supplemented by some additional parameters. M_B^S executes the requested service using resources located at S_B and sends the result back to M_A^C using an additional interaction.

In this paradigm, all components are stationary with respect to execution. The request usually contains the name of the service along with some additional parameters. This concept is comparable to a procedure call in programming languages; therefore, several programming concepts were developed that offer convenient use of the client-server concept in programming languages, for example *Remote Procedure Call* (RPC) [Birrell and Nelson, 1984; Nelson, 1981], CORBA [OMG, 2002], or Java *Remote Method Invocation* (RMI) [Sun, 2002]. In recent years, a new technique for client-server–based distributed computing is gaining more and more popularity, that is, Web Services [Newcomer, 2002]. Whereas CORBA or RMI-based applications are mainly developed to be executed in intranet-scale networks, Web services target at the development of applications that are glued together from software components widely distributed in the Internet.

Remote-Evaluation Paradigm

In the remote-evaluation paradigm the same distinction is made between server and client as in the client-server paradigm (Fig. 2.1(b)). Thus, there is code C^S executed by virtual machine M_B^S at site S_B having access to local resources and code C^C executed by virtual machine M_A^C at site S_A. Important resources are located at site S_B. In contrast to the client-server paradigm, virtual machine M_B^S does not offer a suitable application-specific service that the client M_A^C could use. Instead, the client sends code fragment C^F (which has not been executed so far) to the server to be executed there. Virtual machine M_B^S executes this piece of code, for example, by simply initiating a new virtual machine M_B^F. During execution, local resources at site S_B are used, and afterward the result is sent back to the client using an additional interaction.

In this paradigm the code fragment C^F is mobile and sent from the client to the server. The type of code depends on the concrete implementation of this paradigm and might be either some kind of script language that is transmitted as source code or some intermediate code format that can be easily interpreted at the server. This technique is described by Stamos [1986]; similar approaches were already published earlier. Examples are described in Section 2.2, A Short History of Mobile Agents.

Code-on-Demand Paradigm

In the code-on-demand paradigm, roles are switched compared with those of the remote-evaluation paradigm (Fig. 2.1(c)). Here, virtual machine M_A^C has access to some resources R_A^x but lacks the know-how to access them. The code to access the resources is currently located at S_B. Thus, M_A^C interacts with M_B^S by requesting the information in form of code C^F. The code is executed at S_A by M_A^F.

In this paradigm the code fragment F is mobile and sent from the server to the client. Concerning the type of code, the same remarks as given in the last section apply. Java applets are a very prominent example of this design paradigm.

Characteristics of Mobile Agents

Recalling our definition of mobile agents and considering them as a new design paradigm for distributed systems that supplement more traditional techniques, we can now identify four characteristics of mobile agents:

1. Mobile agents are typically used in wide-area and heterogeneous networks in which no assumptions can be made concerning either the reliability of the connected computers or the security of the network connections.

2. The mobile agent's migration is initiated by the agent (more precisely, its programmer), in contrast to mobile object systems, in which object migration is initiated by the underlying operating system or middleware.

3. Migration of mobile agents is done to access resources available only at other servers in the network and not just for load-balancing, as in mobile object systems.

4. Mobile agents are able to migrate more than once—this characteristic is sometimes called *multi-hop* ability. After a mobile agent has visited the first server, it might migrate further to other servers to continue its task,

whereas mobile code is transferred only once in the remote-evaluation paradigm and the code-on-demand paradigm.

Let's have a closer look at this technical definition before moving on: By the term *code* we mean some kind of executable representation of computer programs. With script languages, such as Perl or TCL, this could be the source code; with the Java programming language [Arnold et al., 2000], it is the portable intermediate Java byte code format; and with the C programming language, it could be the executable machine language format for a single processor. By the term *data* we mean all variables of the agent (in object-oriented languages, it is the set of all attributes of the corresponding object). Finally, by the term *state* we mean information about the execution state of the agent. We leave open what exactly comprises the execution state. It might be quite complete information from within the underlying (virtual) machine about call stack, register values, and instruction pointers. As we will discuss in detail later in this book, most Java-based mobile agent toolkits do not provide a sophisticated determination of the execution stack, because of some limitations of the Java virtual machine.

Mobile Agents as a New Design Paradigm

In the notion we introduced in Section 2.1.2, The Distributed Systems Point of View, we can describe the mobile agents paradigm as follows (see Fig. 2.2). At site S_A a virtual machine M_A^T has the know-how in the form of code, which is then executed. During this execution the code realizes that it needs access to some other resources currently located at site S_B. Thus, M_A^T interacts with M_B^U to transmit the code, together with some information about the current

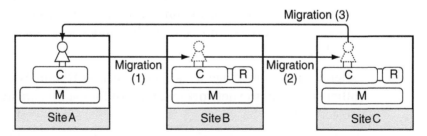

Figure 2.2 The mobile agent paradigm. Agents are represented as small figures, like pieces of a board game and are shown above other, stationary code components (agencies) to indicate that they are dynamically bound to this code.

execution state. At site S_B, virtual machine M_B^U executes the code, providing access to the resources located at S_B. Later, the code may decide that it needs other resources at other sites, (e.g., S_C), in which case the code will migrate to another computer again.

Mobile Agents Need an Environment

Obviously, mobile agents need some kind of environment to become "alive." What we have simplified as *virtual machine* in Figure 2.2 actually consists not only of the interpreter for the programming language but also of the execution environment for agents, which is called the *agent server* or *agency*.

An agency is responsible for hosting and executing agents in parallel and provides them with an environment so that they can access services, communicate with each other, and, of course, migrate to other agencies. An agency also controls the execution of agents and protects the underlying hardware from unauthorized access by malicious agents.

Today, many different types of agencies exist. Many universities and also some companies have developed their own product, and we will use the name *mobile agent toolkit* in the following to describe such a product. The most prominent examples today are Aglets by IBM and Grasshopper by IKV. Later in this book, we introduce Tracy, which is the mobile agent toolkit that was developed by our team at the University of Jena.

A single agency only rarely makes sense, particularly in the case of mobile agents. In addition, even a network of several agencies is still not thrilling unless some mobile agents are roaming the network, using services to fulfill some task. Therefore, we will discuss at least two agencies, which then form a *mobile agent system* that defines the space in which agents live.

2.2 A Short History of Mobile Agents

As we have pointed out, the mobile agent paradigm relies heavily on the idea of mobile code. Thus, to some extent, we must consider mobile code as an ancestor of mobile agents.

2.2.1 The Early Approaches of Mobile Code

The idea of sending code in an architecture-independent format to different hosts via a network was mentioned, probably for the first time, by

Rulifson [1969]. He and his colleagues introduced the Decode-Encode-Language (DEL), which was published as RFC 5.[5] The idea was to download an interpretative program at the beginning of a session while communicating to a remote host. The downloaded program, written in DEL, could then control the communication and efficiently use the small bandwidth available between the user's local host and the remote host. Later, Michael Elie improved this concept and proposed the Network Interchange Language (NIL) as RFC 51 in 1970.

About 10 years later, a group at Linkoping University in Sweden had the idea to build a packet-oriented radio network they called *Softnet*. Each packet sent over the network was a program written in the FORTH programming language, and each network node that received a packet immediately executed this FORTH program. Using this technique, every user was able to instruct every network node to provide new services. More information can be found in a paper by Zander and Forchheimer [1983]. Shoch and Hupp did the first experiments with mobile software at Xerox, where they wrote *worms* to traverse their local area network seeking idle processors [Shoch and Hupp, 1982].

2.2.2 Remote Evaluation

Joseph R. Falcone faced the problem of providing client-specific interfaces to remote services across a heterogeneous distributed system [Falcone, 1987]. In contrast to offering a single interface with many small functions to satisfy the possibly high number of clients, Falcone wanted to enable clients to program their specific interfaces themselves, using a well-defined new programming language NCL (network command language). In NCL a client sends an NCL expression to a server, which then executes this expression using standard functions provided in form of a library. The server sends the result (again an expression) to the client, which can start a computing process again. Thus, what we have here is primitive mobile code in both directions. Independently of Falcone, Stamos developed the *remote-evaluation* (REV) approach, which extends the idea of *remote procedure calls* introduced by Birrell and Nelson (Birrell and Nelson [1984]; Nelson [1981]). The motivation for REV is the same as that for NCL. In REV a client sends a request to a

---

5. Request For Comments, see *www.rfc-editor.org* for more information about RFCs.

server in the form of a program. The server executes the program and sends the result back to the client. Other examples of mobile code sent within networked computer systems are remote batch job submission [Boggs, 1973], *stored procedure* in SQL [Melton, 1998], and the PostScript language used to control printers [Adobe Systems, Inc., 1999].

2.2.3 Mobile Objects

A second step toward mobile agents was the addition of a minimal kind of autonomy to the messaging concept. We refer to this technique as *mobile objects*, although nowadays the term *mobile objects* is often associated with Java RMI. The idea was to create active messages, that is, messages that are able to migrate to a remote host. A message contained data and some program code that was executed on each server. However, the data portion was still dominant in this concept, whereas the active portion (i.e., the code) was more or less an add-on. As opposed to the mobile code approach, a mobile agent typically migrates more than once in its lifetime, and migration is initiated by the agent itself.

The MESSENGERS project [Fukuda et al., 1996] proposed the concept of *autonomous objects*, which were called *Messengers*. Messengers are able to migrate autonomously through a LAN of dedicated servers that accept these objects. The difference from the techniques described previously is that a messenger not only is transferred to a single remote server but is able to autonomously roam a complete network. However, the concept was limited to static LANs and did not include any notion of application-level intelligence. A messenger's autonomy was limited to the level of technological and system-level needs and not targeted at solving a user's problem.

2.2.4 Mobile Processes

A third predecessor of mobile agents are *mobile processes* from which mobile agents inherited the ability to capture the actual execution state of the processor or virtual machine they currently use. The idea was developed in the area of distributed operating systems in the late 1980s. In this framework a process that is currently executed on a single computer system can be moved to another system to balance the load of the distributed system as a whole. An example of operating systems with process migration is Sprite [Douglis and Ousterhout, 1991]. One technique to implement process migration is *checkpointing*. At regular time periods an image of an active process is captured and stored permanently. To migrate a process to another host, the last checkpoint is transmitted and the process is reactivated. If we compare, it has to be noted again that in mobile agents the motivation for migration not only derives from load balancing or other low-level technical goals but is typically driven by the demand to facilitate the use of various available services on the network's application layer via the agent.

2.2.5 Mobile Agents

It was in 1994 that James E. White, affiliated with General Magic Inc. at that time, published a white paper that initiated dedicated research on what we call *mobile agents* today. This paper was later republished in a book edited by Bradshaw [1996]. In it, White introduced the *Telescript* technology, which comprises a runtime environment and a dedicated programming language for mobile agents. This language already offered most of the very important aspects and abstractions of all current mobile agent toolkits. The further development of Telescript was nevertheless dropped when it became clear that this technology would not be able to compete with Java as the common basis for most mobile agent toolkits. For their work on mobile agents, General Magic received a U.S. patent in 1997 [White et al., 1997].

The next milestone in mobile agents research was the paper by Chess et al. [1997a], which described a framework for itinerant agents as an extension of the client-server model. Itinerant agents are dispatched from a source computer and then roam a network of servers until they have fulfilled the user task. Along with a short discussion of the benefits of itinerant agents, the authors describe possible application domains, the architecture of *agent meeting points*, languages to develop such agents, and a discussion of security issues. A second important paper, published at about the same time, discussed the advantages of mobile agents against client-server–based techniques. The paper was later published by Chess et al. [1997b], and the authors conclude:

> While none of the individual advantages of mobile agents given above is overwhelmingly strong, we believe that the aggregate advantage of mobile agents is overwhelmingly strong, because: ... While alternatives to mobile agents can be advanced for each of the

individual advantages, there is no single alternative to all of the functionality supported by a mobile agent framework. ... [Harrison et al., 1995, p. 17]

Since General Magic's initial project, the research community interested in mobile agents has been steadily growing, which is related to many interesting research questions, for example, in the area of security, which are a consequence of the simple idea of moving code.

Available Mobile Agent Toolkits

Many different mobile agent toolkits have been developed since then, and it is impossible to provide even an almost-complete list of available mobile agent toolkits. On the World Wide Web you can find some link lists. Some of them are confined to mobile agent toolkits; others list any kind of agent toolkits.

- As part of the Mole project the University of Stuttgart started to maintain the *Mobile Agent List* several years ago. The list is available at *mole.informatik.uni-stuttgart.de/mal/mal.html* and contains about 70 different toolkits. However, the list was not updated for at least 3 years, and several toolkits listed there are no longer available.

- The AgentLink project (*www.agentlink.org*) maintains a list of ongoing projects with regard to any kind of agent-related topics.

- IEEE distributed systems online (*www.dsonline.computer.org*) also maintains a list of available agent toolkits.

In the following, we will give a very concise and inevitably incomplete list (Table 2.1) of mobile agent toolkits. We selected those toolkits that in our opinion have been or still are very important to the research community and for industrial projects. Later in this book, when describing particular concepts or techniques, we will mention several other toolkits or prototype implementations. See Kiniry and Zimmerman [1997], and Wong et al. [1998] for a comprehensive review of Java-based mobile agent toolkits, although they are quite old. A comparison of object-oriented mobile agent toolkits was done by Gschwind [2000].

One of the mobile agent toolkits developed in the last few years is Aglets, by IBM. Aglets is perhaps the most famous mobile agent toolkit, not least because of the book by Lange and Oshima [1998], which describes

Table 2.1 *Overview of some existing mobile agent toolkits and projects*

Toolkit	Organization	URL
ADK	Tryllian	*www.tryllian.com*
Aglets	Open Source	*aglets.sourceforge.net*
Ajanta	University of Michigan	*www.cs.umn.edu/Ajanta/*
Concordia	Mitsubishi	*www.merl.com/projects/concordia/*
D'Agents	Dartmouth College	*agent.cs.dartmouth.edu*
Grasshopper	IKV	*www.grasshopper.de*
Mole	University of Stuttgart	*mole.informatik.uni-stuttgart.de*
Semoa	Fraunhofer Society	*www.semoa.org*
Tacoma	Uni Tromso	*www.cs.uit.no/forskning/DOS/Tacoma/*
Tracy	University of Jena	*www.mobile-agents.org*
Voyager	ObjectSpace/Recursion	*www.recursionsw.com*

programming concepts for mobile agents chiefly related to this toolkit. The project became an open source project at Sourceforge some years ago. The latest version of Aglets is 2.0.2 (February 2002). Voyager, another toolkit, was originally developed by ObjectSpace, and the product was purchased by Recursion Software, Inc. (USA). The latest version of Voyager is 4.7, and it is available for free from the given URL. Unfortunately, no white paper or any other documentation is available online. Two white papers [ObjectSpace, 1997, 1998] are related to earlier versions of Voyager (1.0 and 2.0). Mitsuibishi was developing a toolkit called Concordia, but the project has been discontinued. See the given URL for more information. The main publication about Concordia is by Koblick [1999].

Two mobile agent toolkits are real commercial products: Grasshopper by IKV and ADK by Tryllian. The Grasshopper mobile agent toolkit was redesigned to become part of a new IKV product, named *enago*; go to *www.ikv.de* for more information. Information about Grasshopper can also be found in Bäumer et al. [1999] and the IKV manuals [IKV, 2001a,b].

Systems have also been developed for university-based research. Mole [Baumann et al., 1998; Straßer et al., 1997] was one of the first Java-based mobile agent toolkits. The project was completed in 2000, but its Web site is still available. Tacoma [Johansen et al., 1995] is an example of a toolkit that supports multiple languages. D'Agents [Gray et al., 2002] is the name of the former AgentTCL [Gray, 1997a] toolkit, which was one of the first mobile agent toolkits. It also supports multiple languages, and the project now focuses on the development of applications in addition to mobile agents. Two toolkits chiefly focus on security issues: Ajanta [Karnik and Tripathi, 2001] and Semoa [Roth and Jalali, 2001]. Finally, our research group has developed its own agent toolkit named Tracy, which will be introduced in Part IV, The Mobile Agent Toolkit Tracy.

All these toolkits differ widely in architecture and implementation, not to mention features related to agent security, communication, and, of course, mobility aspects. Some of these toolkits are tailored to a specific research topic, for example, security, while neglecting several other basic features of a mobile agent toolkit. Interoperability between different toolkits was and still is a major requirement for rapid proliferation of this technology, for which standardization is naturally a good solution.

Standardization

The first standardization approach to mobile agent toolkits was published by Milojicic et al. in 1999. The *Mobile Agent System Interoperability Facility* (MASIF), formerly known as *Mobile Agent Facility* (MAF), was backed by companies and research departments that were active in mobile agent research in the early years (e.g., IBM, GeneralMagic, and GMD Fokus) and was published as an OMG standard in 1998. MASIF bases on CORBA as system infrastructure. Several agent toolkits are available that are, or at least claim they are, MASIF compliant. The two most famous ones are Aglets and Grasshopper.

MASIF is actually a set of definitions and interfaces for interoperable mobile agent toolkits. It consists of an interface for agent transfer and management (MAFAgentSystem) and one interface for locating and naming mobile agents (MAFFinder). The standard defines how to understand notions such as *agent*, *agent system*, *places*, *regions*,[6] and several other basic concepts and notions. MASIF does not define anything related to agent communication, because this issue is extensively addressed by CORBA. To handle security issues of mobile agents, MASIF also relies on CORBA principles. It cannot be said that MASIF failed, but only few toolkits were developed to comply with this standard. One of the reasons for this might be the tight relationship with CORBA.

Another standardization approach in agent technology is FIPA (*www.fipa.org*), which chiefly focuses on issues related to the interoperability of *agents* and, therefore, defines issues on agent communication, including agent communication languages (ACL), message transport

---

6. Some of these notions are used differently in this book.

protocols, and ontologies, but does not consider agent mobility. The basic FIPA specification for an abstract architecture (FIPA 00001) for an agent system explicitly omits agent mobility.

In 2000 a new set of FIPA specifications, which included FIPA 00087 for agent mobility, was released. In the appendix of the specification some issues are discussed related to the problem of integrating MASIF and FIPA. However, the current status of this specification is *deprecated* (May 2002). Refer to Ametller et al. [2003] for more information about the FIPA standard and agent mobility issues.

2.3 Similar but Different Concepts

2.3.1 Internet Agents, Worms, and Spiders

Internet agents, also called worms, robots, spiders, or crawlers, are computer programs used by search engines, such as *www.google.com*, to search the Web and catalog Web pages. When starting the search engine, the user usually defines some keywords and the search engine answers with a more or less useful list of Web pages that contain the given words. We do not want to discuss whether this kind of software is worthy of being called a software agent; we only want to assess whether it is a *mobile* agent.

Let's look at the actual techniques used by common search engines. A Web robot is a program that works on the computer system of the search engine provider. A robot continuously loads Web pages, parses them into words, and stores the result in a very huge database. From each Web page, all hyperlinks are traversed to get new Web pages to archive. When a user wants to search for Web pages, this database is queried with very sophisticated techniques to find the relevant Web pages, that is, the Web pages with the highest information value for the user.

Internet agents are, obviously, not mobile agents according to our definition. They are hardly agents at all. Even if accepted as agents, they would still lack the aspect of mobility, because they work only from the computer system they were started on and never migrate to another platform.

2.3.2 Java Applets

Java applets are Java programs bound to a Web page that is written in HTML. When a user views such a Web page with Web browser software that has a Java plugin installed, the applet is downloaded from the Web server automatically and executed on the client's computer system. Java applets extend the functionality of a common Web browser by offering restricted access to the capabilities of the Java programming language, such as graphical user interfaces, complex business logic, and network access.

In this scenario a well-known mobile code technique is used: *code on demand*. The code of an applet usually consists of a set of single classes that are loaded dynamically on demand; that is, each class is transmitted only if it is really needed on the client's computer system. Since Java 2, several Java byte code classes can be bundled and archived in a so-called *Java ARchive* (JAR) file that is transmitted completely if at least one class from this archive is needed.

Java applets are not mobile agents, because they are not agents at all and have only limited mobility. Applets are not used as a representative of the user that executes some tasks in an autonomous fashion. As mentioned previously, they simply extend your browser's capabilities and work with an application on demand. Applets have limited mobility, because they migrate only once from a server to a client computer system. The migration is not initiated by the applet itself, but by the user (browser) who loaded the corresponding Web page. Applets cannot migrate several times but rather stay on the client computer system until another Web page is loaded or the browser software is terminated. No data is sent along with the applet, only code. Therefore, an applet has no state and is incomplete as an agent. (Although it is possible to send a serialized object as initial starting value for an applet, this is rarely used in practice.)

2.3.3 Java Servlets

Finally, a technology we have mentioned before, but that has no relation to mobile agents at all, are Java servlets. Servlets, and Java server pages as a special form of servlets, are a very popular means to design and program dynamic Web applications.

Java servlets are programs that are executed as part of a Web server or an application container. They form an intermediate layer between the Web browser or other HTTP clients and databases or other types of applications running as part of a Web application. Servlets accept user requests using a CGI interface and produce HTML pages as their result, which are sent back to the Web client.

Java servlets are not mobile agents at all. They are normal Java programs that are executed as part of an application container, and they are immobile.

However, Java servlets could *employ* mobile agents transparently to the user to complete a task.

2.4 Why Are Mobile Agents a Good Idea?

Now we want to describe some major advantages of mobile agents and try to explain why they will meet the demands of future distributed systems.

Although mobile agents provide a new and interesting approach to distributed systems, there must be clear arguments in favor of mobile agents before they are substituted for more traditional techniques. However, although we believe that mobile agents are the most promising technology to solve most of the problems of the networked future, it should be said that we also believe that mobile agents will supplement many older techniques rather than replace them.

We present four major technical advantages in detail. It is this set of basic technical advantages that opens the chance for improved and typical applications.

1. **Delegation of tasks.** Because mobile agents are simply a more specific type of software agent, a user can employ a mobile agent as a representative to which the user may delegate tasks. Instead of using computer systems as interactive tools that are able to work only under direct control by a user, autonomous software agents aim at taking care of entire tasks and working without permanent contact and control. As a result, the user can devote time and attention to other, more important things. Thus, mobile software agents are a good means to cope with the steady information overload we experience.

2. **Asynchronous processing.** Once mobile agents have been initialized and set up for a specific task, they physically leave their owner's computer system and from then on roam freely through the Internet. Only for this first migration must a network connection be established. This feature makes mobile agents suitable for nomadic computing, meaning mobile users can start their agents from mobile devices that offer only limited bandwidth and volatile network links. Because the agent is less dependent on the network, it will be more stable than client-server–based applications.

3. **Adaptable service interfaces.** Current techniques in distributed systems that offer application service interfaces, usually as a collection of

functions, constitute only the least common denominator of all possible clients. As a consequence, most of the interface functions are more or less primitive, and clients will probably have to use a workflow connecting these functions in order to execute a complex, user-driven operation. If the communication overhead for exchanging messages between client and server is high compared with the execution time of each function, it would make sense to offer aggregated and more advanced functions as combinations of the primitive ones. However, because it is difficult to track down every possible scenario in advance or even during runtime, these functions are usually not offered by the server's multi-purpose interface. Mobile agents can help in this situation by offering a chance to design a client-driven interface that is optimized for the client (user) but that is adaptable to different server interfaces. The key is to use a mobile agent to translate the more complex and user-driven functions of the client interface into the fitting primitive functions offered at the server node. The mobile agent will simulate a constant and highly specialized interface for the client (user) while talking to each server in its own language, which will allow servers to become simpler and more generalized.

4. **Code-shipping versus data-shipping.** This is the probably most cited advantage of mobile agents, and it stands in close relationship to adaptable service interfaces. Service interfaces frequently offer only primitive functions to access databases. A single call can therefore result in a huge amount of data being sent back to the client because of the lack of precision in the request. Instead of transferring data to the client, where it will be processed, filtered, and probably cause a new request (data-shipping), this code can be transferred to the location of the data (code-shipping) by means of mobile agents. In the latter case, only the relevant data (i.e., the results after processing and filtering) is sent back to the client, which reduces network traffic and saves time if the code for filtering is smaller than the data that must be processed. This advantage has been scrutinized in the last 5 years by many different research groups for different application domains, and it has generally been verified.

2.5 Possible Application Domains of Mobile Agents

Recently many research groups and companies have participated in the advancement of mobile agent systems. However, because the technology is new and radical in its concepts, some type of *proof* is needed that would show that mobile agents, as a technology, are indispensable. (That this was never done for other technologies that are now widely used seems to be of no interest to those asking for the ultimate *killer application*.)

It is accepted today that mobile agents will not make any applications possible that would not have been possible, using other, more traditional techniques. However, that can be said of other technologies, for example, high-level programming languages: We could still develop all our systems by sticking to plain object code, even though nobody doubts that it was a good idea to develop higher-level languages and introduce design and requirement phases into the software life cycle.

Thus, when we talk about a new technology today, in most cases we talk about improved quality and management of complexity, the efficient use of resources in projects, and the adequacy of concepts and tools. The point is not that something new is possible, but that there are new methods of achieving what is already possible, which may, in turn, lead to new possibilities. For instance, it might be possible to build something similar to the Empire State Building without using cranes, steel, and concrete, but who would want to build it?

We argue that mobile agent systems provide a single framework and a very convenient abstraction—the mobile agent—to build distributed applications more efficiently. See Johansen [1998] for experiences from several mobile agent–based applications. The point is not to look at one specific application but rather to look at the whole set of possible applications and to understand that this new technology will enable a new level of networked software by delivering a sound basis to understand, handle, and implement them, despite their complexity and risks.

Nevertheless, it is possible to identify some application domains where mobile agents have already proved to be highly valuable and that seem to "ask for" that type of technology.

Electronic commerce, be it business-to-business or business-to-customer, suffers from the fact that it simply translates real-world business into electronic processes and data. Neither the advantages of the Web nor the capabilities of software-driven systems are fully utilized. To achieve that, a much higher degree of support for automation and a much better coverage of information sources must be offered. The customer simply wants to state what he or she wants and does not want to direct a system manually to actually implement how this is done. Interfaces need to be unified, but a general standardization has proved to be nearly impossible. Huge amounts of data are shipped, often very slowly, and then thrown away after the most primitive evaluation. In all of these cases, mobile agents can help; they offer delegation and asynchronous task execution, are able to simulate unified interfaces to widely differing sources, and, last but not least, actually were born out of the need to send the evaluation process to the data.

Especially important in this context is that electronic commerce today means, in many cases, that more than a single shopping platform is involved and that we look at a distributed workflow with transaction qualities that involves physically separated data stores. Although we need better certification authorities and repudiation techniques, no doubt, the technological challenge will be to interact with a number of distributed sites and to integrate a set of possibly incomplete results into a coherent solution. Only mobile agents, with their inherent capability for traveling the network and their fully distributed paradigm, provide a conceptually sound basis for this application domain. They do shopping as we like to do it, by visiting the stores, comparing the different offers, and, finally, finishing the acquisition. This also includes the capability to spot a new store and to include it into the acquisition process. Mobility is the key issue. Any centralized approach has to face additional technical challenges, (e.g., increased network load and latency, as well as many unnecessary downloads) and cannot deal with the characteristics of the domain that are distributed and dynamic in nature.

Information retrieval is another popular application domain for mobile agents. Instead of moving large amounts of data to a single point where it is searched, information retrieval moves the data-searching code to the data. Thati et al. [2001] describe a new type of search engine, in which Web pages are analyzed locally by a mobile agent that was sent to the Web server. The agent only sends back a summary of the Web pages, and therefore might reduce network traffic considerably. Other nice examples are search engines for graphic files [Roth, 1999] and music files [Kravtsova and Meyer, 2002], which are data warehouses that will charge for the downloaded data, not the information extracted. These systems also suffer from the problem of the overly simplified and nonstandardized interface for multiple clients, as previously discussed. Again, mobile agents will be able to unify that interface from the client's perspective and offer a higher and well-adapted level of functionality.

Another typical application for mobile agents in the domain of information retrieval is multiple distributed sources. If the relevant information sources cannot be centralized, either because of technical reasons (e.g., in a network of fast updating sensors) or because of business-driven necessities (e.g., if the information at each node is proprietary and the owner does not agree to a centralized solution), mobile agents offer the only chance to develop a flexible solution that accepts the distributed nature of the given environment and offers a solution that is as distributed and scalable as the problem itself.

The real-time aspect of this concept is of major importance, because a mobile agent that resides locally at the sensor's platform does not have to deal with any network latency. It can react on behalf of its owner within given time limits, thus offering the chance to remove itself from any network problems. In addition, each agent has the capability to filter sensor data and to prepare it for use at different customer sites with different needs. This is of major importance if very large amounts of data are to be managed and a transmission of the full dataset to all recepients is economically or technologically impossible. See Umezawa et al. [2002] for a description of a framework for self-configurable sensor networks.

Finally, we briefly mention some specific application areas where the concept of mobile agents has already been used. Sudmann and Johansen [2002] describe how mobile agents can be used for software deployment and updates in a distributed environment. Several research groups have focused on the applicability of mobile agents for network management tasks. As an introduction to this topic, see Rubinstein et al. [2002, 2003] who describe a network management system based on mobile agents. The authors compare the mobile agent paradigm with client-server–based approaches for typical management tasks, with regard to performance and network load.

Summary

In this chapter, we have introduced the term *mobile agent* from the application point of view, without going too much into technical details. We have stressed that mobile agents should be seen from the viewpoint of software engineering and distributed computing rather than from the viewpoint of artificial intelligence.

You might raise objections to the notion *agent*, for, as we have seen, mobile agents do not have much in common with *intelligent* agents. In fact, some people from the mobile agent research community mentioned this problem recently [Gray, 2004]. We would like to add that even the adjective *mobile* might be misleading here, because it is now used to describe objects that can be carried away or have been made for nomadic users. Compare, for example, *mobile* phones and *mobile* Web services. The latter describes a special type of Web services that can be accessed by users over their mobile devices. It may be that other names, for example, *migrating software component* or *migrating software entity*, might be better.

Nevertheless, you should now have some understanding of the term *mobile agent* and also some high-level understanding of the migration process. The next chapter is solely dedicated to a technical description of agent migration. Other concepts that are very important for the rest of this book are:

agency — a software that is responsible to execute mobile agents

agent toolkit — a specific project or product, for example, Aglets, Grasshopper, or Tracy

agent system — all agents and agencies that work together in a specific application

One of the most important advantages of mobile agents is their ability to save network bandwidth as compared with the client-server paradigm. The general idea is to move code close to a large database instead of transferring lots of data to a client. This advantage is often called *code-shipping versus data-shipping*. In the next chapter, we will come back to this advantage and examine it from a more theoretical point of view.

Part II

Mobile Agents— Concepts, Functions, and Possible Problems

Chapter 3

Mobile Agent Migration

After looking at mobile agents from the application point of view, we now focus on the migration process. Earlier we explained agent migration simply as the process of transferring a mobile agent from one computer system to another. In this chapter we go into technical detail on this issue.

First, we develop a generic framework to describe the migration process as it is implemented in almost all mobile agent toolkits today. Along the way, we introduce the main concepts of the Java programming language that are important in implementing the migration process and come back to the main advantage of mobile agents: saving network bandwidth by moving the code close to the data. We develop a mathematical model to compare network load for mobile agents and client-server based systems in a very general case. We will see that the concept of mobile agents has some very useful advantages but also some inherent drawbacks, at least in the way the migration process is implemented in current agent toolkits. Finally, we discuss possibilities for optimization of the migration process for mobile agents and propose a new mobility model named Kalong.

Contents

3.1 The Mobile Agent Migration Process

3.1.1 Generic Framework for Agent Migration

The process of agent migration, although implemented differently in each mobile agent toolkit, can be described using a general framework. Introducing this framework also helps us define some terms, which we use throughout this book.

Basic Terminology

A mobile agent is a software program that is, in most systems, executed as part of a so-called mobile agent server software. This server software controls the execution of agents and provides some basic functionality for agent communication, agent control, security, and migration.[1] In this book we will call this mobile agent server an *agency*. On each computer system that wants to host mobile agents, an agency of the same type must be installed.[2] All agencies that are able to exchange mobile agents form a logical network that we call a *mobile agent system*. To refer to a specific project or product, for example Aglets [Lange and Oshima, 1998] or Grasshopper [Bäumer et al., 1999], we use the notion *agent toolkit*. Each computer system can host several agencies in parallel, and each agency is reachable by at least one URL to which migration is directed. The URL also serves as a name of the agency. For the moment we are not concerned with how the agency is structured. (Some mobile agent toolkits subdivide a single agency into several *places*. If the places are *closed*, agents in different places cannot know, see, or communicate with each other.)

When an agent is created on an agency, that agency becomes the agent's *home agency*. The user who starts the agent is called the *agent's owner*, and the owner also defines the *agent's name*. The owner information is important

---

1. Of course, it is possible to build a system of (mobile) agents by just letting an agent be a *process*. Processes can communicate with each other by primitives offered by the operating system, and even migration can be achieved with special *distributed* operating systems or can be provided as the only service of the underlying mobile agent server software. Tacoma [Johansen et al., 1995] is an example for such a system.

2. Recently, some research groups started to develop methods to make mobile agents interoperable so that two different agencies will be able to exchange agents. See, for example, Pinsdorf and Roth [2002] and Grimstrup et al. [2000] for more information.

in telling foreign agencies how trustworthy the agent is. The agent's name is necessary to identify an agent unequivocally on all agencies of the mobile agent system. All this information about an agent's home agency, owner, and name becomes attributes of the agent. Usually, an agent returns to its home agency after it has fulfilled its task. The other important agency is the one that holds the agent's code; we call this one a *code server*. Usually, the home agency is the code server, but this is not always the case.

Agencies are typically multi-agent systems; that is, a single agency can host many agents in parallel. To provide quasiparallel execution, some kind of scheduling is offered. In most systems this process of scheduling is not programmed within the server software, but is delegated to the programming language and the operating system. For example, it is common for each agent to own a thread. During execution, the agent might be allowed to start new child threads.

The Structure of Mobile Agents

Mobile agents consist of three components: *code*, *data*, and *execution state*. The code contains the logic of the agent, and all agents of the same type use the same code.[3] The code must be separated from the code of the agency so that it can be transferred alone to another agency, and the code must be identifiable and readable for an agency (e.g., in the form of a file from the local file system or a byte stream from the network). Usually, as in other programs, an agent's code consists of more than one file (e.g., in the Java programming language they could be many class files).

The second component of an agent is *data*. This term corresponds to the values of the agent's instance variables if we assume an agent to be an instance of a class in object-oriented languages. The data is sometimes also called the *object state*. It is important to note that not all data items an agent can access are part of its object state. Some variables reference objects that are shared with other agents or the agency software itself, for example, file handlers, threads, the graphical user interface, or other resources and devices that cannot be moved to other servers. Thus, we have to restrict the agent's immediate data to those data items the agent owns and that are movable.

---

3. Here, we have a rather pragmatic and narrow notion of *type* for agents: Two agents are of the same type if they use the same code. More programming language–like definitions would refer to the interface or the communication protocol the agent offers; see Zapf and Geihs [2000] for a detailed discussion on other approaches for defining the notion of a type for agents.

Problems arising from nonmovable resources are discussed in Section 3.3, Design Issues of Agent Migration.

The third component is the *execution state*. The difference between object and execution state information is that the elements of the object state are directly controlled by the agent itself, whereas execution state information is usually controlled by the processor and the operating system. What this means depends very much on the decision of the mobile agent toolkit designer and the underlying execution environment (processor, operating system, virtual machine), as we will see in Section 3.3, Design Issues of Agent Migration. In some toolkits, an agent's execution state is comprised of the current value of the instruction pointer and the stack of the underlying processor. In others it is not possible to determine the execution state of an agent at all. In most Java-based toolkits, for example, the agent itself is responsible for copying information about its current execution state on the level of the programming language into the object state and restoring it after successful migration.

The Migration Framework

The typical behavior of a *mobile* agent is to *migrate* from one agency to another. During the process of migration, the *current agency* (i.e., the one the agent currently resides on) is called the *sender agency* and the other agency (to which the agent wants to migrate) is called the *receiver agency*. During the migration process the sender and the receiver must communicate over the network and exchange data about the agent that wants to migrate. Thus, we can say that some kind of communication protocol is driven, and we call this the *migration protocol*. Some systems simplify this task to an asynchronous communication, comparable to sending an email, whereas other systems develop rather complicated network protocols in addition to TCP/IP.

The whole migration process contains six steps, which are executed in sequence, except for S3 and R1, which are executed in parallel (Fig. 3.1).

The first three steps (S1–S3) are executed on the sender agency:

S1 *Initialize the migration process and suspend the thread.* The process of migration typically starts with a special command, the *migration command*, by which the agent announces its intention to migrate to another agency, whose name is given as parameter of the migration command. The first task for the agency is now to suspend the execution thread

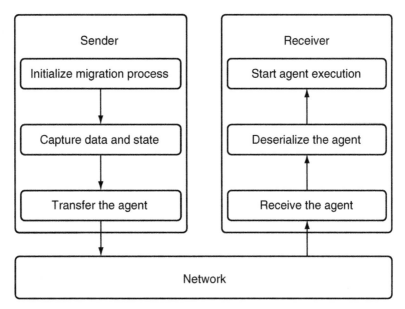

Figure 3.1 The mobile agent migration process.

of the agent and to guarantee that no other child thread is still alive. This requirement is important for the next step, for which it is imperative that data and state be frozen and unable to be modified later on.

S2 *Capture the agent's data and execution state.* The current state of all variables (the data) of the agent is *serialized*; that is, their current values are written to an external persistent representation, for example, a memory block or a file. The agent's state is also stored there so that the point of suspension is known. The result of the serialization process is the *serialized agent*, which is a flat byte stream that consists of the agent's data and state information.

S3 *Transfer the agent.* The serialized agent is transferred to the receiver agency using a migration protocol. Whether any code is sent to the receiver agency depends on different parameters and will be discussed later.

The last three steps (R1–R3) are executed on the receiver agency.

R1 *Receive the agent.* The serialized agent is received using the migration protocol. The receiver agency checks whether the agent can be accepted based on information about the agent's owner and the sender agency.

The receiver agency may filter out agents that come from agencies that are unknown or not trusted.

R2 *Deserialize the agent.* The serialized agent is deserialized; that is, the variables and execution state are restored from the serialized agent. The result of this step should be an exact copy of the agent that existed on the sender agency just before reaching the migration command.

R3 *Start agent execution in a new thread.* The receiver agency resumes agent execution by starting a new thread of control. When resuming execution, the agent's code is needed. In this general framework we make no assumptions about how the code is transferred to the receiver agency. One possible technique is for the receiver agency to load the code from the agent's home agency or its code server. We will discuss those techniques in Section 3.3.

In the next section we look at an implementation of a migration process. As an example we chose our Tracy mobile agent toolkit, which is implemented in the Java programming language.

3.1.2 Migration in the Tracy Mobile Agent Toolkit

In this section we describe the migration process of an existing mobile agent toolkit, which was developed using the Java programming language. We will follow the generic framework introduced in the last section and explain the advantages of Java for programming mobile agent toolkits and mobile agents. We chose the Tracy toolkit as an example here not only because Tracy is the result of our own research but also because the complexity of the Tracy migration process lies between a simple one (e.g., that used in Semoa [Roth and Jalali, 2001]) and a difficult one (e.g., that used in Aglets [Lange and Oshima, 1998]). A detailed introduction into the Tracy mobile agent toolkit can be found in Chapter 9.

Programming Languages for Mobile Agents

The Java programming language [Arnold and Gosling, 2000] has become the *de facto* standard programming language for mobile agents because of its many features that lessen the effort in building mobile agent toolkits. As already described in Chapter 2, any programming language can be used for implementing mobile agents. In most systems there is a restriction that the same programming language must be used for mobile agents as was used for the underlying agency. Only few toolkits, (e.g., Tacoma and D'Agents) allow agents on the same agency to be implemented using different programming languages. The first mobile agent toolkits had mobile agents implemented in interpreted languages (e.g., Telescript [White, 1996]) or script language (e.g., TCL [Gray et al., 1997] or Perl [Wall et al., 2000]). For some time, the question of which languages are suitable for mobile agents was the topic of intensive research in the community. For a detailed discussion about the language requirements for mobile agents, see the dissertation thesis of Knabe [1995] and the papers by Cugola et al. [1997a,b], Knabe [1997a], and Thorn [1997].

Almost all toolkits developed in the last 5 years use the Java programming language for the mobile agent toolkit as well as for mobile agents. Even both projects mentioned previously that do not solely support Java cannot be called opponents of this language, because one of the main research issues in these projects is multi-language support, and both actually do support Java.

The advantage of Java comes from several built-in features that lessen the effort involved in building mobile agent toolkits. In this section we especially focus on features that support the migration process, for example, object serialization, dynamic class loading, and reflection, which we will introduce briefly when describing the migration process. We will also briefly mention foundations of the security architecture of Java. Despite these advantages, some aspects of Java are also imperfect with regard to the requirements of mobile agent systems; we also briefly discuss these drawbacks.

Foundations of Java

Java is an object-oriented language developed by Sun, Inc. Although the original project goal was simply to develop a new programming language (Oak) for a new kind of remote control device with LC display and touch-screen (named "*7"), since 1995 Java has become *the* Internet language. For some time, the most famous application domains for Java were applets that were shipped from a Web server to a Web browser. Today, as a result of major performance improvements, Java has become a widely used programming language for server-based applications, too.

The most important feature that made Java an Internet programming language was its *portability*. Java programs are compiled into a architecture-independent byte-code format [Lindholm and Yellin, 1999], which is executed using a Java virtual machine. Because virtual machines exist for almost all current hardware platforms and operating systems, Java programs have the enormous advantage of being executable on almost all existing computer systems. Portability is a very important requirement for mobile agent systems, because mobile agents must be able to migrate in a network of heterogeneous computer systems.

The byte code is executed by the virtual machine, which completely protects the underlying operating system from direct access by Java programs. This simplifies security control, because an intermediate code format allows easier code inspections for security violations than compiled native code does. As is true for all interpreted languages, Java has a lower execution performance than compiled code. However, very sophisticated techniques were developed for Java to translate intermediate code into optimized native code during execution (just-in-time compilation and hot-spot optimization).

The language itself supports development of *safe* applications, because, in contrast to C, for example, Java has a pointer model that does not support pointer arithmetic and illegal type casting. The *byte code verifier*, a component of the virtual machine, filters out code that violates basic semantics of Java before execution. Even during runtime, a security manager controls all potentially unsafe operations, such as file access, network connections, or access to the graphical user interface. It is dynamically determined whether the given program is permitted to perform these operations.

Java comes with many libraries (e.g., for data structures, network programming, graphical user interfaces). Network programming is supported using sockets as well as using remote method invocation (RMI), which is the object-oriented version of the remote procedure call concept. Java RMI is so powerful that implementing a very simple mobile agent toolkit can be done in less than 100 lines of code (see Avvenuti and Vecchio [2000]).

Unfortunately, Java also has some drawbacks with regard to mobile agent toolkits. The main disadvantage is, perhaps, the fact that it is impossible to obtain the current execution state of a thread in the form of the current instruction pointer and calling stack, making it practically impossible to preserve and later resume execution of a mobile agent in detail. Therefore, Java-based mobile agents can offer only a weak form of mobility, in which the agent is restarted at the receiver agency by invoking a method instead of jumping into it and resuming execution at the first statement after the *go* was invoked. Another drawback is the lack of resource control (e.g., for memory or processor cycles). Therefore, it is not possible to avoid denial-of-service attacks, which is a specific type of security attack in which the attacker tries to consume so many resources that the system is no longer able to handle incoming requests.

Representing Agents in Tracy

In Tracy an agent is an object of a specific class, named *Agent*, which is the main class within the TracyAPI.[4] It is an abstract class that serves as a base for all agents and may not be instantiated by the programmer. Class *Agent* defines methods to control an agent's life cycle, get and set internal data structures, and receive messages. Some of these methods are useful for the programmer (e.g., methods to inform him or her about the current agency), whereas some methods are useful only for an agency to control the agent. Class *Agent* also defines some methods that are supposed to be overridden by subclasses.

To define an agent in Tracy, package *de.fsuj.tracy.agent* must be imported, which includes all basic definitions.

```
1  import de.fsuj.tracy.agent.*;
2
3  public class MyFirstTracyAgent extends Agent
4  {
5    SomeOtherClass other = new SomeOtherClass();
6
7    public MyFirstTracyAgent()
8    {
9      // do some initialization
10   }
11
12   public void startAgent()
13   {
14     // do something
15   }
16 }
```

---

4. We introduce here the high-level programming interface of Tracy, which provides a basic class *Agent*, that already defines some convenient methods, for example, to initiate a migration process or to communicate with other agents. On a lower level, an agent is just an object that implements interfaces *Runnable* and *Serializable* and starts a migration process by using a specific service provided by the hosting agency. See Section 10.1.2, How to Use Services, for more information.

Method *startAgent* is defined `abstract` in class *Agent*. This method is the entry point that is called at the agent's home agency to start the agent; therefore, every user-defined agent must implement this method.

Usually, an agent consists of more than one class. In the preceding example, we see that this agent has a variable named *other* of type *SomeOtherClass*.

Starting the Migration Process and Resuming Execution

In the following we explain the migration process as implemented in Tracy according to the framework introduced in the last section. We do not follow the sequence introduced in the framework, but combine tasks that belong together, for example, S1 and R3, and so on. We do not introduce the network transmission task here. Tracy uses its own migration protocol, called SATP, which is an asynchronous network protocol that is based on the TCP/IP protocol. We introduce this protocol in Chapter 6.

Now we will show how a mobile agent can start a migration to a receiver agency and how execution is resumed at the receiver agency. Actually, a mobile agent can be moved in two ways. The first way is to use the *go* command to initiate migration with a default migration behavior to a single remote agency; the other way is to use so-called migration properties to configure the migration process in detail, for example, to define a complete itinerary. Then the next *go* command automatically chooses the next destination in the given itinerary. In this section we concentrate only on the standard migration technique. See Chapter 10 for an explanation of how to use migration properties.

An agent migration is initiated by calling a method named *go*, with the name of the receiver agency as the first parameter and the name of the method to invoke after migration as the second parameter. Method *go* is defined in class *Agent* and cannot be overridden (defined *final* there).

```
final protected void go( String destination, String methodName )
```
Migrates an agent to the receiver agency destination and restarts it by invoking method methodName.

The name of the receiver agency is just a String, where the protocol should be *tcp* and the host name is the name of the receiver agency. Usually a port number is also required so that, for example, a complete destination address is *tcp://tatjana.cs.uni-jena.de:4040*. Calling method *go* stops agent execution immediately and statements following the *go*, invocation will never be executed, neither in the case of a successful migration nor in the case of a migration error. A *go* command might be included in a try ... catch clause. In this case, neither the Tracy-defined runtime exception *AgentExecutionException* nor any super classes of this exception must be caught. If they are caught, the *go* method will have no effect.

```
 1 try
 2 {
 3   // some code that might throw an IOException
 4
 5   System.out.println("Running on server \"tatjana.cs.uni-jena.de\"");
 6   go( "tcp://domino.cs.uni-jena.de:4040", "runAtRemote" );
 7
 8   // statements below will never be executed
 9   System.out.println("This message will never be seen.");
10 }
11 catch( IOException e )
12 {
13   System.err.println( e.getMessage() );
14   e.printStackTrace();
15 }
```

There are two other methods that are shortcuts for the previously mentioned *go* method:

> final protected void *go_home(String methodName)*
> Migrates an agent to its home agency and restarts it by invoking the method with name methodName.

> final protected void *go_back(String methodName)*
> Migrates an agent to the agency it came from and restarts it by invoking the method with name methodName.

If migration is not successful (e.g., because the receiver agency does not accept agents from the current agency, or both agencies use different versions of the migration protocol), the agent must be reactivated at the current agency. In that case, method *migrationFailed* is called, which is defined empty in class *Agent*.

> protected void *migrationFailed()*
> Is called in case of any migration error.

The default behavior of this method is to do nothing, which lets the agent wait for new messages to become active again. Usually, this method will be overridden and could try to migrate again.

Agent execution at the receiver agency is resumed using the Java *reflection* technique. After the agent was deserialized and the agent's main class is at the receiver agency (so that the agent object can be successfully instantiated), agent execution is resumed. In Tracy, the agent is resumed by starting a method whose name was given as the second parameter in the *go* statement. The name of this method was transmitted as part of the state of the agent.

Java reflection is a powerful technique to determine information about classes, their variables, and methods during runtime. In addition, it is possible to invoke a method of an arbitrary object only by having its name in a *String* variable. In the following example, we show an extract from the Tracy source code in which a method with name *methodName* is invoked for a given mobile agent object.

```
1 import java.lang.reflect.Method;
2
3 protected void startAgent( Agent mobileAgent,
4                            String methodName ) throws Exception
5 {
6   Class agentClass = mobileAgent.getClass();
7   Method method = agentClass.getMethod( methodName, new Class[0] );
8   method.invoke( mobileAgent, new Object[0] );
9 }
```

In line 6 we first determine the class name of the given mobile agent object, then ask this class for a method of name *methodName*. The second parameter of method *getMethod* contains an array of types that the wanted method must accept as parameters. An empty array, as in the example, indicates that the method should accept no parameters. If the agent's class has such a method, it is stored in variable *method*. If not, an exception is thrown. In line 8 this method is invoked with the mobile agent as a parameter and an empty array of objects, which means that this method has no parameters at all. Method *startAgent* is called within a new thread, which is assigned to the agent.

Object Serialization and Deserialization

After a mobile agent has been instructed to migrate to another agency, serialization of the agent takes place. Serialization means that all variables of the agent, together with all recursively referenced objects and their variables, are traversed and put into a flat byte array. The set of all objects to be serialized is called the *object closure*.

In the current version of Tracy we use the standard object serialization technique that is already implemented in Java [Sun, 1999]. To use this technique, each class whose objects should be serialized during their lifetimes must implement interface *java.io.Serializable*. Class *Agent* already implements this interface so that all agents in Tracy can be serialized. In addition, all variables that a mobile agent class defines must be either marked serializable too or marked as *transient*, which means that they are not elements of the object closure. If a nonserializable object is found during the serialization process, an exception will be thrown. Note that class variables (i.e., those marked as static), are not part of the serialized object. Thus, the object will probably retrieve different values of class variables at the destination agency.

Java object serialization determines only the object state of an agent, not its execution state. In Tracy only the name of the method that should be invoked at the receiver agency is part of the agent's state.

The following extract from the Tracy source code shows how simple the task of object serialization is in Java. Method *serializeAgent* gets a reference to the mobile agent as a parameter and returns the serialized agent as a byte array. In the case of an error, the method returns null.

```
 1 private byte[] serializeAgent( Agent mobileAgent )
 2 {
 3  ByteArrayOutputStream baos = new ByteArrayOutputStream();
 4  try
 5  {
 6   ObjectOutput oos = new ObjectOutputStream( baos );
 7   oos.writeObject( mobileAgent );
 8   oos.flush();
 9  }
10  catch( IOException e )
11  {
12   return null;
13  }
14
15   return baos.toByteArray();
16 }
```

The most important statement is line 7, where the agent is serialized to an output stream. In line 15 this output stream is converted into a flat byte array.

The result of the serialization process is the so-called serialized agent, which is now transferred to the receiver agency. To instantiate a new mobile agent from a byte array is only slightly more complicated. The standard Java object serialization technique allows you to instantiate a new object simply from a byte array containing the serialized object. This procedure is correct because the serialized object contains all the information about used classes that is necessary to define and initialize the object correctly.

```
 1 private Agent deserializeAgent( byte[] bytestream )
 2 {
 3   try
 4   {
 5     ByteArrayInputStream bais = new ByteArrayInputStream( bytestream );
 6     ObjectInputStream ois = new TracyObjectInputStream(
 7                                      new TracyClassLoader( this ),
 8                                      bais );
 9
10     mobileAgent = (Agent)ois.readObject();
11     return mobileAgent;
12   }
13   catch( Exception e )
14   {
15     return null;
16   }
17 }
```

This method uses two Tracy-specific new classes to instantiate mobile agents. Class *TracyObjectInputStream* is a subclass of the standard Java class *ObjectInputStream*, which is responsible for conducting the complete deserialization process. If a class must be loaded during deserialization, then method *resolveClass* is called. In class *TracyInputStream* this method is overridden so that our new class *TracyClassLoader* is used for this task. If the process of deserialization fails, value null is returned.

Finding Classes and Dynamic Class Loading

Tracy's default migration technique transfers the serialized agent together with the state information, which is only the method name to invoke at the destination, and all classes the agent might ever use to the receiver agency.

Therefore, the first problem before an agent can migrate is to determine which classes must be transferred to the next agency. Comparable to the definition of *object closure,* we can define *code closure* as follows: The code closure consists of the agent's main class (e.g., *MyFirstTracyAgent* in the previous example) and all classes that are used for variables, method parameters, method return values, and local variables of any class of the code closure. Unfortunately, Java does not provide an easy way to determine this set of class names automatically. Class *Class* of the Java API provides method *getDeclaredClasses* which returns only an array of classes that are used for member variables. Using method *getDeclaredMethods,* we can obtain information about all methods, and, using this information, we can determine classes that are used for parameters and return values. But Java does not provide a method to determine information about local variables defined within methods. Therefore, we implemented our own technique that looks at the byte code of the class. There we find the *constant pool* [Lindholm and Yellin, 1999], which is a table that contains all names that are ever used in this class. To read this table we use a tool named ByCal (byte code analyzer), which was developed within our project. This tool offers several services to analyze Java byte code, transform it, and even perform sophisticated control and data-flow analyses on it.

Obviously, the code closure should not contain classes that are not to be transferred because they can be assumed to be already in the receiver agency (e.g., classes of the Java API or classes that are part of Tracy). Before the byte code is collected for each class of the code closure, those redundant classes are deleted from the code closure. Java does not provide a way to read the byte code for each class that is an element of the code closure. Therefore, we search for the class in the agent's code base, which is defined when launching an agent (this can be a directory, a JAR file, or any URL; see Chapter 10 for more information).

After the agent is received at the destination agency, its code must be linked to the code of the already running agency. This is another advantage of the Java programming language that allows dynamic class loading and linking. This mechanism allows the virtual machine to load and define classes at runtime.

In Java an instance of class *ClassLoader* is responsible for loading and defining classes. Each class loader defines its own name space so that different classes with the same name can be loaded into a single virtual machine without conflicts. The default class loader, which is used unless the user specifies one, loads classes from the local file system (i.e., from directories or from Java archives that are listed in the *CLASSPATH*). Each object knows the class loader it was created by and a single class loader has usually created many objects. (If an object creates new objects, the same class loader is used.)

When a class loader has to load a class, it looks for the corresponding class code according to the following rules:

1. The class loader checks whether the class has been loaded before and, if it has, gets the byte code from the cache.

2. The system class loader is asked to load the class from the system JAR file.

3. The class loader looks at the *CLASSPATH* variable and searches all directories and Java archives.

4. It delegates the task to a user-defined class loader by invoking method *findClass*.

When the class code is found, it is defined by calling a special method *defineClass* of the class loader. User-defined class loaders must override method *findClass* and can load the byte code for the given class name by using an HTTP or FTP server or any other technique. As a result of the default Tracy migration technique, all class files are already at the destination agency, so the *TracyClassLoader* has to look for the byte code only in a local repository, where all incoming classes are stored.

Summary

In this section we introduced a generic framework for the description of the migration process in many, if not all, Java-based mobile agent toolkits. You have learned about the basic steps that are executed at the *sender agency* and *destination agency*, respectively, and you have learned how basic Java techniques such as *object serialization* and *dynamic class loading* are employed in those toolkits. We presented some simple examples to illustrate how to program mobile agents and how to initiate the migration process. Every mobile agent toolkit has implemented the migration process differently, and we will discuss different design issues in Section 3.3, Design Issues of Agent Migration.

3.2 Effective Migration as a Core Feature of Mobile Agent Toolkits

We now discuss one of the main advantages of mobile agents, that is, the ability to save network load as compared to client-server based applications. According to this argument, mobile agents are able to save network traffic by shipping the code close to data, instead of shipping data to the code as is done in the client-server paradigm. Although this argument can be proved by experiments, there are also cases in which mobile agents produce higher network load than client-server techniques. This leads to the very important question for software designers: "Which paradigm produces lower network load?"

In the first section, we describe two approaches from the literature to answer this question. The first approach proposes a design decision between mobile agents and client-server applications on the basis of mathematical models. The second approach argues that only a mixture between mobile agent migrations and remote procedure calls can achieve the smallest network load. Neither approach provides a detailed analysis of the reasons for the mobile agents' bad performance.

Our theory is that mobile agents suffer from several drawbacks that are all related to the technical bases used to provide the ability to migrate. Therefore, we will carry out a detailed network-load analysis using mathematical models in Section 3.2.2, Performance Analysis of Simple Mobile Agents versus Client-Server. We compare both paradigms in typical scenarios to identify reasons for the higher network load produced by mobile agents. The result is an enumeration of inherent drawbacks of mobile agents as compared to client-server techniques, which all involve the details of the migration process. In the last section, we discuss our results and mention a few other papers that also focus on network-load analysis of mobile agents.

3.2.1 Mobile Agents versus Client-Server

Static Decision between Mobile Agents and Client-Server

This approach proposes a static decision between the two paradigms according to a mathematical analysis of the network load for a concrete application. The approach was published several times for different applications. Carzaniga et al. [1997] and Vigna [1998] discuss this approach for an application from the information-retrieval domain, whereas Baldi et al. [1997], Picco [1998], and Baldi and Picco [1998] use it for an application from the network-management domain. This approach compares network load for client-server, remote-evaluation, code-on-demand, and mobile agents.

Picco and Vigna's main thesis is that no paradigm is better than the others in every application scenario, but "The choice of the paradigm to exploit must be performed on a case-by-case basis, according to the specific type of application and to the particular functionality being designed within the application" [Vigna, 1998, p. 42].

We describe Picco and Vigna's approach using the example of a distributed information system. To give an expression on the mathematical model, we also mention some of the most important parameters here. In the distributed information system, N servers each hold D documents. The client's task is to download the *relevant* documents, which are identified using keywords. The server offers a header for each document that also contains the keywords for the document. For the sake of simplicity, the authors allow the following constraints: (1) The relation between relevant documents and all documents equals i for all servers; (2) The header information has length h bits for each document, and each document has length b bits; (3) requests sent from the client to the server have length r bits. Then the authors model each approach using these parameters and finally gain an expression for network load for each paradigm, for example, the network load using the client-server paradigm equals $((D+iD)r+Dh+iDb)N$ and the network load for the mobile agent approach equals $(r+C_{MA}+s+\frac{N}{2}iDb)(N+1)$, where C_{MA} is the agent's code size and s is the size of the state. Based on an evaluation of these models, with estimated values for all parameters, the authors select a single design paradigm to recommend for the implementation of this application.

Concerning an analysis of the drawbacks of mobile agents, Picco and Vigna found that mobile agents always produce the highest network traffic because an agent carries all documents already found, whereas in all other paradigms, documents are sent back to the client immediately. Thus, a mobile agent's data grows continuously with each hop, so it grows quadratically with the number of servers.

They assume a network in which transmission costs depend only on the number of bytes to transmit and not on bandwidth and latency values. According to the authors themselves, this is unrealistic, but it is necessary to keep their model simple. Using such an uniform network, it is rather impossible for the mobile agent approach to produce less network traffic than the remote-evaluation approach, because code in the remote-evaluation approach is smaller and mobile agents have to migrate $N + 1$ times, whereas in the remote-evaluation approach, only N migrations are necessary. In our opinion it must be considered that networks for real-world applications are heterogeneous, meaning that, for example, a migration between two remote servers is faster than sending two requests from the client. In addition, the authors can only estimate values for the parameters of their model, for example, the size of the mobile agent's code, *before* having implemented this agent and do not explain how to obtain reliable values. They do not consider the possibility that parameters might change in the future, which might reverse their recommendation.

Mixture between Agent Migrations and Remote Procedure Calls

The second approach is proposed by Straßer and Schwehm [1997]. Their thesis is that only a mixture between agent migrations and remote procedure calls leads to minimal network traffic.

Straßer and Schwehm develop a simple mathematical model for network load and execution time of client-server– and mobile agent–based approaches for a given application scenario. Several parameters are known in advance, for example, the amount of communication necessary between client and server(s), as well as bandwidth and latency for all network connections. They model the ability of mobile agents to filter or compress server results before sending it back to the client with a so-called compression factor, σ. Agent migration is modeled as implemented in their Mole mobile agent toolkit [Baumann et al., 1998], where agent code is not always transmitted along with the agent's state but is usually dynamically loaded from the agent's home server if it is necessary. Class downloading can be avoided if the necessary class is already available at the destination agent server. Therefore, a parameter, P, models the probability of downloading any class from the agent's home server. Nevertheless, the authors do not evaluate their model with regard to class downloading probability P.

First, they evaluate a single client-server–like interaction with regard to different values for the server result size and the compression factor. The result is as expected and shows that, for example, with low compression factors, mobile agents produce a greater network load, because sending code to the server causes a fixed overhead, whereas with high compression factors, mobile agents produce a smaller network load. After that they consider a scenario in which a sequence of interactions between a single client and several servers is processed.

The authors' main idea is that only a mixed sequence of agent migrations and remote procedure calls produces the minimum network load. The agent migrates to only a subset of all servers to be visited, whereas the other servers are accessed using remote procedure calls. The optimal sequence depends on the sizes of requests and results and on the network quality between each pair of nodes. All these parameters are assumed to be known in advance.

To assess this technique, Straßer and Schwehm compute the network load for all possible combinations of migrations and remote procedure calls using a mathematical model. With the assumption that network bandwidth and latency are known in advance, they are able to show that minimal network load is actually produced by a mixture. Finally the authors prove their theoretical findings through experimental validation. Here, an agent is able to compute its optimal communication pattern by itself, using the developed mathematical model. Values for bandwidth and latency are measured by the underlying mobile agent toolkit, Mole. The authors compare three *mobility strategies* in which the agent migrates always, never, or varies according to the results of the mathematical model. The measured execution times show that the optimized mobility strategy always has the shortest execution time. The results were not compared with a pure client-server solution. Iqbal et al. [1998] continue this work and present several algorithms to compute the optimal migration sequence of a single agent. The approach is based on an algorithm to determine the shortest path in a directed and weighed graph.

Both papers show that only a mixed sequence of remote procedure calls and agent migrations lead to an optimal network load. Thus, to determine the optimal communication sequence, knowledge of several parameters, about network bandwidth, latency, request, and result size, for example, are assumed. However, it is not clear how these values can be obtained in general and how well the approach works with variations of these values.

3.2.2 Performance Analysis of Simple Mobile Agents versus Client–Server

In this section we develop a simple mathematical model in order to compare network load for both client-server–based and mobile agent–based paradigms. Our aim is to show under which circumstances the use of mobile agents causes lower network load and which characteristics of mobile agents are responsible for sometimes higher network load. Therefore, we do not consider the remote-evaluation and the code-on-demand paradigms here, although the remote-evaluation paradigm might produce less network load than the mobile agent paradigm (see Picco [1998]). We want to keep the model as simple as possible. Therefore, we focus our analysis on network traffic in terms of transmitted bytes and do not consider transmission time, except in one scenario in which we consider a heterogeneous network.

The application scenario we will use consists of a set of computers, where one system takes the client role and all other systems are servers. The client sends *client requests* to servers to obtain data items that are sent back as *server results*. The size of a single client request is B_{req}, and the size of a server result is B_{res}. If no data matches the request, the server has to send some kind of error notification about this case, which has size B_{rep}. A mobile agent that is sent from a client to a server has code of size B_c and state information of size B_s. In addition, an agent carries data items (e.g., the client request or the results found at previously visited servers).

There are two individual advantages of mobile agents, both able to reduce network load:

1. The ability to avoid network protocol overhead (e.g., avoiding many communication steps in a network protocol)

2. The ability to filter and compress data at the server site

In our model we describe data filtering and compression by a single parameter, σ, $0 \leq \sigma \leq 1$, which stands for a *compression factor*. The compression factor is applied to the server result, B_{res}, so that only $(1 - \sigma)B_{res}$ must be sent back to the client and carried by a mobile agent. Table 3.1 gives an overview of all used symbols.

For the sake of simplicity, we make the following additional assumption: When a mobile agent migrates to another computer, it carries all its code, all state information, and all data with it. Only if an agent migrates to its home agency is code transmission omitted, because the code can be assumed to be already there. This corresponds to a migration technique that is implemented in most mobile agent toolkits. For the moment, we do not consider the impact of other techniques for agent migration, for example, the one implemented in Mole (see Section 3.2.1, Mobile Agents versus Client-Server) and we do not take into account additional costs that might arise from sophisticated security solutions. We also do not consider any kind

Table 3.1 *Overview of the symbols used for the mathematical model in Section 3.2.1*

Parameter	Unit	Description
B_{CS}	Byte	Network load in the client-server approach
B_{MA}	Byte	Network load in the mobile agent approach
T_{CS}	Sec	Response time in the client-server approach
T_{MA}	Sec	Response time in the mobile agent approach
B_{req}	Byte	Size of a client request
B_{rep}	Byte	Size of a server error reply
B_{res}	Byte	Size of a server result
B_c	Byte	Size of a mobile agent's code
B_s	Byte	Size of a mobile agent's state
σ	$0 \leq \sigma \leq 1$	Compression factor
m	Number	Number of servers to be visited
m^*	Number	Number of servers at which client-server and mobile agents produce the same network load
n	Number	Number of communication steps
p_i	$0 \leq p_i \leq 1$	Probability that data is found at server i
$\delta(L_i, L_j)$	Sec	Delay (latency) between network nodes L_i and L_j
$\tau(L_i, L_j)$	Byte/sec	Throughput between network nodes L_i and L_j

of manual optimization that might be possible on the application level to optimize the migration behavior, for example, to distribute code manually to several code servers in advance.

Our model of network load is placed on top of the TCP/IP stack, so we neither model TCP or IP headers nor network load that is caused by data retransmission and other factors.

We will now discuss the behavior of mobile agents in the following three scenarios:

1. Network of one client and one server, in which the client accesses the server one or many times

2. Network of one client and m servers, in which the client is searching for a single data item that might be stored on any server

3. Network of one client and m servers, in which the client is searching for data items on all servers

Scenario 1: Network of One Client and One Server

We first consider the case of reducing network load through data filtering and compression. In the client-server approach the client sends a request of size B_{req} to the server, which answers with a result of size B_{res}. Here, no data filtering or compression can be applied. Thus, the number of bytes that are sent over the network is:

$$B_{\text{CS}} = B_{\text{req}} + B_{\text{res}} \qquad (3.1)$$

In the mobile agent approach, the client sends an agent to the server. The agent consists of code of size B_c and state information of size B_s. The agent carries the request object of size B_{req} as a data item. On the server, the agent communicates locally with the server, which does not produce any network load. The agent has the code to filter or compress the server result, so only $(1-\sigma)B_{\text{res}}$ must be carried to the agent's home server. Note that the agent does not carry code or the request object during the home migration, because the code is already available at the home server and the request object is no longer needed. However, state information must be sent back to the agent's home. Thus, the amount of bytes for the mobile agent approach is:

$$B_{\text{MA}} = B_c + 2B_s + B_{\text{req}} + (1 - \sigma)B_{\text{res}} \qquad (3.2)$$

From Equations 3.1 and 3.2 we can derive a verification of the thesis that mobile agents produce less network load than client-server approaches.

$$B_{\text{MA}} \leq B_{\text{CS}}$$
$$B_c + 2B_s + B_{\text{req}} + (1 - \sigma)B_{\text{res}} \leq B_{\text{req}} + B_{\text{res}}$$
$$B_c + 2B_s \leq \sigma B_{\text{res}} \qquad (3.3)$$

We see that a mobile agent produces lower network load if, and only if, its code (including double the state) is lower than the number of bytes of the server result that the agent could save through compression and/or filtering.

We evaluate this scenario with the parameters found in Table 3.2 (Scenarios 1.1 and 1.2). The result is shown in Figure 3.2. Figure 3.2(a) compares the network load of the client-server approach with the mobile agent approach for a fixed compression factor of $\sigma = .7$ while varying the server result size between 0 and 5000 bytes. The diagram shows that the use of mobile agents produces less network load only if the server result size is large. The reason for this is the fixed network load overhead for transmitting mobile agent's code and state to the server, which is, in this scenario, 2100 bytes. Figure 3.2(b) compares the network load of the client-server approach with

Table 3.2 *Typical values of model parameters, which we use for all scenarios in Section 3.2.1*

Scenario	B_{req}	B_{rep}	B_{res}	B_{c}	B_{s}	σ	p_i	Network	Figure
1.1	50	20	var.	2000	100	.7	n/a	hom.	3.2(a)
1.2	50	20	3000	2000	100	var.	n/a	hom.	3.2(b)
1.3	50	20	100	2000	100	n/a	n/a	hom.	3.3
2.1	100	50	10,000	3000	200	.8	$\frac{1}{m}$	hom.	3.4(a)
2.2	100	50	10,000	3000	200	.8	$\frac{1}{m}$	hom.	3.4(b)
3.1	100	n/a	10,000	3000	200	.8	n/a	hom.	3.5
3.2	100	n/a	var.	3000	200	var.	n/a	hom.	3.6
3.3	100	n/a	10,000	3000	200	.8	n/a	hom.	3.7
3.4	100	n/a	10,000	3000	200	.8	n/a	het.	3.8

"n/a" indicates that this parameter is not needed in this scenario and "var." indicates that this parameter is varied in this scenario.

the mobile agent approach for a fixed server result size of 3000 bytes while varying the compression factor σ between 0 and 1. This diagram shows that the use of mobile agents produces less network load only if the compression factor is high.

We now look at the advantage of avoiding several network protocol steps. A typical scenario is for a client to need to check a server periodically to keep informed about changes, for example, when a stock rate goes below a given limit. Therefore, the client sends requests of size B_{req} to the server, which answers with a server reply of size B_{rep} if there are no changes and with a server result of size B_{res} if there has been a change. Let us assume that the change happened after n requests were sent. For the client-server approach, the network load amounts to:

$$B_{\text{CS}} = nB_{\text{req}} + (n - 1)B_{\text{rep}} + B_{\text{res}} \qquad (3.4)$$

The agent has to migrate to the remote server, which costs $B_{\text{c}} + B_{\text{s}}$, and it carries the request of size B_{req}. After processing, the agent migrates back, which costs $B_{\text{s}} + B_{\text{res}}$. Note that we consider neither filtering nor data compression in this scenario. For the mobile agent approach, the network load amounts to:

$$B_{\text{MA}} = B_{\text{c}} + 2B_{\text{s}} + B_{\text{req}} + B_{\text{res}} \qquad (3.5)$$

We evaluate this scenario with the parameters found in Table 3.2 (Scenario 1.3). The result is shown in Figure 3.3, which compares the network

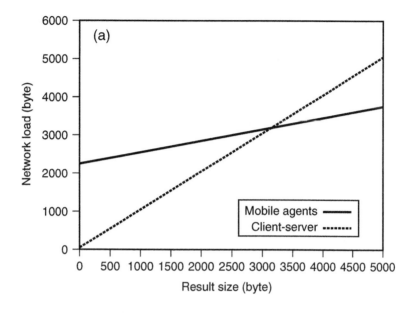

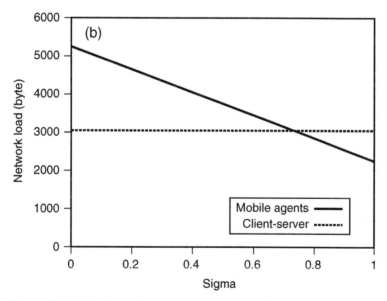

Figure 3.2 Evaluation of Scenario 1.1 and 1.2: Mobile agents produce less network load only if the server result is large or the compression factor is high. (a) Server result size versus network load for fixed compression factor. (b) Compression factor σ versus network load for a fixed server result size.

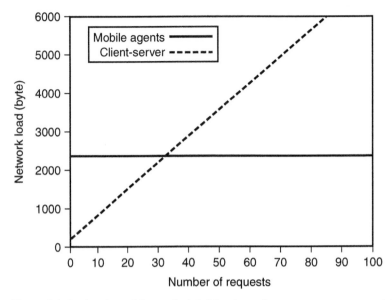

Figure 3.3 Evaluation of Scenario 1.3: Number of request versus network load. Mobile agents produce less network load only if the number of requests is high.

load of the client-server approach with the mobile agent approach for fixed request, reply, and result size while varying the number of times request n is necessary until the event occurs. It can be seen that in the client-server approach, network load increases in proportion to the number of requests, whereas mobile agents produce constant network load. Thus, mobile agents produce a smaller network load only if the number of requests exceeds the threshold. This is again because of the fixed network load overhead for transmitting code to the server.

Scenario 2: Network of *m* Servers, Searching for a Single Data Item

In this scenario the client searches for a single data item that is currently available on only one out of a set of *m* servers. Thus, in the client-server approach the client must access each server sequentially until the information is found. We denote the set of all servers with $\mathcal{L} = \{L_1, \ldots, L_m\}$. The probability that the information is found at server L_i equals p_i, where $0 \leq p_i \leq 1$. Therefore the order in which the servers are accessed is important, and for our comparison, we will use the same order for the client-server approach and the mobile agent approach. After the information is found at server L_i, servers $L_{i+1}, \ldots, L_m$ will not be visited.

Let us first consider the client-server approach. If the information item is found at the first server, then only a single client request of size B_{req} and a single server result of size B_{res} are sent. If the information is found at the second server, two requests of size B_{req}, a single error reply of size B_{rep} (from the first server), and one server result of size B_{res} is sent. We weight each single case with its probability and obtain the following network load:

$$
\begin{aligned}
B_{\mathrm{CS}} = {}& p_1(B_{\mathrm{req}} + B_{\mathrm{res}}) + p_2(2B_{\mathrm{req}} + B_{\mathrm{rep}} + B_{\mathrm{res}}) + \cdots \\
& p_m(mB_{\mathrm{req}} + (m-1)B_{\mathrm{rep}} + B_{\mathrm{res}}) \\
= {}& \sum_{i=1}^{m} p_i(iB_{\mathrm{req}} + (i-1)B_{\mathrm{rep}} + B_{\mathrm{res}})
\end{aligned}
\tag{3.6}
$$

We now look at the mobile agent approach. If the information is found at the first server, the agent migrates only to the first server and comes back with the compressed result. Remember that the agent does not carry its code when migrating home. If the information is found at the second server, the agent has to migrate three times; it does not need to carry any reply message from the first server, so it carries only the compressed server result from the second server. Again, each case is weighted with its probability to obtain the network load.

$$
\begin{aligned}
B_{\mathrm{MA}} = {}& p_1(B_{\mathrm{c}} + 2B_{\mathrm{s}} + B_{\mathrm{req}} + (1-\sigma)B_{\mathrm{res}}) + \\
& p_2(2B_{\mathrm{c}} + 3B_{\mathrm{s}} + 2B_{\mathrm{req}} + (1-\sigma)B_{\mathrm{res}} + \cdots \\
& p_m(mB_{\mathrm{c}} + (m+1)B_{\mathrm{s}} + mB_{\mathrm{req}} + (1-\sigma)B_{\mathrm{res}} \\
= {}& \sum_{i=1}^{m} p_i(iB_{\mathrm{c}} + (i+1)B_{\mathrm{s}} + iB_{\mathrm{req}} + (1-\sigma)B_{\mathrm{res}})
\end{aligned}
\tag{3.7}
$$

We evaluate this scenario with the parameters found in Table 3.2 (Scenario 2.1). The result can be found in Figure 3.4(a). The diagram compares network load for the client-server approach and the mobile agent approach for fixed request, reply, and result size while varying the number of servers m. For a small number of servers, mobile agents produce less network traffic, because in that case data filtering and compression have a positive effect on the overall network load. Beyond a specific number of

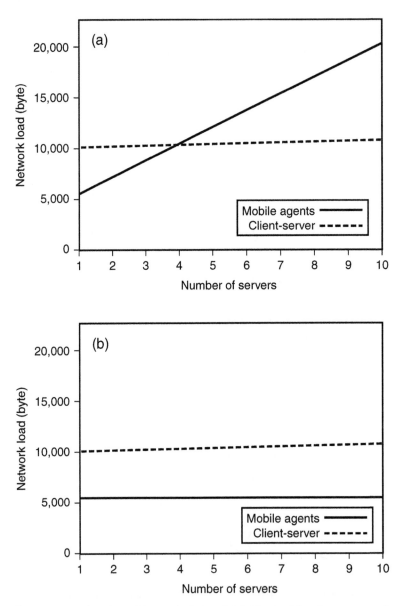

Figure 3.4 Evaluation of Scenario 2.1 and 2.2: Network load versus number of servers. (a) When network load between all nodes is considered, mobile agents only produce smaller network load if the number of servers to be visited is small. (b) When network load at the uplink is considered, mobile agents always produce smaller network load.

servers, mobile agents produce a greater network load because of the overhead of sending code and state information to each server. Thus, network load increases in proportion to the number of servers in the mobile agent approach, whereas network load increases only slightly in the client-server approach.

We will now evaluate the same scenario in a network in which only the costs at the client network interface are considered. For example, if the client is a mobile phone that has a GPRS connection to the Internet, costs depend on the number of bytes sent from the mobile phone to the Internet service provider. We denote this network connection as an *uplink*. Of course, the network load of the client-server approach is identical to the one represented by Equation 3.6. For the mobile agent approach in this scenario we can ignore all costs related to migrations between servers in the network. Thus, the network load amounts to:

$$B_{MA} = p_1(B_c + 2B_s + B_{req} + (1 - \sigma)B_{res}) + \cdots$$

$$p_m(B_c + 2B_s + B_{req} + (1 - \sigma)B_{res})$$

$$= \sum_{i=1}^{m} p_i(B_c + 2B_s + B_{req} + (1 - \sigma)B_{res}) \qquad (3.8)$$

$$= B_c + 2B_s + B_{req} + (1 - \sigma)B_{res} \qquad (3.9)$$

Figure 3.4(b) shows that network load is now much smaller in the mobile agent approach, because data filtering and compression have a positive effect. Network load is constant in the mobile agent approach, because only uplink costs are considered; therefore, it is irrelevant on which server the information is found, whereas network load increases slightly in client-server approach. Note that a scenario in which only uplink costs are considered is the only case in which mobile agents produce a lower network load for a large number of servers than client-server techniques—in all other scenarios, the reverse is true; the higher the number of servers, the higher the network load for mobile agents. Thus, it is very profitable to use mobile agents if only uplink costs must be considered.

Scenario 3: Network of *m* Servers, Select Information at All Servers

In this scenario the client has to collect data items from all servers in the network, so in any case all *m* servers are visited. In the client-server approach, the client sequentially accesses each server, sending a request and receiving a server result. The total network load amounts to:

$$B_{CS} = m(B_{req} + B_{res}) \qquad (3.10)$$

In the mobile agent approach, the agent migrates from its home server to server L_1, which produces costs for code, state, and request transmission. On server L_1 the agent selects and filters data, so the cost for the next migration to server L_2 increases by $(1 - \sigma)B_{res}$. At each succeeding server, new data items of cost $(1 - \sigma)B_{res}$ must be added, so for the migration from server L_i to server L_{i+1} data items of size $i(1 - \sigma)B_{res}$ must be taken along. Therefore, network load for the mobile agent approach equals:

$$
\begin{aligned}
B_{MA} = & B_c + B_s + B_{req} + \\
& + B_c + B_s + B_{req} + (1 - \sigma)B_{res} + \\
& + B_c + B_s + B_{req} + 2(1 - \sigma)B_{res} + \cdots \\
& + B_s + m(1 - \sigma)B_{res} \\
= & mB_c + (m + 1)B_s + mB_{req} + \frac{m(m + 1)}{2}(1 - \sigma)B_{res} \qquad (3.11)
\end{aligned}
$$

We evaluate this scenario using the parameters given in Table 3.2 (Scenario 3.1). The result is shown in Fig. 3.5. The diagram compares the network loads of the client-server approach and the mobile agent approach for a fixed size of client requests and server results while varying the number of servers to be visited. Network load increases in proportion to the number of servers in the client-server approach, whereas it grows quadratically in the mobile agent approach. The reason for this is that a mobile agent collects data items from *each* server and must carry all the results. Mobile agents produce lower network load only when the number of servers to be visited is small.

As shown in Figure 3.5, for a certain number of servers, both paradigms produce the same network load. We denote this number of server with m^*. We are now interested in how m^* changes when the server result size B_{res} and the compression factor σ vary. We evaluate this scenario using the parameters found in Table 3.2 (Scenario 3.2). Figure 3.6 shows the relation between m^* and the server result size for four different compression factors. It can be seen that the number of servers up to m^* has an upper bound for each value of σ, which depends on the size of the server result. This upper bound is higher when the compression factor is higher.

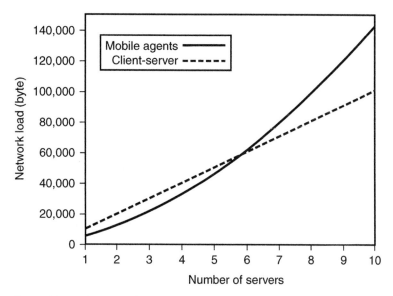

Figure 3.5 Evaluation of Scenario 3.1: Network load versus number of servers. Network load for mobile agents increases quadratically with the number of servers.

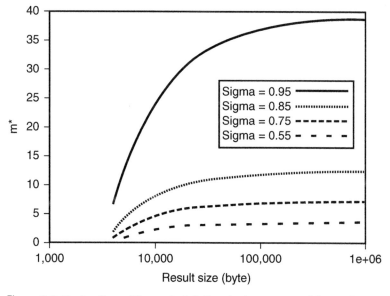

Figure 3.6 Evaluation of Scenario 3.2: Result size versus m^* for various compression factors. There is an upper bound for m^* for each value of σ.

Now we evaluate Scenario 3.1, but consider only costs at the client-network interface. Network load for the client-server paradigm is the same as in Equation 3.10. The network load for the mobile agent approach equals:

$$B_{\mathrm{MA}} = B_{\mathrm{c}} + B_{\mathrm{s}} + B_{\mathrm{req}} + B_{\mathrm{s}} + m(1 - \sigma)B_{\mathrm{res}}$$

$$= B_{\mathrm{c}} + B_{\mathrm{req}} + 2B_{\mathrm{s}} + m(1 - \sigma)B_{\mathrm{res}} \tag{3.12}$$

We evaluate this scenario using the parameters found in Table 3.2 (Scenario 3.3). The result can be seen in Figure 3.7. As in Scenario 2.2 we can see that mobile agents produce a much smaller network load than client-server techniques as a result of data filtering and compression.

Finally, we discuss the influence of network parameters on the response time in both approaches. We want to show that in a heterogeneous network it is not valuable to assess a paradigm solely on basis of network traffic, especially when the network connection between the client and any server has lower bandwidth than interserver connections. Therefore, we introduce $\delta : \mathcal{L} \times \mathcal{L} \rightarrow \mathbb{R}$, where $\delta(L_{\mathrm{i}}, L_{\mathrm{j}})$ describes the delay (latency) of a network connection between node L_{i} and node L_{j}, and $\tau : \mathcal{L} \times \mathcal{L} \rightarrow \mathbb{R}$, where $\tau(L_{\mathrm{i}}, L_{\mathrm{j}})$ describes the throughput between node L_{i} and node L_{j}. For the moment

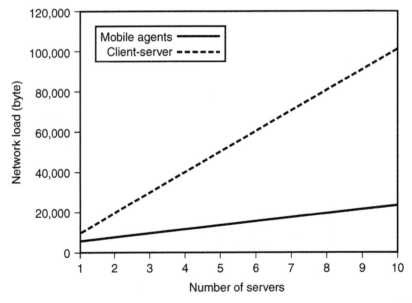

Figure 3.7 Evaluation of Scenario 3.3: Number of computers versus network load, only considering network load between client and any server.

we omit processing time. From Equation 3.10 we obtain the following equation for the response time:

$$T_{CS} = \sum_{i=1}^{m} 2\delta(L_0, L_i) + \frac{B_{req} + B_{res}}{\tau(L_0, L_i)} \tag{3.13}$$

We assume the client is node L_0. The execution time for a simple client-server call is the sum of the time for transferring the request and result plus the delay for this network connection.

In the mobile agent approach we can derive the following equation from Equation 3.11:

$$T_{MA} = \left(\sum_{i=1}^{m} \delta(L_{i-1}, L_i) + \frac{B_c + B_s + B_{req} + (i-1)(1-\sigma)B_{res}}{\tau(L_{i-1}, L_i)} \right)$$
$$+ \delta(L_0, L_m) + \frac{B_s + m(1-\sigma)B_{res}}{\tau(L_0, L_m)} \tag{3.14}$$

We will now evaluate this scenario using the parameters given in Table 3.2 (Scenario 3.4). The result is shown in Figure 3.8. We assume delay time to be 90 ms between the client and each server and 30 ms between a pair of servers.

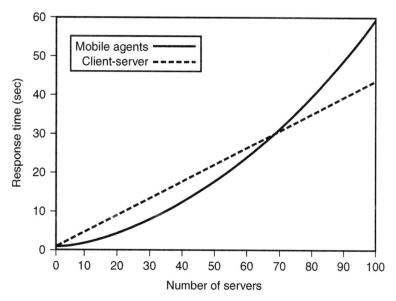

Figure 3.8 Evaluation of Scenario 3.4: Response time versus number of servers. The number of servers for which response time of client-server and mobile agents are equal is higher than in Scenario 3.3.

Throughput is assumed to be 40,000 byte/sec for the client-server link and 200,000 byte/sec for interserver connections.

The only difference between this evaluation and the evaluation of Scenario 3.1 is the heterogeneous network, as evidenced by the fact that the break-even point between client-server and mobile agents increased from about 5 to nearly 70 servers. Because the slow link between the client and all servers is used very often in the client-server approach, response times are very high. However, beyond a certain number of servers, mobile agents are slower because they carry so much data.

3.2.3 Discussion of Our Results and a Further Literature Review

In the last section we developed a mathematical model for network traffic and response time of client-server– and mobile agent–based approaches for three general application scenarios. Our evaluation of this model confirms the thesis that mobile agents produce less network load than client-server techniques only if their code, together with the state, is smaller than the network load that can be saved by their use.

The general result of our mathematical model is that within the same application scenario we can find situations in which smallest network traffic is achieved by either client-server or mobile agent approaches. We must conclude that which paradigm produces the best result depends on the values of several factors, for example, code size, server result size, number of servers to be visited, and so on. In this difficult situation, software designers would surely benefit from any rule of thumb to decide which paradigm should be used in a given situation. However, in our opinion, this does not make sense, because we have omitted several factors from our model for the sake of simplicity, and these parameters would undoubtedly influence the decision and would invalidate such a rule or at least make it inaccurate outside our model.

Limitations of Our Model and Other Approaches

Some factors that also influence network traffic and response time in real applications are those considering network quality. One important aspect is the error probability of a given network connection, especially in the case of wireless connections. A mathematical model including this parameter is presented by Jain et al. [2000]. Another factor we did not model is server processing time. Because we ignored this factor, our model assumes response time to be equal to agent migration and data transmission time, which is of course inaccurate for all processing-intensive tasks. To extend our model with processing time would make it indispensable to model server scalability too — but this would have been clearly beyond the scope of our intention for the moment. Nevertheless, we are aware of this factor; Gray et al. [2001] pointed out that scalability of a mobile agent server software is a major drawback for the overall performance of mobile agent–based applications.

In contrast to our general mathematical model in which we tried to figure out the main parameters influencing the performance in both paradigms, some authors focus on parameters that are very specific to the examined application. For example, Puliafito et al. [1999, 2001] consider an example from the information retrieval domain in which a fixed number of servers must be accessed. After the first request is processed and the server result is sent back to the client, the client decides whether another request must be sent to the server. The authors analyze the influence of the probability, p_r, of reusing the same server for a subsequent request. Such a subsequent request produces network load and therefore transmission time in the client-server approach, whereas in the mobile agent approach, only processing time must be added. The evaluation shows that with a low value for p_r, the client-server approach performs better because of the overhead of mobile agent migration. However, with increasing probability, p_r, the client-server approach results in higher processing time than the mobile agent approach.

Several other papers also discuss trade-offs between client-server and mobile agent approaches, which we will not mention in detail here, because they would not contribute any new results: Spyrou et al. [2000], Outtagarts et al. [1999], Papastavrou et al. [1999], Knudsen [1995], Spalink et al. [2000], Theilmann and Rothermel [1999], and Samaras et al. [1999].

Advantages of Mobile Agents

We evaluated our model using several scenarios, and we identified the following limited advantages of mobile agents with a simple migration capability only. Mobile agents produce lower network traffic:

1. if the number of requests during a communication is high, so many data transmissions of the client-server paradigm can be avoided by using mobile agents, or

2. if the size of the server result is high combined with a high compression or filter factor, so a much smaller number of bytes must be sent back to the client.

As already stated, the concrete value of the threshold beyond which mobile agents produce lower network load depends on several factors. Therefore, we are unfortunately not able to be more precise at this point than to say that the number of requests or the compression factor must be *high*.

It is obviously easier to give concrete numbers if, instead of a mathematical model, real-world experiments are conducted. For example, Ismail and Hagimont [1999] present results of experiments with the Aglets mobile agent toolkit and a client-server implementation based on Java RMI. The authors consider an example from the information retrieval domain consisting of a single client and two servers. The first server offers information about hotels, and the second server is a telephone directory. The task is to get a list of hotels in a given town and their telephone numbers. The client first requests a list of hotels from the hotel database, then selects the hotels in the given town, because it is assumed that the interface of the first server does not offer any filter function. For each selected hotel, the second server is asked for the hotel's telephone number. Measurements were taken in a network of three computers located in different European cities. The results show that the overall execution time depends on the number of hotel records returned by the first server. If there are fewer than 30 records, the RMI-based client-server approach has a lower execution time, but if there are more than 30, the mobile agent approach performs better. The experiment shows that mobile agents are a good choice only if *a lot of* data must be processed. Otherwise, mobile agents may produce more network load than client-server techniques.

The other two scenarios deal with cases in which multiple servers must be accessed. In these cases, mobile agents work completely differently than client-server–based techniques. Whereas in the latter approach the client accesses each server, resulting in a star-shaped communication flow, mobile agents hop from server to server, not visiting the client in the meantime. In Chapter 2 we identified this behavior as a major difference between mobile agents and mobile objects. The main advantage of this behavior comes from the fact that the network connection between the client and any server is not used frequently by mobile agents, so mobile agents produce:

1. smaller network load if only network traffic at the client-interface is considered, and

2. shorter response time if the uplink has a smaller bandwidth (or higher latency) than all inter-server connections.

We investigated a scenario in which only data transmission at the client interface, the so-called uplink, is considered. The result was that mobile agents have advantages if the user is interested in minimizing uplink costs, which might be the case if the user has a GPRS mobile phone. In this case we do not consider all the network traffic that is produced between servers, so all these transmission costs for code and data transmission are not taken into account. Of course, this advantage can exist only in combination with one of the advantages mentioned previously. For example, if an agent were not able to reduce the server result, its network load would be smaller only for a very high number of servers.

The second advantage deals with the case of heterogeneous networks, that is, networks in which network connections do not have the same quality. We concentrated on those networks in which the uplink (i.e., the connections between the client and any server) has lower bandwidth or higher latency than connections between servers. A typical example for such a network is of a mobile client that must use a wireless LAN connection with a bandwidth of 2 to 11 Mbit/sec rather than Ethernet with 100 Mbit/sec. In such a heterogeneous network, we showed that mobile agents have a shorter response time than client-server techniques. The reason for this is that mobile agents need this small bandwidth connection only twice, for the migration from the client and back to the client when they have completed the task, whereas in the client-server paradigm, each server is accessed using this bottleneck connection. In our evaluation we did not analyze the impact of network bandwidth and network latency on the performance of mobile agents in detail, because this has already been done.

Rubinstein and Duarte [1999] evaluate trade-offs of mobile agents in network management tasks. Performance of mobile agents is compared with an approach using SNMP. The network topology used in these simulations is a LAN of Managed Network Elements (MNE) connected to a management station by a bottleneck link. Simulations are done using a network simulation software. The application scenario the authors look at is simple network management tasks, such as retrieving SNMP variables from all MNEs. The authors consider the network load at the bottleneck link and response time of a single task as performance parameters. The authors have conducted several experiments, varying network latency and bandwidth, the initial mobile agent's size, and the number of bytes to select at each MNE.

The result is that the performance of mobile agents does not change with the latency, because mobile agents use the bottleneck link only twice, whereas all SNMP messages must traverse the bottleneck link. Varying bandwidth of the bottleneck link has the result that, for a small bandwidth, both mobile agents and SNMP messages present larger response times. Here the authors found that for a lower number of MNEs, SNMP messages perform better, but when the number of MNEs is increased, mobile agents have shorter response times. Increasing mobile agents' size has the expected effect of higher response times, whereas response times for SNMP messages remain constant.

Drawbacks of Mobile Agents Using a Simple Migration Technique

We will now discuss the reasons that mobile agents sometimes produce higher network traffic. The first obvious reason is the size of the code that has to be transmitted to each server the agent visits. Agent code is usually larger than a simple client-server request, because agents not only carry the code for data filtering and/or compression but also need additional logic implemented to decide which servers should be visited. In a few applications, this order might be a fixed itinerary, implemented as a primitive array of URLs. In most applications the decision for the next server to visit is made dynamically during runtime. On the other hand, large code size is not a drawback in all cases. There is often a simple relation between the quality of filtering and/or compressing data at the server site and agents' code size. Simply speaking, the more sophisticated the data filtering task (which results in a higher compression factor), the larger the code that is necessary to achieve this compression factor. Higher network traffic of mobile agents as compared with that of client-server techniques can be caused by situations with low achieved compression factor, although a lot of code was sent to the remote server—and those situations are not always avoidable.

A second drawback of the mobile agents paradigm is that sending code to each server causes a fixed overhead in network traffic for each agent migration. Therefore, there can be several client-server interactions that produce less traffic than a single mobile agent migration, as long as they are in sum smaller than this fixed overhead. If the advantage of mobile agents comes from data compression or filtering, then this data reduction must save network traffic at least in the size of agent's code.

A third drawback deals with the migration technique. One simplification of our model is that we do not consider different techniques for agent migration. We assume the widely used technique that sends code as one unit to each server. In some cases this might include pieces of code with low execution probability on specific servers; that is, it is improbable that these pieces of code will be executed on a specific server. As an example, just think of a task divided into several subtasks. On a specific server only one of these subtasks is executed; therefore, code for all other subtasks is transferred superfluously. Kotz and Gray [1999] describe this as following: "Thus, ... mobile agents (especially those that need to perform only a few operations against each resource) often take longer to accomplish a task than more traditional implementations, since the time savings from avoiding intermediate network traffic is currently less than the time penalties from slower execution and the migration overhead." We will come back to this drawback of mobile agents in Section 3.3, in which we extend our model to include several migration techniques.

The last three drawbacks for mobile agents were deduced from the first scenario (p. 56) of our model evaluation, where only a simple interaction between a single client and a single server was examined.

If a mobile agent has to migrate to many servers instead of only one, we can find further drawbacks. First, it is clear that a higher number of servers to be visited does not have any positive impact on code migration. The agent's code must be transferred to each server that the agent visits; we could therefore repeat all the drawbacks of mobile agents presented earlier, even in the multi-server case. But another drawback of mobile agents becomes obvious. If more than one server must be visited, the result collected at server L_{i-1} is transferred as part of the mobile agent's data to server L_i. If the result of server L_{i-1} is not needed at any server $L_i, \ldots, L_m$, then it was superfluous to transfer it. The same is true if data originally created at the client must be transferred to all servers $L_1, \ldots, L_{i-1}$, even if server L_i is the first one that needs them (e.g., to create an appropriate request).

Our evaluation showed that mobile agents are useful only if there is a *small number of servers to be visited*, a fact that contradicts the general idea of mobile agents as multi-hop entities. Besides, we have shown mathematically that there is an upper bound for the number of servers and that beyond this bound mobile agents are unable to *ever* produce lower network traffic. For example, in a typical scenario of a very high compression factor ($\sigma = .95$), mobile agents are better than client-server only if fewer than 40 servers are to be visited.

Summary

In this section we presented a mathematical evaluation and examined a performance analysis of simple mobile agents as compared with the client-server approach. The evaluation showed that mobile agents have the possibility of reducing the network load and processing time compared with client-server–based applications, because code is shipped to the data instead of data being shipped to the code. However, we also showed some severe drawbacks of mobile agents, features that are responsible for higher network load and longer processing time in certain situations.

All these drawbacks are caused by the simple migration technique used in our mathematical model, which, however, reflects the current state of the art in agent migration. We learned that code migration is a very expensive task that must be optimized and has to become more flexible. We also learned that data migration has an important effect on the performance of mobile agents. It is our thesis that *the migration process of mobile agents must be optimized to let them migrate in a more flexible and fine-grained way.* What we mean is that a mobile agent should not always migrate as one unit that consist of all code, state, and data information but that it is sometimes useful to let the agent decide which code and data items should be transferred to the next server. In the next section we will therefore focus on the migration process of mobile agents and consider possible optimizations.

3.3 Design Issues of Agent Migration

Now that we have introduced the technical details of the migration process and shown how the migration process is implemented in the Tracy mobile agent toolkit, we can discuss other approaches to implement mobile agent migration. The main goals of this section are to examine the design issues and to discuss design alternatives of agent migration. We introduce the term *mobility model* to describe the migration technique of a specific mobile agent toolkit, and we propose a language to describe mobility models. As an example we describe the mobility models of two existing mobile agent toolkits, Aglets and Grasshopper, using our new language. The chapter concludes with a brief review of other approaches to classify mobile agent migration techniques.

In this chapter we will consider only those design issues that are related to agent mobility. Of course, there are many other issues a designer must take into consideration when implementing a mobile agent toolkit, as, for example, agent naming, agent communication, security, monitoring, fault-tolerance, and so on. We know that there are several interdependencies between all these issues, and we agree that it would be very useful to propose a complete list of design issues for mobile agent toolkits. Some attempts have been made in this direction, for example, by Picco [1998], Hammer and Aerts [1998], and Karnik and Tripathi [1998]. However, in this book we will focus only on mobility issues. The very important relationship between agent migration and agent security is discussed in a later chapter.

3.3.1 Mobility Models

The migration technique of Tracy that we introduced in the last chapter was only one option for implementing migration in mobile agent toolkits. Actually, all mobile agent toolkits have implemented their own migration techniques, and differences can be found in all phases of our generic framework for agent migration. We already mentioned some of them in Section 3.1, as, for example, other migration initiation commands than *go*, different understandings of the elements of an agent's state, other techniques to relocate classes, and different migration protocols.

The goal of this section is to gather information about other migration techniques in order to:

1. discuss the design issues and design alternatives for agent migration, show pros and cons, and discover dependences between different design issues, and

2. develop a language to describe the migration technique of an existing mobile agent toolkit.

The first point is important for a designer of a new mobile agent toolkit, because he or she must decide which migration technique the new system should provide. The second aspect is to describe the migration technique of an existing mobile agent toolkit in a unified way, which makes it easy to compare different approaches.

To structure our discussion, we introduce the term *mobility model*. The mobility model of a mobile agent toolkit describes almost all the important features concerning agent migration. A mobility model defines three views on migration issues, and each view corresponds to two phases of our six-phase generic framework presented in the last chapter (Fig. 3.9).

1. User's view: How is agent migration initiated?

2. Agent's view: How are data and code relocated in the network?

3. Network's view: How are data and code transferred over the network?

The first view focuses on all issues that are related to the user interface of agent migration (phases S1 and R3). Design issues are the migration command, the technique to resume agent execution, and how the receiver agency is addressed. The second view focuses on the technique for data and code relocation (phases S2 and R2). Here, we introduce the term *migration strategy*, which describes which pieces of code migrates to which other agency and how data is handled in each case. The last view focuses on the technique for transmitting data over the network (phases S3 and R1). We already introduced the term *migration protocol*, which is an important part of this view.

To describe a mobility model, we propose a language named *Mobility Language* (MoL) for which we will give a definition using *Extended Backus-Naur Form* (EBNF). A description of a mobility model consists of several lines, and each line comprises a key-value pair. The key is the name of a design issue, and the value is either a single design alternative or a collection of design alternatives, separated by a semicolon, that were chosen for the mobile agent toolkit to be described.

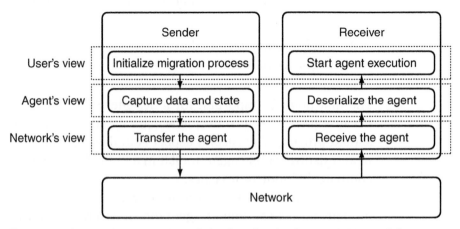

Figure 3.9 The migration process and the three levels of our mobility model.

For example, the following excerpt of a description in MoL defines that an *AgencyName* consists of a *SymbolicName* together with a *HostName*. The second line defines that this agency can be addressed using either a *Protocol* and the *SymbolicName*, or a *Protocol*, the *SymoblicName*, and a *PortNumber*.

```
1 AgencyName = SymbolicName + HostName .
2 AgencyAddress = Protocol + SymbolicName ;
3                 Protocol + SymbolicName + PortNumber .
```

To describe the grammar of MoL, we use EBNF. We will write ⟨MobilityModel⟩ to denote a design issue (nonterminal symbol) and "weak-migration" for a design alternative (terminal symbol). We use the following meta symbols: A sequence of symbols is separated by +, alternatives are printed using brackets [. . . | . . .], repetitions with at least one element are printed using braces { . . . }, and finally an optional symbol is marked with parenthesis (. . .). So, to start our definition of MoL, we define that a mobility model consists of three views and that each view must be defined.

1. ⟨MobilityModel⟩ ::= ⟨User⟩ + ⟨Agent⟩ + ⟨Network⟩

In the following three sections, we discuss each view of a mobility model in detail.

User's View

The first view is considered with all aspects of migration that are related to the agent programmer.

2. ⟨User⟩ ::=   ⟨Naming⟩ + ⟨Creating⟩ + ⟨Code⟩ + ⟨Data⟩ + ⟨Migration⟩

Naming and Addressing

The first design issue, ⟨Naming⟩, considers the aspects of the agency name and the types of addresses that can be used for agent migration.

3. ⟨Naming⟩ ::= ⟨AgencyName⟩ + ⟨AgencyAddress⟩

The aspect of *agent naming* is not considered in our description, because it is part of the design issues for the whole mobile agent toolkit. Each agent has a name to be identified during its lifetime. The name is used by other agents to set up a communication channel and is used by the agency itself to control the agent. In some mobile agent toolkits, the name is also used for agent tracking and for remote communication between agents currently residing at different agencies. Therefore, the agent name must be unique and immutable for the agent's entire lifetime. The structure or scheme for an agent name can be very different. Beside a symbolic name (e.g., *Blofeld*) it usually also contains the name of the home agency and the name of the underlying host system to make the name globally unique. The symbolic name can be explicitly given by the agent's owner in the form of an easy-to-read name or implicitly computed by the agency (e.g., as a digest of the agent's code, together with some random element to make the name unique). In the latter case, a human-readable alias might be provided by the agent's owner. Concerning migration, it is not important how an agent's name is structured or obtained as long as it is guaranteed that each name is globally unique. The agent name is very important for successful migration, because the constraint that no two agents can have the same name can be best validated during the migration process. Therefore, the agent's name is an element of the migration protocol, and the receiver agency checks whether there is an agent with the given name already registered with the agency.

More important with regard to agent migration is the structure of the agency's name. Each agency must have a name so that it can be identified whenever the agency itself or any of its resources must be addressed. If the mobile agent toolkit allows only a single agency on each host, then it is sufficient to have the "Hostname" as the agency name (e.g., `tatjana.cs.uni-jena.de`). For some application areas it might be more convenient to have more than a single agency on each host, so each agency must have a "SymbolicName" (e.g., `fortknox`). If an agency is further structured into several smaller units, sometimes called places, then each place must also have a name, which becomes part of the symbolic name (e.g., `whyte/penthouse`). The symbolic name without the host name is sufficient for agency addressing if there is a technique for name resolving comparable to the domain name resolving of Internet names. If such a technique is not available, then the agency name must consist of the symbolic name and the host name.

4. `<AgencyName>` ::= "AgencyName" + "=" + `<AddressNameScheme>` + "."

5. `<AddressNameScheme>` ::= ["SymbolicName" | "HostName"
      | "SymbolicName" + "+" + "HostName"]

For migration it is necessary to address a single agency. Addressing requires more information than naming, because a network connection usually requires the name of a network protocol and a port number to which communication is directed. To require a protocol makes sense if the mobile agent toolkit provides more than a single transmission protocol. If a port number is required too, then the mobile agent toolkit should require that this port number never be changed and that all agencies use the same port number, because a change forces changes at all agent's source codes (assuming that addresses are hard-coded in the agent's sources and not given by the user). Because this usually cannot be guaranteed, perhaps because another software system already uses this port number, it is wise to allow a dynamic resolution of port numbers according to the required protocol. For example, in Tracy there is a *port resolution service* from which information about used port numbers and network protocols can be obtained, so the user never has to deal with port numbers. Thus, in addition to the source code presented on p. 45, we could also write `go("tcp://tatjana.cs.uni-jena.de", "runRemote")`.

In Grasshopper the *region registry* is responsible for resolving port numbers. In a system where such service is not available, protocol and port number are mandatory if the agency offers several transmission protocols in parallel. A mobile agent toolkit might allow more than one addressing scheme.

6. `<AgencyAddress> ::= "AgencyAddress" + "=" + <AddressSchemes> + "."`

7. `<AddressSchemes> ::= <AddressScheme> + ({";" + <AddressScheme>})`

8. `<AddressScheme> ::= ("Protocol" + "+") + <AddressNameScheme> +`
   `( "+" + "PortNumber")`

Creating Agents

When an agent is created, it must be decided where the agent is started first. Usually, the agent is started at the current agency, that is, the one on which the agent's owner placed the creation command. In this case the current agency becomes the agent's home agency. Sometimes it might be useful to start the agent immediately at a remote agency (e.g., if the current host has only enough resources to execute some kind of loader instead of a fully equipped agency software). To allow this feature, other agencies must support remote starting by offering a communication interface for that purpose.

9. `<Creating> ::= "CreateAt" +`
   `"=" + "CurrentAgency" + ( ";" + "RemoteAgency") + "."`

Agent Code

The next important issue that must be decided is the place from which code can be loaded. We call such a place a *code source*. The code source is used to load classes when the agent is created at its home agency as well as whenever classes are not available at any remote agency and must be loaded dynamically on demand.

The most natural way is to add the directory where agent class files can be found to the *CLASSPATH* variable so that the Java virtual machine can find it. This solution is not the best, because it makes it necessary for *CLASSPATH* to contain all directories for all agents that might ever be started at this agency *before* starting the whole agency software. This comes from a limitation of the Java virtual machine, which does not allow modifications of *CLASSPATH* during runtime. The consequence is that the entire agency must be shut down to make changes of the *CLASSPATH* variable visible. It is more flexible to allow agent class files to be stored anywhere in the file system and to give their location as parameter during agent creation. It is not easy in either case for remote agencies to load classes, because direct access to the file system of a remote agency is usually prohibited if class loading is not part of the migration protocol. The most flexible way is to store class files somewhere in the file system where they are reachable using standard network transmission protocols such as HTTP or FTP.

Next, the file format for the agent's code must be chosen. The easiest way is, of course, to store each class file separately, because this is the output of the Java compiler. Java also allows many class files to be bundled into a single JAR file, which might be compressed and digitally signed.

10. `<Code> ::= "Code" + "=" + <CodeSources> + "."`

11. `<CodeSources> ::= <CodeSource> + ({ ";" + <CodeSource>})`

12. `<CodeSource> ::= ["ClassPath" | "FileSystem" | "HTTP" | "FTP"`
    `| "MigrationProtcol"] + "+" + ["Class" | "Jar"]`

Agent Data

Next it must be decided what types of data the mobile agent can access and use. Each type of data has its own behavior during agent migration.

We distinguish four types of data that are useful for mobile agents:

Proxy Proxy is nonmobile, and remote access is possible. Data items of this type exist only at the agent's home agency and cannot be moved to other agencies. However, mobile agents can access these data items transparently from any other remote agency, and any modifications are transmitted to the agent's home agency. We name this data type *proxy* because there is a proxy object[5] on each agency that is part of the serialized agent and that is responsible for transparently forwarding modifications to the home agency. Access to files or the graphical user interface might be more efficient using this type of data.

Static Static data is nonmobile, and remote access not possible. Data items of this type exist only at one agency and cannot be taken along during migration, because they are physically bound to their agency. This data type is common for files or the graphical user interface, whenever they are not of type proxy. In Java these data items can be marked as *transient* so that they are not part of the serialized agent.

Moving Moving data is, mobile and source removed. This data type is used for all local or member variables of the agent that are not shared with other agents or the agency. Data items of this type are part of the serialized agent. After migration, data items of this type no longer exist at the sender agency.

Copying Copying is mobile, and the source is not removed. This data type is used for all variables for which the agent has a reference and that are shared with other agents or the agency itself. A copy of the data item is part of the serialized agent, so at the remote agency the agent has still access to it but modifications are not visible at the original data item at the last agency.

13. `<Data> ::= "DataTypes" + "=" + <DataTypes> + "."`

14. `<DataTypes> ::= <DataType> + ({ ";" + <DataType>})`

15. `<DataType> ::= [ "Proxy" | "Static" | "Moving" | "Copying"]`

---

5. Compare the proxy design pattern described in Gamma et al. [1995].

Migration

We subdivide design issues concerning migration into the following items:

16. `<Migration> ::= <Initiator> + <Mobility> + <DestinationAddress> +`
    `<Effect> + <Error>`

The first design issue that must be discussed is the initiator of an agent migration. Migration can be initiated by the agent itself or by some other instance (e.g., another agent or the agency). Usually, it contradicts the autonomy of software agents for an external instance to decide to migrate an agent. Nevertheless, in some situations it does make sense to allow this, for example, for load balancing or in the case of severe errors, which make it necessary to shut down a complete agency. In this case the agent should be forced to migrate to another system to prevent severe damage to the agent. The other scenario, in which migration is initiated from outside the agent, is when an agent is forced to migrate back to its home agency. If migration is initiated from outside the agent, it might be useful to allow the agent to vote against the migration.

17. `<Initiator> ::= "MigrationInitiator" + "=" + "Agent" +`
    `<OtherInitiator> + "."`

18. `<OtherInitiator> ::= (";" + "OtherAgent" + ("withVeto")) + (";"`
    `+ "Agency" + ("withVeto")) + (";" + "Owner" + ("withVeto"))`

The next issue is the type of mobility. Existing mobile agent toolkits can be distinguished by the type of mobility they offer to the programmer, and, actually, this is the most discussed design issue concerning agent migration. Each type of mobility can be characterized by the interpretation of the term *state*. The type of mobility can be *weak* or *strong*, and in both cases further issues must be decided.

19. `<Mobility> ::= "Mobility" + "=" + [ "Weak" + "." + <Weak> | "Strong"`
    `+ "." + <Strong>]`

The weakest form of mobility transmits only the instance variables (object state) and the code of the mobile agent to the destination platform. The mobile agent is initialized and started by invoking a designated method. This kind of mobility is used in Aglets, Grasshopper, Mole [Straßer et al., 1997], and Discovery [Lazar and Sidhu, 1998]. We call this type of mobility *weak mobility with fixed method method invocation*.

In a stronger form of mobility the mobile agent toolkit allows the programmer to define the name of a starting method within the `go` command. On the destination site the agent is initialized and started by invoking the given method. This kind of mobility is used in Voyager [ObjectSpace, 1997]. The drawback of these two forms of mobility is that the programmer has to exert additional effort to implement state marshaling and unmarshaling of local variables. Consider the following example:

```
1 public class AMobileAgent extends Agent
2 {
3   private int copyOfLocal = 0;
4
5   protected void anyMethod()
6   {
7     int local = 10;
8
9     // some code
10
11    // before we can migrate, we have to save variable local
12    copyOfLocal = local;
13
14    go( "tcp://tatjana.cs.uni-jena.de", "runAtRemote" );
15  }
16 }
```

This example shows how to save the value of local variables in object variables so that the value is part of the serialized agent. Method *runAtRemote* can use variable *copyOfLocal* again.

In both mobility levels the migration command has to be the last instruction within a method, because changing the platform induces invoking a new method. The difference between these two types of mobility is not really evident, because it is very easy to map the latter type of mobility to weak mobility in the Java programming language. We show an example of an agent that simulates the latter form of mobility, although the mobile agent toolkit only provides weak mobility.

```
1 public abstract class GoWithMethodName extends Agent
2 {
3   private String nextMethod = null;
4
```

```
 5   protected void go( String destination, String methodName ) throws Exception
 6   {
 7     nextMethod = methodName;
 8     go( destination );
 9   }
10
11   public void run()
12   {
13     Method method = this.getClass().getMethod( nextMethod, new Class[0] );
14     method.invoke( this, new Object[0] );
15   }
16 }
```

The *go* command stores the name of the method to be invoked at the remote agency in a variable that is part of the serialized agent. At the remote agency, the designated method *run* is started as usual for weak mobility. This method uses the Java reflection mechanism to call the given method. We call this type of mobility *weak mobility with arbitrary method invocation.*

20. `<Weak>` ::= "WeakMobility" + "=" ["FixedMethod" | "ArbitraryMethod"] + "+" + ["Command" | "Ticket"] + "."

When only a weak form of mobility is offered, the command to initiate the migration can be a specific command or predefined method of the agent, or a *ticket*. The first way is to use a migration command, for example, *go* or *move*, in which parameters define to which agency the agent should migrate. The other way is to store necessary information about the destination as a data structure that is called a ticket. When agent execution terminates, the agency reads the ticket and migrates the agent. Using a migration command terminates agent execution at exactly the point where the migration command occurs. All statements following the migration command are never executed, unless a migration error occurs, which we will discuss later. Using a ticket does not give direct control of migration to the programmer. A ticket can be redefined several times, which makes it not obvious to the programmer what the agent really will do when execution terminates.

Mobile agent toolkits that offer the highest level of agent mobility can marshal not only all instance variables but also all local variables of the current method, together with the program counter and the call stack. On the destination agency the agent is initialized and started at the first instruction after the *go* command. We call this type of mobility *strong*. Early mobile agent toolkits, such as Telescript [White, 1996] or AgentTCL [Gray, 1996], offered this kind of mobility, because it is the most natural one for the programmer. It is comparatively easy to add all the features that support strong mobility to a mobile agent toolkit if full access to the underlying programming language, the compiler, and the runtime system is available. A new command go can be supplemented that initiates the complete marshaling process, or open access to call stack and program counter can be granted to the programmer of the mobile agent system.

To implement strong mobility in mobile agent toolkits that are written in the Java programming language, the source code of the Java virtual machine (JVM) must be modified or the agent's source code has to be transformed to simulate modification. Modifying the JVM is difficult, although it is said to be done in Ara [Peine and Stolpmann, 1997], Sumatra [Acharya et al., 1997], and D'Agents. (See also the Merpati project at University of Zurich, Switzerland [Suri et al., 2000].) A modification of the JVM must be considered strategically imprudent. A customer can use the resulting mobile agent toolkit only if he uses the modified JVM, not to mention problems of licensing the JVM source code.

The other way to offer strong mobility to the programmer is agent source code transformation. Fünfrocken [1999] transforms the agent's source code by a preprocessor that inserts code to save and recover the execution state. Another comparable attempt has been made by Sekiguchi et al. [1999]. The drawback of both methods is a longer source code and an unnegligible performance decrease. Other techniques to achieve strong mobility were developed by Illmann et al. [2001], Bettini and Nicola [2001], Wang et al. [2001], Fukuda et al. [2003], and Chakravarti et al. [2003].

Strong mobility, in the way we have described it, only means that the agent can interrupt itself to start the migration. The reverse case, that the agency can interrupt an agent (e.g., to perform load balancing or to start an emergency migration to a neighbor platform because of a system failure) is not possible with any of these migration concepts. Because it is currently impossible to achieve this *transparent* type of mobility, we do not add a design alternative for this case. (See Walsh et al. [2000], who describe how to achieve this type of mobility in principle in Java.)

```
21.  <Strong> ::= "StrongMobility" + "=" + ["SourceCodeTransformation" |
                  "VMModification"] + "."
```

Whether weak or strong mobility should be implemented in mobile agent toolkits has been a major issue. Baumann [1995] states that strong mobility is useless in most cases, because "a migration step is a major break in the life of an agent." Usually, a mobile agent works in phases, and each phase is completely executed at a single agency. Migration at the transition between phases, takes place not within a single phase. Cabri et al. [2000] argue along the same line while stressing that weak mobility leads to a "clean programming style, ... resulting in a more clear and understandable program." Advocates of strong mobility argue that it has a more natural programming style and more possible advantages in agent engineering; see, for example, Belle and D'Hondt [2000]. Walsh et al. [2000] argue that the advantage of strong mobility is "that long-running or long-lived threads can suddenly move or be moved from one host to another," which immediately leads to the question of agent autonomy.

Next, the target of a migration must be discussed. Each migration is directed to some target, whose address must be defined using a migration command or a ticket. Usually, migration is directed to a remote agency whose name is known. Migration can also be directed to another agent or a resource that the agent wants to use. Then we must take into account whether only the next destination is specified or a complete itinerary or route can be defined. In some application scenarios it might be very useful to have a mechanism to define a route, because the agent has to repeat a single task on several agencies to collect data. The route can be defined by the programmer of the agent and can be fixed (i.e., not modifiable by the agent during runtime) or fully flexible, allowing the agent to define the route by itself.

22. `<DestinationAddress> ::= "DestinationAddress" + "=" +`
     `<DestinationType> + ({ ";" + <DestinationType>}) + "."`

23. `<DestinationType> ::= <Resource> + "+" + <Cardinality>`

24. `<Resource> ::= ["Agency" | "Agent"]`

25. `<Cardinality> ::= ["Single" | "Fixed Route" | "Definable Route"]`

The next issue is the effect of an agent migration. Usually, in a migration, the agent is moved completely to the remote agency and there is still only a single instance of this agent. One alternative is to make a fresh copy of the agent, which is sent to another agency and started as if it has not existed before. Another option is to clone the agent. In this case a copy is sent to a remote agency, but this copy already has the same data as the original agent. The latter technique is used in AgentTCL and is called *forking* there.

26. `<MigrationEffect> ::= "MigrationEffect" + "=" + <Effects> + "."`

27. `<Effects> ::= <Effect> + ({ ";" + <Effect>})`

28. `<Effect> ::= ["Move" | "Copy" | "Cloning"]`

The final design issue is related to an agency's behavior if there is a migration error. The technique to use here depends on the type of mobility chosen. For the first technique the agent restarts, and a local variable indicates that an error has occurred. If a weak form of mobility was chosen, then this kind of error notification is used. If the system allows an arbitrary method to be invoked after successful migration, then invoking an error method is a good alternative. The reason of the migration failure can be given as a parameter. If a system provides strong mobility, then throwing an exception is the best technique. Grasshopper offers this technique too, although it offers only a weak form of mobility.

29. `<Error> ::= "MigrationError" + "=" + ["Restart" | "ErrorMethod" | "Exception"] + "."`

Agent's View

In this section we look at the way code can be relocated within the network. Data transmission is not an issue here, because the types of data supported by the mobile agent toolkit were already defined previously and the only technique currently available is that in which the serialized agent is sent as a single unit from the current agency to the next remote agency.

Migration Strategies

The type of code relocation that is used for agent migration is named *migration strategy*. In the following we describe four common migration strategies with regard to transmission type, site location and code granularity (Fig. 3.10).

Some toolkits offer a migration strategy that we call *push-all-to-next strategy*. The code of the agent (together with the code of all referenced objects) and the serialized agent are transmitted simultaneously. Some toolkits do not transmit the whole code but rather filter out those pieces of code already available on each platform (e.g., ubiquitous classes) like the standard classes of Java and code of the mobile agent toolkit. This migration strategy is used in Voyager 2.0 [ObjectSpace, 1998], Ara [Peine, 1997], and

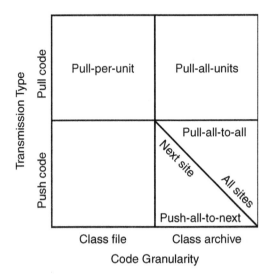

Figure 3.10 Overview of migration strategies.

Extended Facile [Knabe, 1997a]. It corresponds to one of the main characteristics of mobile agents—autonomy. The agent needs no connection to the home agency, from which it was started. At a first look this strategy seems fast, because only one transmission is necessary for the complete agent. However, a major drawback is that code that is probably never used is transmitted to the destination site.

The second approach does not transmit any code with the data transmission. We call this the *pull strategy*. After receiving and unmarshaling the agent's data, the mobile agent server on the destination site tries to invoke the given method and then starts loading the corresponding class files dynamically. The pull strategy can be further divided into *pull-per-unit* and *pull-all-units*. The first strategy dynamically loads code on a per-class policy, whereas the second strategy loads all class files as one package immediately if even one class file must be loaded. The pull strategy is used in Mole [Straßer et al., 1997] and in Grasshopper. This strategy can be slower than push-all-to-next, because several network connections may be necessary to load all the required class files. When delegating this task to the Java virtual machine, one network connection per class is needed (pull-per-unit), unless several classes have been combined into one Java archive (pull-all-units). The major drawback of both pull-oriented migration strategies is that there must be an open network connection, or at least a fast way to reconnect, either to the home agency or to the last agency the agent came from. If it is impossible to connect to any of these platforms, the agent cannot be executed.

The fourth migration strategy is the *push-all-to-all* strategy. As in the push-all-to-next strategy, the complete code of an agent is transmitted, but it is sent to all destination platforms the agent is going to visit, not only to the next destination. Of course, this requires that the agent know all its destinations in advance (e.g., by a given itinerary). When an agent arrives on a destination platform, the execution can start immediately, without any further code downloading.

Besides these four different strategies, combinations of push and pull techniques are used in some toolkits, as we describe in detail later, for example, Aglets offers a technique in which classes with a high probability of use at the next agency are pushed and missing classes are pulled from a code server later on demand. The MASIF standardization approach suggests that only the agent's main class be pushed and that all other classes be loaded on demand. However, the decision of which classes are pushed and which are pulled is made by the system. In contrast, in Sumatra [Acharya et al., 1997], the programmer can combine push and pull strategies manually.

Almost all mobile agent toolkits offer only one of these strategies, and an interesting question is whether it makes sense to adapt the migration strategy to fit an application scenario. We already mentioned some qualitative arguments in favor of each migration strategy, but we have not provided exact quantitative arguments. For the moment, we only mention that our own research [Braun et al., 2001b] has come to the conclusion that there are unnegligible performance differences between all strategies—we come back to this question in the next section.

Code Transfer

We now discuss the following issues concerning code relocation:

30. `<Agent> ::= <CodeTransfer> + (<CodeCache>) + (<UbiquitousClasses>)`

As described in the last section, code relocation strategies can be divided into push strategies and pull strategies. Some toolkits offer both approaches, which means that some classes are pushed to the next destination and other classes are pulled on demand.

31. `<CodeTransfer> ::= "CodeRelocation" + "=" + <CodeStrategies> + "."`

32. `<CodeStrategies> ::= <CodeStrategy> + ({ ";" + <CodeStrategy>})`

33. `<CodeStrategy> ::= [<Push> | <Pull>]`

When the system offers a push strategy, it must be decided which classes must be sent to the agency. We call this issue `<ClassClosure>`. The first technique is to determine all classes the agent might ever use during its lifetime based on the agent's main class file. How to determine an *agent class closure* in Java was already described in Section 3.1. The next technique collects only those classes for which an object exists in the serialized agent (`"SerializedAgentClosure"`). Because these classes are necessary to deserialize the agent successfully at the remote agency, it is a good compromise between sending all classes at once and sending none. However, the fact that some classes are *in use* does not say anything about the probability of other classes being in use at the next agency. Some systems allow the user to bundle classes in a JAR file, and whenever a class from a JAR file must be transmitted, the whole JAR file will be transmitted (`"JarClosure"`). The last technique allows the user to make the decision of which classes will be transmitted transmit dynamically during runtime.

The next design issue that must be decided is whether code can be pushed only to the next agency or to all agencies that were defined in a route or that are available within the logical network.

34. `<Push> ::= "Push" + <ClassClosure> + "To" + <PushTarget>`

35. `<ClassClosure> ::= ["AgentClassClosure" | "SerializedAgentClosure"`
`| "JarClosure" | "UserDefinedClosure"]`

36. `<PushTarget> ::= ["NextServer" | "ManyServers"]`

When a system offers a pull technique, it first must be decided what transmission unit will be used. Usually, only single class files will be transmitted. Although not implemented in any mobile agent toolkit, it is possible to download a complete JAR file. The next issue is the place where the remote agency looks for the class to be loaded. Here, a mobile agent toolkit must define a strategy for which instances are to be asked for the code and in which order. A possible component is, for example, the class loader, which is responsible for loading all the agent's classes. A class loader should have a local cache of all classes already loaded. Next, the local *CLASSPATH* variable could be checked for a class with the given name. Then, an agency-wide class cache, which is shared by all class loaders, can be asked, and finally, several other agencies, for example, the last agency visited or the agent's home agency, can be asked.

37. `<Pull> ::= "Pull" + [ "Jar" | "Class" ] + "From" + <PullTargets>`

38. `<PullTargets> ::= <PullTarget> + ({ "+" + <PullTarget>})`

39. `<PullTarget> ::= [ <AgencyType> | "ClassLoader" | "ClassPath" |`
    `"Cache" | "CodeSource"]`

40. `<AgencyType> ::= ["Home" | "Remote" | "LastServer"]`

An important design issue is to decide which classes are never transmitted, even if they are members of a class closure, because they are assumed to exist at every agency already. Those classes were named *ubiquitous* in Section 3.1. A mobile agent toolkit might define that by itself, for example, it could determine that all class from Java packages (which have specific prefixes) and all classes of the mobile agent toolkit are never transmitted. Sometimes it might be useful to allow the user to add package prefixes or class names to this list ("`UserDefined`"), because mobile agents are part of some application that can also be assumed to exist on every remote agency. The most flexible way is to allow the agent to define its own filter list.

41. `<UbiquitousClasses> ::= "UbiquitousClasses" + "=" + ["SystemDefined"`
    `|"UserDefined" | "AgentDefined"] + "."`

Finally, it is important to decide whether class code is cached by the agency after it was loaded for the first time. Although caching is a good technique to save time when loading the same classes very often, it has the negative effect that class code changes might not become visible to the agency, because the cache is not informed about changes. Caching can be found most often when an agent's code is reachable using the *CLASSPATH* variable, because all classes of the *CLASSPATH* are loaded by the system class loader of the Java virtual machine. For other classes it must be decided whether the agent class loader or a component of the agency manages the class cache. In the first case, agents of the same type are not able to share code, which means that the same class might be loaded more than once. In the latter case, agents might share classes, which might lead to problems with different class versions. In this case it must also be decided whether any kind of version management will be implemented. Another design issue concerning code caches is whether the class cache is checked only before loading classes or also before class transmission. The first approach can prevent only class downloading, whereas the second approach can also prevent classes from being pushed to the agency. This technique must be supported by the migration protocol, because class names must be sent before pushing any agent code. The remote agency could determine for which classes the code is already available.

42. `<CodeCache> ::= "CodeCache" + "=" <Instance> + "+" + ["BeforeTransfer"`
     `| "BeforeLoad"] + "."`

43. `<Instance> ::= [ "ClassLoader" | "Agency" ] + "+" + ("VersionManagement")`

Network's View

The last view considers all aspects related to data transmission. The *transmission strategy* defines the way an agent is actually transmitted to the destination platform. Some Java-based mobile agent toolkits (e.g., Mole) use a proprietary and very simple migration protocol that is based on *remote method invocation* (RMI) [Sun, 2002] for this task. The destination agent server is an RMI server that provides a method to accept a mobile agent. The drawback of using RMI is its poor performance. Most toolkits use migration protocols in addition to TCP/IP or HTTP.

It must be decided whether an asynchronous or synchronous migration protocol is used. The advantage of an asynchronous protocol is performance, whereas it can also be more unreliable, because the remote agency does not acknowledge reception. The second issue is whether migration is failure atomic, that is, whether the migration protocol guarantees that the mobile agent is transmitted completely or not at all. The next issue is the network protocol. Several protocols are listed; the most common are perhaps TCP/IP and RMI. Grasshopper defines some kind of meta-protocol, which can be used to determine which protocols the receiver agency supports before sending the agent.

44. `<Network> ::= <MigrationProtocol> + <TransmissionProtocols>`

45. `<MigrationProtocol> ::= "MigrationProtocol" + "=" + ["Synchronous" |`
     `"Asynchronous"] + ("FailureAtomic") + "."`

46. `<TransmissionProtocols> ::= "TransmissionProtocol" + "="`
    `<NetworkProtocols> + "."`

47. `<NetworkProtocols> ::= <NetworkProtocol> + ({ ";" +`
    `<NetworkProtocol>})`

48. `<NetworkProtocol> ::= [ "TCP/IP" | "CORBA" | "SSL" | "RMI" | "RMISSL"`
    `| "SOAP" | "META" | "HTTP" | "Other" ]`

3.3.2 Examples for Mobility Models

In the following section we describe the mobility model of the mobile agent toolkits Aglets and Grasshopper. We chose these two toolkits, because they are the most famous and are used for real-world application development. We will not describe the Tracy mobility model here; a detailed introduction into the migration technique of Tracy will be part of the next chapter.

Aglets

Aglets is a mobile agent toolkit that was developed by IBM in 1995. The first announcement was made at the JavaOne conference in 1996, and the first version of Aglets was published in 1998. Since 2000, Aglets has been an open-source project at Sourceforge and is no longer supported by IBM. The Aglets toolkit supports the MASIF standard.

Aglets provides a weak form of mobility, in which a method named *run* is called whenever an agent is started or restarted at an agency. The migration initiation command is named *dispatch* and gets as a single parameter the URL of the destination agency. To address agencies, a protocol and a host name are mandatory and a symbolic agency name can be added if more than one agency exists at the destination. The port number is predefined and cannot be changed. Route management is not supported by the *dispatch* method but can be implemented by the user with use of a specific design pattern.

When an agent is created, only a single code source can be defined, but the type of code source is very flexible. It usually contains a URL to a resource that can be accessed using the HTTP protocol or the Aglets migration protocol ATP. Classes must be stored in a directory that is listed in the *AGLET_EXPORT_PATH* environment variable to be fetched from any agency using the ATP protocol. If the code source contains a file system path, classes cannot be downloaded from remote agencies. If no code source was defined at all, then the agent's code is loaded using the environment variable *AGLET_PATH*, which contains a list of directories of the local file system. These classes cannot be transferred to other agencies.

The migration strategy of Aglets is not just a simple push or pull strategy but a sophisticated combination of both. When an agent migrates, all classes for which an object exists in the serialized agent (Aglets calls these *classes in use*) are pushed to the next agency. If the code source is a JAR file, then the entire JAR file is pushed to the next agency without regard for whether a class is in use. At the destination agency, missing classes are loaded on demand (pulled). To load a class, the following strategy is used. First, it is determined whether the current class loader has already loaded this class, then the class is searched in the local *CLASSPATH*. Because of this, local class might be loaded even though the agent has pushed its own class file. Third, the local cache manager is checked, which is, in the current version of Aglets, able to cache only JAR files. Finally, the agent's code source is checked for the code. Code downloading is always based on single class files and never on complete JAR files. Classes that are not supposed to migrate must be defined using one of the two environment variables, *CLASSPATH* or *AGLET_PATH*.

The user can influence the migration strategy used for the next migration only by modifying the object state of the agent. If a class is not to be transferred to the next agency, none of its objects may exist in the serialized agent. The most flexible way to achieve this is to set all variables of this class to `null`. Then the Java serialization process will not consider this class. The other way is to define a variable as `transient`, which has the same effect. The reverse case, to transmit a class although no object of this type currently exists, can be achieved just as easily. It is necessary only to add a variable of type *Class*, which must be initialized with the name of the class to transmit, for example, *Class forceTransmission = MyClass*`.class`.

Other important issues of the Aglets mobility model are that an agent's owner is able to retract an agent from any agency, if he or she knows its current location. Aglets uses the standard Java serialization technique, so data types static, copy, and move are supported. The class cache is requested only before class downloading, and the migration protocol is defined in addition to TCP/IP, and can also be tunneled within an HTTP protocol to get through firewalls.

Here is the complete description of the Aglets's mobility model:

```
1 // Programmer's view
2 //
3 AgencyName = SymbolicName + HostName .
```

```
 4 AgencyAddress = Protocol + HostName ; Protocol + HostName + SymbolicName .
 5 CreateAt = CurrentAgency .
 6 Code = ClassPath + Class ; ClassPath + Jar ; FileSystem + Class ;
 7      FileSystem + Jar ; HTTP + Class ; HTTP + Jar ;
 8      MigrationProtocol + Class; MigrationProtocol + Jar .
 9 DataTypes = Static ; Copy ; Move .
10 MigrationInitiator = Agent ; OtherAgent ; Owner .
11 Mobility = Weak .
12 WeakMobility = FixedMethod + Command .
13 // Agent's view
14 //
15 DestinationAddress = Agency + Single .
16 MigrationEffect = Move .
17 MigrationError = Restart .
18 CodeRelocation = Push SerializedAgentClosure To NextServer ;
19                  Push JarClosure To NextServer with base Jar ;
20                  Pull Class From ClassLoader + ClassPath + Cache + CodeSource .
21 UbiquitousClasses = SystemDefined .
22 CodeCache = ClassLoader + BeforeLoad .
23 // Network's view
24 //
25 MigrationProtocol = Synchronous .
26 TransmissionProtocol = TCP/IP ; HTTP .
```

Grasshopper

The Grasshopper mobile agent toolkit was developed by IKV++, in Berlin, Germany. The first version was developed at GMD FOKUS in 1995. Since 1998 the product has been maintained by IKV, which is a GMD spin-off company. Currently, Grasshopper has been shared to a be part of a new product called enago. Grasshopper supports both MASIF and FIPA standards.

Grasshopper provides a weak form of mobility, in which a method named *live* is invoked to start the agent. The migration initiation command is *move*, which gets as a parameter the URL of the next destination. Grasshopper's technique for catching migration errors is interesting: An exception is thrown. Grasshopper does not provide techniques for route management.

When an agent is created, several code sources can be defined from which code can be loaded on demand. A user definable code source can be on the local file system or can be accessed via the HTTP protocol. In either case it seems impossible to define a JAR file as the code source.

When an agent migrates, *no* classes are transmitted with object state migration, which means that Grasshopper does not support any kind of push strategy. When the agent is deserialized, classes must be pulled according to the following strategy. First, the agency's *CLASSPATH* is checked by the system class loader. If code is reachable using this class loader, no two different classes with the same name can exist. Next, the last agency from which the agent has come is asked for the class. If it is still not found, all the agent's code sources are checked sequentially, and finally the agent's home agency is asked for the code. In all of these cases, class files are cached only by the agent's class loader, so transmission of the same class for different agents cannot be avoided. Because Grasshopper provides only a single pull migration strategy, there is no chance for the user to change the migration behavior of its agent. It is even impossible to modify the class downloading strategy, for example, to bypass the last agency to be asked for the code.

Another important issue of the Grasshopper mobility model is that an agent can be forced to migrate by other system components, but the agent is able to vote against a migration. Grasshopper's transmission strategies are very interesting. Grasshopper not only supports several network protocols but also has a meta-protocol by which two agencies can communicate to ascertain which network protocols are supported by both systems. A service called *region registry* is responsible for maintaining a directory of all agencies active within the local subnetwork. Using this region registry makes it possible to omit port numbers in the agency address.

```
 1 // Programmer's view
 2 //
 3 AgencyName = HostName + SymbolicName .
 4 AgencyAddress = HostName + SymbolicName ; Protocol + HostName + SymbolicName ;
 5               Protocol + HostName + SymbolicName + PortNumber .
 6 CreateAt = CurrentAgency .
 7 Code = ClassPath + Class ; HTTP + Class ; .
 8 DataTypes = Static ; Copy ; Move .
 9 MigrationInitiator = Agent ; System WithVeto .
10 Mobility = Weak .
11 WeakMobility = FixedMethod + Command .
12 // Agent's view
13 //
14 DestinationAddress = Agency + Single .
15 MigrationEffect = Move .
16 MigrationError = Exception .
```

```
17 CodeRelocation = Pull Class From ClassLoader + ClassPath + LastServer +
18                  CodeSource + Home.
19 UbiquitousClasses = SystemDefined .
20 CodeCache = ClassLoader + BeforeLoad .
21 // Network's view
22 //
23 MigrationProtocol = Synchronous .
24 TransmissionProtocol = TCP/IP ; CORBA ; SSL ; RMISSL ; META .
```

3.3.3 Related Work—Other Classification Approaches

In this chapter we proposed a classification scheme for the migration issues of mobile agents. Although almost every mobile agent toolkit has implemented a different migration technique, as far as we know, no sophisticated approach has been developed to classify these different techniques. Some authors describe design issues of mobile agent toolkits in general (e.g., related to agent communication, agent naming, security). Concerning agent mobility, these approaches remain superficial and in most cases mention only the difference between weak and strong mobility.

For example, Hammer and Aerts [1998] discovered several design issues concerning mobile agent toolkits, but detected only three issues concerning migration. First, according to Hammer and Aerts, it must be decided whether migration is *state preserving*. The next issue is whether migration is *failure atomic*, and the last issue is whether the agent can define an itinerary. Karnik and Tripathi [1998] distinguish only between strong and weak mobility; whether the agent is moved, cloned, or forked; and whether code is pushed to the next agency or pulled from the home agency. Cabri et al. [1998a] decide only between strong and weak mobility and whether migration is initiated explicitly by the agent itself or implicitly by the underlying agency software.

Fuggetta et al. [1998] have proposed the best approach so far to classify different techniques for mobile code. Unfortunately, their approach is not suited to classify mobile agent migration techniques; it mainly tries to cover all types of mobile code approaches, such as code-on-demand, remote-evaluation, and mobile agents. The authors distinguish strong and weak mobility; they use the term *weak mobility* to mean remote-evaluation, in which, except for some initialization data, no *state* information is shipped to the remote server. In our definition, weak mobility contains the object state of the agent. Fuggetta et al. define strong mobility as supported in two forms: migration and remote cloning. The first form is comparable to our migration effect of *moving* an agent, whereas the latter is comparable to our migration effect of *cloning* an agent. Weak mobility is divided into code shipping (remote-evaluation) and code fetching (code-on-demand)—do not confuse this with our distinction between push and pull migration strategies. Finally, the authors distinguish between asynchronous and synchronous techniques, in which the sending execution unit is either nonblocking or blocking and waiting for the result. The authors also classify data-space management, which results in an enumeration of alternatives comparable to our approach for the *data* design issue.

3.4   Reasoning about Improved Mobility Models

In the previous section we presented information about current implementation techniques for mobile agent migration. We can now address new mobility models and migration techniques that surmount the drawbacks of simple mobile agents, as discussed in Section 3.2.3.

In Section 3.4.1 we discuss these drawbacks against the background of current implementations and evaluate whether today's mobility models are able to solve any of these problems. Then, in Section 3.4.2, we will examine factors influencing mobile agents' performance and discuss how this performance can be improved. One important aspect of Section 3.4.3 is to investigate whether the migration strategy has an effect on the overall performance of mobile agents. In Section 3.4.4, we will describe our new mobility model, named Kalong. Using the Kalong mobility model gives the mobile agent programmer and the mobile agent itself the possibility of influencing the migration strategy in a very fine-grained way and offers other very important new features to increase migration performance.

3.4.1   Drawbacks of Simple Migration Techniques, and Current Implementations

In Section 3.2.3 we discussed the results of our mathematical model for network load and transmission time for mobile agents using a single, very simple migration technique (push-all-to-next). We detected several inherent drawbacks of mobile agents that are responsible for a higher network load and higher processing time as compared with client-server approaches.

The inherent drawbacks of mobile agents are:

- An agent's code is typically larger than a simple client-server request and causes a fixed overhead for each migration. It is only practical to send large code to remote agencies if server results can be decreased dramatically by data filtering or compression.

- An agent's code is transmitted to a remote agency, even if it is never used there. In the case of the push-all-to-next migration strategy, transmission of never-used classes cannot be avoided. However, even in the case of a pull migration strategy, code might be loaded superfluously because of the object state serializing technique used by all Java-based mobile agent toolkits. We will present an example of this later.

- An agent's data is transmitted as a single unit, which means that a mobile agent carries data items to all servers of the given itinerary, even if they are never used before reaching the home agency again. In the other case, the agent carries data items to several agencies, although they are never used at the first agencies. This was the reason for poor performance in the case of a high number of agencies.

However, we have also already detected a major advantage of mobile agents. For small-bandwidth network connections, a mobile agent rarely needs to use this bottleneck for migration, whereas client-server approaches have to use it several times.

It is fair to assume that using migration strategies other than the simple push-all-to-next strategy could be a solution for the problem of superfluously transmitted class code. For example, in the pull-per-unit strategy, code is never transmitted with an agent's state transmission and is always loaded dynamically on demand. Therefore, classes are transmitted only if they are imperative at the remote agency. It is important to understand what it means for a class to be imperative at a specific agency. Usually, we would expect to load a class, only if the corresponding object is accessed, that is, used or defined. In Java, at least as long as the Java object serialization technique is used, code must also be downloaded if an object of this type is part of the serialized agent. Look at the following example for a mobile agent:

```
1 import de.fsuj.tracy.agent.*;
2
3 public class SomeTracyAgent extends Agent
4 {
```

```
 5    protected SomeClass first = new SomeClass();
 6    transient SomeOtherClass second;
 7
 8    public MyFirstTracyAgent()
 9    {
10     // do some initialization
11    }
12
13    public void startAgent()
14    {
15     // do something
16     go( "tcp://tatjana.cs.uni-jena.de", "runAtRemote" );
17    }
18
19    public void runAtRemote()
20    {
21     // do something
22     if( /* ... */ )
23     {
24       AnotherClass third = new AnotherClass();
25       // do something
26     }
27     go( "tcp://domino.cs.uni-jena.de", "runAtNext" );
28   }
29 }
```

After initialization, the agent immediately migrates to *tatjana.cs.uni-jena.de*, and execution is resumed by invoking method *runAtRemote*. Variable *first* is part of the serialized agent, whereas variable *second* is not, because it is marked as `transient`. We assume that the agent migrates using strategy pull-per-unit, so no classes are sent with the object state. When the agent is deserialized at the remote agency, besides the agent's main class *SomeTracyAgent*, class *SomeClass* is also loaded, because it is needed to reconstruct the agent correctly. Thus, this class *is* loaded, although method *runAtRemote* does not use variable *first* at all. Class *SomeOtherClass* is also loaded, because it is necessary to create an object of type *SomeTracyAgent*, although variable second was not part of this serialized object and is not used in method *runAtRemote*. An example in which code downloading really depends on use is variable *third*, which is a local variable defined within method *runAtRemote*. If we assume that no other object variable uses *SomeOtherClass*, then only if the expression in line 22 is `true`, will code for class *SomeOtherClass* be loaded. What we have learned from this example is that when using the standard Java serialization technique, the agent and the programmer do not have precise control over which classes are downloaded at the destination agency. Even if strategy pull-per-unit is used, classes might be downloaded that are not really necessary at the remote agency.

We now want to discuss whether the disadvantages of the two simple migration techniques just described can be resolved by any mobility model presented in the last section. The first point—mobile agents' code being larger than a simple client-server request—can of course not be solved by any mobility model automatically. The problem is that an agent's code usually contains other methods that are not needed at the next destination, which lengthen the code. An agent's code size would surely benefit from a code split so that each piece of code would contain only methods with high coherence. Code transmission would then work on the basis of code pieces. As long as such a *code-splitting technique* is not available, the programmer can attach importance to this problem only when designing his or her agents.

The second point—superfluously transmitted classes—cannot be solved either in the Aglets toolkit or in the Grasshopper toolkit. For example, in Grasshopper, classes are never pushed to next agencies but rather always loaded dynamically on demand. Because Grasshopper uses the standard Java serialization technique, some classes might be loaded even though their code is not needed at the destination. Classes are also loaded superfluously if two agents of the same type reside at the same agency. Code is loaded twice in this case, because Grasshopper does not provide code caching on the level of agencies. In Aglets, classes in use are pushed, and other classes are loaded on demand. The user is able to influence only which classes are pushed to the next agency (e.g., by storing class code in different directories on the local file system and defining environment variables appropriately). Because the Aglets toolkit is also based on the Java serialization technique, classes are downloaded.

The third point—fine-grained data transmission—cannot be solved by either system's mobility model, because both use the standard Java serialization technique, in which the object closure always contains all data items that are in use and not marked transient. The user cannot download data items from the agent's home agency during the agent's tour or send data items back to the home agency when it is known that they are not used at the next agencies, unless he or she uses application-level techniques.

Our conclusion after this brief analysis of current mobility models and toolkits is that none of them is even close to solving the problems we identified as inherent drawbacks of simple migration techniques. Although neither of the inspected mobile agent toolkits uses the simple push-all-to-next migration strategy, they are not able to solve the problems of superfluously transmitted code and data transmission.

3.4.2 Improving the Performance of Mobile Agents

Before we examine specific techniques to improve the migration process using new sophisticated mobility models, we need to think about performance optimizations for mobile agents in general. In the next section we concisely discuss several approaches to improve the performance of mobile agents. Then, we discuss the influence of different migration strategies on the performance of mobile agents.

Overview of Mobile Agents' Performance Aspects

The performance of mobile agents is influenced by several factors, and within the life cycle of a typical mobile agent, we find several areas where performance can be improved (e.g., its task given by the user, the route or itinerary, its code size, the size of collected data, network parameters like bandwidth and latency).

To structure our discussion, we developed the following classification schema (Fig. 3.11). We first divide *runtime aspects* and *transmission aspects*.

Runtime Aspects

In runtime aspects we place techniques by which an agent's execution time can be improved. The first important aspect is the format, used to send an agent's code to destination agencies.

Code Format

The code format influences code size, and therefore, code execution time, and, to a lesser extent, transmission time. We can distinguish here among source code, intermediate byte code, and machine code. *Machine code* is specific to a processor architecture family and cannot be executed on processors that do not belong to this family. In heterogeneous systems like mobile agent systems, it is very important to have code in a format that can be

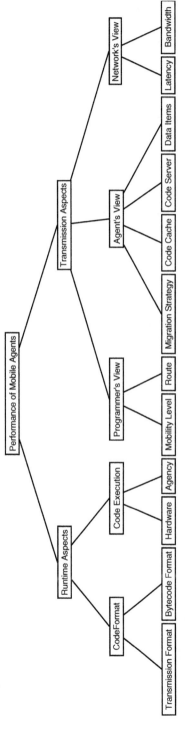

Figure 3.11 Classification of mobile agents' performance issues.

understood and executed at all or almost all nodes. Therefore, machine code is not a good format to transmit mobile agents' code, unless some kind of simulator or translator is used that is able to translate code among different architectures. However, because most computer systems are based on Intel Pentium, Compaq Alpha, or Sun SPARC processors, techniques that send an agent's code in multiple representations to destination agencies could be used. In the distributed operating system community this was implemented in systems described by Dubach et al. [1989] and Shub [1990]. In the mobile object system Emerald [Steensgaard and Jul, 1995], not all code representations are sent; instead, only one is selected to be used at the next destination. This technique is not suitable for mobile agents, because a later migration would not be possible unless the code representation for the destination platform could be downloaded from some code server on demand. Knabe [1997a] describes several drawbacks of these approaches, for example, that the addition of a new processor architecture type requires a new compilation of all agents. In addition, he points out that the number of different processor architectures is too high to allow code transmission for *all* processor types.

A better solution is to transmit an agent's code in a format that is independent of the underlying processor architecture. This might be *source code* or some *intermediate code* representation, if such is available for the language used. In the first mobile agent's toolkits, for example, AgentTCL code was transmitted in source code format. Source code must be compiled at each agency and translated to an executable format, which increases execution time and becomes very uneconomical if a huge amount of source code must be compiled to execute only a few lines of code at an agency. An advantage of this code format is high execution performance because of the imperative compilation process.

Intermediate code is the result of a compilation process that is performed at the agent's home agency. Intermediate code is a low-level representation, which consists of commands for a virtual machine. Java byte code is the most popular example of an intermediated code format, especially for mobile agent toolkits. Intermediate code is usually more compact than source code and can contain several architecture independent code optimizations (e.g., dead code elimination or loop unrolling [Aho et al., 1986]), which increase execution performance. Intermediate code is either interpreted by some kind of virtual machine or immediately translated into machine code at the destination agency. Java uses a mixture of both techniques: Code is interpreted when executed for the first time and then translated into machine code during runtime (just-in-time compilation). Later, this code is further analyzed to detect performance bottlenecks, and the problem code areas are individually optimized (hot-spot-optimization).

An approach that combines transmission of source code, intermediate code, and machine code has been proposed by Knabe [1997a]. In his mobile agent toolkit, which uses the programing language Extended Facile, the agent programmer can influence in which transmission format the agent will migrate. The decision might be based on the agent's task, as can be seen in the following example, which we take from Knabe [1997a]: In the case of a so-called batch agent, which has to execute a long-running process, the destination agency will benefit from a highly optimized machine code which can be produced only if high-level source code is available for compilation. Another example is related to code size versus network quality. If the network connection has low bandwidth, for example, if it is a dial-up connection, transmission time is more important than execution time; therefore, the smallest code representation should be sent, regardless of execution time.

If we now look at Java as a programming language, another issue that influences the performance of mobile agents is its byte code format. Although it is very easy to produce and interpret, Java byte code has some major drawbacks with regard to code optimization and security. For example, the stack-based architecture of the Java virtual machine makes it difficult to optimize code for RISC processors, and the built-in byte code verifier provides only some simple code checks for violations of the basic semantics of Java. Alternatives to Java byte code that allow easy code annotations for code optimization and provide sophisticated security checks have been discussed in the programming language community. See Amme et al. [2001] for a new, safe, intermediate code format for Java, based on static single assignment, that can be translated to highly optimized machine code very quickly.

Code Execution

Another aspect that influences execution performance is the underlying hardware architecture (e.g., CPU, memory, system load). Hardware parameters are especially important in the case of Java, because the virtual machine itself needs a huge amount of memory. Unfortunately, this cannot be influenced by the agent or agent programmer. A second aspect is the agency software and its optimizations on the level of Java code. Some drawbacks of the Java virtual machine can be resolved through skillful programming within the agency software. Most of these techniques are not restricted to programming of mobile agent toolkits but rather are applicable in all Java programs. We want to mention only two techniques here: improved object serialization techniques and thread pools. Some authors propose new object serialization techniques for Java, which either speed up the entire serialization process or produce a smaller serialized object. See Philippsen and Zenger [1997] for an example of such a technique.

Because mobile agent toolkits are multi-threaded systems, every software agent usually controls at least one thread. To achieve parallel execution of agents, thread scheduling is provided by the Java virtual machine and by the underlying operating system. Unfortunately, thread creation is very expensive in Java and should therefore be minimized to save execution time. The problem is aggravated if mobile agents have only a very short visiting time at each agency because that makes a thread's lifetime very short. It is a well-known technique to use so-called thread pools to solve this problem. A thread pool is more or less a data structure that manages a stock of sleeping threads. Whenever a new thread is needed, an already existing thread from the thread pool is resumed and associated with the new task. When the task is finished, the thread is put back into the pool again. The technique of thread pools is described by Soares and Silva [1999], and its influence on the overall execution performance is measured using several experiments.

Transmission Aspects

In transmission aspects, all techniques that influence network load and transmission time during agent migration are summarized. According to the three views of mobility models, we distinguish three optimization issues.

Programmer's View

From the programmer's point of view, the most influential factor is what level of mobility is supported. Whereas weak mobility is very easy to achieve and works very quickly in Java-based systems, it is very complicated to achieve strong mobility in Java, as already mentioned in Section 3.3.1. Strong mobility not only increases code size and lengthens transmission time but also increases execution time, as can be seen from the experiments made by Fünfrocken [1999]. Another concern from the programmer's point of view is the itinerary an agent has to execute. The optimization goal within this level is to find suitable agencies and services, and to optimize the route to all of these agencies. The order in which agencies are visited is most important, and there are several trade-offs to be considered. For example, is it more useful to go to neighboring agencies first, because they are easy to reach, and to risk that information will not be found there or go to far-away agencies first where the probability of finding right information is high but migration costs are also high and transmission may be untrusted? Moizumi and Cybenko [2001] define the *Traveling Agent Problem,* which is NP-complete in its general formulation. We named this level of migration optimization the *macro* level (see Erfurth et al. [2001a,b]).

An example of an optimization on the macro level is given by Barbeau [1999]. He uses the term *migration strategy* to describe the way of relocating an agent's state and code within the network. Barbeau uses a more coarse-grained approach, because he still views an agent's code as one transmission unit, whereas we consider code to consist of multiple pieces that can migrate (almost) independently. He compares three strategies: (1) An agent visits all nodes sequentially; (2) all nodes are visited sequentially but the agent's state is uploaded to its home server periodically; (3) the agent is sent in parallel to all nodes that it has to visit, using a multi-cast protocol. Barbeau evaluates these migration strategies using mathematical models and is able to show that it makes sense to upload the state of an agent to its home agency under certain circumstances. He also shows that the parallel strategy performs better than any sequential strategy.

Agent's View

From the agent's point of view, a mobile agent's performance is influenced by code and data relocation techniques; we call this the *micro* level of optimization. The issue of optimization here is the amount of network load that is produced by a single agent migration between two agencies. Migration time may not depend directly on the number of bytes that are transmitted, because in networks with varying values for bandwidth it might be even faster to send a larger number of bytes through a high-bandwidth network connection than to send a small number of bytes through a low-bandwidth network connection.

Techniques to optimize network load and transmission time can be easily deduced from the problems of the simple migration technique. The first problem is related to the actual size of the code, which can be reduced by using sophisticated compression techniques that have been developed for

Java byte code, see Bradley et al. [1998] and Pugh [1999].[6] The second problem is raised by code that is superfluously transmitted to a destination agency, either because it is not needed there or because it already exists there as a result of a prior code transmission by its agent or another agent of the same type. However, besides the *qualitative* arguments against this technique, we can also mention *quantitative* arguments. An extension of our model of network load and transmission time to consider different migration strategies is beyond the scope of this section, so we postpone it to the following one, in which we compare all migration strategies presented in Section 3.3.1 in two application scenarios. The result of this evaluation is that no migration strategy works best in every situation; that is, no one migration strategy is able to produce lowest network load and transmission time in all application scenarios.

The result is that it is not sufficient to make a simple exchange of strategies, but a dynamic choice for which migration strategy should be used for the next migration must be made. As we have seen, current mobility models are not able to provide techniques that allow a dynamic decision between different migration strategies (e.g., in Aglets it is not possible to decide which class should be pushed or pulled, and in Grasshopper it is not possible to push classes at all).

Another technique to avoid class transmission is a class cache. The limitations of current class caches used in Aglets and Grasshopper have already been described. Class cache techniques are able to avoid class downloading only from the agent's home agency, not code transmission as used in push strategies. An evaluation of class caches was done by Soares and Silva [1999]. In the case of push strategies, current class caches are completely useless. A solution would be a class cache technique that becomes active when an agent migrates. For example, in the first step, the names of classes that should be transmitted are sent to the destination agency as part of the migration protocol. The destination agency answers with information about which classes are already available. In practice we would have to deal with the problem of equal class names for different classes and different class versions.

If class downloading cannot be avoided, then it should be made as fast as possible. To do that, it is important to load classes from a nearby server, because a shorter distance could improve the time needed for downloading.

---

6. Regarding byte code compression techniques, you might also want to look at Java Specification Request (JSR) 200, where a new and dense network transfer format for Java archives is proposed.

Current mobile agent toolkits allow only a single code server (Aglets) (which in most cases is the agent's home agency) or multiple code servers (to which code must be transmitted using techniques outside the mobile agent system, e.g., a simple FTP file transfer) to be defined. Hohl et al. [1997] describe techniques to improve migration performance by using multiple code servers in the Mole toolkit. These code servers need not to be located on the same host as the agent server. If a destination agency must download classes during the execution of a mobile agent, it first looks for them at neighboring code servers before loading them from the home agency. Code servers communicate to exchange information about existing classes. Hohl et al. assume that classes are registered at a code server by the programmer manually. They do not provide any performance measurements to prove their concept.

The last drawback of the simple migration techniques used so far is data handling. We saw that it creates a huge network load to carry data items to servers, although these data items are never used at this agency. We already have seen that this drawback cannot be avoided using the standard Java object serialization technique, which is used in all current mobile agent toolkits. A technique to transmit data items independently of the object state of the agent is necessary, so that an agent can dynamically download data items from its home agency when they are really needed. Later, the agent can upload these data items again to avoid carrying them to more agencies.

The last aspect we would like to mention here is the way code is transmitted from the sender agency or a code server to the destination agency. Usually, code transmission is completed before code execution is started. An optimized code transfer starts code execution *before* code transmission is completed, so the phases overlap. This can be easily achieved with Java applets if the JAR file is reordered so that classes that are needed first at the destination are placed at the beginning of the file. Krintz et al. [1999] and Stoops et al. [2002] describe approaches to implement this technique, but only for mobile object systems, not for mobile agent systems.

Network's View

From the network's point of view, we see three factors that influence mobile agents' performance: network bandwidth, network latency, and the overall architecture of the network in which the agent operates. As we will see in detail in the next section, the type of network (e.g., whether all network connections have the same quality) has a great impact on performance. Of course, the agent or agent programmer has no means to influence these values, but it is very important to be able to react to them.

3.4.3 Performance and Migration Strategies

In this section we evaluate the relationship between the performance of mobile agents and the migration strategies used. Section 3.3.1 introduced the two main classes of migration strategies: push and pull strategies. We also learned that in most cases they are used alone, but in rare cases they are also used in some kind of combination.

An interesting question is how the migration strategy influences the migration performance of mobile agents. One severe simplification of our mathematical model for network load and transmission time was a scenario in which only push-all-to-next was supported. To evaluate the influence of the migration strategy on the performance of mobile agents, we will now extend our model to allow dynamic class downloading. Prior versions of this model have been published (see Braun et al., 2001b).

We extend our model so that the agent has to visit m servers $\{L_1, \ldots, L_m\}$ to collect data from each server. In contrast to our first model, we now assume that an agent consists of several class files, which can be dynamically loaded during execution from the agent's home agency. The decision of which class files must be loaded is influenced by the communication between the agent and the local agent server.

To model network load, we assume that an agent consists of u units (classes) of code, each of length $B_c^k, k = 1, \ldots, u$, some data of length B_d (which contains at least the request of length B_{req}), and state information of length B_s. A request to load a specific code unit has length B_r for all units B_c^k. The probability of dynamically loading code unit k on server L_i is $P_{L_i}^k$. With this we can model two aspects. First, it expresses the probability that a specific code sequence will be executed. Second, we can also model a case in which code is already in a local code cache. On server L_i the agent's data increases by $B_{res} \geq 0$ byte.

The migration process consists of marshaling data and state; transmitting data, state, and code to the destination agency; and unmarshaling of data and state information. To model round-trip time, we make the following simplifications. The time necessary for marshaling and unmarshaling data correlates with the number of bytes and modeled by $\mu : \mathbb{N} \to \mathbb{R}$. For each pair of servers we know throughput $\tau : \mathcal{L} \times \mathcal{L} \to \mathbb{R}$ and delay

$\delta : \mathcal{L} \times \mathcal{L} \rightarrow \mathbb{R}$ in advance. We assume both τ and δ to be symmetric, that is, for all $L_i, L_j \in \mathcal{L} : \tau(L_i, L_j) = \tau(L_j, L_i) \wedge \delta(L_i, L_j) = \delta(L_j, L_i)$.

We divide the migration process into three steps. First, the agent migrates from its home agency, L_0, to the first server, L_1, of the given itinerary. Second, the agent migrates from server L_i to server L_{i+1}, where $i = 1, \ldots, m - 1$. Last, the agent migrates back to its home agency. For the following we assume that $L_0 \neq L_i, i = 1, \ldots, m$. We define $B_c = \sum_{k=1,\ldots,u} B_c^k$. $S \in \{$pushnext, pushall, pullunit, pullall$\}$ stands for a migration strategy. The network load for a migration from an agent's home agency is calculated by:

$$B_{\text{leave}}(\mathcal{L}, S) = \begin{cases} B_d + B_s + B_c & \text{if } S = \text{pushnext} \\ B_d + B_s + |\mathcal{L}|B_c & \text{if } S = \text{pushall} \\ B_d + B_s + \sum_{k=1,\ldots,u} P_{L_1}^k (B_r + B_c^k) & \text{if } S = \text{pullunit} \\ B_d + B_s + B_r + B_c & \text{if } S = \text{pullall} \end{cases} \tag{3.15}$$

A migration from L_a to L_{a+1}, with $a \in \{1, \ldots, m - 1\}$ has network load of:

$$B_{\text{mig}}(\mathcal{L}, a, S) = \begin{cases} B_d + aB_{\text{res}} + B_s + B_c & \text{if } S = \text{pushnext} \\ B_d + aB_{\text{res}} + B_s & \text{if } S = \text{pushall} \\ B_d + aB_{\text{res}} + B_s + \sum_{k=1,\ldots,u} P_{L_{a+1}}^k (B_r + B_c^k) & \text{if } S = \text{pullunit} \\ B_d + aB_{\text{res}} + B_s + B_r + B_c & \text{if } S = \text{pullall} \end{cases}$$
$$\tag{3.16}$$

When an agent migrates to its home agency, network load amounts to:

$$B_{\text{home}}(\mathcal{L}, S) = B_d + |\mathcal{L}|B_{\text{res}} + B_s \tag{3.17}$$

Finally, the whole network load equals:

$$B_{\text{MA}}(\mathcal{L}, S) = B_{\text{leave}}(\mathcal{L}, S) + \sum_{l=1,\ldots,m-1} B_{\text{mig}}(\mathcal{L}, l, S) + B_{\text{home}}(\mathcal{L}, S) \tag{3.18}$$

To derive transmission time from network load, it is necessary to consider time for marshaling and unmarshaling of data, state, and network latency. All network load must be divided by network throughput. To make the following formulas more lucid, we define the following abbreviations.

The time necessary to load all necessary code units dynamically on server L_s from the agent's home agency is:

$$\phi_s = \sum_{k=1,\dots,u} P^k_{L_s} \left(\delta(L_s, L_0) + \frac{B_r + B^k_c}{\tau(L_s, L_0)} \right)$$

If not only some but all code units must be downloaded at server L_s, we can write:

$$\Phi_s = \delta(L_s, L_0) + \frac{B_r + B_c}{\tau(L_s, L_0)}$$

The time necessary to push code to all agencies equals:

$$\varphi = \sum_{l=1,\dots,m} \left(\delta(L_0, L_l) + \frac{B_c}{\tau(L_0, L_l)} \right)$$

The corresponding time necessary for migrating an agent from its home agency is:

$$T_{leave}(\mathcal{L}, S) = \begin{cases} 2\mu(B_d + B_s) + \delta(L_0, L_1) + \dfrac{B_{leave}(\mathcal{L}, S)}{\tau(L_0, L_1)} & \text{if } S = \text{pushnext} \\[2ex] 2\mu(B_d + B_s) + \varphi + \dfrac{B_d + B_s}{\tau(L_0, L_1)} & \text{if } S = \text{pushall} \\[2ex] 2\mu(B_d + B_s) + \delta(L_0, L_1) + \dfrac{B_d + B_s}{\tau(L_0, L_1)} + \phi_1 & \text{if } S = \text{pullunit} \\[2ex] 2\mu(B_d + B_s) + 2\delta(L_0, L_1) + \dfrac{B_d + B_s + B_r + B_c}{\tau(L_0, L_1)} & \text{if } S = \text{pullall} \end{cases}$$

$$(3.19)$$

Note that marshaling and unmarshaling of date and state information takes $\mu(B_d + B_s)$ of time. For example, in the case of a *pullunit* strategy, time comprises the time to gather and parse the agent's state, open a network connection to the home agency, transmit all the agent's state information to the first agency, and load missing classes from the home agency (ϕ_1).

We define $B^a_{d,s} = B_d + aB_{res} + B_s$, which is the amount of accumulated data and state information at server L_a. The time needed to migrate from L_a

to L_{a+1}, with $a \in \{1, \ldots, m-1\}$, is:

$$
T_{\mathrm{mig}}(\mathcal{L}, a, S) = \begin{cases}
2\mu(B_{d,s}^a) + \delta(L_a, L_{a+1}) + \dfrac{B_{\mathrm{mig}}(\mathcal{L}, a, S)}{\tau(L_a, L_{a+1})} & \text{if } S = \text{pushnext} \\[2ex]
2\mu(B_{d,s}^a) + \delta(L_a, L_{a+1}) + \dfrac{B_{\mathrm{mig}}(\mathcal{L}, a, S)}{\tau(L_a, L_{a+1})} & \text{if } S = \text{pushall} \\[2ex]
2\mu(B_{d,s}^a) + \delta(L_a, L_{a+1}) + \dfrac{B_{d,s}^a}{\tau(L_a, L_{a+1})} + \phi_{a+1} & \text{if } S = \text{pullunit} \\[2ex]
2\mu(B_{d,s}^a) + \delta(L_a, L_{a+1}) + \dfrac{B_{d,s}^a}{\tau(L_a, L_{a+1})} + \Phi_{a+1} & \text{if } S = \text{pullall}
\end{cases}
$$

$$(3.20)$$

Note that $B_{\mathrm{mig}}(\mathcal{L}, a, S)$ refers to the amount of network load produced by a normal migration using strategy S; see Equation 3.16.

The time required to migrate to the home agency is:

$$
T_{\mathrm{home}}(\mathcal{L}, S) = 2\mu(B_{\mathrm{home}}(\mathcal{L}, S)) + \delta(L_m, L_0) + \frac{B_{\mathrm{home}}(\mathcal{L}, S)}{\tau(L_m, L_0)}. \tag{3.21}
$$

Finally, the whole transmission time amounts to:

$$
T_{\mathrm{MA}}(\mathcal{L}, S) = T_{\mathrm{leave}}(\mathcal{L}, S) + \sum_{l=1,\ldots,m-1} T_{\mathrm{mig}}(\mathcal{L}, l, S) + T_{\mathrm{home}}(\mathcal{L}, S). \tag{3.22}
$$

To evaluate an agent's round-trip based on this model, we consider two network scenarios (Fig. 3.12). In the first scenario we assume a homogeneous network, where all network connections have the same quality. We assume network bandwidth as $\tau = 800$ Kb/sec and delay as $\delta = 5$ ms. In the second scenario we assume a heterogeneous network (ring topology),

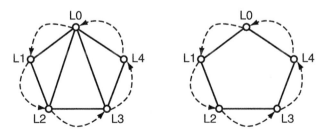

Homogeneous network   Heterogeneous network

Figure 3.12 Examples for the network model used for the evaluation. Agencies are drawn as circles, network connections as solid lines, and agent migrations as dashed lines.

Table 3.3 *Code size and download probabilities in four different scenarios*

Class	Class size (bytes)	Class download probability			
		Sc. 1	Sc. 2	Sc. 3	Sc. 4
1	10,000	1	1	1	1
2	15,000	0	.5	1	1
3	15,000	0	.2	.8	1
4	15,000	0	0	.5	1
5	15,000	0	0	.2	1

where connections between neighboring servers are as fast as in the homogeneous case, but all other network connections have only a small bandwidth of $\tau = 250$ Kb/sec and a delay of $\delta = 10$ ms.

The agent consists of five classes; the first class is the agent's main class, and the other four classes are to process specific subtasks and are necessary only on a few servers. The code size of each class can be seen in Table 3.3. The initial data size (B_d) of the agent is 1000 bytes and the initial state size (B_s) is 100 bytes. The agent has to migrate to four servers, and on each server it has to communicate to the local agent server. As a result, the agent's data increases by the value of the server result, which is 3000 bytes on each server. A class request has length $B_r = 20$ bytes.

Figures 3.13 and 3.14 compare transmission times of four different migration strategies while varying class download probabilities in four scenarios. The probabilities for class downloading of these four scenarios can be seen in Table 3.3. In the first scenario only one class (the agent's main class) is downloaded, whereas in the last scenario all classes must be downloaded. The second and third scenarios model cases in which only a subset of classes must be downloaded.

In a homogeneous network, the mobile agent's transmission time using strategies push-all-to-next, push-all-to-all, and pull-all-units are almost identical, because all code is transmitted whether or not it is needed. The additional time to open a network connection and to transmit a code request is only a few milliseconds when using strategy pull-all-units to the home agency. In contrast, strategy pull-per-unit grows linearly with the download probability. It is faster than all other strategies in a homogeneous network, even if more than one class must be downloaded. This strategy leads to a higher transmission time only in the case of downloading all class files because of several code requests that must be sent to the home agency.

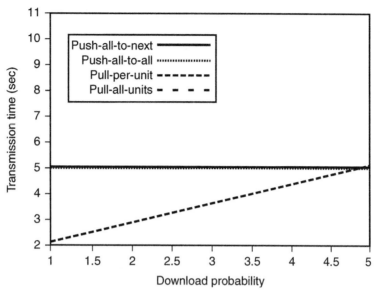

Figure 3.13 Transmission time versus class download probability in a homogeneous network for four different migration strategies. Note that transmission times for *push-all-to-next*, *push-all-to-all*, and *pull-all-units* are almost identical.

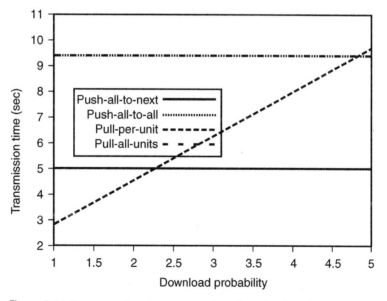

Figure 3.14 Transmission time versus class download probability in a heterogeneous network for four different migration strategies. Note that transmission times for *push-all-to-all* and *pull-all-units* are almost identical.

In a heterogeneous network, strategies push-all-to-all and pull-all-units take the same amount of time. However, transmission time is higher than that when using strategy push-all-to-next, because in these strategies all class files must be transmitted using slow network connections, whereas in strategy push-all-to-next, code and data are sent via neighboring network connections. The diagram shows that in a heterogeneous network strategy pull-per-unit is slower than push-all-to-next, even if not all classes must be downloaded. Again, this is because code must be download from the home agency via slow network connections.

What we have learned from this evaluation is that no migration strategy produces the shortest transmission time in every situation. In homogeneous networks, pull-per-unit is a good strategy, because code downloading is cheap, whereas in a heterogeneous network, code downloading from a far-away agency is expensive and should be avoided. In such a network, it is useful to push code in most cases. Of course, the decision for a migration strategy is influenced by several factors, such as code size, code download probability, and so on.

3.4.4 The Kalong Mobility Model

In this section we introduce our new mobility model, named Kalong, which is the synthesis of most ideas for improved mobility models proposed in the last two sections. The main feature of Kalong is its flexible and fine-grained migration technique, which allows an agent or its programmer to define new migration strategies for each individual migration. In this section we confine our discussion to the foundations of Kalong without going into technical details. In Chapter 6 we formally describe the migration protocol and explain how to program migration strategies in detail.

Kalong differs from current mobility models in three main aspects:

1. Kalong defines a new agent representation and new transmission units. In our model, mobile agents not only consist of their code and an object state but also have an *external state*, which comprises data items that are not part of the object state. A mobile agent's code is no longer transmitted in the form of classes or JAR files but in a new transmission format that we call a *code unit*. A code unit comprises at least one class which is supposed to migrate as a unit. A single class can be a member of several units.

2. Kalong defines two new agency types in addition to the already-known *home* and *remote* agencies used in current mobility models. We introduce a *code server* agency, from which an agent can download code on demand, and we introduce a *mirror* agency, which is an exact copy of an agent's home agency. It is important to understand that agency types are valid only for a single agent; that is, a single agency can be a mirror for one agent and a remote for another agent at the same time. A mobile agent can define an agency as a code server or mirror and later release it again dynamically during runtime.

3. Kalong defines a new class cache mechanism that prevents not only class downloading in the case of pull strategies but also code transmission in the case of push strategies. Our class cache is able to avoid transmission of identical classes used in different agents and can distinguish between different versions of the same class.

All these new features are accompanied by new commands for agents to define their own migration behavior.

Kalong does not define anything related to mobile agent security and leaves this to an implementation of this model.

Agent Representation

We start our introduction with the new agent representation (Fig. 3.15). Because of the problems with the Java serialization process, we allow agents to have other data items besides their object state, and we call these data

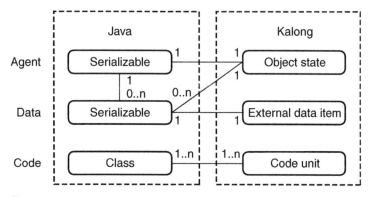

Figure 3.15 Mapping of the Java agent representation to elements of the Kalong mobility model.

items the *external state*. Elements of the external state are plain Java objects that must be serializable. Each data item of the external state must have a name to be stored and accessed by its owner. The external state is private for a single agent instance, and it is not possible to share the external state with other agents (with blackboards, for example) even if they are of the same agent type.

We introduce two new commands by which mobile agents can access their external state.

```
protected void setData( String name, Serializable data )
```
Stores a data item under the given name in the external state.

```
protected Serializable getData( String name )
```
Receives a data item of the external state.

For a data item to be deleted, it must be set to null.

When an agent migrates, elements of its external state do not migrate automatically, in contrast to the elements of its object state. However, an agent can define one or many items of its external state to be part of the state that is sent to the destination agency. Such data items become invalid at the sender agency if migration is successful. Using this technique of external data items, an agent or its programmer can select data items for migration that have a high probability of being used at the next agencies. Data items that most likely will not be used are not transferred, which can reduce network load.

Data items that were not sent as part of an agent's state remain at the sender agency only if it is the agent's home agency. If the sender agency is a remote agency, all data items of the external state will be transferred along with the agent's state, because they may not be left at an agency other than the agent's home agency. A data item that remains at an agent's home agency is not accessible by its owner if the owner is residing at another agency. Thus, there is no possibility for remote access. Instead, Kalong provides a technique to transmit data items from the agent's home agency to the current agency. First, a data item can be downloaded using method *loadData*.

```
protected void loadData( String data )
```
Loads a data item of the external state from the agent's home agency.

When the data item is transferred from the home agency to the current agency it becomes invalid at the home agency. No class code is sent with this data transmission. It is possible to transmit multiple data items in one shot using either a list of names or wildcards.

Data items of the external state can be sent back to the agent's home agency using method *uploadData*.

```
protected void uploadData( String data )
```
Uploads a data item from the current agency to the agent's home agency.

After this, the data item is no longer available at the current agency and becomes valid at the home agency again. This makes it possible to reduce network traffic by uploading data items that will not be necessary at the agencies visited in the near future. It is possible for an agent to later request the same data item from its home agency. On this low level of the description of our model we define that a data item is not loaded automatically when method *getData* is invoked.

Using the concept of external data items, we solve not only the problem of superfluously transmitted data items but also the problem of superfluously transmitted code caused by the Java serialization technique. As we have seen in Section 3.4.1, for each element of the object state, code is necessary when deserializing the agent, even if the variable is not used at this agency. Using data items stored in the external state, code that is necessary to instantiate this object at the current agency is downloaded most quickly when the data item is deserialized.

A further advantage of external data items is security. One problem in the area of security of mobile agents is the fact that an agent's data must be protected against illicit reading and any manipulation by malicious agencies. Using our technique of an external state, it is possible to integrate sophisticated techniques to protect the data items that an agent has to carry. The agent can, for example, leave data items that might be the target of unauthorized reading attempts at the home agency until they are really needed.

Kalong also introduces a new code representation in which the basic code transmission unit is not a single class file or a JAR file. Because we observed that often several classes migrate together, we introduce a new transmission unit, which we call a *code unit*. A code unit consists of at least one Java classes, comparable to a JAR file. Classes that are part of the same code unit should have a common criterion that qualifies them for transmission as a single unit. A good reason to bundle classes is if they have the same execution probability, for example, because all classes belong to the same subtask. Each code unit has at least one *code base*, from which it can be loaded.

The decision of which class belongs to which code unit is made by the agent before its first migration. This distribution cannot be changed afterward because it would contradict some other fundamental aspects of our mobility model. We come back to this issue later. It is important to understand that such a distribution of classes into units is done by each agent instance itself and that two agents might have different code units even if they belong to the same type.

Code transmission always works on the basis of code units. In the case of push strategies, the agent can define which code units will be sent to the next agency. If a code unit migrates, all classes of this code unit migrate. Code downloading, which is necessary when using pull strategies, works as follows: If a class is needed, for example, during the agent deserialization process, it first must be determined to which code unit the class belongs. This might not be clear, because it is possible to let a single class be part of more than one code unit. Second, it must be decided from which code base the code unit should be loaded. The technique to make this choice will be explained later.

Migration Process

We now describe how a migration is processed in Kalong. Kalong provides a very flexible and fine-grained technique to describe the migration strategy of a mobile agent. It is possible to define the migration strategy not only for a type of agent or a single agent instance but for each single migration that the agent has to perform. For the moment we will introduce only the general concept of defining migration strategies in Kalong. A detailed introduction into programming migration strategies will be part of Chapter 6.

The parts in which an agent is transmitted during a migration are:

1. State, which consists of the object state and some other agent-defined data items of the external state, and

2. Code units, which contain the code in the form of Java class files.

As already stated, it is not necessary for the agent to carry all of the data items of the external state as well as all code units. It is possible and sometimes advisable to send only code units and no state information at all, which would make the destination agency a code server—we will explain this in detail later.

If only state information is sent, then the agent uses a pull strategy. In this case a description of all code units that contains at least the names of all classes and code bases is sent to the destination agency.

After an agent has left its home agency, no information about this agent is deleted, except the object state and data items that were part of the state. At the destination agency, code units are received and stored so that the agent's class loader can access code using a class name. If the state was sent during the migration, then the agent is deserialized. Classes not already available at the destination agency must be downloaded as previously described.

When an agent migrates from an arbitrary remote agency to another agency, it can define a new migration strategy in terms of state and code units. The agent is free to define which data items will be part of the agent's state and which code units will migrate, with one exception concerning data items. Because data items cannot be left at an arbitrary remote agency, the migration strategy must define for each data item whether it will be part of the state or be uploaded to the agent's home agency. We define a rule that all data items that are still valid at the current (remote) agency when an agent migrates are a mandatory part of the state. With code units, we do not have this problem, because they may be safely deleted at the remote agency after a successful migration. After an agent has left a remote agency, all information about the agent is deleted. Thus, this agency cannot be used for code unit downloading in the future.

It should be obvious that, using these two primitives of state and code unit transmission, together with the ability to define which elements of the external state should be part of the agent's state, it is possible to describe all the migration strategies that we have introduced in this chapter. For example, to describe the push-all-to-next strategy, we define all classes to form a single code unit, which is sent along with the agent's data to the next agency. To describe the pull-per-unit strategy, we define that each class forms a single code unit, which is not transmitted along with the agent's code.

Types of Agencies

In the last section we mentioned that Kalong also defines some new types of agencies. So far, mobile agents can migrate only from their home agencies to visit the so-called remote agencies. One very important rule we introduced in the last section was that all information about an agent is deleted at a remote agency after the agent has left it. Now, we will introduce two new types of agencies, which are both able to keep or remember data and/or code for a single agent.

First, we introduce the *code server agency*. When an agent leaves a remote agency, it can define within the migration strategy that some code units will be stored at the current agency. Code units must be already available to be stored, so they must already have been downloaded by the migration strategy. If at least one code unit is copied, this agency becomes a code server agency for this agent. The effect is twofold: The name of this agency is added to this list of *code bases*, and after a successful migration these code units are not deleted and can in future be downloaded from this agency. As already mentioned, the agent must decide which base to download code units from, which will be explained later. The range of possible strategies goes from a simple one that always uses the last code server agency defined to very complex one that considers network metrics and compares the cost of downloading code units from different agencies.

When it uses code server agencies, an agent has the chance to deposit code at several agencies that are near the ones it will visit in the future. For example, in Figure 3.16, we assume the cluster of agencies on the right side to be in the United States and those on the left side to be in Europe. Now, when the agent migrates in the United States, if it is known that many servers should be visited there and it is also worthwhile to use code downloading, then the agent can define a code server there.

This is not possible with any other mobility model currently available. In Aglets it is not possible to define anything resembling a code server. All classes

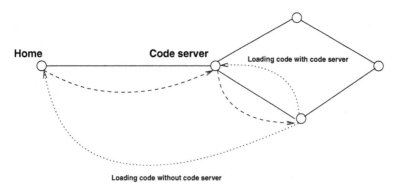

Figure 3.16 Example to show the advantages of a code server. Agencies are drawn as circles, network connections as solid lines, migrations as dashed lines, and code requests as dotted lines.

must be downloaded from a single code base, which must be defined during agent creation. In Grasshopper it is possible to define multiple code servers, but only when starting the agent, and not during runtime.

One question remains, and that is how to release code servers again. Therefore, we introduce the technique of sending commands between agencies. To send a command to another agency is a new primitive. Using this command it is possible for the agent to release a previously defined code server at any time. This results in all code units being deleted and this agency being deleted from the list of code bases of all units.

If there is no user-defined code sever release, Kalong has a rule that code servers must be released before an agent terminates. Because agents can get lost during execution (this is actually an issue of the agent manager and not of the mobility model), each agency should implement techniques to release code servers automatically, for example, when they were not used for a predefined time.

As a direct consequence of the concept of a code server for *code* we introduce the *mirror agency*, which can keep information about *code* and *data*. The mirror agency is a copy of all data items of the external state and all code units. If a mirror agency exists, it takes the role of the home agency as long as it is defined. The necessity of a mirror agency becomes obvious when looking at the previous example and assuming that the agent wants to download and upload data items. It would be very expensive if the agent were forced to communicate with its home agency for exchange of data items. Therefore, an agent can define a mirror agency so that all data items and all units of the home agency that are not already at the current agency are downloaded to the new mirror agency. All data items then become invalid at the home agency.

If there is already a mirror agency, the agent cannot define a new mirror agency until it has loaded all data items and all units from the old mirror. The last mirror agency must be released by the agent, which is done by sending a command to this agency, as described previously for code servers.

Code Cache

The third important aspect of our new mobility model is the code cache. Code caching is a technique to decrease network load by avoiding class transmission between two agencies if code is already available at the destination agency. We are already familiar with the Java code cache technique, which is implemented as part of the class *ClassLoader* and which can avoid multiple downloading of code for the same agent instance. In contrast to this technique, our class cache will not only work for a single agent instance but will also be able to share classes between several agents.

The cache works on the basis of classes instead of units, because agents of the same type could use different unit definitions so that for one agent instance a specific class is in one unit and for another instance it is in another unit. If we used a cache on the basis of units, it would work only for a single agent instance and therefore would be quite useless.

The goal of our code cache is to check during the migration protocol whether code that belongs to the migrating agent is already available at the destination agency, without sending the whole code. We use the technique of *digests* or *hash values* to check whether two classes are equal. A digest is a sequence of bytes of fixed length, for example, 16 bytes in the MD5 [Rivest, 1992] algorithm, which is produced from a stream of data of variable length. A digest algorithm must ensure that it is computationally infeasible to find two data streams that produce the same digest.[7]

As part of the SATP migration protocol, which we will discuss in detail in Chapter 6, the sender agency transmits the so-called *Agent Definition Block* to the receiver agency. This block contains information about all units, all classes within these units, a digest for each class, and information about code bases from which units can be downloaded. At the destination agency, each class is now checked against the local class cache. If it contains a class with an equal name and equal digest, it can be assumed that code for this class is already available. The destination agency informs the sender about this fact by a specific reply message so that the sender will not send this class. Otherwise, code for this class is not available yet, and the sender is informed to send the code.

Which units and classes are really sent to the destination agency depends on the migration strategy. If, for example, a unit is not pushed from the sender agency and code is not yet available at the destination, code for these classes will inevitably be pulled later. If code is already available at the destination, it will be discovered by the cache algorithm and then we will not need to send code for these classes at all.

---

7. This does not mean that it is impossible but that the probability is very low that there exists a pair x, y for which $H(x) = H(y)$, when H is the digest (hash) function.

3.4.5 Kalong's Advantages

Until now, mobile agent toolkits have provided only very simple migration strategies. The *push* strategy always transmits all code classes of the agent and the agent's state to the next destination [Fig. 3.17(a)]. In contrast, the *pull* strategy never transmits any code class, but only the agent's state and imposes the task of downloading code on the receiving agency [Fig. 3.17(b)].

Using the new Kalong mobility model, the agent has the opportunity to select classes that should be transmitted to the next destination agency, while other classes can be downloaded from the agent's home agency later. With regard to data items, Kalong provides new functions to select which parts of the agent's data state should be sent to the destination agency, while others remain at the home agency (Fig. 3.18). If the agent needs a specific data item that is not yet available, it can be downloaded from the agent's home agency. The advantage of this technique is a reduction of network load, because the data items and the corresponding class code are transmitted only if the data item is really used. We call this feature the *adaptive transmission of code and data*, which gives the agent's programmer the chance to react to certain execution or network scenarios. No other mobility model currently allows the programmer to influence the migration process to such an extent. The necessity for adaptive transmission has already been discussed. For example, in the case of a low-bandwidth and unreliable network connection, the agent should migrate with all its classes to avoid dynamic class loading later. However, if it is already known from the current execution state of the agent

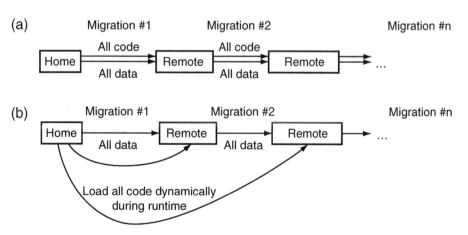

Figure 3.17 Traditional migration strategies. (a) Push migration strategy; (b) Pull migration strategy.

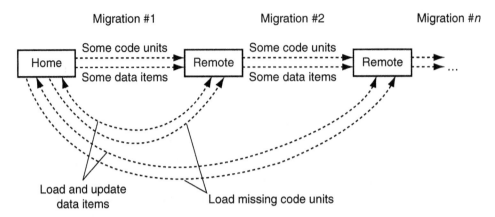

Figure 3.18 Adaptive transmission of code and data in Kalong.

that specific classes or data items will not be used under any circumstances at the next destinations, their transmission is superfluous and should be avoided. With Kalong it is possible to implement migration strategies that take such concerns into account.

The second advantage of Kalong as compared with all other mobility models is its ability to dynamically define *code server* and *mirror* agencies. All other mobility models distinguish between only the agent's *home* server and the *remote* servers, which are all the servers that the agent visits. The home server has the very important role of providing all of the agent's code so that it can be downloaded from this server later. In most mobile agent toolkits, the home server is also the only server that provides the agent's code, although in some systems the programmer can manually deploy agent code to other servers.

In Kalong it is possible for the agent to dynamically define a server to become a code server (Fig. 3.19). This means that all of the agent's code is copied to this server and therefore can be also loaded from this server in the future. The advantage is that it is faster to load code from a nearby agency than from the far-away home agency. The agent can decide, based on its itinerary, which server should become a code server. When the agent terminates, it has to release all code servers to free resources.

A mirror agency is an extension of a code server agency. Not only the agent's code but also selected data items of the external state are moved to this agency. A mirror agency completely overrides the existence of a home agency, so all data and code loading requests are directed to the mirror instead of the

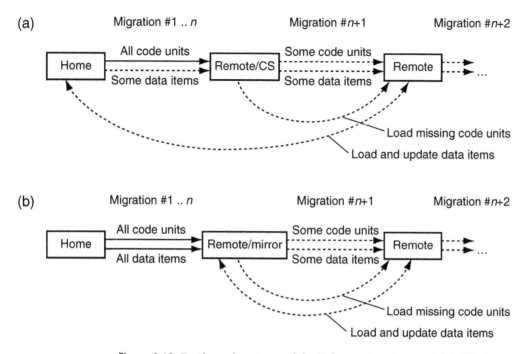

Figure 3.19 Further advantages of the Kalong migration model. (a) Code Server; (b) Mirror.

home agency. Like a code server, a mirror server should be used to reduce the time needed for code and data transmission.

The third advantage of Kalong is a comprehensive technique for code caching. Before any class is transmitted to a destination agency, it is determined whether this class is already available there. If the destination agency already has this class, the sender agency does not send it again. When this technique is used, network load and transmission time can be decreased if many agents of the same type (using the same classes) roam the network and visit the same agencies. The equality of classes is checked using a hash value, which also guarantees that different versions of the same class can be distinguished.

3.4.6 Migration Optimization Techniques Proposed in the Literature

As far as we know, there is only one paper available in the literature that discusses the concept of an adaptable migration process.

Picco [1999] proposed a lightweight and flexible mobile code toolkit named μCode. The main principle of μCode is the flexibility to control code relocation. The unit of transmission is called *group*; it can contain single classes, class closures, and objects. The programmer can choose which classes and objects will be part of the next migration—a technique that is comparable to the possibilities a programmer has with Kalong. A migration is started by invoking method *ship* of class *Group*. Classes that are not already available at the destination server are downloaded from a single server that is given as a parameter in method *ship*. μCode does not provide the ability to load data items dynamically during runtime or to update data items at the agent's home server. It does not allow more than one server from which code can be downloaded to be defined and therefore does not allow code servers to be defined during runtime. Because of the lack of individual data transmission, μCode also does not provide a mirror concept. The source code of μCode is available as an open source project at Sourceforge.[8]

The idea of introducing *code servers* to load code from nearby agencies instead of the home agency was presented by Hohl et al. [1997]. However, their concept can be called static, because the code server must be initialized manually by the agent programmer and cannot by initialized by the agent during runtime.

Other papers available do not focus on the adaptation of the general migration process but rather on optimizations for specific aspects of mobile applications. For example, Tanter et al. [2002] discuss the problem of determining the data items that a mobile application (which could be an agent) should take along during a migration or leave at the source environment to be accessed remotely. They explain techniques a programmer can use to specify the type of data migration for each instance. The authors work toward a technique in which the kind of migration can be exchanged dynamically during runtime.

Another paper discusses techniques to determine the itinerary of a mobile agent during runtime [Satoh, 2001, 2002] using the new concept of mobile agents as the providers for the migration service in a mobile agent system. The MobileSpaces system is a framework for building network protocols for migrating mobile agents over the Internet. It is characterized by two new concepts. First, mobile agents are organized in a hierarchy, which means that agents can contain other agents, resulting in a tree structure. Second, mobile

---

8. Visit *mucode.sourceforge.net* for more information.

agents can migrate to other mobile agents (interagent migration) as a whole, together with all their inner agents. A mobile agent migrates into another agent, which itself implements a network protocol for migration. Satoh only describes applications of this system on the level of route determination, not the lower level of an optimized agent transmission.

Summary

In this section, we proposed our new mobility model, named Kalong, which gives the mobile agent programmer more possibilities to influence the migration process.

The main differences of Kalong as compared with other mobility models are:

- Adaptive transmission of code and data; that is, the programmer or the agent can define during runtime which classes and which data items should be transferred to the destination agency.

- Code server and mirror agencies, that is, places agents can unload code classes and data items to improve their performance for the next migration steps.

- Code caching, which is implemented as part of the mobility model and will be part of the network transmission protocol and improves the performance of the migration process by preventing transmission of identical code units.

We believe that it will be possible to improve the performance of the migration process of mobile agents greatly when using Kalong. We devote the third part of our book completely to the specification and a critical evaluation of Kalong. We also introduce a flexible software component that implements this mobility model and that we designed to be added to any other mobile agent toolkit.

Chapter 4

Mobile Agent Communication

In previous chapters we have focused mainly on examples in which a single agent roams the Internet in order to fulfill a user's given task. Although in many application scenarios a single agent is sufficient as a representative of a human user, other domains may have many agents, possibly of various types, that must work together to solve a single problem. In these situations, agents need some technique to coordinate and to collaborate, for example, to synchronize their activities or to exchange provisional results. In fact, agent communication problems might be seen as differing from agent coordination problems, because the latter can occur without communication [Franklin and Graesser, 1996]. In the rest of this chapter, we do not further distinguish these two aspects.

Because we are solely interested in problems regarding the mobility of agents, we focus our discussion on the problem of providing *location-transparent communication*; that is, how can two or more mobile agents that are frequently migrating communicate to each other in a reliable way? We identify and discuss five different solutions to this problem, which are all particularly suitable for different classes of application scenarios and different types of mobile agents.

Contents

4.1 Introduction

Problems related to agent communication have been extensively discussed in the area of distributed intelligence and multi-agent systems. However, it should be obvious that communication is also one of the most important challenges in mobile applications. Applications beyond a specific level of complexity should not be built using only a single agent that carries all knowledge and all strategies. Rather, it would be better to model a world of different agents, where each one is specialized to solve a specific problem [Glaser, 2002].

Let's look at a simple example in which an agent will arrange a business trip for a human user. The business trip consists of booking a flight and a hotel, renting a car, arranging a meeting with the business partner, and later checking in with the airline if the flight is delayed or canceled. In this case the agent should react to the situation appropriately by informing the business partner and the hotel.

A possible architecture for this application might consist of several specialized agents to find information regarding flights, other agents that are responsible for finding an adequate hotel, and so forth. These are the *slave* agents, which are instructed by a single *master* agent that communicates to the user and monitors the entire process. Obviously, all these agents must exchange information about their tasks and intermediate results. Not only does the master instruct slave agents, it also sometimes terminates slave agents or changes some parameters in response to a change in the user requirements. The main problem in enabling *mobile agents* to communicate with each other is to *locate* agents that can move through the network without knowing their current location in advance. In addition, the slave agents might want to periodically check if their master agent is still "alive," thus performing some kind of orphan detection that also might require locating the master if it is allowed to be mobile too.

In fact, agent communication includes several issues—most of them beyond the scope of this book. (They are common in all multi-agent systems and have therefore already been discussed in other, more specialized books.) For example, the problem of how to design such multi-agent systems affects parts of software engineering [Plekhanova, 2002], and the problem of designing suitable communication paradigms for agents is part of research that is done in distributed artificial intelligence [Ferber, 1999]. Also, the definition of languages that are appropriate to communicate between agents is part of existing research in the area of multi-agent systems and is not a problem that is specific to *mobile* agents. The semantic layer for knowledge sharing is beyond the scope of this book, and we are interested only in the delivery of opaque application data between mobile agents. Therefore, rather than discuss the well-known languages such as KQML [Fritzson et al., 1994; Finin et al., c1994] or FIPA ACL [O'Brien and Nicol, 1998],[1] we refer you to the available literature for more information.

In this chapter we discuss only techniques that enable *mobile agents* to communicate with each other and focus on the problem of *locating* mobile agents. We are not interested in techniques used by agents to communicate with services that are located at specific agencies. As we have already learned, mobile agents should migrate to these physical hosts, where a specific service is offered, so that agent-to-service communication is always local—it is up to the concrete mobile agent toolkit to provide any suitable technique, for example, message passing or method invocation. We only marginally discuss techniques that can be used by agent owners to communicate with their agents. The latter problem is mainly addressed in the area of *mobile agent control problems* [Baumann, 2000], which includes the task of verifying whether agents are still alive or terminating agents that are no longer necessary. Agent control problems and agent communication share a single basic challenge—locating mobile agents.

Here, we are interested only in problems that are singular to mobile agents that need to communicate. With this in mind, we can define the following requirements with respect to the main problems:

■ Where is my communication partner? Because mobile agents can move through the underlying network autonomously, it is generally impossible to predict where a specific agent needed for communication is at a given time. The most user-friendly solution to this problem is, of course, to have a *location-transparent* communication service. This makes it necessary to know only the name of the agent with which we want communicate—not its current location.

■ Even if we knew the current location of an agent, delivering a message to this agent might cause an error, because the agent could relocate as the message is being delivered. The goal is to ensure that all messages be forwarded to the migrated agent (i.e., to the new location). This requirement

---

1. Visit *www.fipa.org* for more information and the specification of the FIPA standard.

is typically named *reliability* of communication. One possible way to provide reliable information systems is to increase the degree of redundancy and avoid fault situations. This is not so in mobile agent systems. As Murphy and Picco state, it is important to understand that the typical techniques to achieve some degree of toler- ance toward communication faults are not sufficient, because agent mobility cannot be classified as fault but rather must be seen as a typical behavior of highly mobile agents. The authors state, "it is the sheer presence of mobility, and not the possibility of faults, that undermines reliability" [Murphy and Picco, 2002, p. 82]. If reliability cannot be guaranteed, messages might be lost.

■ What are the semantics of the communication model? If the model guarantees that a message is delivered to an agent but the agent might receive the same message several times, we have an *at-least-once* semantic. In certain situations this might be sufficient according to the application domain, but if the internal state of the receiver has already been changed by the first message, the second instance of the same message might cause an error or might lead to an undesired state of the receiver. Some RPC protocols support semantics that are called *zero-or-more*, which means that each call of a remote procedure is processed not at all or possibly many times. It is obvious that this might result in problems with procedures that change a local state, for example, if you initiate a bank transfer. If the model provides an *at-most-once* semantic, which is supported by some RPC protocols, we have to accept that message can get lost. The ideal form is an *exactly-once* semantic, which might be difficult to achieve because of technical restrictions.

■ How efficient is the communication model? As we will see in detail later, communication models must provide solutions for two different actions. The first one is when an agent migrates from agency to agency. This causes some processes to update a location directory, for example. The second action is to deliver a message, which involves locating the target agent and sending a message to the agency on which it currently resides. Each communication model provides different solutions for these two actions, which differ significantly in terms of network load. Other measures of the efficiency of a communication model include how it scales if the number of agents or agencies is increased and whether it distinguishes between local migrations between hosts in a single subnetwork and migrations in wide-area networks. We believe that this issue of communication models has been neglected in recent years by the community, and it might be an interesting point for future research in this area to create performance models and evaluate different communication models in simulations or real-world experiments.

Almost all mobile agent toolkits that are currently available provide some kind of *local communication* in which agents that reside at the same agency are able to communicate. Only a few toolkits also provide a *global communication* mechanism in which agents that reside at different agencies and especially at different physical hosts are able to locate each other for message exchange or to share a common information space. In the case of global communication we denote the communication mechanism to be *location-transparent*.

An interesting question and starting point for debate on the principles of mobile agents is whether mobile agents should be able to communicate globally at all. One of the main benefits of using mobile agents is to reduce network traffic by replacing communication between two components residing at different hosts in a network with code mobility. Thus, it could be argued that mobile agents should migrate only to the host where the communication partner currently resides and then communicate locally [cf. Murphy and Picco, 2002]. On the other hand, it can also be argued that mobile agents benefit from having the capability to communicate with remote agents transparently because migration is not always cheaper than remote communication.

If we accept that the overall goal of using mobile agents is to reduce network traffic and thereby increase application performance, then we must accept the trade-off between remote communication and agent migration in every single case. As shown in earlier chapters, this decision might be difficult because of many factors that are known only at runtime. Consider an example in which an agent, α, on agency A_1 has to communicate with another agent, β, on agency A_2. Even without developing a mathematical model for this type of scenario, it is clear that migrating agent α from agency A_1 to agency A_2 is in most cases slower than communicating globally, because in both cases the same information—the message—must be transmitted; however, in the first case, code transmission must be added. Some experiments have stressed that mobile agents should be complemented with remote communication capabilities [Gray et al., 2001; Straßer and Schwehm, 1997]. An alternative is to reduce code transmission to such a degree that a performance difference can no longer be measured. How effective such techniques will be in future remains to be seen. Thus, we can conclude that, even for mobile agents, global communication is a matter of relative importance and a further means to reduce network costs, although it might be considered contrary to the principles of mobile agents and it is unclear how expensive it would be to use techniques that enable global communication for highly mobile agents.

From the viewpoint of programming, it is evident that a communication model greatly simplifies the programming of mobile agents, which uses primitives to guarantee reliable and effective delivery of messages to a communication partner independent of its current location and movement through the network. In some application scenarios, for example, when mobile agents are used solely to deploy code to remote agencies, global communication is the most appropriate form of communication. As we will demonstrate in the next chapter, where we discuss security problems of mobile agents, there are also some algorithms that are built on the requirement of global communication. An example is Roth's technique of cooperating agents to mutual record their itineraries [Roth, 1998].

Let's now return to the issue of controlling mobile agents. The *control problem* is twofold: (1) it must be possible to locate a mobile agent roaming the Internet in order to modify the agent's task and send a termination signal when its has became obsolete, and (2) it must be possible to detect agents that are orphans (i.e., their owners are no longer interested in the result or are not available because of a host error). The latter can occur when a master agent assigns a subtask to a slave agent and the master agent's agency crashes. In this case it would be helpful to have some automatic orphan detection that would terminate the slave agent as soon as possible to avoid unnecessarily consuming resources.

Both problems are intensively discussed in the thesis of Baumann [2000]. The first problem—locating mobile agents—is similar to the first problem in agent communication. The second problem is not discussed in this book, and we mention only a straightforward algorithm called *energy concept.* Every agent maintains some *amount of energy,* which it consumes during its life. When its energy is used up, the agent must contact some component, named *dependency object* by Baumann. If the dependency object no longer exists, the agent is considered an orphan and must terminate. Two things are left open. First, what is energy? In principle, any kind of counter can be used for this, for example, a counter that is decreased after every migration. Other resource counters are also possible, for example, for every service access, each message sent, and so forth. Second, the dependence object must be defined. This could, for example, be the master agent in the case of specific applications or the home agency, which must be periodically contacted to refresh living energy. In addition to this straightforward concept, several optimizations and design issues can be considered. We refer to the given literature for more information.

4.2 Classification of Communication Models for Mobile Agents

As for software agents in general, communication techniques for mobile agents can be classified into two kinds of communication models.

4.2.1 Message Passing

The first type of communication model is *message passing*, which allows agents to send messages to each other. It is a form of direct communication in which the *sender* of a message must know the *receiver* by name and its current location. Message passing is a powerful communication concept that forms a flexible foundation for any kind of complex communication strategy. It does not define the structure and the semantics of the message content. Therefore, this technique can be used as a foundation to implement an exchange of text messages, Java objects, or any other message structure according to some Agent Communication Language (ACL), such as KQML or FIPA.

As part of the message-passing model, there must be some kind of service in which agents can find names of other agents with respect to the descriptions of services that other agents provide. If no service is available that provides this information, then this type of communication is practicable only for a group of agents who know each other in advance.

The simplest form of message passing is a *point-to-point* connection in which a single agent sends messages to exactly one receiver agent. The sender asks the agency (to be exact, a software component responsible to provide this kind of communication) to deliver a message to the receiver's message box. Only the receiver agent will be able to read the message. Messages can be removed from the mailbox and delivered to the addressee agent in two ways. With the *push technique* the mailbox actively delivers messages to agents. With the *pull technique* an agent retrieves messages from its mailbox. If the receiver agent is not available locally, the message component is responsible for locating the receiver agent and delivering the message to it. Techniques for locating agents are discussed in the following section.

Another form of message passing is *multi-point* communication (sometimes also called *multi-cast* or *broadcast*). For example, we may have a group of agents that are working together to solve a problem. They must communicate to coordinate their activities. A common communication technique here is the *point-to-multi-point* technique, in which a sender agent wants to deliver a message to many or all agents of the group. We can specify whether only local agents are included or all agents in the entire agent system are possible receiver agents. The difference between multi-cast and broadcast is the same as in network protocols: Multi-cast messages are sent to a set of receivers that have registered with a virtual group in advance, whereas broadcast messages are sent to all agents. Multi-cast messages are implemented in some mobile agent toolkits already (e.g., Aglets), but it is often restricted to local agents because of the complexity of the necessary message-delivery protocol.

Another criterion that needs to be established for message-passing techniques is whether messages are sent synchronously or asynchronously. In synchronous communication the addresser sends a message to the addressee and blocks its own execution until the addressee has answered with a reply message. Synchronous communication guarantees that messages are delivered and in case of a delivery error; for example, if a time-out occurs, the sender will be informed and an exception could be thrown. Synchronous communication naturally implies that both agents remain static during the communication. The Mole toolkit, for example, does not prevent agent migration in the case of synchronous communication but terminates the communication channel if at least one agent migrates.

In asynchronous communication the addresser sends a message to the addressee and continues its own execution. However, the addressee might also switch to a state in which it waits for new messages. Note that the distinction between synchronous and asynchronous communication is not defined by *waiting until the addressee answers* but rather by the even harder condition that it blocks its own execution thread. Asynchronous communication allows the receiver agent to decide autonomously how to react to incoming messages; for example, it can be temporarily in a state in which it does not want to receive messages. The drawback is that communication is temporally delayed and the sender agent has no guarantee that the message was delivered and read by the receiver. Asynchronous message passing is considered harder to program than synchronous message passing, because most programmers are simply unfamiliar with this type of communication because the semantics of the common procedure call or method invocation are synchronous. Most of the today's mobile agent toolkits provide an asynchronous model of message passing, whereas Aglets provides both types in parallel.

4.2.2 Information Space

The second communication model is named *information space*. Here we must distinguish between *blackboard*-oriented approaches and *tuple space*-oriented approaches.

The information space model provides all agents a single space where they can exchange information, data, and knowledge with one another. It is an *indirect* form of communication, because agents do not directly interact; that is, they do not have to address their posting to any agent—an agent simply writes a piece of data into the information space and other agents can read it. In some implementations, even the name of the agent that has posted into the information space is unknown, resulting in an anonymous form of communication.

The most important difference in regard to message passing is that an agent does not have to decide *which* piece of information must be sent to *whom*. With message passing, the responsibility of defining which information must be sent is made by the sender agent. In addition, each receiver agent must decide what information or results it has received from other agents, what results must be remembered in its own repository, and how to react to each message. It might be said that the control and data flow of an application is more or less predefined when using the message-passing paradigm.

In contrast, with the information space approach, an agent posts into the common information space all or almost all data that might be of any interest for the group. It is each agent's responsibility to watch the information space and react to any kind of modification or new data. If an agent finds a new and interesting data item, which might be some kind of intermediate result produced by another agent, it starts its own process to transform it into another intermediate result. The result is then posted into the common information space again. Thus, this communication model can be defined to be nondeterministic, because it is not predefined which agent will process new information.

All *information space* approaches temporally decouple communication between agents; that is, the writer and reader agent do not need to synchronize to communicate. The basic primitives are to write and read pieces of information. Some systems also provide functions to register for specific updates. To ensure that agents are notified when new and possibly useful information is written into the information space, agents can register their desires with the information space. When such information is published, the information space will notify the appropriate registered agents of its arrival.

In *blackboard*-oriented systems, each piece of information is stored under an identifier that must be specified by the writer and that must be known by all reader agents so that they can later find this information. Blackboard-oriented systems have a long history in software engineering [Buschmann et al., 1996] and artificial intelligence [Ferber, 1999]. Blackboards are a good model for collaborating software, especially when tackling problems that do not have a deterministic solution (i.e., no clear control and/or data flow exists between several modules of a program). However, blackboards still provide only a spatially coupled type of communication. The group of agents that use the information space to collaborate must have some common knowledge, at least about the structure of the blackboard and the identifiers under which certain data is published.

Tuple space–oriented approaches expand upon blackboard systems by adding associative mechanisms to the shared information space. Data items are organized as tuples, which are ordered collections of information, for example, ("Sean Connery," "Goldfinger"). The tuple space contains a set or multi-set of tuples. Tuples are identified by their contents rather than by their name. They can be retrieved in an associative way via a pattern-matching mechanism. One can access the aforementioned tuple by providing parts of the contents, for example, ("Sean Connery," ?movie), and obtaining the rest of it. Tuple space models have become popular with the Linda language [Carriero and Gelernter, 1989], which was developed in the parallel programming domain and which was also made available for mobile computing environments [Picco et al., 1999].

To further structure an information space, some approaches allow you to define regions or subspaces that are devoted to a single application and that are protected against illicit access. Tuple spaces can also be distributed over several network nodes, especially when combined with mobile agents. These models typically provide multiple spaces, each one on a separate agency. As a consequence, locality of agents is supported, which improves the performance of the application. An agent can then access only the tuple space that is located at the same agency. If the agent wants to access another tuple space, it must migrate to the remote agency [Cabri et al., 1998b] or explicitly access the remote tuple space [Omicini and Zambonelli, 1998].

To make the distribution of a tuple space transparent to the agent, Rowstron proposes, for example, to migrate parts of the tuple space to another location [Rowstron, 1998]. An overview of tuple space–oriented approaches for mobile agents can be found in Ciancarini et al. [1999] and Omicini et al. [2001].

4.3 Solutions to Provide Location-Transparent Communication

In this section we discuss several approaches to solving the problem of global and reliable communication. The main issue we are tackling here is location-transparent communication using asynchronous message passing between mobile agents.

As we mentioned at the beginning of this chapter, early systems published in the mid to late 1990s provide only local communication between agents residing on the same agency or some kind of remote communication without location transparency. In the latter case, different concepts for local and remote communication were often provided. In Telescript [White, 1996], local communication is offered by *meetings*. An agent—the petitioner—initiates communication by calling the specific method `meet`, which defines the target agent—the petitionee. If another local agent is available and matches the petition, the method `meeting` is called to allow the target agent to decline the communication. In the other direction the petitioner agent gets a reference to the other agent so that it can call methods. Global communication is implemented by *connections*, which are point-to-point connections between agents residing at different agencies. If the target agent accepts the connection, both agents can exchange Telescript objects via this channel. In Agent Tcl [Gray, 1997a] agents were allowed to communicate remotely by using remote procedure calls—tracking of mobile agents was not an issue, and the programmer had to implement his own techniques for this. Ajanta, a Java-based mobile agent toolkit, also provides remote method invocation [Karnik and Tripathi, 2001] as the only choice. Other toolkits, for example, Mole, do provide some kind of remote communication, but they restrict the mobility of agents. After an agent has accepted a so-called session, it is not allowed to migrate. If it migrates, the session is terminated immediately [Baumann et al., 1997].

Some of the mobile agent toolkits developed in recent years provide a means to let mobile agents communicate with other agents independent of their current location. Before we discuss some of these approaches, we want to point out the wide range of possible solutions related to the design space for global communication. First, we can determine that any approach for location-transparent communication must provide solutions for both of the following actions:

- Agent tracking, which involves recording the current position of an agent to make it possible to find the agent later

- Message delivery, which dictates that the message must be sent to the agent's current location if the target agent is not residing at the same agency as the sender agent

We can immediately present two solutions with opposite behavior. The first one, the *full information approach*, assumes that every agency has full knowledge about the current location of all agents in the system. Agent tracking becomes a very expensive task in this approach, because for each migration, all agencies in the network must update their local location directory. To make this protocol reliable, an agent must notify all agencies about its forthcoming migration so that they can buffer messages to this agent during the migration process. After the agent has reached its new location, a second update message must be sent to all agencies. This approach is also very expensive in terms of used storage, because the location directory contains entries for all agents currently active in the system independent of their real behavior in terms of messages sent to it. This location directory also contains the same data on each agency, so we have a high level of redundancy. In contrast, delivering a message is extremely easy in this approach, because it involves accessing only a single directory and sending the message to the current agent's destination.

The opposite solution is the *no information approach*. With this approach, we assume that no agent tracking is established and therefore no agency has direct knowledge of the current location of any agents other than those residing locally. Obviously, agent migration is now very cheap, because no location directory must be updated. However, to locate an agent to deliver a message becomes extremely expensive. The only way to do this is to search for the target agent either sequentially or in parallel using multi-cast or broadcast mechanisms of the underlying network infrastructure. In wide-area, Internet-scale networks, this technique is impracticable, which has resulted in this approach being discarded as well.

Even if in reality neither approach is feasible, we want to use them as examples to discuss a metric that is possibly interesting when assessing the quality of a global communication model. For any agent we can measure the number of migrations in relation to the number of messages sent to it, and we name this the *migration-to-receipt relation* (MRR). If there is a highly mobile agent that frequently changes its location but rarely receives messages (i.e., it must be found by other agents), the MRR is high. In this case the no information approach would be the better choice, because associated migration costs are low. If an agent is rather immobile and often receives messages by other agents, the MRR is low and the full information approach would produce lower communication overhead.

Clearly, the world is not as simple as we have described it here. Several other factors affect which approach actually produces the lower communication overhead. For example, in both approaches the number of agencies and the distance between them must also be taken into account. However, the general idea of using the MRR as a possible gauge to assess the quality of any communication model remains correct. If the MRR is high, an approach with low tracking costs is preferred, whereas with a low MRR, an approach with low delivery costs should be chosen.

An interesting question in this context is how a software designer should choose the correct communication technique. Wojciechowski and Sewell [2000] argue that the choice of the communication model should be application-specific. The authors assume that the behavior of all agents could be predicted to a certain extent, making a single MRR valid for the entire application. Together with additional requirements (e.g., scalability and reliability), this enables us to select a single communication model at design time. We affirm this and want to mention the consequence that a mobile agent toolkit should be built in such a manner that the communication model, as before with the migration model, is exchangeable so that it can be adapted to the specific application. This requirement has never been realized in any mobile agent toolkit thus far.

Nevertheless, we believe that we need to go a step further. Given that this situation is similar to that seen with agent migration, we are not convinced that it will be possible to develop a sufficient and appropriate decision model for communication techniques. It would be necessary to have a mathematical model, comparable to our model developed to describe agent migrations, for communication techniques. This model depends on several factors, some of which might be not be assessable before developing the application. Here we have the same line of argumentation as with agent migration. It is likely that even within the same application scenario, no single technique will be able to solve all problems. Or, to state this using the *migration-to-receipt relation:* We believe that there are many application domains where each agent will have its own typical MRR that might be diverse from those of other agents. Thus, it is highly probable that each agent has its own optimal solution, and it is an interesting problem for upcoming research—is it possible to develop an adaptive communication model that covers many of the current approaches transparently? According to Wojciechowski [2001], such an approach is currently used only in the context of mobile users in telecommunications.

4.3.1 Central Server and Home Agency Solutions

We start our discussion with an approach that uses a single location server to keep track of mobile agents while they are roaming the network. We can further distinguish between the approaches based on whether the location server is responsible only for tracking or also for message delivery.

In both approaches a mobile agent informs the server before it leaves an agency and after it has reached its new location. If the central server is responsible for tracking only an agent's location, a sender requests the target agent's current location and sends the message to this agency (see Fig. 4.1). If the current location cannot be determined, for example, if the agent is currently in transit or has not updated its directory entry correctly,

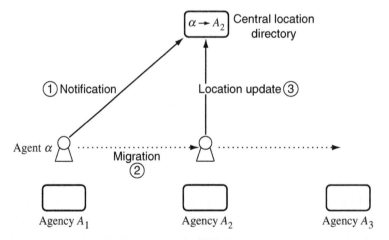

Figure 4.1 Central server approach. The central server contains a mapping of agents to their current locations. The picture shows the situation after agent α has updated its new location at the central server.

no messages can be delivered. The sender agent and its hosting agency can then buffer the message and try to locate the target agent later. If the target agency does not know the target agent, the message is sent back with an error notification, which results in a new query against the location directory. This approach is described by Wojciechowski and Sewell [1999], who use their NomadicPict language. The Semoa mobile agent toolkit, which actually focuses on security issues, also provides such a central server solution, named *Atlas*. This tracking solution also considers security aspects (e.g., that agents are not allowed to update location information of other agents) [Roth and Peters, 2001]. Atlas is also used as a foundation for Semoa's communication model.

The second approach not only stores the location but also delivers the message. In this case the sender agent transmits the message to the central server, which then looks up the current location of the agent and delivers the message. If the agent is not registered, the central server might store the message and wait a specified time or send the message back to the sender along with an error notification.

Agent tracking is expensive with any kind of central server solution. For each migration, the server must be contacted twice: once to invalidate the last location and once to publish the new one. In the second approach, the central server must also be contacted for each message. Neither of these approaches scales with the number of agents and the number of messages—it is a bottleneck for the entire agent system and a single point of failure.

An example of an extension of the central server solution that scales better is the *home server* approach. This scheme is comparable to the central solution scheme but differs in that each agent now has its own central server that is located at its home agency. Remember, the home agency is the agency where the agent was started. The general course of actions is the same as described previously. Even with home servers, we could distinguish between a simple query solution and the message delivery solution (see Fig. 4.2).

This technique is comparable to mobile IP [Perkins, 1996], which is designed to route IP packets to mobile hosts. The mobile host registers with a remote network and obtains a *care-of-address*. This address is forwarded to the *home server*. The home server then forwards all IP packets directly to this host using the care-of-address. A similar technique is used in operating systems using process migration, for example, in Sprite [Douglis and Ousterhout, 1991]. Referring to agents, the entire protocol is comparatively straightforward to implement and is used, for example, in the Aglets toolkit.

Both the central server solution and the home server approach disregard locality between sender and receiver agents. In the domain of mobile IP, this

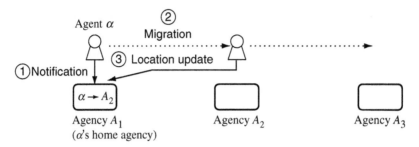

Figure 4.2 Home-server approach. Each agency contains a mapping of agents that were started on this agency to their current locations. The picture shows the situation after agent α has updated its new location and has reached agency A_2.

is known as a *triangle problem*. If two agents located at the same or proximate agencies want to communicate, location inquiries must be sent to a possibly distant server, which might be located at the other side of the globe. Some approaches were developed for mobile IP to solve the triangle problem by using cache-based techniques. They might be also adapted to mobile agent communication. The home agency then not only forwards messages to the agent's current location but also informs the sender agency about its current location (comparable to *binding-update* messages in mobile IP). Later, the sender agent can then send messages to this agent directly. If the agent has left the agency, messages cannot be delivered correctly and the new address of the agent must be requested from the home agency.

The home server approach scales better than having only a single tracking server and is a good choice in small or medium agent systems. Message delivery is easy to implement and can be fast because only a single inquiry against the location directory is necessary. With caching of addresses, message delivery can be further improved. However, this solution uses a single point of failure, and it still poorly scales when a large number of agents start at the same agency. The home server approach is not practical when home agencies are intended to be cut off the network once the agent has left it.

4.3.2 Forwarding Pointers

We now come to a solution that reduces the cost of keeping up-to-date location-related information, making it more suitable when agents are highly mobile. For each agent, the home agency provides an anchor that can be used to address messages. Whenever an agent migrates, it leaves a pointer to its new location at the agency it left. The *forwarding pointer* approach was probably first proposed in Desbiens et al. [1998].

We assume that each agency maintains a local directory that contains a "guess" as to current location for each agent that has visited the agency. In addition, we assume that each agency knows which agents are currently residing on it. If agent α migrates from agency A_i to A_k, the source agency first has to withdraw agent α from the list of locally available agents. If this agency is requested to deliver a message to this agent, the message must be stored locally, because the current location of agent α is not known. After the agent has arrived at the destination agency A_k, it registers with the local messaging service, which promptly sends an acknowledgment message back to agency A_i. Agent α is now known to be local at A_k, and the former agency, A_i, has updated its local directory so that it now contains a *forwarding pointer* to the new agent's location. If any messages were buffered at A_i, they are all forwarded to A_k. Also, new messages arriving at A_i can be immediately forwarded to the agent's new location (see Fig. 4.3).

When a message needs to be delivered to an agent, the sender delegates this process to the target agent's home agency. The name of this agency is typically part of the agent's name. The home agency then forwards the message along the chain of forwarding pointers until the agent is eventually reached.

We can immediately identify the following problems:

■ Is the forwarding pointer chain cycle-free? If not, a message might get caught within a cycle and never reach the target agent.

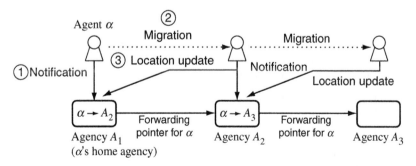

Figure 4.3 Forwarding pointer approach. Each agency maintains a forwarding pointer to the agent's next location. The pictures shows the situation after agent α has arrived at agency A_3 and has updated its new location at the last agency.

- How long can a forward pointer chain be? If an agent frequently migrates to new agencies, forwarding pointer chains will grow in size, thereby decreasing the performance of message delivery. It is reasonable to think about techniques to reduce the length of these chains from time to time. These techniques are also called *chain-compaction* techniques.

- What if the home agency is placed on a mobile host and is intentionally cut off the network after the agent has left it?

- What if the forwarding pointer chain breaks because of a failure in a listed agency?

- When can forwarding pointers be removed and garbage collected?

- Is this approach reliable? When an agent migrates faster than the message can be delivered, the message will probably never reach the agent. We have a race condition, which is not acceptable for a reliable communication model.

The algorithm we described previously is not reliable if agents migrate back to an agency they have visited before. According to Moreau et al. [2001], such an approach is implemented in Voyager [ObjectSpace, 1998]. Assume a situation in which agent α has left agency A_i at time t to migrate to A_{i+1}. This agent later comes back to A_i at time t' and migrates further to agency A_{i+k}. We assume that $A_{i+1} \neq A_{i+k}$. According to the algorithm, both agencies A_{i+1} and A_{i+k} are expected to send acknowledgment messages back to A_i and it might happen that for any reason the acknowledgment message from A_{i+k} reaches A_i before the acknowledgment message of A_{i+1}—we have a potential race condition between two acknowledgment messages. If the acknowledgment message from A_{i+1} arrives after the other one, there will be a cycle in the forwarding chain, which prevents reliable message delivery to this agent from now on. Moreau suggests using a *mobility counter* to solve this problem. The counter increases each time an agent migrates and is attached to acknowledgment messages, making it possible for every agency to distinguish between new and old messages. In the scenario described earlier, A_i will now update its local directory with only the new acknowledgment messages sent from A_{i+k}. Other messages with lower mobility counter are discarded [Moreau, 1999].

Let's now discuss approaches to collapse the forwarding pointer chain to improve performance of message delivery. The general idea is to update location information at each agency to skip intermediate agencies and point to the agent's current location, if possible, thereby reducing message hops. The range of possible solutions is manifold. We can distinguish between approaches that send location update messages as an effect of agent migration or delivery of a message. However, we can also distinguish between approaches that send updated notifications either to all agencies in the network, selected agencies (e.g., those that the agent has visited so far), or only a single agency (which could be for example the agent's home agency). Let's discuss some examples in more detail.

First, every time an agent migrates, the new hosting agency broadcasts update messages to all agencies in the network. Every agency then has up-to-date location information for every agent in the form of a forwarding pointer that directly points to the agent's current location—which is equivalent to the full information approach. In Internet-scale networks, this approach is clearly impractical. Another extreme solution is to have an agent send its new location only to its home agency after every migration—which makes this approach identical to the home server approach presented in the last section. However, we can combine the home agency approach with forwarding pointers if we reduce the number of update messages. For example, the agent carries a counter that decreases with each migration. As long as the counter is not zero, the agent leaves a forwarding pointer at each visited agency, as described previously. In the other case, the agent sends an update message to its home agency. Instead of using a migration counter, other metrics can be used, such as time, the number of messages received, or the distance between the home agency and the new location.

In a more "lazy" update strategy, update notification messages are sent upon receipt of messages. For example, when a message should be sent from A_i via the target agent's home agency and along the forwarding pointer chain finally pointing to agency A_k, then A_k could send an update message to the sender agency, A_i, so that all following messages can be delivered directly. Instead of updating the sender's location directory, it is also possible to update the agent's home agency or send update messages back to the forwarding pointer chain so that all agencies on the agent's path are updated [cf. Moreau and Ribbens, 2002].

Concerning the fault tolerance of agencies and the reliability of the communication techniques, Moreau [1999] uses a special type of message, named *inform* message. This message is sent between agencies only to update location directories. The concrete strategy of sending *inform* messages is not defined and is intentionally left to the application designer, because which policy will serve best depends on the application-specific parameters, such as the network type, the relation between migrations and messages received, and so on. Moreau uses *inform* messages in a later publication to provide a fault-tolerant communication model based on forwarding pointers. Moreau [2002] presents an approach in which location information is replicated so that agency A_i holds a pointer not only to A_{i+1} but also to $A_{i+2}, A_{i+3}, \ldots, A_{i+k}$. This approach is able to tolerate failures of up to $k - 1$ consecutive agencies. However, migration costs increase with this approach.

The next problem that we are faced with is that of the single home agency serving as an anchor for the forwarding pointer chain. As Moreau and Murphy and Picco state correctly, to rely on such an anchor makes the approach impractical in peer-to-peer networks, where single hosts are mobile and can be cut off the network temporarily. Moreau's solution makes use of *inform* messages that are sent to arbitrary agencies in the network. In contrast, Murphy and Picco use a broadcast-based approach, which we will discuss in the next section.

A forwarding pointer approach has the advantage that agent tracking costs are relatively low. In contrast, message delivery can be expensive, because a potentially long forwarding pointer chain must be followed unless reasonable chain-compaction algorithms are available. Although many strategies and policies are conceivable, we are not aware of any in-depth comparisons in terms of network or other attributes. Although the algorithm is relatively straightforward to implement, adding fault-tolerance and code-compaction techniques makes this approach conspicuously more difficult. This approach seems to be good for agents that migrate frequently but only within a small area and to a small number of agencies.

Another approach that also uses forwarding pointers but does not use forwarding chains [Cao et al., 2002] splits a mobile agent from its mailbox in such a way that the agent can migrate independently from the mailbox. The mailbox is a kind of buffer, where incoming messages are stored. The mailbox can migrate on request of its agent if the agent thinks that it is worthwhile to have the mailbox close to it—but only along the agent's migration path. Thus, all agencies that a mailbox visits is a subset of all agencies that its agent visits. The mailbox migrates with lower frequency than the agent. On each agency that the *mailbox* visits, there will be a forwarding pointer to the current location of the mailbox. The agent always knows the location of its mailbox and communicates with its mailbox either by occasionally fetching messages or by being informed actively by the mailbox about new messages. It can even decide which of these two protocols should be used.

If an agent migrates, it can decide to move its mailbox to the destination agency as well. In this case the agent informs its mailbox about the forthcoming migration, and the mailbox then informs all agencies that it has visited before (including the agent's home agency) about a forthcoming mailbox migration. All these agencies now activate their local buffer for messages that are directed to this mailbox. After the mailbox has reached its new location, it sends an update message to all these agencies again, presenting its new location address. These agencies now update their local address cache, close the internal buffer, and deliver all accumulated messages.

If a message should be delivered to agent α, the sender agency first looks up its local directory. If the agent is not residing on this agency, it checks to see whether a forwarding pointer to α's mailbox is available. If so, the message is forwarded directly to the mailbox. Otherwise, the message is forwarded to α's home agency, whose name is part of the agent's name.

We thus have an approach in which forwarding pointers that always have length 1 are used. The mailbox is split from the agent, and the goal is for the mailbox to migrate with lower frequency than the agent itself. Therefore, the number of forwarding pointers can be reduced even for a highly mobile agent. This approach is interesting because it provides some parameters that allow the protocol to be adapted to the local circumstances of the agent. Parameters that might influence the overall performance of this approach are as follows:

■ The frequency of mailbox migration compared with the number of agent migrations

■ The technique to transfer messages between the mailbox and the agent (push versus pull)

Further work in this area is needed to determine whether these parameters really do significantly influence the overall performance of the protocol and whether it really has a positive effect.

4.3.3 Broadcast–Based Approaches

In this section we discuss approaches that are based on broadcast protocol messages (not to be confused with agent messages), that is, sending messages from a single agency to many agencies in the logical agency network (see Fig. 4.4). The general advantage of broadcast-based approaches is that they

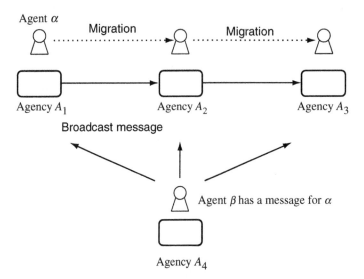

Figure 4.4 Broadcast-based approach in which a message is broadcasted to all agencies.

do not require a specific agency to serve as a location directory or as a starting point for a chain of forwarding pointers. Thus, these approaches work well in scenarios of peer-to-peer networks and mobile hosts, where we cannot make any assumptions about the availability of any host or infrastructure. Agent tracking is completely neglected in these approaches, which makes agent migration very cheap. However, for each agent message to be delivered, the target agent's location must be determined using the broadcast protocol— and this can be considered a brute-force method to locate agents. Some of the following approaches use broadcast and multi-cast protocols provided by the underlying network infrastructure [Peterson and Davie, 2003]; others implement their own broadcast protocols. The latter requires having some kind of logical agency network, that is, some neighbor relation between every pair of agencies.

We start again with a presentation of the design space and later point out problems and shortcomings of the broadcast-based approach. Finally, we discuss possible improvements of the protocol.

Broadcast-based approaches can be distinguished from one another according to the type of information that is broadcasted. First, the message itself can be broadcasted from the agency the sender currently resides on to all agencies in the network. If an agency receives a broadcast, it checks to see whether the target agent is currently on this agency; if it is, it delivers the message to the agent. If the target agent is not on that agency, the message is forwarded to all neighboring agencies until all agencies have received the broadcast message. Next, not the message itself but only a location query concerning the target agent is broadcasted. If an agency receives the query and the target agent resides on this agency, the agency acknowledges receipt of the query by sending back the target agent's current address to the sender agency. The agency also prohibits any migration attempts of the target agent to guarantee that arriving messages can be delivered correctly. After the message has arrived, the agent is allowed to migrate again. Finally, migration notification messages can also be sent through the network. After an agent has arrived at a new agency, it sends its new location, together with a time-stamp (e.g., a migration counter) as broadcast messages to all agencies in the network. Messages with stale location information are discarded.

In the first two approaches, an agent migration does not produce any costs to update location directories. In contrast, the effort to deliver a message is very high, because network broadcasts are extremely expensive and, in a global network, almost impracticable. Both broadcast approaches should be used only if the number of migrations is much larger than the number of messages to be sent within the agent system. The differences between these two approaches are related to the size of the broadcast message. Location queries are relatively small compared with agent messages. Therefore, the first approach works well if messages are small, whereas the second approach should be used in all other cases. The third approach makes agent migrations extremely costly, because the agent's new location must be propagated through the entire agent system. In contrast, message delivery is straightforward and inexpensive. Exactly opposite to the first two approaches, the third approach works well whenever the number of migrations is low in relation to the number of messages to be sent.

As already mentioned, broadcast approaches are useful in small to medium networks but not in Internet-scale agent systems. Broadcast-based approaches seem to qualify as a fall-back mechanism (e.g., to supplement any of the techniques described in the last sections). It can also be combined with the home-server approach under the assumption that there is some kind of logical and hierarchical agency network.

The main idea is that the logical network contains regions, and each region comprises a small number of agencies. Within a single region, all agencies know each other (the technique necessary to create such a logical network is not of interest here). When an agent crosses regions, it informs its home agency it is leaving the *old* region and entering the new one. When the agent migrates between agencies of the same region, the agent does not contact its home agency to update its location.

In contrast to the home agency approach presented previously, migration now becomes less expensive because the agent's new location is updated only with every n-th migration. How does message delivery work now? The sender agent and its hosting agency contact the agent's home agency to obtain the target agent's latest address, which is not more than the region out of which the agent has announced its location last time. The message is then forwarded to the representative of this region. This representative then uses broadcasts within its own region to find the actual location of the target agent.

Let's now discuss some improvements of the basic broadcast approach. We have already identified the most important drawback—the number of agencies that must be informed. If we were able to reduce the number of agencies to which an agent message or location query must be sent, the overall approach might become worth reconsidering.

The concept works assuming that an agent's itinerary is known in advance and that messages must therefore be sent only to all agencies on the agent's current route. This approach can be further optimized if we are able to guess on which of these agencies the agent resides when the message is sent. It might be possible, for example, to estimate how far the agent has already processed its itinerary. Agencies at the beginning of the route could then be neglected.

4.3.4 Hierarchical Approaches

In this section we expand the approaches based on central or distributed location directories that we introduced so far. Those approaches mentioned previously can be characterized as two-tier approaches, where location directories are placed in the topmost tier and all other agencies are located in the lowermost tier.

Hierarchical approaches are characterized by additional tiers in which more location directories are placed. Usually, the hierarchy is tree-structured, with nodes representing agencies, and the tree structure is built according to the geographical structure of the network (i.e., agencies that have a common ancestor are also geographically proximate). An agency at a leaf covers only those agents that are currently located at this agency. At higher layers, an agency maintains a location directory that contains tracking information for all agents currently residing at any agency in its subtree. All agencies form the *location tree*. As usual, we name agencies at lower levels the *children* and agencies at higher levels the *ancestors* of an agency. The single agency at the highest layer is named the *root* of the location tree.

According to Pitoura and Samaras [2001], we can distinguish the following two approaches. In the first one, each location directory contains a pointer to the current address for all agents in its subtree. In the second approach, each location directory contains a pointer only to an agency at a lower level, which also contains location information for the given agent. To discuss both approaches in detail, we first define the *least common ancestor, LCA(i, j)*, of two agencies, A_i and A_j, to be the first agency that lies on both paths from A_i and A_j, respectively, to the root of the location tree.

The first approach, named *Pointer to Leaf* (PTL), maintains a pointer to an agent's current location at each agency. Let's assume that the current location of α is A_k. There is a path from the root A_r to A_k. Each agency on this path has a pointer for agent α that points to A_k. If the agent migrates from A_k to A_m, then all entries concerning agent α at agencies on the path from A_k to $LCA(k, m)$ must be removed. All agencies on the path from A_m to $LCA(k, m)$ must add an entry concerning the new location of agent α. Finally, all agencies on the path from $LCA(k, m)$ to A_r must modify their location directory concerning this agent (see Fig. 4.5).

To deliver a message sent by agent β residing at A_l to agent α residing at agency A_k is straightforward. Along the path from A_l to A_r, each agency simply delegates message delivery to its ancestor until agency $LCA(l, k)$ is reached. This agency must have a pointer to the current address of target agent α. Thus, the message is forwarded to this agency and then delivered to the agent.

In the second approach, named *Pointer to Child* (PTC), each agency maintains only a pointer to an agency at a lower level for all agents in its subtree. If agent α migrates from agency A_k to A_m, entries concerning agent α on all agencies on the path from A_k to $LCA(k, m)$ must be removed. All agencies on the path from A_m to $LCA(k, m)$ must add a new entry for agent α that contains a pointer to the lower level. The entry at agency $LCA(k, m)$ must be updated. It is not necessary to update entries at agencies on the path from $LCA(k, m)$ to A_r.

To deliver a message sent by agent β residing at A_l to agent α residing at agency A_k is only a little more complex than in the PTL approach. The message is forwarded from agency A_l to its ancestor until agency $LCA(l, k)$ is reached. Then the path from $LCA(l, k)$ to A_k must be followed until the agent is found.

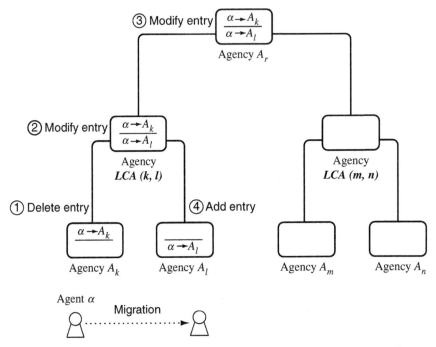

Figure 4.5 Hierarchical approach in which each agency on the path up to the root agency maintains a pointer to an agent's location. The pictures shows the situation in which agent α has migrated from A_k to A_l, making several updates necessary. Directory entries above the line are valid before the migration; those beyond the line are valid after the migration has completed.

Both approaches differ slightly according to their migration and message delivery costs. With the PTL approach, for each agent migration, all location entries on the path up to the root of the location tree must be updated. In contrast, with the PTC approach, only agencies up to the least common ancestor of the source and destination agency must update their location directory. Thus, the latter approach considers the distance between source and destination agencies and is faster (if agents migrate only locally). In general, hierarchical approaches scale better according to the number of agents and number of agent migrations than when using central server approaches. Message delivery is faster with the PTL approach than with PTC because the pointer to the agent's current location can be found at the least common ancestor already. The second phase of forwarding the message along the path down to the leaf can be neglected. One shortcoming of PTL is that it requires reachability of all agencies on the network layer. If an agency is part of a subnetwork and can be accessed only by using a gateway agency, messages cannot be delivered directly starting from the least common ancestor.

Hierarchical approaches can also be combined with forwarding pointers to reduce the number of location updates. Let's take the PTC approach as a starting point. The general idea is to update only those directories on the path from the source agency, A_i, and the destination agency, A_k, respectively, up to some level l, which is lower than that of $LCA(i, k)$. We name the ancestor of A_i at level l agency $A_{i'}$ and the ancestor of A_k at level l agency $A_{k'}$. A forwarding pointer is installed from $A_{i'}$ to $A_{k'}$, and all agencies on the path from A_k to $A_{k'}$ add their location directory with an entry for the migrating agent. As a consequence, the number of agencies where location information must be updated is less than that needed in the original PTC approach. The forwarding pointer makes message delivery only slightly more complicated. For more technical details, refer to Pitoura and Samaras [2001].

Summary

We identified mobile agent communication as another key problem in mobile agent research. Although it might be argued that mobile agents do not necessarily have to be able to communicate remotely (i.e., between two agents located on different agencies), it eases programming of mobile agents if we use a reliable and location-transparent communication technique.

In this chapter we proposed five techniques from current literature, in addition to two simplistic approaches:

1. Central server approach, which stores the current location of all agents in a central database

2. Home server approach, which stores the current location of an agent at the agent's home agency

3. Forwarding pointer approach, which forwards messages along the visited agency

4. Broadcast approach, which broadcasts messages to all agencies in parallel

5. Hierachical approach, which uses tree-structed location directories that are based on the geographical structure of the network

As far as we know, these approaches have not been compared with each other using either mathematical models and simulation or real-world experiments. Obviously, there are considerable differences between these approaches, for example, regarding reliability, performance, and security. We believe that conducting some kind of evaluation would be very important to identify dependences between agents' behavior or application and the type of communication they should use. We discussed that each approach may work well in some scenarios but not in others. For example, the home-server approach is not applicable in scenarios in which a mobile agent is started on a mobile device, because it usually has a wireless low-bandwidth network connection to the Internet. The broadcast approach is not suited in large networks. We believe that mobile agents would benefit from being able to select a communication technique that matches their application dynamically during runtime. It is an interesting and still open question whether this can be done in an intelligent way without influencing the agent's programmer.

Chapter 5

Mobile Agent Security

This chapter focuses on a very important part of mobile agent research—security. Many research groups worldwide have focused on security aspects of mobile agents and published a large number of papers. In fact, most research in the area of mobile agents was done in security issues. However, the actual state-of-the-art technology has not yet reached a level that could provide an applicable set of best practices with industrial strength. We really talk about basic research and miss out, in most cases, on a complete framework of integrated concepts and tools. We cannot provide such an integrated framework in this book; our goal is to provide an overview of the current state-of-the-art technology as it relates to our perspective on mobile agents.

First, we introduce security requirements for computer systems in general. We also discuss some basic cryptographic techniques, such as encryption, signing, and hash values. We then concentrate on the problems specific to mobile agents and present the currently available solutions.

Contents

5.1 Security Requirements and Cryptographic Techniques

Security is one of the most important factors influencing software quality. It is as important as correctness, reliability, and efficiency. In general, security as a requirement translates into the ability of a software to prevent unauthorized access, be it by mistake or deliberately, to both code and data. Software designers must ascribe importance to security in the early phases of software development and in tight relation to the customer. The goals of this introductory section are to further break down the general requirement of secure computer systems and enlist several key issues from the perspective of a user.

Security cannot be seen in a simple "black and white" manner—a computer system is neither completely secure nor, hopefully, completely insecure. It must be determined against *which* security problems or sort of attacks a specific computer system is safe. It is an invariable attribute of every computer system that only a subset of all possible security problems are solved. Some problems may not yet have been foreseen. Others, for example, those that are outside system boundaries or that have a low probability of occurring, are not solved. This must not be viewed as a failure but as an intention of the developer, who must accept certain types of risks that have a limited probability.

For example, a commonly used means to protect private data is to demand a authentication from users such as a password, before granting access. The software will be able to avouch that only the owner of the data will have access to it. An example of a type of attack that the software designer has rated with low probability is a brute-force search for the correct password of a specific user. Searching through all possible sequences of characters will take more time than the attacker might find worth spending, making the probability of a successful attack low. The better the quality of the password, the better the protection against even dictionary attacks, where the attacker simply iterates through a list of frequently used passwords. If the software designer had rated the probability of such an attack as being high, he or she would have chosen another authentication procedure, such as using smart-cards or biometric identification.

On the other hand, some types of attacks affect the computer system's environment instead of the system itself. The important difference here is that neither the software nor the computer designer is responsible for developing countermeasures against such an attack. For example, someone may observe the user entering the password and later try to gain access using the password he or she observed. This type of assault cannot be solved by the software designer; rather it is the user's responsibility to prevent such attacks. Thus, a computer system protected by passwords for authentication purposes is not generally secure but rather offers tailored security against a hacker who tests out passwords. Or, as Schneier pointed out in his book *Secrets and Lies,* a computer system might be secure against a lot of attacks but never against a hand grenade being thrown on it.

It is important to stress that the level of security that a software system can and must provide always strongly depends on the application domain and the application scenario. It is not necessary—and from the economical point of view, usually not advisable—to build a system that is safe against all types of attacks. As usual in software development, it is mandatory to analyze which security problems might occur and to find solutions for these specific problems.

The use of mobile agents generates a lot of security problems, sometimes new and regrettably still unsolved problems. Some opponents of mobile agents cite these problems as reasons not to use mobile agents, which in our opinion is unfair. Although each new technology has potential, it usually also has new security problems. The key is to develop a focused set of countermeasures against identified threats, not a generalized damnation of the entire technology. Following their logic, we would have to unplug the nodes of the World Wide Web to prevent the further spreading of worms.

The mobile agent systems must be seen as embedded in an application scenario, and the best way to evaluate an agent-based approach is to determine whether the specific security problems for this application scenario are solved. To give a simple example, consider the case of malicious agencies. A *malicious agency* is one that tries to attack mobile agents; for example, it may try to steal private data of the agent's owner. This is a problem only in open mobile agent systems, where anybody is allowed to start a mobile agent server on his or her home computer. Some people see this as the only real application scenario for mobile agents, but many application scenarios focus on a closed mobile agent systems, in which such an attack is unlikely to occur.

We start our discussion with a brief overview of the general security requirements of software systems, with some emphasis on distributed systems. These requirements are always named in relation to computer security and cryptography. Each of these requirements is mandatory for the acceptance of computer and software systems or systems in general.

5.1.1 Authenticity

Authenticity is a major requirement and the foundation of many security solutions. It demands that each partner in a communication be able to prove that he or she is who he or she claims to be. When we say that A *authenticates* against B we mean that A identifies himself or herself against B to allow B to decide whether A can be trusted.

In the real world, authentication is a matter of social rules that everyone must learn and accept. It is a kind of protocol that has been developed over time and that depends on the situation in which it happens. When you enter a jewelery store to buy an expensive present for someone, you signal that you are someone who has enough money to pay by wearing good clothes, carrying your briefcase, or presenting your credit card. At the same time, the owner of the jewelery authenticates himself or herself by his or her expertise or by the quality of the shop so that you can believe you can trust the quality of the object you buy. Obviously, you will not buy an expensive ring from a hawker. In some cases, it is even necessary to authenticate yourself by providing a signature, such as when signing a contract to buy a car or a house.

Authentication in the Internet is far more complicated. How can you be sure that the Web page you have requested is really from the company you wanted to contact? *Spoofing* is a technique in which a malicious host claims to own a specific IP address to intercept requests to that IP address and take the role of the other computer. If there was a technique in place to force the remote Web server to authenticate, you could be sure that the information is genuine. We need something similar to an electronic passport for our software.

The equivalents to a passport and signature in the electronic world are certificates and electronic signatures. This authentication process depends on secrets, for example, a private key that is used to electronically sign a document and that is by definition not known to anybody else. Some basic cryptographic techniques are introduced next.

Symmetric cryptosystems use a common key, K, which is shared between the sender Alice and the receiver Bob to encrypt messages but must be kept secret against other entities. Alice uses key K to encrypt a message, which is then sent to Bob, who is able to decrypt it with the same key K. An eavesdropper, Eve, may be able to read Alice's message, but without key K, she cannot understand it. The advantage of symmetric cryptosystems is speed, whereas secret key distribution between Alice and Bob is a considerable technical problem.

In *asymmetric cryptosystems* or *public-key cryptosystems*, each principal has two keys. A *public key* is shared with all other principals (e.g., by posting it on a public-key directory service). A corresponding *private key* must be kept secret by the owner. The concept of public-key cryptosystems is that messages can be encrypted using either key and can be decrypted only by using the second key of the key pair. For example, Alice encrypts a message to Bob with Bob's public key, K_B^+, which she obtains by looking at a public directory. This message can be deciphered only by using the corresponding private key K_B^-, which is known only by Bob. The advantage of asymmetric cryptosystems is a comparatively easy key distribution—the public key can be published anywhere in the network and only the private key must be kept secret. The disadvantage is its slow speed. In practice, public-key distribution is supplemented by techniques to verify the identity of the owner using so-called certificates so that Alice can trust that the public key she has obtained from the directory service actually belongs to Bob.

Authentication using a public-key infrastructure is now very easy. We assume that Alice and Bob want to authenticate each other. Both know the public key of the other person but know only their own private key. Thus, Alice sends a message to Bob that consists of a random number that was encrypted with Bob's public key. Bob proves he possess the corresponding private key by decrypting the message, and then he sends it back to Alice. Bob can verify the identity of Alice using the same protocol afterward.

Authentication between mobile agents and agencies is a major concern as well. A mobile agent must authenticate on each visited agency so that the agency can decide whether the agent is trusted. After this first line of defense, the agent is then authorized; that is, a specific set of permissions is granted to it. Vice versa, the agency must authenticate against the agent so that the agent can be sure it is on the correct agency. A malicious agency could, for example, masquerade as another agency to deceive the agent about its real host. As a consequence, the agent could disclose sensitive information, because it assumes it is on a known and trusted agency.

However, here we have a major problem when using mobile agents. How can a mobile agent protect a secret, as, for example, a private key, when it is roaming the Internet and is executed in a possibly malicious environment (i.e., a hacked agency)? The mobile agent must at least present all data and all code to that agency because it is needed to execute the agent. Is there any chance that a mobile agent can sign a legally binding contract as a delegate of its owner? To electronically sign a document requires a secret that will be no longer a secret if the agent enters a malicious host.

5.1.2 Confidentiality

Confidentiality demands that information be protected against unauthorized access. Many techniques have been developed to gain confidentiality between communication partners. Recall the various techniques that can be used to conceal the fact that any information was transmitted at all, such as writing a message with invisible ink. Such techniques are called steganography and are used today, for example, to embed sensitive information in pictures using a technique called digital watermarking.

If it is necessary not only to enwomb the message but also to conceal the sense of it, the message must be encrypted. Encryption techniques have been known for a very long time, probably beginning with the Skytale that was used by the government of Sparta about 2500 years ago. They used a cylinder lagged with a piece of leather or parchment paper. It is an example of a so-called transposition algorithm, where the order of characters is changed to encrypt the message, but not each character itself. An example of a later technique, called substitution algorithm, is the Caesar code, which maps each character to another character of the underlying alphabet.

Although all these techniques were used by governments and militaries, confidentiality is now also a major concern for companies and private persons. Banks must encrypt money transfers, companies must encrypt trade negotiations or business reports, and so forth. The technique that is most commonly used today is encryption using public-key cryptosystems, as introduced previously.

With regard to mobile agents, we can again find several examples where confidentiality is to be guaranteed. Assume a shopping agent that travels to several online stores. The agent carries some kind of confidential trading algorithm. Otherwise, the store could reveal the trading strategy of the agent and react to it. Now assume that the agent has already visited several stores and carries various offers within its data package. This information must be confidential to prevent a store from using this information to produce its own offer, which, of course, would be only marginally lower than the current lowest price.

5.1.3 Integrity

Often it is necessary to be sure that a particular piece of information has not been modified at some point in time. In the real world this may be realized by numbering all pages of a contract and binding them together so that no piece of paper can be exchanged, added, or removed. Or, a notary might sign a contract and then impress it with a seal. Manual modifications are either not allowed or must be signed by all parties. All these techniques ensure that no modifications can be made to the contract after it has been signed.

The digital equivalent of these techniques are digital signatures. Using *digital signatures* makes it possible to verify that a message was originated by the sender and to simultaneously check the integrity of the message.

For example, let's say Alice encrypts a message with her private key, K_A^-. When Bob receives the message, he can decrypt it using Alice's public key, K_A^+. If the decryption is successful, he can be sure that the message was encrypted using the corresponding private key, which is known only by Alice. Thus, Bob can be sure that Alice is the author of the received message. Because of the low speed of public-key cryptosystems, message signing is often combined with *digests*.

A *digest* or *hash value* is the result of a *one-way hash function* computed over a message. Such a hash function maps any arbitrary-sized byte sequence to a fixed-sized byte sequence, for example, 16 bytes in the case of the MD5 function. An important feature of a hash function is that there is not a simple technique to find the original value x when only the hash value $h(x)$ is known. In addition, it also is computationally infeasible to find another y so that $h(x) = h(y)$. In other words, if two hash values are the same, it can be inferred that the two original values are identical. Digests are often used in combination with digital signatures. Because digests are a good means to condense data while keeping its uniqueness, it is the message's digest that is encrypted using private key K_A^- rather than the original message. Digests alone verify the integrity of a message but provide no information about the sender. Therefore, this must be combined either with digital signatures as described earlier or with *message authentication codes*.

A message authentication code (MAC) is computed over a sequence of bytes and requires a secret key that is shared between the sender and the receiver of the message. The MAC is sent along with the message; therefore, the receiver can be sure about both the integrity of the message and the sender's identity. The advantage of MACs, compared with digital signatures, is that they are easier and faster to compute because they are based on a secret key rather than a public-private key pair.

Integrity is also an important issue for mobile agents. For example, the owner of an agent starts an agent with some initialization data, let's say with the itinerary that the agent should process. It is very important that the integrity of the itinerary not be attacked; otherwise, the agent could be sent to arbitrary hosts.

5.1.4 Accountability

Accountability means that each subject is responsible for any action it has taken and cannot deny responsibility later on.

Assume that Alice and Bob have performed some price negotiations. They ultimately agree that Alice is going to buy a particular good from Bob for a specific price. Accountability now enforces that neither Alice nor Bob can later repudiate that this negotiation has happened. Both partners are bound to the result of the negotiation and must comply with the contract.

A possible solution might include cryptographic techniques, such as digital signing of the contract by both partners. Using this technique, we might have encountered a problem with regard to mobile agents. As we have already noticed, it might be impossible for mobile agents to carry a secret, such as a private key, but this is required to sign a contract.

5.1.5 Availability

Availability aims to ensure that access to a service cannot be restrained in an unauthorized way. Availability guarantees a reliable and prompt access to data and resources for authorized principals. Availability can be reached, for example, through redundancy of computer systems, hardware, and software. In the case of mobile agents a malicious host can, for example, refuse to execute an agent, which would be a denial of service. Or the malicious agency could refuse to let the agent migrate to another agency.

5.1.6 Anonymity

Anonymity means that you do not have to identify yourself and therefore must be seen in contrast to authenticity that was introduced previously.

The interesting question from the technical point of view is, can we reach anonymity in the digital world, and if so, at what cost?

In the real world, it is not always necessary to identify ourselves to conduct business. For example, it is not necessary to identify yourself when you want to buy something and plan to pay in cash. Anonymity in this situation can be achieved because we have other mechanisms to authenticate ourselves. This is not so in the digital world. As we have seen, authenticity is a major concern, especially in electronic commerce. Sure, there are techniques that enable you to pay for a service without authentication against the seller, especially for smaller amounts of money—so-called micropayments. Such a technique introduces a so-called trusted third party. When you want to buy a newspaper, for example, you must authenticate only against the third party, which then will give notice to the newspaper. The newspaper itself has no information about you except for the IP address of your computer. Thus, browsing the Web is still not completely anonymous. See, for example, the JAP project at the University of Dresden,[1] in which software was developed that guarantees anonymity on the level of IP addresses when surfing the Web.

5.2 Taxonomy of Possible Attacks

In this section we give an overview of possible problems that can occur when using mobile agents. We use the common classification scheme found in similar papers, such as Hohl [1998b] and Jansen [2000], which distinguishes between malicious agents and malicious agencies.

5.2.1 Malicious Agents

Malicious agents are those that try to attack the hosting agency. We further classify malicious agents according to the target they attack.

Attacking the Hosting Agency

The most obvious example of a malicious agent is one that consumes resources of the hosting environment in an improper way. Examples of such

---

1. See *anon.inf.tu-dresden.de* for more information.

resources are all computational resources—memory, CPU cycles, or network bandwidth. These resources are consumed with the result that the agency eventually is not able to provide its usual service to other agents. Such attacks are therefore called denial-of-service attacks. In a less severe case the agent merely wants to annoy the agency's administrator by opening windows on its screen. In this case the agent is authorized but does not comply to the unwritten rules of a benevolently behaving agent. It should be obvious that it is difficult to decide whether an agent performs a malicious act or not without a clear model of access authorization to resources. The Java programming language does not yet provide such a model. Consider the following example of a correct Java code:

```
1 public void run()
2 {
3   synchronized( Thread.class )
4   {
5     while( true );
6   }
7 }
```

This piece of code holds a lock on the object *Thread*.class (remember that every class is an object in Java too). Actually, it prevents other threads from being executed. An agent that carries this piece of code can freeze the entire agency.

The second type of attack to the hosting agency is when an agent tries to gain unauthorized access to the agency. Agents can try to pilfer or alter sensitive information stored on local hard disks. For example, it may try to access a local key store file, which includes private keys of the agency or its users. An agent could also try to disclose the agency's code or even try to terminate the agency completely. Such attacks are made possible either by an inadequate access control mechanism or by improper agent authentication and authorization, which allows any agent to masquerade as an authorized agent and then (mis)use services or resources of the underlying agency. If, for example, agent authorization is done only using the agent's name, then the attacking agent needs access only to the name of another agent with more permissions.

At this point, it is worthwhile to compare mobile agent technology with Java applets—this time from the point of security. In both cases, mobile code is transmitted to a host that is going to execute it, therefore making it a possible target of attacks initiated by the mobile code. The decisive difference, however, is that an applet loaded from Web server A is executed on host B on behalf of a user at host B. In contrast, a mobile agent started by a person at host A migrates to host B and is then executed on behalf on its owner. Here, the administrator of host B has a great interest to protect the platform against all kinds of attacks initiated by mobile agents.

This problem of malicious mobile agents can be solved to a great extent by using the Java sandbox technique that we will explain later in detail. Although the Java sandbox is quite comprehensive, it does not solve all problems with malicious agents; for example, in Java it is not easy to control memory access or CPU usage.

Attacking Other Agents

A malicious agent that wants to attack other agents currently residing at the same agency has several possibilities. Some of these possibilities result from the programming language; others are possible because of the hosting agency and the communication infrastructure and services provided there.

First, no agent must have access to any other agent on the programming language level. If we assume object-oriented programming languages, this means that no agent should ever obtain a direct reference of another agent. Otherwise, the malicious agent would gain full control of the referenced agent, could invoke methods outside the agent's own life-cycle model, and could modify accessible object variables. In Java it is reasonably easy to protect each agent (seen now as an object) by defining a separate class loader for it. Other problems are shown later, when we discuss pitfalls of the Java programming language in detail.

Second, a malicious agent can mask its identity to cheat other agents and gain sensitive information from them or to use services on behalf of the betrayed agents without paying for them. This problem is comparable to the masquerading attack described previously, but it might be even easier to achieve. Consider the case that, because of a lack of adequate programming, an agent is allowed to forge the addresser name of a message. Note that in this case, both the cheated agent and the one under whose identity the malicious agents does work now are shammed.

Third, a malicious agent could initiate denial of service attacks on other agents, for example, by sending thousands of spam messages. On one hand, the attacked agent is not able to work properly; on the other hand, in environments where agents have to pay for CPU and/or memory use, for example, the agent owner also suffers from these attacks.

Finally, we have here an example for the accountability requirement introduced earlier. An agent rejects the result of a communication with another agent. This can be done intentionally or unintentionally. In either case there will be a quarrel about this, and the agency should prevent that by logging all agent activities.

5.2.2 Malicious Agencies

A malicious agency is one that tries to attack mobile agents currently residing on it or other agencies by attacking the communication link.

Attacking Other Agencies

Attacks against other agencies are directed at the communication link between agencies. Using passive attacks, the adversary does not interfere with the messages sent over the network. No data is modified by such an attack, but the data is monitored to extract useful information. Because neither communication partner notices this attack, it is usually difficult or impossible to detect. The simplest variant of a passive attack is *eaves-dropping,* where in which the adversary monitors the communication link between two agencies and captures agents to extract useful information from the agent's state or code. This might result in a leakage of sensitive information. Another form of attack is *traffic analysis,* which also works when each message is encrypted because it is not important whether the data is readable (understandable) to the attacker. Here, the adversary attempts to find patterns in the communication between two agencies, which might allow the adversary to derive certain assumptions based on these patterns.

Active attacks include security threats in which an agency tries to manipulate agent code or data while it is transmitted between agencies. The most common examples of this kind of attack are *alterations,* in which an agent's data is deleted or tampered with by an agency, and *impersonation,* in which a malicious agent impersonates another agent instance that has more comprehensive permissions than the malicious agent itself.

Sometimes malicious agencies attack an agent to cause another agency to malfunction. Farmer et al. [1996a] describe an interesting example for this case. Assume that two airlines are providing ticket-booking services. An agent that travels to these two airlines (among others) could be manipulated by the first airline agency in a way that the agent, rather than reserving 2 seats, reserves 100 seats for a specific flight. The agent will execute the reservation at the second airline, booking all available seats and thereby preventing other agents from being able to book a seat at the second airline. These later agents must then book at the first airline.

Attacking Agents

Attacks against agents involve malicious agencies that try to tamper with an agent's code or data. Unfortunately, this type of attack is much more difficult to prevent than malicious agent attacks.

The general problem is that a mobile agent must disclose its information about code and data if it wants to be executed. Chess et al. [1997a] note: "It is impossible to prevent agent tampering unless trusted (and tamper-resistant) hardware is available in AMPs [Agent Meeting Point—comparable to an agency]. Without such hardware, a malicious AMP can always modify/manipulate the agent." Therefore, no general guarantee can be given that an agent is not maliciously modified; see also Farmer et al. [1996b]. However, the situation is not so irremediable as it seems to be. With use of cryptographic techniques, especially data signatures and data encryption, a situation can be achieved in which some types of illegal access to an agent's code and data can be detected—but not prevented.

Possible attacks include simply spying on the agent's data or code and modifying the agent's data, code, or control flow. More comprehensive attacks include terminating the agent or capturing an agent's state before it migrates off the agency. In the latter case, the agency could restart the agent later, in effect actually cloning the agent. We further distinguish this type of attack with regard to the type of information that is targeted.

Agent's Data

Assume a scenario in which an agent roams the Internet to collect prices for an airfare. This scenario was introduced by Yee [1999] and is used in many papers dealing with the security issue of a possible attack by a malicious agency. The agent visits several agencies according to a fixed itinerary, or it decides dynamically to which agency it should migrate next. In its data package, the agent collects information about the agencies visited and the airfare offered there.

A malicious agency might now intend to influence the agent in such a way that its airfare will be the lowest. Therefore, the agency's first step is to spy out the agent's data. It is unlikely that the agent will communicate this information voluntarily, so the agency will access the agent's data in an unauthorized way. The obvious problem with spying out data is that it is completely invisible to the agent. The agent does not realize that some of its data has been stolen. This type of attack seems to make it completely unrealistic that mobile agents can carry any type of secure, sensitive information, such as a secret or private key of its owner. Besides price information, the malicious agency might also spy out the agent's itinerary and thereby collect information about other agencies that offer the same type of service. Later, this information could be used to attack those agencies by using the techniques previously described. This is also a general problem. It is not necessary that the result of such spying attacks become visible in the near future. The agency could steal a secret key and use it much later.

Another type of attack is called *cut and paste*. This attack works even if data has been encrypted so that it can be read only at specific agencies. Assume the following example. An agent, α, carries a data item protected with the public key of an agency, A_i, that the agent is going to visit. Because only this agency has the corresponding private key, the agent can read this data item only at exactly this agency. However, a malicious agency, A_m, which currently is hosting agent α, could cut the data item, paste it into a new agent, and let this agent migrate to A_i. The new agent decrypts the data item and carries it back to agency A_m.

Once the agency has this information, it could either increase each price collected so far or modify its own fare so that this becomes the lowest fare. If the agent has a fixed route, then the malicious agency could further modify this route so that it was the last agency to be visited.

From this example we learn that an agent typically carries two types of data. First, a static part contains data that is unmodifiable during agent transmission. This data may be public or private static data. Public static data can be read by anyone, especially by all agencies visited, whereas private static data is readable only by the agent itself. The major requirement for public static data is integrity, whereas for private static data the major requirements are confidentiality and integrity. A typical example of public static data is the name of the flight the agent is searching for airfare information. Private static data is typically the agent's itinerary or some configuration parameter defined by the agent's owner, for example, parameters for price negotiations. Second, an agent carries dynamic data that is modifiable during agent transmission.

In the airfare example, the list of visited agencies with the associated price information is an example of this type of data. Again, this type of data may be public or private dynamic data.

Although not part of our example, we can identify yet another class of data. In some application scenarios it might be wise to send some parts of the agent's data back to the agent's home agency before the agent migrates to the next destination. The requirements here are confidentiality and integrity for private data.

Agent's Code and Control Flow

We now consider the agent's code as a target of an attack of malicious agencies. The general requirements for code are integrity and confidentiality. However, because the agent must disclose at least parts of its code to be executed, code cannot be confidential for the hosting agency.

Even if we assume we have a technique to protect the agent's code completely from the interpreter, it would still be possible for the agency to perform so-called black-box attacks on it. In a black-box attack, the agent is executed several times, every time with different input parameters and different calls to services. Another attack would be sabotage, in which the malicious agency alters code at arbitrary points to corrupt the agent.

When code cannot be protected as a whole, we might be able to disclose only each line of code. There is a difference between knowing each line of code and understanding the overall semantics of the program. However, even if we have a technique to ensure that the Java interpreter has access only to the next line of code, the agency could learn the overall semantics if large parts of the agent are executed.

The agency can spy out the code to analyze the agent's intended behavior. Say you developed an agent with a new algorithm for protein folding. Your achievement should, of course, be protected against malicious agencies that want to steal your code and provide a service based on your code. Spying out an agent's code becomes even easier if the agent is built from reusable software components or uses code libraries that are already available at each agency. One solution might be to have the agent carry along its own libraries for data encryption instead of using those provided at the agency.

As a result of code analysis, the agency might then manipulate the agent's code. For example, it could implant some piece of possibly malicious code into a formerly benevolent agent. The agency could insert a component that makes it possible to remotely control the agent later, even if it has migrated to other agencies. If the malicious agency has successfully analyzed the code, it might even *understand* the strategy of the agent, for example, in price negotiations. In our airfare example, the agent could be manipulated so that no later price offer could be lower than the one of the malicious agency.

Whereas all the aforementioned attacks seek to modify the agent's code permanently, the agency can also change code temporarily and can modify agent execution by attacking the agent's control flow. Attacks targeted at the agent's control flow include direct manipulations of the control flow and malicious execution of the agent in general. A useful manipulation of the control flow could be to skip security checks or other conditionals by returning wrong results to system calls. The malicious agency could even return wrong addresses of other agencies to misguide the agent. Second, the agency could refuse to execute the agent correctly; for example, it may execute the agent several times until it eventually accepts the offer.

5.3 Introduction to the Proposed Solutions

After giving a concise overview of possible attacks, we now present possible solutions for these problems. We start with the reasoning for the range of countermeasures that might apply.

During this discussion we exclude any arguments about how each countermeasure might influence performance, storage usage, or network traffic. At this time, it can only be said that a certain, most likely fairly high, price with regard to these aspects of the system will have to be paid to reach a high level of security. However, hard evidence from actual applications is still missing and would thus reduce any arguments to the level of educated speculations.

The cheapest alternative is to install *no protection* and to gamble that everything will work well. The advantage of having no security protection is that no additional effort is necessary for encryption and signing of data or any further security protocol.

Although the concept might look strange at first sight, there might also be some good arguments to risk attacks as discussed previously. The type of application affects the level of security you want to achieve. Consider an application in which your agent is travelling to several agencies to collect information about products you are interested in, but it is not allowed to buy anything. You do not use any sophisticated security solution to protect your agent against malicious agencies, so the agent's code and data can by spied out and modified. The important trade-off is between the effort to install such security solutions versus the problems that may arise if a manipulation occurs. What is the risk? Why should an agency try to modify your agent when it is just collecting information? Sure, the agency could guess that after the phase of gathering product information there might come a phase where you, as owner, will buy a product. Thus, the agency could, for example, provide some offer that attracts your attention. However, your risk when using an unprotected mobile agent is that you must spend time visiting the Web page of the purchaser and detecting that the offer was bogus. Your agent did not reveal more information about its owner than you would have given to the online store when surfing through the Internet anyway.

The best security solution would be a technique to prevent all types of attacks. As we have already indicated, it is doubtful that a solution based only on software algorithms will be powerful enough to protect mobile agents against all types of attacks undertaken by malicious agencies. Therefore, most researchers in the area of mobile agents are content with developing techniques to detect attacks after they have occurred, for example, when the agent returns to its home agency. Some authors recommend using hardware-based security solutions, for example, using a tamperproof co-processor. See, for example, Wilhelm et al. [1998] for such an approach.

Starting with the next section, we will discuss countermeasures to mobile agent security challenges. Countermeasures consist of all techniques, procedures, and protocols to diminish the vulnerability of mobile agents hosting agencies. We will see that many techniques can be adopted from the area of distributed systems. Many techniques are based on the cryptographic techniques we introduced in the last section (i.e., encryption, digital signatures, and hash values). Therefore, many of the proposed solutions build on the assumption that there exists a public-key infrastructure (PKI), where, to simplify matters, public keys and certificates of any principals can be loaded. Other techniques require different presumptions. Some of them can be taken for granted, for example, that the home agency is trustworthy—maybe it's the only trustworthy agency in the entire mobile agent system.

5.4 Organizational Solutions

We start our overview of solutions with the description of some approaches that can be characterized by the absence of any technical countermeasure to prevent or detect attacks but that provide organizational rules for how mobile agents systems should be built. Organizational solutions confine the openness of mobile agent systems to achieve some level of security. None of these techniques solves security problems—they only circumvent them.

5.4.1 Trusted Agencies

Until now we have used the term *trusted agency* to refer only to an agent's home agency. In general, an agency can be trusted if we have strong evidence to assume that this agency will not attack our agent or any other agency in our mobile agent system. If we now assume that we could distinguish *a priori* between trusted and untrusted agencies, then we would have a very straightforward solution to all security problems. We let our agent migrate only to trusted agencies! To achieve this, our agent must have a predefined itinerary that includes only trusted agencies, or in the case of dynamic routing of agents, we can assume that the logical agency network consists of trusted agencies only and no agency will allow a mobile agent to migrate to an untrusted one.

From the viewpoint of an agency, we must ensure that the only mobile agents accepted are those that have solely visited trusted agencies before. This will prevent our agency from being attacked and possibly becoming vicious later. Aglets enforces such a trust-based policy, whereby hosting environments will not accept or dispatch agents to remote hosts they do not trust.

As you have guessed, of course, the problem is to differentiate between trusted and untrusted agencies in advance. However, in a closed network environment, such as that of a company, we can achieve such a situation smoothly. An example of this approach is the PersonaLink application proposed by GeneralMagic some years ago.

Nevertheless, to make this solution applicable in general, rules that are positioned outside the mobile agent systems must be established to build a network of trusted agencies. One problem remains, though. How can an agent and all agencies be informed if it is discovered that an agency has become malicious?

If it is not possible to bar mobile agents from visiting untrusted agencies, it might still be possible to design the agent in a way that secure sensitive computations, for example, are moved to trusted agencies. Such an approach should be always applicable, because we assume we have at least one trusted agency in the system, that is, the agent's home agency. Of course, the problem of spying out an agent's data and those pieces of code executed at an untrusted agency remains. Besides, to artificially split an agent's activities on two or more hosts might contradict the mobile agent paradigm and ruin performance advantages, for example, if a large amount of data must now be moved to a trusted agency to process it instead of processing it locally.

Although many authors devalue this approach, as we will see, it might be the only one that is worthwhile to pursue. It is a solution for the problem that an agent might want to carry secure sensitive information, such as a secret of its owner. This information can be encrypted with the public key of the trusted agency, making it possible for only the agency to read it. Therefore, an agent can carry even a private key of its owner, as long as the agency is really trusted.

5.4.2 Agency Reputation

Agency reputation can been seen as an approach to allow mobile agents to decide which agencies are trusted in an open network environment. Rasmusson et al. [1997] suggest that agents can complain about any agency with a central registration agency. Malicious agencies lose reputation, causing other agents to stop visiting these agencies. Rasmusson et al. denote their approach as *social control*, which is defined as a type of behavior that enforces all members of a social group to behave according to rules that were defined within this group.

The authors compare their approach with the population of a small village, where people know each other and unethical behavior of one person immediately becomes known by all and is extremely embarrassing for that person. Such a village could therefore be interpreted as a type of closed social system, whereas, in contrast, a typical mobile agent system could be seen as a big town, where people might be more willing to be deceitful, knowing they live in a anonymous microcosmos.

During their lifetime, agencies can obtain some level of reputation when acting benevolently to visiting agents. Conversely, they lose reputation when an agent gives notice about an attack. The agents themselves will propagate the information about whether they were treated in a pleasing way or were attacked from other agents; thus, malicious agencies will be bypassed in the future. The problem with this approach is that only agents can complain about agencies; agencies have no means to decline a bad reputation.

For example, it might be possible for an agent to deliberately complain about an alleged malicious agency. Another problem is that behaving benevolently for a long time does not necessarily mean that an agency is not malicious. The agency might work properly over a long time, accumulating a high reputation, and then begin attacking agents without warning.

5.4.3 By Law

The last organizational approach we want to mention here is based on laws legislated by the government or individual contracts between agency providers and users to guarantee that agencies are not spying out an agent's data or code or otherwise tampering with agents. In addition, a provider could be forced to ensure that his or her agency is not attacked by third parties. Refer to the approach that was proposed in the Telescript project [Tardo and Valente, 1996].

This approach does not need any techniques to prevent attacks, but it does require techniques to detect them and later be able to verify whether attacks have taken place. The agency must audit all activities of visiting agents so that the agency administrator can prove the behavior of its agency if an agent owner makes claims about malicious behavior. These audits could be used as evidence later in court. This means that this solution does not really improve the situation in which we have no security protection but provides only a trusted procedure for the case of an attack.

5.5 Protecting Mobile Agents

We divide our introduction of techniques and protocols to protect mobile agents from malicious agencies to address the best possible prevention of attacks and the detection of attacks after they have occurred.

5.5.1 Preventing Attacks on Mobile Agents

Encrypted Functions

Sander and Tschudin [1998a] propose a technique to encrypt an agent while still allowing it to execute at remote agencies. Their technique is called *encrypted functions*. Using this technique makes it possible to create mobile agents that are able to compute functions securely even in an untrusted environment. The general idea is to let an agency execute the mobile agent carrying an encrypted function without knowing the original function. Unfortunately, it can be shown that, so far, only basic mathematical functions can be protected with this approach. The technique is not sophisticated enough to be used in mobile agents in general. However, with the development of enhancements to their approach, in the future, this technique might work with mobile agents in a generalized setting.

The general scheme can be described as follows:

1. Alice has a mathematical function, f, and encrypts this function, resulting in $E(f)$.

2. Alice sends the program $P(E(f))$ that executes $E(f)$ to Bob.

3. Bob executes $P(E(f))$ using input x.

4. Bob sends $P(E(f))(x)$ back to Alice.

5. Alice decrypts $P(E(f))(x)$ and obtains x.

This idea seems simple at a glance; however, it is difficult to find a suitable encryption function E, and until now, no such encryption function has been developed. Sander and Tschudin [1998b] present a protocol that works for polynomials over rings $\mathbb{Z}/M\mathbb{Z}$ with smooth integers M, where smooth integers are those that consist only of small prime factors.

However, even if function f is encrypted and an agency has access only to $P(E(f))$, this does not prevent the agency from undertaking so-called black-box attacks. Here, the agency simply executes $P(E(f))$ several times to obtain pairs of input and (encrypted) output of the underlying function f. Thus, any algorithm that can be easily detected from such a table could be reconstructed. As the authors point out, the only difficulty might be the size of the table necessary for reconstructing f.

For a complete understanding of this approach, some basic knowledge in algebra is necessary, which is outside the scope of this book. The interested reader is pointed to the available literature.

Time-Limited Black Boxes

The last approach results in an encrypted program that will be completely protected against spying out code and data for the lifetime of an agent.

We now discuss a technique proposed by Hohl [1998a] that assures protection only for a limited time.

First, we define the term *black box* according to mobile agents. An agent is a black box if at any time code and data of the agent cannot be read and modified. We see that Sander and Tschudin's encrypted functions fulfill this requirement and therefore make agents into black boxes according to this definition. Hohl now relaxes the requirement that an agent must be a black box for its entire lifetime and introduces a new property that he calls *time-limited black box*. The difference of a time-limited black box is that an agent must be a black box only for a specified time interval. After this time interval, any attacks to such an agent will have no effect.

The goal of this approach is to make it hard to analyze an agent, that is, to understand the agent's code and data to attack the agent in an expedient way. As we have stated, there is a difference between understanding every line of code and understanding the semantics of an entire program. This is the point of Hohl's approach. The goal cannot be to protect the agent's code against understanding each line of code but rather against understanding the sense of the agent as a unit. Therefore, the author proposes to obfuscate, or mess up, code so that an automated program analyzer will need a large amount of time to understand the code. Without being able to grasp the code and data, a malicious agency cannot modify the agent in its own favor. The only type of attack that would still be possible is sabotage of the agent.

The second important issue of this approach is the need to take precautions for the time after the protection interval. It is clear that there can be either an automated analyzer or a human being who is able to understand the code, regardless of what type of obfuscation has been used. Therefore, almost all data stored within the agent's state or data package must be attributed with an expiration date. This expiration date must be encapsulated with each data item in an unforgeable way so that other agencies will be able to verify it and reject the agent and the agent's data item, if necessary. Note that not all data has to be protected by such expiration intervals, only those that are needed to interact with other parties.

Hohl proposed three mess-up techniques: The first targets the agent's code, the second the agent's data, and the third the agent's control flow. All examples are taken from the paper by Hohl [1998a]. For the first technique, no specific algorithm is given, but an example is presented to demonstrate the idea of code obfuscating. Consider the following piece of code and assume that variables a and b are arrays of integer values.

```
1 b[6] = a[3] - a[5];
2 b[7] = a[2] * 256;
3 b[8] = b[7] + b[6];
4 b[5] = b[8] - a[4] * 256;
5 a[0] = b[5] DIV 256;
6 a[1] = b[5] MOD 256;
```

This code fragment computes the difference of 2-byte values stored in a[2] and a[3] (high byte and low byte) and a[4] and a[5], respectively. At the end, the difference is stored in a[0] and a[1]. To recover this is very easy when you resolve b[5] recursively. This example also shows the basic idea of *variable recomposition,* which Hohl proposes to protect data items. The technique works on a set of variables and cuts each variable into pieces, let's say a sequence of bits of variable length, and creates new variables that are composed of segments from different original variables. Access to these variables must be rearranged accordingly.

Finally, Hohl suggests converting control flow elements, that is, conditionals or loops to value-dependent jumps. The result is evocative of finite state machines, where in each state some atomic expression is calculated. A more interesting approach is called *deposited keys,* in which deciding parts of the agent's code remain at a trusted server and the agent has to communicate to this server from time to time to advance in its flow of control.

The drawbacks of this approach are manifold, the most important of which is the exact determination of the expiration date. The time needed for an automated analyzer to determine the semantics of a piece of code greatly depends on the quality of the mess-up algorithm and on the expertise of the attacker in program analysis using, for example, monotonic data flow systems. Second, only the existence of such an expiration date makes it impossible to use long-living mobile agents and contradicts one of the principles of software agents in general. The longer the interval is, the higher is the probability that the agent will be attacked. The shorter the interval is, the shorter the agent's itinerary can be.

Environmental Key Generation

Now we consider a scenario in which agents roam the Internet, and we examine whether it is possible to protect the agent's private data (i.e., code and data) from being analyzed by the hosting agency. For example, let's say your agent will make a patent search against a database. It is your intention that the type of request will not be visible to the patent server because it might already contain enough information about your future patent that another person could steal it from you.

The goal is to have clueless agents [Riordan and Schneier, 1998]—agents that actually do not completely know what their behavior will be because portions of their code or data are encrypted with a secret key. The basic scenario is as follows: The agent has a cipher-text message and a method to search the environment for the data needed to generate the secret key for decryption. When the information is found, the agent can generate the key and decipher the message. Without this key, the agent has no idea about the content and the semantic of the encrypted message; that is, the agent is clueless.

So, we see, the general idea is to give the agent only hash values of some information and let the agent compare this hash value with computed hash values at the remote agency. If they match, the hash value is used as a key to decrypt additional information or code that should be processed now.

Thus, the goals of this method are (1) to protect the intention of the agent by not giving it full knowledge about its task and (2) to protect further against actions by using encryption. It is obvious that the hosting agency can still attack the agent after it has decrypted the message, but to do this, it must be executed. An analysis *a priori*, for example, by a dictionary attack, is very costly.

The authors also propose more protocols, for example, considering the time when keys are generated. These protocols can be used to ensure that a particular data item can be encrypted only before or after, and in combination with these two protocols, during a time interval. All rely on the existence of a minimally trusted third party that is used for key generation but that does not need to understand of the semantics of the information.

These protocols all have the same structure and distinguish between three steps:

1. The programmer interacts with the trusted server to obtain an encryption key based on particular parameters.

2. The programmer initializes the agent, giving it an encrypted message (code or data), some additional data required to decrypt the message later, and information about the trusted server to let the agent access the environmental information necessary to generate the key.

3. The agent afterward contacts the server for the information necessary to generate the key.

We first discuss the *forward-time* approach, which permits key generation only after a specific point in time. After that, we discuss the *backward-time* approach, which permits key generation only before some point in time. Let S be a secret known only to the server. According to the pattern just presented, the protocol works with the following steps:

1. The programmer sends the target time, t_* (i.e., the time after that key generation is permitted), and a nonce, R, to the server. The server generates a key using the current time, t_{cur}: $h(h(S, t_*), h(R, t_{cur}))$, and sends the key together with t_{cur} back to the programmer.

2. The programmer sets $P = h(R, t_{cur})$. It uses the key received from the server to encrypt the message to the agent and also gives the agent a copy of P. The agent then starts roaming.

3. At each agency, the agent continuously requests the secret from the server. At point t_i the server returns the hash value $S_i = h(S, t_i)$. The agent tries to decrypt the message using key $h(S_i, P)$. It will succeed only when $S_i = h(S, t_*)$, which is when $t_i = t_*$

The *backward-time* approach works according to the same pattern:

1. The programmer sends the target time, t_*, and a nonce, R, to the server. The server returns $h(S, R, t_*)$ if and only if t_* is in the future.

2. The programmer uses the returned value as the key, encrypts the message, and gives it to the agent, together with a copy of R and t_*.

3. At time t_{cur} the agent sends the target time, t_*, and the nonce, R, to the server. Only if the correct time t_* is sent will the server be able to return the valid key, and it does this if and only if t_* is later than t_{cur} with regard to the server time.

Forward- and backward-time approaches can be combined to use closed time intervals in which the encrypted information can be deciphered.

The major concern with this approach is that it protects data and code but does not protect the behavior of your agent. Consider the example of an agent performing a patent search. Rather than carrying keywords describing the patent, the agent carries only hash values. It searches through the complete patent data store, computes hash values of keywords, and compares them with the hash value that it is carrying. The agency will not be able to analyze which type of patents the agent is interested in, but it can observe the agent and find out for which result the agent will perform an action, such as sending information back to its owner. Another problem with this approach is that decrypting pieces of code at runtime implies that it must be allowed to create code dynamically, which might be prohibited by the hosting agency and/or the underlying execution environment.

5.5.2 Detecting Attacks on Mobile Agents

Detecting through Replication of Agencies

We start with the discussion of two approaches presented by Schneider [1997] and Yee [1999], both of which rely on replication to detect any type of attack. The general idea is to replicate the agent so that not only a single but many agents of the same type roam the network with the same task.

Schneider [1997] argues that a malicious agency may corrupt a few copies of the agent but that there will be enough replicas that the encounter can be avoided and the task successfully completed. We assume a situation in which a mobile agent executes in a sequence of so-called stage actions, S_i, where $0 \leq i \leq n$. Usually, the mobile agent processes an itinerary that consists of several agencies, A_i, $0 \leq i \leq n$. Let A_0 again be the home agency and A_n be the destination, which might equal the home agency. There is a strong relationship between stages and agencies as S_i is processed at agency A_i. Schneider now assumes that for each stage S_i there will be not only a single agency A_i but many of them providing the same set of services and behaving the same, as intended. More formally we can write that in each stage there will be a set $S_i = \{A_0^i, A_1^i, \dots\}$ of agencies.

The agent's home agency replicates the agent and sends copies to all agencies $A_i^1 \in S_1$. Each replicated agent processes the same action, but each does so on a different agency. Eventually, the agent wants to migrate to another agency. The protocol now dictates that the agent is to be sent not only to a single agency but to all agencies $A_i^2 \in S_2$. In general, at stage i, each agency A_k^i sends a copy of the agent to all agencies of stage $i + 1$ (i.e., S_{i+1}).

Each agency at stage S_i receives many copies of the same agent, probably with different state or data packages (because they might have been attacked). It compares all agents with each other and assumes that not more than half of all agencies in stage S_{i-1} were malicious. It then chooses the agent with the most frequent state to execute. The problem now is to determine which agencies form stage S_{i-1}. Otherwise, malicious agencies could behave as if they were on the penultimate stage and foist some bogus agents to the destination or the home agency.

Schneider denotes an agency on state i as a voter that must be able to select its *electorate*, that is, the agencies of stage $i-1$ from which it will accept agents as input. Each agent must carry a kind of privilege to identify itself as sent by an authorized agency. Bogus agents will be detected because they will not carry such a privilege. The privilege consists of the set of so-called forwards. When an agent is sent from agency A_k^i of stage S_i to some other agency A_j^{i+1} at the next stage S_{i+1}, it will carry a *forward*, which is digitally signed by agency A_k^i: $K_{A_k^i}^-(\mathbf{A_k^i} \to \mathbf{A_j^{i+1}})$. Here, $\mathbf{A_k^i}$ is the id, or name, of A_k^i.

It is now easy for an agency on stage S_{i+1} to determine which agencies do belong to stage S_i. An agent carries a *forward* $K_{A_m^{i-1}}^-(\mathbf{A_m^{i-1}} \to \mathbf{A_k^i})$, which contains this information. However, an agency on stage S_{i+1} might be foist with some other (bogus) agents carrying other *forwards*. To check this, the agency must verify the list of *forwards*, beginning with the one signed by A_k^i and ending with the home agency, A_0. Here, we assume that each agency knows the home agency, A_0. Because bogus agents will not have this information (they cannot carry an information signed by A_0), they can be identified. From the rest of agents, we are taking the majority value from S_i.

Finally, after all bogus agents are discarded, agency A_j^{i+1} determines whether a majority of the remaining agents are equivalent. All these agents are augmented by the new forward $K_{A_j^{i+1}}^-(\mathbf{A_j^{i+1}} \to \mathbf{A_l^{i+2}})$.

The main problem with this approach is that it might be unrealistic in common application domains to assume that agencies can be replicated. Although agency replication is not a problem if the replicated agencies are within the same application domain, this is not sufficient for the proposed approach. Agencies within the same domain will certainly run the same hardware and software. Why should an agent then be attacked only at a subset of these replicated agencies? In addition, agents must be replicated as well, and it depends on the agent task whether this is possible or not. Consider, for example, a scenario in which an agent is supposed complete a bargain. This task is better not replicated. Another problem is that the author does not provide information on how the agent should find different agencies for each stage.

Detecting through Replication of Agents

Yee [1999] proposes another solution that is also based on replication. However, this approach does not work with agency replication, only with replication of agents. The scenario is that of an agent configured to search for the lowest price of an airfare. The user has predefined the itinerary of the agent and proved some parameters to describe the flight to search for. Let the agent's itinerary be the following set of agencies, $\{A_0, A_1, \ldots, A_n\}$.

We start with two mobile agents, α and β, each processing the predefined itinerary in a different order. The first agent will process the itinerary as given, and the second agent will execute the itinerary in exactly the reverse order (i.e., the sequence $A_n, A_{n-1}, \ldots, A_0$).

Yee now argues that if there is only a single malicious agency on the agent's tour, using this approach will make it possible to detect any tampering with the agent by comparing the results of the two agents α and β. The user will then be able to decide which of the agents was attacked and can be certain that the other agent has presented the correct result of its search—the lowest airfare.

First, we consider the case that there is exactly one malicious agency, A_i. The agency that will provide the overall lowest fare is A_j, and we first assume that $i < j$. Agent α processes its itinerary in the given order and will therefore visit the malicious agency before it reaches the agency providing the lowest fare. If we assume that agency A_i is malicious according to data integrity and does not kill the agent completely, then it cannot attack agent α successfully because agent α does not have any sensitive data yet. Later on its tour, agent α gets the lowest fare from agency A_j and will report this to its owner. Agent β visits the agencies in the inverted order. It first reaches agency A_j, getting the lowest fare. Later it reaches the malicious agency A_i and becomes attacked, for example, by modifying the information about the lowest fare. If agent β returns home, it will report an incorrect value to its owner. A comparison of both results shows that they are not equal, but the owner can see which fare is lower. Therefore, he can infer that agent β was attacked and agent α has presented the correct result. It is obvious that case $i > j$ works analogously.

Finally, we must consider the case that $i = j$, that is, that the malicious agency would be the one to present the lowest fare, even without any type of attack. Agency A_i, however, now benefits in that it need not present its real price but can alter it to be just marginally lower than the second-lowest fare. Note that in this case, the owner will not get the real lowest fare but only the second-best price.

This approach seems to be more applicable than assuming that agencies can be replicated. However, it requires that the agent's itinerary be predefined and immutable until the second agent starts. The approach does not work if more than a single malicious agency is present. For example, consider the case that the agency providing the lowest price is in the middle between two malicious agencies. In this case, neither agent can determine the real price.

Detecting Black-Box Attacks

We have introduced the black-box property of mobile agents and presented two approaches to convert mobile agents into black boxes. We distinguished between a time-unlimited approach using encrypted functions and a time-limited approach working with mess-up algorithms. However, one problem remains: Even if a malicious agency is no longer able to determine the semantic of an agent, it might still be able to run so-called black-box attacks on them, for example, by executing the agent several times with different input parameters and therefore different results of system calls to test the agent.

By re-executing a mobile agent, a malicious agency can gain information about the agent's behavior; that is, it can determine how it reacts on the given input parameters. Consider a scenario in which an agent travels to an agency, asks for an airfare, and accepts the deal if the proposed price is lower than a user-defined threshold. The malicious agency might now execute the agent and start with a comparatively high price. If the agent does not conclude the bargain, it decreases its own price and restarts the agent until the threshold is reached.

Hohl and Rothermel [1999] propose a technique to make agents themselves capable of detecting such attacks. The main idea is to let the agent verify that the agency delivers the same result for equal system calls and any inquiries to the agency. Therefore, for each input, the agent sends a message to a trusted registry, such as that located at the agent's home agency. The message contains a unique statement identification number associated with the agent's source or byte code and a hash value of the data response. Thus, the registry collects information about all results to inquiries of the agent. When the registry receives a new message, it looks up the statement identification number and compares the hash value of the data response entry. If they match, it acknowledges the message; otherwise, it returns an error code to the agent. If the agent receives a nonacknowledge message, it knows that the hosting agency has tried to re-execute it and reacts accordingly.

For details of the protocol implementation, we refer to Hohl and Rothermel [1999].

Detection Using Cryptographic Techniques

In the following sections we will discuss techniques to detect tampering with an agent's data by malicious agencies.

Protect an Agent's Read-Only Data

The read-only part of an agent's data is characterized by the fact that these are immutable during the lifetime of the agent. Consider, for example, the itinerary that is predefined by the agent's owner and contains addresses of all agencies the agent should visit. This information should be unmodifiable.[2]

For the following we assume that the name of the agent's owner and the name, or id, of the agent's home agency are carried by the agent as part of the agent's name or state. Both are examples of immutable data items and therefore must be protected against modifications. Thus, the main requirement here is integrity of the data. To achieve such *read-only* data items, the following technique based on asymmetric cryptosystems can be used. At the agent's home agency, A_0, the data item is signed with the private key of the owner. According to the notion just presented, we can write $signature = Sig_O(data) = K_O^-(h(data))$, where $h(data)$ is the digest of the data item, computed using a one-way hash function (e.g., MD5), and O is the owner of the agent. The signature must be computed at the agent's home agency because the owner's private key is available only there and becomes part of the agent. The same technique can be used to detect any tampering with the agent's code.

When the agent accesses this data item, the host agency verifies whether the read-only data item has been tampered with. To do this, the agency needs the public key, K_O^+, of the owner, usually in the form of a trusted certificate. It computes the digest equally to the home agency and compares it with the signature that the agent carries. Thus, it checks to see whether $h(data)$ equals $K_O^+(signature)$. If both match, the agency can assume that the data item was not modified.

---

2. Of course, a malicious agency has other techniques to manipulate an agent's route, for example, by simply sending the agent to a destination other than that requested.

A malicious agency can attack this technique in several ways. The most trivial way is to modify the data item but not the corresponding signature. The modification will be detected at the next agency, which tries to verify the data item using the given signature. Next, the malicious agency could modify the data item in a way that the digital signature is still valid. Although this is possible because of the hash function used, it is assumed to be computationally infeasible to find another data item with the same digest. Third, the agency could modify the data item and the signature so that the data item seems to be valid even though it is not. Because it is a fundamental concept of the whole public-key cryptography that the private key is known only to the owner, this attack can be ruled out. Finally, the malicious agency can modify the data item and sign it with its own private key. As in the first case, such an attack can be detected very easily because the signer of the data item will not match the given owner name. If the malicious agency also changes information about the agent's owner and the agent's name (forging the agent's home agency), then we have a special type of attack, where the malicious agency steals the complete agent and executes it on behalf of the kidnapping agency.

Reveal an Agent's Data at Specific Agencies

The next problem is to protect data items in such a way that they can be read only at certain agencies. This is necessary when data items are defined at the home agency but will be read only at other agencies. It is also necessary when a data item is defined at any agency and readable only at the agent's home agency.

This problem can be solved by encrypting the data item with the public key $K_{A_T}^+$ of the agency for which the data item is targeted. An additional signature $Sig_O(h(data) + \mathbf{A_T})$ that binds the name ($\mathbf{A_T}$) of the target agency A_T to the encrypted data item using the onwer's private key can be used to ensure that the target address has not been tampered with. The target agency, A_T, can decipher the data item with its own private key and verify the signature using the owner's public key, K_O^+, and comparing hash values. This approach has been proposed by Karnik [1998].

The disadvantage of this solutions is that the data item must be encrypted n times if it must be readable at n agencies. A better solution is proposed by Roth and Conan [2001], who use a *hybrid* encryption technique. The data item is encrypted using symmetric encryption, where only key k (which is much shorter than the original data item) is encrypted n times using the public key of all target agencies.

Another problem detected by Roth and Conan [2001] is the vulnerability of this approach to a simple *cut and paste* attack. A malicious agency could copy a data item that is encrypted for agency A_T into a fresh agent β and send this agent to the target agency. There, the agent decrypts the data item and carries it back to the malicious agency.

A possible solution proposed by Roth and Conan uses a MAC that binds the agent owner's public key with a symmetric key, k, and lets this MAC be transmitted as a static part of the agent (i.e., signed by the agent owner). In detail, the authors propose to encrypt a data item using a secret key, k, which is encrypted with the public key of the target agency. The agent therefore carries the encrypted data item, $k(data)$, together with the encrypted key, $K_{A_T}^+(k)$. A message authentication code is computed over the agent owner's certificate and the symmetric key k: $m = MAC(K_O^+ + k)$. This MAC is signed by the agent's owner and is sent along with the agent. Target agency A_T can then decrypt key k, recompute the MAC using k and the owner's certificate, and then compare it with the MAC that was signed by the owner. Both MACs must match to ensure that the correct agent is going to reveal the encrypted data. In the case of a cut and paste attack, a fresh agent β is started at a malicious agency and carries the data item to be revealed at agency A_T. Agency A_T will then decipher key k and recompute the MAC over the key and owner's certificate. However, agent β will, of course, be signed by the malicious agency or some owner. Obviously, this MAC will not match the one that the agent carries.

Agent's Dynamic Data

An agent's dynamic data is typically the result of an inquiry to the hosting agency. It consists of data that the agent wants to carry to other agencies on its itinerary or that it wants to send home to its owner. For dynamic data, of course, the same requirements apply as for static data. Data items must be protected against being spied out at later agencies, which can be solved by using encryption. In addition, data items must be protected against modifications, which can be solved by using digital signatures. However, the difference with dynamic data is that there will be other principals to encrypt and sign than in the case of static data. The general idea is to let the agency digitally sign each data item it has transferred to the agent and encrypt some data items with the public key of a destination agency.

For example, data items that are readable only by the agent's owner later can be encrypted using the public key of the agent owner. Only the owner will be able to decipher the data item because only he or she has access to the corresponding private key. However, a malicious agency could attack data items by deleting the data item, even if it does not understand the sense of it, together with the corresponding signature. Another type of attack could be to modify the value, sign it with its own private key, and encrypt it with the owner's public key. If the agent has no additional protocol to detect that a data item has been deleted or modified, such attacks will remain invisible. Another problem with this approach is that the size of the agent increases with each hop. In sum, the agent must carry a huge amount of encryption data, the cipher text, where only a small portion is real information. One solution to this problem is called *sliding encryption,* in which an agent can gather small amounts of data from several agencies and encrypt them using a public key without wasting an excessive amount of storage space [Young and Yung, 1997].

Karnik [1998] proposes so-called append-only logs as part of an agent's state to make a data item unmodifiable for the rest of the agent's itinerary. We assume a situation in which agent α has travelled to many agencies and now resides on agency A_i. It has obtained a new value (denoted as *data*) that it wants to protect against later modification. The new object is inserted in an *AppendOnlyContainer* and signed by the current agency. In addition, a *checksum* is carried by the agent. This is initialized at the agent's home agency with a nonce, R, that is encrypted with the agent owner's public key, $K_O^+(R)$. This nonce must be kept secret at the agent's home agency. This checksum is updated after a new data item has been added as follows: $checksum = K_O^+(checksum + Sig_{A_i}(data) + \mathbf{A_i})$. The data item is still readable at later agencies, if it is not only integrity that should be protected. If confidentialiy also must be guaranteed, then *data* can also be encrypted by using the public key of the owner. When the agent returns home, the owner can verify the integrity of all data items by unrolling the encrypted checksums. This also includes comparing hash values of the data item, which then makes it possible to detect, any tampering with data. After unrolling is complete, the original nonce should appear. One drawback of this approach is that the verification process relies on the owner's private key and can therefore be performed only on the agent's home agency. Another drawback is that this protocol is also vulnerable to a cut and paste attack if a malicious agency, A_m, that knows a checksum as computed by any agency visited earlier. For details, we refer to Roth [2001].

Another approach, presented by Yee [1999], is called *PRAC,* which stands for *partial result authentication code.* Rather than relying on asymmetric key encryption of partial results, this technique relies on secret keys, which are faster to compute. The goal is to ensure forward integrity of partial results. If a mobile agent will visit several agencies $A_1, A_2, \ldots, A_n$ and the first malicious agency is A_i, $1 \leq i \leq n$, then none of the partial results generated at agencies A_x, where $x < i$, can be forged.

First, we introduce simple MAC-based PRACs. When the agent is started, the home agency provides the agent with a list of PRAC keys, where, for each agency the agent is going to visit, a key is designated. Before the agent leaves an agency, it summarizes its partial result from its stay at this agency in a message. To provide integrity, a MAC is computed for this message using the key that was associated with the current agency. The PRAC now consists of the message itself and the MAC. Then the key used must be deleted. Next, the message can be sent back to the agent's owner directly or carried along to further agencies. With this technique, it is ensured that no partial result that was originated by a previously visited agency can be modified without detecting it later. If a malicious agency, A_i, wants to modify the content of a partial result, P_a, with $a < i$, it must know the PRAC key of agency A_a to recompute a valid PRAC.

Yee also proposed two modifications of his technique. First, a key need not be generated for all agencies in advance. It is possible to start with only one key for the first agency, A_1, and to generate a new key used at the second agency, A_2, dynamically before leaving agency A_1 using a m-bit to m-bit one-way hash function. A second modification works with public and private keys. A key pair is generated for each agency. At an agency the associated private key is used for encryption and then dropped. If the agent carries all certificates, it is even possible for the agent to decrypt and verify partial results at later agencies. Again, it is possible to defer key creation to a later time and start with only one key pair.

One of the drawbacks of this approach is that a malicous agency could retain copies of the agent's original key. If the agent visits the agency again (or another agency conspring with the malicious agency), a previous result might be modified with notification to the agent.

Detecting Code and Control Flow Manipulations through Execution Tracing

If we cannot guarantee that code and data are unmodified, at a minimum, we want to be able to detect any modifications later. Vigna [1998] has developed a technique called *execution tracing*. This technique makes it possible to trace an agent, that is, to save the history of execution at a single specific agency in an unforgeable way. The owner of the agent can verify that its agent has been executed correctly, that is, that it has been executed in the correct order of statements and that the correct data has been used. Execution traces help to prove that some malicious agency has tampered with the agent.

The general idea is that each visited agency sends messages to the agent's home agency or some other trusted agency after it has received the agent (and before it starts to execute the agent) and after the agent has terminated (and before it migrates to the next agency). With the first message the current agency gives notice about what it has received from the sender agency. With the second message it signs for the agent that now will leave this agency.

We will use the following notation: Agent α visits several agencies on its route I_α. Each agency is denoted with A_i, where the number i corresponds to the iteration step; that is, A_0 is the home agency, A_1 is the agency that is visited first, and so on. The agent's code is α_c, and the agent's state after it has been executed at agency i is $\alpha_s^{A_i}$. Each agency is able to compute a trace, that is, the sequence of all statements executed by the agent. This list is denoted by $T_C^{A_i}$.

The protocol uses three types of messages that we will now describe step by step. We assume a situation in which an agent is currently executed at agency A_{n-1} and now wants to migrate to agency A_n. The agent's state is denoted by $\alpha_s^{A_{n-1}}$. Agency A_{n-1} has computed an execution trace for this agent that is described by $T_C^{A_{n-1}}$. The trace is stored so that it can later be retrieved by the agent's owner for verification of the execution. Before agency A_{n-1} actually sends the migration message to the next agency, it informs the agent's home agency, A_0, about the fact.

Notify Home Agency about Forthcoming Migration

Agency A_{n-1} sends a message to agency A_0 with following content:

$$\{\mathbf{A_{n-1}}, K_{A_{n-1}}^-(\mathbf{A_n}, h(\alpha_s^{A_{n-1}}), h(T_C^{A_{n-1}}), i_\alpha)\}$$

The message consists of the following parts:

■ The name of the sender agency, A_{n-1}

■ The name of the next agency, A_n; a hash value of the current state, $\alpha_s^{A_{n-1}}$; a hash value of the execution trace, $T_C^{A_{n-1}}$; and the unique identifier, i_α, that remains equal during the agent's lifetime—all signed by agency A_{n-1}

The home agency does not send such a message to itself. Agency A_0 stores the hash values of the current agent's state and the execution trace. The second message sent by agency A_{n-1} is directed to the next destination that the agent will visit, which is agency A_n.

Migrate

With migration from agency A_{n-1} to agency A_n, the message has the following contents:

$$\{\mathbf{A_{n-1}}, \mathbf{A_n}, \mathbf{A_0}, K_{A_n}^+(\alpha_c, \alpha_s^{A_{n-1}}), K_{A_{n-1}}^-(h(\alpha_s^{A_{n-1}}), \mathbf{A_n}), K_{A_0}^-(h(\alpha_c), t_0, i_\alpha)\}$$

The message consists of six parts:

- The first three parts consist of the name of the sender agency, the name of the destination agency, and the name of the agent's home agency.

- The fourth part contains the code, α_c, and current state, $\alpha_s^{A_{n-1}}$, of the agent. Both are encrypted with the public key of the destination agency. Therefore, only the destination is able to read the code and data. Thus, code and state are both protected against tampering and eavesdropping during transmission, but it is unclear whether they come from the sender agency or some other agency (man-in-the-middle attack).

- The fifth part of the message contains the hash value of the agent's current state, $\alpha_s^{A_{n-1}}$, and the name of the destination agency, A_n. Both are encrypted with the private key of the sender agency, A_{n-1}. The sender signs all information, so the destination agency, A_n, can be sure that it is from A_{n-1} because only this agency has access to the private key, $K_{A_{n-1}}^-$.

- The last part of the message contains information that was signed by the home agency, A_0. With the first migration, (when the agent leaves agency A_0), this information is actually signed by A_0. All other agencies visited later merely copy this piece of information. The message consists of a hash value of the agent's code, a time stamp to guarantee freshness, and a unique identifier to prevent replay attacks. As in the preceding point, the destination agency, A_n, can be sure that all information is from the home agency, A_0, because only this agency has access to the private key, $K_{A_0}^-$.

Agency A_n decrypts the fourth part of the message using its own private key, $K_{A_n}^-$, to obtain the agent's code and the agent's last state. Then it uses the name of the last agency, A_{n-1}, to retrieve public key $K^+_{A_{n-1}}$ and to decrypt the fifth part of the message that contains the hash value of the agent's last state. Agency A_n computes the hash value of the agent's last state, $\alpha_s^{A_{n-1}}$, and compares it with the hash value that was encrypted by A_{n-1}. If both are equal, agency A_n can be sure that the state is unmodified. In addition, because the sender agency A_{n-1} has signed the information to which agency the migration is directed, A_n can be sure that it is the correct addressee. Finally, A_n retrieves the public key of the agent's home agency, A_0, and decrypts the last part of the message. It computes the hash value of the given code and compares it with the hash value given in this part of the message. If both values match, A_n can be sure that the code is unmodified.

After authentication has been performed, agency A_n sends an acknowledge message to the agent's home agency, A_0.

Acknowledge the Receipt of the Agent

By this message, agency A_n confirms that is has received the agent (i.e., the agent's code and current state) in a specific state. Later, this agency could not deny having received the agent in this specific state. The message has the following format:

$$\{\mathbf{A_n}, K^-_{A_n}(K^-_{A_{n-1}}(h(\alpha_s^{A_{n-1}}), \mathbf{A_n}), K^-_{A_0}(h(\alpha_c), t_0, i_\alpha))\}$$

This message contains the name of the current agency, A_n, and the fifth and sixth part of the migration message, both signed by this agency. Using this message, the home agency can verify that agency A_n has received the migration message with the agent's code, α_c, and the last state of the agent, $\alpha_s^{A_{n-1}}$, correctly by comparing the hash values for the state and the code with the ones received in the migration notification sent by A_{n-1} to A_0.

Then the agent is executed until it wants to migrate to the next agency. The protocol starts again by sending the migration notification to the agent's home agency and then sending the migration message to the next destination. Finally, the destination agency acknowledges receipt by sending a message to the home agency. The protocol repeats itself until the agent wants to terminate. If the agent is self-maintained to its home agency, there is no difference to the message described previously. Otherwise, instead of the migration message, another message must be sent to transmit the current agent's state to the home agency but to indicate that the agent does not want to be executed at the destination agency again.

In the original work by Vigna [1998], the author proposes additional message types to consider the case that the agent leaves its home agency or returns back to it. We have tried to summarize these cases in classifying only the three main types of messages. It is obvious that one possibility to optimize the protocol (i.e., to reduce the network load) is that information could be summarized and dropped.

Finally, we have to explain how the agent's owner can now prove correct execution of his or her agent. This is done by retrieving the execution trace of the suspicious agency and simulating agent execution at the home agency. Simulation must start at the point when the agent was started at A_0. Because the home agency is by definition trusted, the agent is simulated without comparing it to an execution trace. Before the agent wants to migrate to A_1 simulation of this agent is in state $\alpha_s^{\tilde{A}_0}$.

For all agencies A_i with $1 \le i \le n$, when n is the last agency that the agent will visit, do the following:

1. Retrieve the acknowledge message from A_i. Compute a hash value of the agent's last simulated state $h(\alpha_s^{\tilde{A}_{i-1}})$ and compare it with $h(\alpha_s^{A_{i-1}})$ that was sent as part of the acknowledge message by A_i. If they do not match, state $\alpha_s^{A_{i-1}}$ was manipulated.

2. Compare the hash value of the agent's code with the one that was acknowledged by A_i. If they do not match, the code was manipulated.

3. Retrieve the original execution trace $T_C^{A_i}$ from A_i. Simulate agent execution as on agency A_i until it wants to migrate or die. Trace agent execution in $\tilde{T}_C^{A_i}$. All values that are the result of systems calls are stored in the trace. These values are therefore used for the simulation. If there is any conflict, agency A_i has cheated with the control flow. However, if the agency has returned a wrong value for system calls, this cannot be detected.

4. Compare the hash values of the state that is the result of the simulation $\alpha_s^{\tilde{A}_i}$ with the one that A_i has sent in the notification message. If they do not match, A_i has cheated with the state.

5. Otherwise, A_i has executed the agent correctly.

Drawbacks of This Approach

Execution tracing is a very interesting approach, but it also has some severe drawbacks. First, the size of the trace might be large and must be transmitted from each agency to the trusted server and its respective home agency, which slows the overall performance of mobile agents. To reduce the trace, Vigna [1998] proposes several techniques, for example, not tracing the entire program but only selected statements that were marked by the programmer or only the points where control flow changes. Second, if the agent is allowed to use threads on its own, execution tracing becomes more complex. Third, the code must be static. An agent is not allowed to use code generation on the fly and the underlying execution environment, a virtual machine, in the case of Java must not use Just-in-Time Compilation unless the tracing technique was adopted. Finally—and this is a drawback of all approaches that *only* detect attacks but do not prevent them—there must be some kind of legal or organizational framework that now comes into terms. For example, if an agent was manipulated but has already bought a good, there must be a procedure that the agent owner could use to obtain a refund.

Some of these drawbacks are solved by using an extension of this technique presented by Tan and Moreau [2002]. Yee presents some theoretical ideas to reduce the effort to transmit and prove the trace sent by a suspicious agency using holographic proof-checking techniques [Babai et al., 1991] or computiationally sound proofs [Kilian, 1992; Micali, 1994]. Neither technique is currently applicable, so we will skip a detailed introdcution here and refer you to Yee [1999] for more information.

Detecting Itinerary Manipulations

Finally, we want to discuss a technique proposed by Roth [1998] to detect attacks on agents, in which the agency prevents an agent from migrating to some other agency.

The general idea is to let two agents migrate independently within the mobile agent systems and exchange information about their current, their last, and their next agency. In a special scenario, one of the agents could even be immobile and remain, for example, at its home agency. In the following an agency is denoted as usual as A_i, and the name, or id, of this agency is denoted as $\mathbf{A_i}$. We assume that at each agency A_i, agent α can request the name of the agency from which it came, $\mathbf{prev_i}(\alpha)$. The name of the next agency to which agent α wants to migrate to is denoted by $\mathbf{next_i}(\alpha)$.

Both agents start at the same agency, A_0, which becomes their home agency. At each agency A_i that agent α visits, it sends the information about the last agency visited, $\mathbf{prev_i}(\alpha)$, and the information about the next agency the agent is going to visit, $\mathbf{next_i}(\alpha)$, to agent β using an authenticated communication channel. Agent β, therefore, also knows the name of the agency $\mathbf{A_i}$ that α is currently visiting. Now, agent β can verify that $\mathbf{prev_i}(\alpha)$ equals $\mathbf{A_{i-1}}$. If they do not match, we have two possible error situations. First, A_{i-1} could have sent agent α to agency A_x instead of A_i—or A_i is returning wrong information for $\mathbf{prev_i}(\alpha)$. For example, agency A_i may be malicious and want to incriminate agency A_{i-1}, which is actually not malicious at all. It is not possible to determine which of the two agencies cheats.

Then, agent β can verify that $\mathbf{A_i}$ matches $\mathbf{next_{i-1}}(\alpha)$; that is, it checks that the current agency is really the one to which agent α wanted to migrate. In this case, agency A_i must masquerade its identity or deny communication between the two agencies to mask the error situation. On the other hand, if agency A_i does not deny communication and does not masquerade, then β will discovers that A_{i-1} has sent the agent to a wrong agency.

This protocol has some drawbacks. First, communication between the two agents is expensive. Second, the agent might be killed after the agent has sent its position message to β but while it is still on agency A_i or after the agent has been received by A_{i+1} and before the agent has sent its new position message.

To make this protocol work, it must be guaranteed that both agents α and β are at each point in time on two hosts for which it is clear that they do not work together. In the other case, the two malicious agencies might cooperate to attack the protocol. For example, it could be possible that simply both agents are killed at the same time.

Roth, therefore, proposes to mark all agencies with the colors white, gray, and red. White agencies are benevolent. Possibly, only the home agency is marked white. Gray agencies are not completely trusted, and red agencies are those that might collaborate with some other agency to attack an agent. Then, Roth defines the following condition to make his protocol work: The two agents migrate into two disjunct sets of agencies, and no red agency from one set is willing to cooperate with a red agency from the other set. The question that remains is how this condition can be guaranteed.

5.6 Protecting Agencies

We now consider the problem of how agencies can be protected against malicious agents. Actually, this problem is played down and regarded as almost solved in large parts of the literature, because Java as a programming language and execution environment already provides several techniques that can be used to protect the underlying agency from several types of attacks carried out by malicious agents. In fact, the problem of malicious agents seems to be better understood than the reverse problem of malicious agencies.

One of the main concerns is how the underlying operating system and hardware can be protected against unauthorized access by agents. Although Java's *sandbox* concept provides an already-sophisticated solution for this problem, we will show that many problems still remain and that the sandbox in its current version is by no means a complete solution.

In this section, we start with an introduction to Java security and then present techniques for agent authentication and authorization. Finally, we present techniques to protect an agency from malicious agents during runtime.

5.6.1 Introduction—Java and Security

In Chapter 2 we introduced some of the major benefits of Java as a programming language for mobile agent toolkits. In this section we extend this introduction and provide a deeper overview of Java security aspects. For a full introduction to Java security, we point the interested reader to Oaks [2001].

Java as a Safe Programming Language

One of the major benefits of Java—and not only for mobile agent toolkits—is that it can be considered a safe programming language compared with C or C++, for example. Many typical programming flaws that result in severe runtime errors in C or C++ simply cannot occur in Java. With regard to security, one of the main differences between Java and C is that Java is a strictly typed programming language and has a pointer model that does not allow illegal type casting or pointer arithmetic. For example, in Java the programmer has no chance to access arbitrary memory locations and overwrite and destroy data there. In Java it is impossible to access arrays beyond their boundaries, as can be done in C, for example.

Code Signing

Code signing is a technique used to verify the integrity of mobile code, and it can also be used as one step in the agent's authentication process.

Typically, the agent programmer or owner (i.e., the person who starts the agent on his or her behalf) signs a hash value of the agent's code with his or her private key and sends the signature along with the code to a destination agency. The destination agency can then verify the integrity of the code by recomputing the hash value on the code and comparing it with the decrypted signature. If both match, the agency can use this as input for the agent authorization process and grant privileges to the agent.

However, what is really verified here is only code integrity—not that the code is nonmalicious. If the code signer is in fact the owner and he or she is not equal to the programmer, then the owner can sign only that the agent belongs to him or her and not that the agent behaves properly. This difference is used in the *state appraisal* approach that we introduce in the following section. Thus, code signing is an important step in the agent authentication and authorization process—at least you know whom to blame if something goes wrong.

The Bytecode Verifier

When a Java class is loaded into the virtual machine, it is verified on the level of bytecode. This verification process includes several steps to guarantee that the loaded class or interface is structurally correct with regard to the semantics of the Java virtual machine. Among other things, bytecode verification includes ensuring that only valid instruction opcodes are used, no final method is overridden, local variables are not accessed until they have been defined with an appropriate value, and control flow instructions target the beginning of an instruction.

Bytecode verification is very time-consuming because, for example, an expensive data flow analysis must be performed for some of the checks. Therefore, some researchers propose other intermediate code representations competing with Java bytecode, where type safety can be guaranteed just by the structure of the code representation and without an additional verification process. See, for example, Amme et al. [2001]. For more information about Java bytecode and the verification process, we refer to Lindholm and Yellin [1999].

Sandboxing to Protect the Runtime Environment

Bytecode verification is done before the Java program is executed. If a program has passed the verification process, it is executed and further security checks are performed during runtime. This technique is called *sandbox*, and it includes the following elements:

- Each Java class is loaded from a specific *code source* that is specified by a URL (which is called *codebase*). If the code is signed, the code source also includes information about the signer.

- A *permission* is a specific action that a code is allowed to perform. In Java, permissions have a type (a class name), a name, and an action. For example, to access all files in directory */foo/bar,* the code must have the *java.io.FilePermission* with the directory as name and *read* as action string.

- A *protection domain* is an association of code sources and a set of permissions. A protection domain defines, for example, that all code that is loaded from *http://www.mobile-agents.org* is allowed to do anything (that can be described by the permission *java.security.AllPermission*) and code that is loaded from *http://www.devil.org* has permission only to open file for reading but not for writing.

- *Policy files* are used to define protection domains. They can be plain text files in which you define which permissions a code loaded from some URL will have.

- *Keystores* contain certificates that can be used to verify signed code.

The agent authorization process defines which permissions a mobile agent should have. We will present techniques to decide on the set of permissions later in this section. One problem with the Java sandbox concept is that assigning permissions to protection domains is done statically per default; that is, it is not possible to withdraw a permission from an agent once the agent has been started. However, there are techniques to handle this drawback and make permissions dynamic.

Finally, we must explain how the runtime environment of Java verifies that some code C has permission to execute a possibly harmful statement, such as opening a file for reading. When control flow reaches this statement where a file should be opened, for example, by creating an object of type *FileInput-Stream,* a component of the runtime environment, referred to as the *security manager,* is called. The security manager itself now verifies that code C has the permission to open a file as described earlier. However, code C in turn might have been called by methods in other classes so that the security manager iterates through the complete calling stack. If any of the classes on the stack do not have the necessary permission, the security manager throws an exception and the file cannot be opened.

Some Shortcomings of Java

In this section we present some examples of malicious agents that exploit shortcomings of the Java programming language and the Java virtual machine.

We start with a problem with agent serialization. As already described, each Java object that implements the interface *Serializable* can be marshaled in a plain byte array to be sent over the network. What we have not introduced so far is the possibility to implement specialized methods for the serialization process, as well as for the deserialization process. For example, in an agent class the following methods could be defined:

```
1 public class AnAgent implements Runnable, Serializable
2 {
3  // ...
4
5  private void writeObject( java.io.ObjectOutputStream out )
6              throws IOException, ClassNotFoundException
7  {
8    // an own serialization process for this class
9  }
10
11  private void readObject( java.io.ObjectInputStream in )
12              throws IOException, ClassNotFoundException
13  {
14    // an own deserilization process for this class
15  }
16 }
```

In this case, rather than using the default deserialization technique, the one that is provided by the class is used. Here we have a severe loophole because now a part of the agent's code is executed *before* the agent has been started. Remember that deserialization happens immediately after receiving the agent via a network and before the agent is registered with the hosting agency. It must be guaranteed that the deserialization process is invoked with the permission of the agent rather than with that of the agency. Otherwise it would be possible for the agent to start first attacks on the agency even before it was really started and registered with the hosting agency.

A similar problem considers class initialization. A class is initialized immediately before an instance of this class is created, a static method of this class is invoked, or a nonconstant static field is used or assigned. The static initializers are executed before the agent instance is created and before the agent is registered with the agency.

Next, we will present two examples of malicious code by which an agent can run denial of service attacks on the hosting agency. The first one shows an agent that locks the object *Thread.class* and never releases it again.

```
1 public class CaptureThread implements Runnable
2 {
3  public void run()
4  {
5    synchronized( Thread.class )
6    {
7      while( true );
8    }
9  }
10 }
```

After the agent has reached the **synchronized** statement, access to class *Thread.class* is impossible, which prevents other threads from being started.

The next example shows an agent that captures the garbage collector thread. If the garbage collector detects that there no longer exists any strong reference to some object, then this object becomes garbage collected. However, any object and its respective correspondig class might define a method *finalize*, which is invoked by the garbage collector to give the object a chance to close resources (e.g., file handlers). The following agent implements such a method and does not terminate, which eventually leads to a memory overflow.

```
1 public class CaptureGCThread implements Runnable
2 {
3  public void run()
4  {
5    //
6  }
7
```

```
 8  protected void finalize()
 9  {
10    while( true );
11  }
12 }
```

As Binder and Roth [2002] point out, it is not enough to simply reject incoming agents that have implemented a method *finalize,* because there exist classes as part of the Java API, where the finalizer calls other methods that might be overridden in subclasses. For example, class *FileInputStream* implements method *finalize* by actually calling method *close.* An agent might bring a class that inherits from class *FileInputStream* and has overridden method *close* so that it does not terminate.

Java has other shortcomings as well; for example it is allowed to lock a monitor and never release it. We do not want to discuss these in detail here. The interested reader is pointed to the paper by Binder and Roth [2002]. One other and very important drawback of the current version of Java is that it does not provide an adequate means for resource control. The examples of infinite agents we presented can also occur within the business logic of an agent, even if previously the programmer had not intended such. To decide between an attack and still proper behavior of an agent is obviously very difficult. Nevertheless, some research targets the problem of resource accounting, and we will present approaches on that in Section 5.6.3.

Because of these limitations of Java, Roth, in a panel at the MDM conference in 2004, stated that Java *has simultaneously been a fortune and a misfortune.* Without the many features of Java, it is undoublty more difficult to develop a mobile agent toolkit—but on the other hand, all these limitations and shortcomings of Java with regard to security make it *next to impossible to build and maintain a publicly deployed and dependable mobile agent system* [Roth, 2004].

5.6.2 Agent Authentication and Authorization

In this section we discuss techniques that can be used to authenticate and authorize a mobile agent that has migrated to an agency. Agent authentication includes the verification of the agent's identity and the identity of the agent's owner or sender. Code signing, as introduced earlier, is used in almost all mobile agent toolkits for this purpose. Inspection of the agent's data and code, for example, by using the *state appraisal* technique we will introduce later or code inspection to detect possibly malicious agents, are also done in this phase. The result of agent authorization is the assignment of privileges to the agent according to its identity.

Proof-Carrying Code

Proof-carrying code (PCC) is a technique proposed by Necula and Lee to enable a host to be absolutely certain that it is safe to execute an untrusted piece of mobile code. The work was initiated outside the research of mobile agents. The authors refer to problems in the field of operating systems, where a code fragment should be installed in the operating system kernel. They also mention possible applications in the field of distributed and Web-based computing, where mobile code is sent from a *code producer* to a *code consumer*. Necula and Lee [1998] illustrate their technique by using an example of a mobile agent that visits several online stores. In the following we use the term *mobile code* to refer to a piece of code that is transmitted from the code producer to the code consumer. It is irrelevant how the code is transmitted.

The general idea is that the code consumer publishes a *safety policy* that describes properties that any mobile code has to comply with by using an extension of first-order logic. In practice, it is reasonable to publish several safety policies tailored to different scenarios or application domains. The code producer must formally prove that his or her code behaves in accordance with the safety policy. The PCC itself is a special form of intermediate code representation that consists of the mobile code and an encoding of a formal proof that the code complies with the safety policy. Then, the PCC is sent from the code producer to the code consumer, who is able to verify the PCC without using any cryptographic techniques or consulting with an external trusted third party.

The code consumer receives the PCC, validates the proof that is part of the PCC, and loads the code. This check must be done only once, even if the code is going to be executed several times. Afterward, the code can be executed without any additional checking. Any attempt to modify either the code or the proof is detected and the mobile code can be rejected.

PCC is an alternative to other techniques that protect the hosting environment against potentially malicious code by using runtime checks. Until now, PCC has not been adopted to work in Java-based environments and mobile agents. The most severe drawback of PCC is that even in the latest paper

[Necula and Lee, 1998], the problem of proof generation is not completely solved. In some cases it might be done only semi-automatically. Another drawback is the size of the proof. Experiments showed that it can become even larger than the code that it has to prove and, in the worst case, can be exponentially larger than the size of the program. Finally, we would like to mention that the concept of PCC has not been adopted to multi-threaded programs. Further information can be found in Necula and Lee [1998], Necula [1997], and Necula and Lee [1996].

Path Histories

We now consider the problem of how an agency should decide on the level of trust it offers to a mobile agent, which is a prerequisite to agent authorization. Trusting an agent depends on the identity, which is verified in the process of authentication and, as Ordille [1996] argues, where the agent has been so far (i.e., which agencies it has visited). The general idea of *path histories* is therefore to supplement an agent with information about the agencies it has visited. When an agent arrives at an agency, the list of previously visited agencies (the path) can be verified. The question of whether an agency can trust an agent can now be refined into the question of whether an agency can trust all agencies on the agent's path. In addition, the agency will ask for further information about the agent to finally decide on the level of trust.

Ordille suggests two techniques. In the first one, each agency, A_i, adds itself to the path history of an agent and signs the complete path. The destination agency, A_{i+1}, verifies the signature and then determines whether it can trust every agency on the path, whether it has forwarded the agent properly, and whether it has authenticated its immediate predecessor. This must be done—it is not sufficient to assume that it can trust the authentication procedure of all its predecessor.

In the second technique, agency A_i signs a *forward* (see Section 5.5.2) $\mathbf{A_i} \rightarrow \mathbf{A_{i+1}}$ with the information to which agency the agent will migrate. To prevent tampering with the path, A_i must sign not only the new forward but also the previous entry. The destination agency then authenticates each agency on the path.

Obviously, neither technique prevents an agency from behaving maliciously. It is rather a matter of deterrent, because the agency's signed entry in the agent's path is nonrepudiable. A drawback of this approach is that the size of the path history increases with the number of hops, and in the same manner, the time for verification also increases.

We see as a major drawback of this approach that each agency already must have a sense of trust; in addition, some technique must be available to determine whether it can trust another agency. However, *path histories* as a concept have already influenced some other techniques, for example, Roth's technique to securely record the itinerary of a mobile agent (see Section 4.1).

State Appraisal

If a mobile agent must visit several agencies during its tour, it might have been attacked by a single agency or several malicious agencies. The technique we present in this section can be used to assure agent owners and agencies, to some extent, that an agent's state has not been tampered with. In the overall process of receiving incoming mobile agents, this technique is placed after agent authentication and before agent authorization, for which this technique actually produces an input. Ideas for this approach were first presented in Farmer et al. [1996a] and later revised in Berkovits et al. [1998].

This technique is based on the idea that illicit modifications of an agent's state can be predicted, described, and later verified. Therefore, several state appraisal functions are defined, which verify specific conditions or invariants in the agent's state. After an agency has received a mobile agent, it verifies the state appraisal functions. This results in a set of privileges that the agent will have while executing on this agency or even in rejecting the mobile agent to protect the agency.

The general idea is that an agent should carry two so-called state appraisal functions by which the agency can determine the agent's privileges with regard to the agent's state. The first function, $max(\Sigma)$, where Σ is the current state of the agent, must be developed by the agent owner and is sent as part of the agent's code. It is signed to prevent later modification by an agency. This function determines the set of permissions that the agent owner would like to see granted to the agent. In other words, using max, the owner can limit his or her responsibility and liability. The second function, $req(\Sigma)$, is provided by the sender (the person or entity that instantiated the agent and on whose behalf the agent is executed) and contains the desired set of permits. Usually it holds that $req(\Sigma) \subset max(\Sigma)$ because the sender might not be sure about the effect of the agent in detail and would like to limit his or her liability further more.

Farmer et al. enlist the following purposes of their technique:

■ It can protect agencies from attacks where the agent's state has been altered in a detectable way, for example, by verifying state invariants.

■ It can protect the agent's owner and sender from malpractice of the agent in their name.

■ It enables the agency to assign privileges to agents with regard to their state.

Both functions could, for example, check that some conditionals are true or invariants have the expected value.

Before proceeding, we would like to present an example from Farmer [1996a]. Recall the airfare example previously introduced in which an agent travels to several airlines to gather information about the airfare. To apply the technique of state appraisal in this scenario, we first consider the different types of data items. Obviously, we have static and immutable data items. However, as we have shown, such static data can be protected against alteration by using signatures by the agent owner. Dynamic data items are harder to protect—remember the attack in which the second airline increases the airfare artificially. Here, even with state appraisal, the agent cannot be protected and modifications cannot be detected, because it is impossible to decide whether an airfare is in fact high but still valid. This is not a problem and not in the scope of this approach, because the agencies that the agent will later visit will not be affected by a wrong price information and will therefore not suffer any damage.

Now, consider a scenario in which an agent will reserve two seats on a specific flight. The agent might be programmed in such a way that it is not necessary to book both seats at the same airline. Now, the number of seats to book is no longer static, and a malicious agency could manipulate the number of seats by increasing it from 2 to 100. However, in this case a state appraisal function would help: The number of seats to book plus the number of seats already booked must be constantly 2.

After an agency has executed both state appraisal functions *req* and *max*, it can grant privileges to the agent according the following conditional:

```
if   req(Σ) ⊂ max(Σ)   then grant   req(Σ)  else grant   Ø
```

If either *req* or *max* detects tampering of the agent's state, the function will return ∅. Likewise, if the sender requests more privileges than the owner has allowed with *max*, this function will also return ∅.

In our opinion, this is an interesting approach and it can be combined with the concept of detection objects, as presented by Meadows [1997]. The author proposes to set baits, called detection objects, which are any data that the agent carries but that is not used for processing. If the agent does not notice any manipulation of this detection object, it can be sure that it was not tampered with. However, this technique depends on the type of application, and the detection object must not be so obvious that it cannot deceive the agency about the real usage.

However, this approach also has some drawbacks. In both papers, the authors do not provide detailed descriptions about how to develop such state appraisal functions. The examples presented in this paper show that the technique is applicable in specific application domains but that it remains vague whether this technique can be used in general. Even in specific application domains, the decisive issue is whether it is possible to find suitable appraisal functions that can distinguish normal results from deceptive alternatives. Another concern is whether a malicious agency can analyze the appraisal functions and modify the agent in a way that will not be detected by either function.

History-Based Access Control for Mobile Code

In the last two sections we presented techniques that determine a static set of privileges dependent on the path history or state verification functions. Now we present a technique in which the agent's privileges are determined on the basis of the agent's behavior at runtime.

The goals of *history-based access control* are to maintain a selective history of access requested by the code and to use this information to decide between trusted and untrusted code. The approach presented by Edjlali et al. [1998, 1999] targets mobile code, especially Java applets, and is motivated by the following examples: In some application scenarios it might be too restrictive to prohibit all access to the local file system or to open a socket to a remote host. With static privileges it is possible only to define that the code has either both privileges or neither of them. The authors argue that it is worthwhile to define mutual exclusive privileges so that the code is allowed to first open a file for reading but it is not allowed to open a network connection later, where the file might be sent to a remote host. Another example is access to a database, where the code is allowed to read only one of two relations but not both of them.

The concept presented by Edjlali et al. [1999] is based on unique identifiers for programs, which are computed using hash functions over the entire code of the program. This prevents the applicability of the approach for programs that use dynamic code loading during runtime. In our opinion, history-based access control needs some extensions to be applicable with mobile agents. Consider the previous example in which a program has opened a file for reading. In contrast to Java applets, which can open network connections only to remote hosts in case they want to *steal* data, mobile agents have other means, such as simply carrying the file as part of their own code. Therefore, some kind of firewall is needed to examine the mobile agent before it leaves the current agency.

5.6.3 Agent Execution

After the agent has been authenticated and authorized, it is finally started. Each agent should be executed in a separate environment, where each access to host resources is verified against the agent's permissions and no agent can access any other agent instance on the level of Java objects. We have already introduced the concept of Java sandboxes and the possibility to grant an agent individual permissions.

The sandbox also includes that each agent gets a separate class loader and thread group. Both are necessary to distinguish agents from each other and to establish a border between agents. The class loader is necessary to create an individual name space for each agent and to ensure that agent classes are removed after the agent has left the agency. Each agent is started within a separate thread group, and if the agent is allowed to create new threads at all, they must all be members of this very same thread group. Conversely, if all agent threads belong to the same thread group, an agent could enlist all threads of this thread group and lock a thread or invoke method *stop* (which is actually deprecated) on it, resulting in a denial of service attack against other agents.

Finally, the problem of malicious agents that consume resources in an unauthorized way must be mentioned. Java does not provide any means to restrict memory allocation or CPU usage. Future versions of Java will provide built-in solutions for this problem; until then, other techniques that are based on modified virtual machines or that rewrite the code of an agent must be used. Czajkowski and von Eicken [1998] describe a technique that relies on native code implementation, a different implementation of several Java packages, and code rewriting to track memory usage and CPU and network bandwidth consumption. Because this approach is not fully implemented in Java, it is not applicable to mobile agent toolkits. This would require, at a minimum, installation of modified packages from the Java API.

Villazon and Binder [2001] propose another solution that relies completely on Java bytecode rewriting, making it suitable for mobile agent toolkits. Their approach can also be applied for CPU, memory, and network control. It creates a so-called meta-agent for each mobile agent currently residing at the agency. Reification of network bandwidth, for example, consists of redirecting calls to the component that provides network services to the meta-agent, which itself then calls the network service. Reification of memory works in a similar manner but is more difficult because every object creation and disposal must be taken into account. Finally, reification of CPU usage is done by analyzing the agent's code and inserting accounting instructions at selected points in the control flow. The drawback of this approach is that execution time increases because of the process of bytecode rewriting and additional inspections. The authors report an overhead of about 20% only for CPU reification.

Summary

In the last sections we presented a range of countermeasures for the problem of malicious agencies and malicious agents in mobile agent systems. As we have seen, techniques for the latter problem are highly developed, with the effect that some authors consider this problem to be more or less solved. However, as we have shown using some examples of malicious Java code, details are still tricky to solve. Only a few toolkits, for example Semoa [Roth and Jalali, 2001], face the problem of malicious agents that exploit shortcomings of the Java language environment though *content inspection*. However, even the measures implemented in Semoa can be outwitted by more inscrutable code. Resource accounting is also a problem that is addressed in only a very few mobile agent toolkits.

Countermeasures for the problem of malicious agencies range from *organizational solutions,* which are highly pragmatic but do not provide the necessary level of security, to *encrypted functions,* which provide an excellent level of security but are still not applicable to mobile agents in general. It is still an open research question: Which of all these techniques can be combined to later form some kind of general security solution?

We sorted the solutions for the problem of malicious agencies in techniques that can prevent an attack and techniques that can only detect that an attack has happened, usually as soon as the agent has returned to its home agency. Obviously, prevention is preferable because it provides an overall solution to the given problem, whereas all techniques that only detect attacks must be supplemented by laws, contracts, or rules that are defined outside the technical solution and therefore outside the mobile agent system. They must define how agent owners and agencies shall behave in the case of a well-founded suspicion.

Table 5.1 lists all countermeasures that we have introduced in the preceding sections and classifies each with regard to several categories.

The first category defines the subject of the countermeasure; that is, is it the agent or the agency that can be protected by it? Next, we distinguish between prevention and detection. Here, it is worth mentioning that we

Table 5.1 *Overview of countermeasures*

Countermeasure	Subject	Type	Code or Data
Encrypted functions	Agent	Prevent	Both
Time-limited black boxes	Agent	Prevent	Both
Environmental key generation	Agent	Prevent	Both
Agency replication	Agent	Detect	Both
Agent replication	Agent	Detect	Both
Detecting black-box attacks	Agent	Prevent	Data
Read-only data	Agent	Detect	Data
Target agencies	Agent	Detect	Data
Forward integrity	Agent	Detect	Data
Detecting objects	Agent	Detect	Data
Execution tracing	Agent	Detect	Both
Secure itinerary recording	Agent	Detect	Data
Sandbox	Agency	Prevent	Code
Code signing	Agency	Detect	Code
Proof-carrying code	Agency	Prevent	Both
Path histories	Agency	Detect	Both
State appraisal	Agency	Detect	Data
History-based access control	Agency	Prevent	N/A
Content inspection	Agency	Detect	Code
Resource accounting	Agency	Prevent	Code

found only a single technique—agent replication—that not only detects an attack but can also recover the error. The next column distinguishes between techniques that address an agent's code or agent's data. Here, we can find techniques that address the agent as a whole, including its code and data.

In the last few years, security issues of mobile agents have been a rapidly evolving area of research. Although many of the problems we introduced in Section 5.2 can be solved by using state-of-the-art cryptographic protocols already known from research in distributed systems, some problems are unique to mobile code and even a few problems are singular for mobile agents. We have to concede that our overview of countermeasures for mobile agent security is not comprehensive. We chose to review those techniques that, in our opinion, have been widely accepted and cited frequently in the literature.

Notwithstanding, we would like to mention a few points missing in mobile agents security research so far, as we could identify them: We believe that the general pattern to exchange information permanently between the mobile agent and some trusted communication partner, be it another agent or the agent's home agency, contradicts the general idea of mobile agents. If, for example, the agent has to publish its current location at each hop with a central trusted agency, we have a star-shaped communication pattern typical of client-server applications with the already-known drawbacks of having a single point of failure and performance bottleneck. Actually, the influence of security solutions to the performance of mobile agents, especially as compared with client-server applications, is not considered in the literature thus far. As we have mentioned in earlier chapters of this book, it is difficult to find real-world application domains where the *network load argument* in favor of mobile agents can be verified in general. If we now add the network overhead invoked by security protocols, this might shift the balance even further.

To summarize, we believe, as was pointed out to us also by others, that there currently exists no single common security solution. We also mentioned that the applicability of each countermeasure will have to be evaluated in the light of detailed performance tests. Finally, it should be acknowledged that some of the concepts discussed in this chapter are still waiting to be fully implemented. Therefore, the truly important aspect of integration and mixing of security technologies must remain open at present, even though we put forward that, in our view, it is exactly this integration that will be of the utmost importance.

Part III

The Kalong Mobility Model– Specification and Implementation

Chapter 6

Specifications of the Kalong Mobility Model

The third part of this book is completely devoted to the specification and evaluation of the Kalong mobility model. First, we specify Kalong by defining some application programming interfaces (APIs) and the Simple Agent Transmission Protocol (SATP). You might want to skip this technical chapter and continue with Chapter 7, in which we will introduce the Kalong software component, which is the reference implementation of the Kalong mobiliy model. Finally, in Chapter 8, we will report on several experiments we conducted to assess the performance of the Kalong software component.

Contents

6.1 Introduction

This chapter defines the Kalong[1] mobility model.

Kalong provides an efficient technique for migration of mobile agents between computer platforms. It is designed to be ported on demand on

---

1. Kalong is the name of a fruit-eating flying fox, lat. *Pteropus vampyrus*, inhabiting Java island. The Kalong is remarkable for its wingspan and its flying speed. The latter was the reason we chose this name for our mobility model, besides the relation to Java.

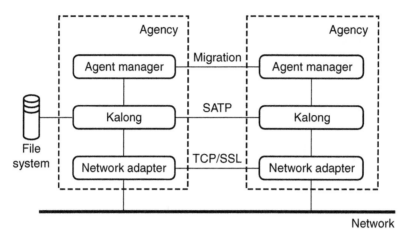

Figure 6.1 Kalong and its environment.

different machines, operating systems, network architectures, and network transport protocols. In the current version, Kalong is based on the Java programming language. We plan to translate Kalong to other programming languages later.

Kalong is supposed to be embedded in an agency software and to communicate with three other components, see Figure 6.1.

1. The *agent manager* is responsible for agent execution and other basic functions of a mobile agent server. It tells Kalong when to start a migration process and how the migration should work. Kalong notifies the agent manager about received agents.

2. The network is not directly accessed by Kalong; a *network adapter* component sorts through the details of a network protocol and works as a dispatcher for a different set of protocols. Kalong communicates with the network adapter using a very limited interface, which only provides functions to open and close a network connection and to send and receive byte sequences. For each network protocol, the network adapter launches a server that listens to a network port for incoming migrations. The network adapter informs Kalong about incoming requests.

3. Kalong must have access to a file system in order to load class files, or they can be loaded from remote network resources, accessible using a URL address and an HTTP or FTP connection. The latter is not pictured in Figure 6.1.

Kalong defines a new migration protocol, named *Simple Agent Transport Protocol*[2] (SATP), which is an application level protocol that transfers agent information to a single destination agency. SATP works according to a simple request/reply scheme and must be used in addition to a connection-based network protocol that provides a reliable flow of data, for example, TCP. It can be embedded in any other application-level protocol that also uses TCP, such as SSL, HTTP, and SOAP. This specification defines SATP commands as well as the message format to be used, in contrast to the specification of SMTP, in which the definition of the message format is moved to a companion protocol (RFC 822).

Kalong is responsible for the entire migration process and all tasks related to agent migration. Kalong must provide functions to serialize and deserialize agents, it must define a class-loader object for each agent, which directs requests to load classes back to Kalong. Kalong is *not* responsible for any kind of agent thread management. In the case of an agent migration, it is the agent manager that must control thread suspension and guarantee that no agent thread is able to still modify the agent's state. After an agent has been received successfully, Kalong only notifies the agent manager to start the new agent.

Kalong defines the following models, interfaces, and protocols:

1. An agent model that introduces the concept of *external state* and a new level of granularity for class transmission (see Section 6.3).

2. An interface, *IKalong*, (see Section 6.4.1) for the agent manager to conduct a migration; an interface, *IAgentManager*, (see Section 6.4.2) for Kalong to access the agent manager.

3. An interface, *INetwork*, (see Section 6.4.3) for Kalong to use the network adapter; an interface, *IServer*, (see Section 6.4.4) for the network adapter to access Kalong.

4. A migration protocol, named SATP, which defines messages sent over the network and their formats (see Section 6.5).

Regarding our definition of mobility models, Kalong focuses on issues of the agent's and network's views. Kalong's new agent model partially refers to the programmer's view too. However, Kalong does not define anything related

---

2. The name was chosen in the tradition of other application-level protocols, like *Simple Mail Transfer Protocol* and *Simple Network Management Protocol*, and to distinguish it from Aglets's *Agent Transfer Protocol* (ATP). Unfortunately, SATP became more complex than ATP.

to the mobility level (which is part of the programmer's view) and it is the task of the agent manager to map requirements of the mobility level to the preferences of Kalong as described in the following sections.

6.2 Kalong Vocabulary

Kalong uses the following terms:

Agent An *agent* is a mobile agent as defined in this book. We will often use the term *agent instance* to denote a single agent object in contrast to the set of all agents of the same type, or the agent's type.

Agency An *agency* is software that is necessary to execute and migrate mobile agents on a computer system. We distinguish between the *sender agency*, which starts a *transfer*, and the *receiver* agency, to which the transfer is directed.

Agent Manager An *agent manager* is a subcomponent within an *agency* that conducts a migration process.

Context Kalong maintains for each agent a *context* data structure that is composed of all information necessary for Kalong (e.g., its name, its home agency, its data units, its state, etc.).

Message A *message* is the basic unit of SATP communication. It is a sequence of bytes matching the syntax described in the following sections.

Migration *Migration* is a special form of a *transfer*, in which agent execution is stopped at the sender agency and resumed at the destination agency. We define two new verb phrases to describe the direction of a migration. When an agent leaves an agency, it *migrates out* and when an agent is received by an agency, it *migrates in*.

Migration Strategy A *migration strategy* defines what agent information should be sent to which agency; it can consist of one transfer or many transfers. The agent manager defines the migration strategy by using the methods of interface *IKalong*.

Network Connection A *network connection* is a virtual communication channel between two computers that is used to transmit SATP *messages*.

Object State The *object state*, or *agent object state*, is equal to the serialized agent.

Reply A reply is an SATP *message* that is sent from the receiver agency to the sender agency as answer to a request.

Request A request is an SATP *message* that is sent from a sender agency to a receiver agency.

Transaction A *migration strategy* might consist of several *transfers.* Because a migration strategy must be an atomic process, which is either executed completely or not at all, Kalong provides *transaction* management according to a *Two Phase Commit* (2PC) protocol.

Transfer A transfer is the process of sending agent information from a single sender agency to a single receiver agency. If the transfer includes an agent's state information, then it is a *migration.*

URL Each *agency* must have one or many addresses in the form of a *URL.* Kalong does not require a specific format of URLs, because addresses are only forwarded to the network adapter.

6.3 Agent Model

6.3.1 Agents and Agent Contexts

In Kalong, an agent must be a Java object of type `Serializable` or any subclass, because an agent's object state must be marshaled to be sent to a destination agency. The object state contains all the agent's attributes, which must also be serializable.

Agent Names

An agent must have a globally unique name that does not change during its lifetime. To be globally unique means that there must never be two agent instances with the same name in the entire agent system. Kalong does not specify how to obtain such a name and does not define any structure for a name, except that a name must be codeable into a Java `String` object. Kalong can only verify that no two agent instances with the same name exist when new agents are registered with Kalong and when agents migrate in. The agent manager is responsible for guaranteeing uniqueness with an appropriate algorithm for generating agent names.

Data Items

Besides the agent's object state, agents also have an *external state*, which is defined as a set of serializable Java objects that are accessible by the agent but are not part of the object state. Each element of the external state must have a unique name to be stored and accessed by its owner. A name must be codeable as a Java *String* object. Data items of the external state must not be accessible to other agent instances. A single data item should not be shared with another agent instance, because it is copied when it migrates.

Each data item has a status that can be *defined* or *undefined*. If a data item is transferred to another agency, it is locally set to *undefined* and set to *defined* at the destination agency. Thus, it is possible to let data items remain at the home agency even if the agent has migrated to another agency. The agent can request those data items from its home agency later. Kalong must ensure that a data item currently set to *undefined* is never read or written by the agent manager.

Another potential problem is that a data item could be uploaded to the wrong agency. For example, data items could be overwritten accidentally at a home agency, when the agent has already defined a mirror agency. Additionally, we have to consider a security problem. A malicious agency might send forged data-upload messages to a home or mirror agency and thereby manipulate data items. The problem could also occur if a malicious agency requests a data item from a home agency. If the state of this data item is set to *undefined* at the home agency, the agent will not be able to download the same data item later.

Unfortunately, we cannot solve this problem completely; we cannot protect the home agency against malicious access. However, we can provide a two-step technique that will allow the agent to notice a malicious access and be able to react.

1. Downloading and uploading data items always changes the state of the data item. If a data item is downloaded, then its state is set to *undefined* at the home agency. If the agent later tries to download this data item again, it receives an error message.

2. If a malicious server loads a data item, modifies it, and then uploads it again, the state is set to *defined* at the home agency. The agent would not notice the manipulation in this case. Therefore, we introduce a

data-item key that is necessary for data uploading. This key is created at the home agency when the agent is started, and is carried by the agent as part of the state. In case of a data-upload message, the key must be sent to the home agency, where it is compared to the key locally stored. If they match, the upload is successful, if not, the upload is rejected. In the case of a successful upload, the reply message contains a new key that was computed by the home agency. It is possible for a malicious agency to steal the key that the agent carries. Using this key, the server would be able to upload a data item. However, if the agent later wants to upload a data item by itself, the message is rejected because it knows only an outdated key.

Code Units

An agent's code is transferred in the form of code units. A code unit contains one class or many classes, which will always be transferred together. Each code unit has a locally unique identifier, that is, no two units of the same agent instance have the same identifier.

Each agent instance divides its own distribution of classes into units. The same class may be included in more than one unit. It is the task of the agent manager to make sure that classes are completely separated onto units. Code distribution cannot be modified after the *agent-definition block* (see Section 6.4.1) was sent the first time. Each code unit has a list of *code bases* from which it can be loaded. A code base is an agency and is described by one or many URL addresses. The home agency should not be a member of any code base, because it would be redundant.

Agent Context

All information about the external state and code units of an agent is stored within Kalong in a data structure named *agent context*. There is a single agent context for each agent instance. Kalong must provide the agent manager with access to data items of the external state, but it does not specify how an agent manager provides an agent instance with access to its data items. Kalong does not define the detailed structure of an agent context. All implementation details are left to the programmer.

It is important to understand the difference between the lifetimes of an agent instance and an agent context. An agent is created by a user within the agent manager. It has a *global* lifetime, which lasts from its creation to its termination (which is not necessarily at the same agency). The time an agent spends visiting an agency, starting after the agent has migrated in and stopping after the agent has migrated out, is called the *local* lifetime. Thus, the local lifetime is bound to a single agency.

Agent context objects are created when the agent manager registers an agent with Kalong or when an agent migrates in. However, the lifetime of an agent context might not terminate at the same time as the local lifetime of an agent. For example, a home agency is supposed to keep information about code units so that the agent can load necessary classes later. We will see two more examples in Section 6.3.2 of agencies that retain agent information beyond an agent's local lifetime. To summarize, the lifetime of an agent context is not bound to either the local or the global lifetime of an agent, but it is at least as long as the local lifetime of the corresponding agent.

This can be best explained using an example; Figure 6.2 shows global and local lifetimes for an agent visiting agencies A, B, and C. Its global lifetime is the striped bar, its local lifetime is the nonfilled bar, and its context lifetime is the solid bar. The agent is created at agency A, which automatically becomes the agent's home agency. It migrates to two other agencies, named B and C, and finally returns to agency A to terminate there. After the agent is created, an agent context object is created for it. When the agent migrates to agency B, the local lifetime terminates, but the agent context's lifetime continues. At agency B, the local lifetime and the agent context's lifetime are started when the agent migrates in. After it has migrated out, the local lifetime terminates, whereas the agent context's lifetime continues. This is because the agent has defined agency B as a code server, that is, some code units of this agent are still available at agency B for later download. Before the agent leaves agency C, it releases the code server again, which terminates the context's lifetime at agency B. Finally, after the agent has returned home, the context's lifetime at agency A terminates too.

We can also describe the lifetime of an agent context using a state diagram, (Fig. 6.3). After creation, an agent context is first in state *AgentRunning*, which indicates that the agent is currently being executed. After the state has been sent to another agency, the context switches to state *AgentRoaming*, which means that the agent is no longer being executed at this agency. If an object state is received later, it switches back to state *AgentRunning*. On a remote agency, the context is first in state *AgentRoaming* (because a remote agency may be initialized as a code server by only sending code units), until an object state is received. Then it switches to state *AgentRunning*.

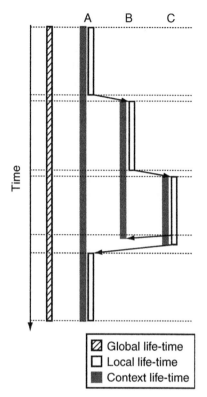

Figure 6.2 Comparison of the global and local lifetimes of an agent with the lifetime of an agent's context. A, B, and C are agencies to which the agent migrates. The row beneath each agency name shows the local lifetime of the agent and the agent's context lifetime.

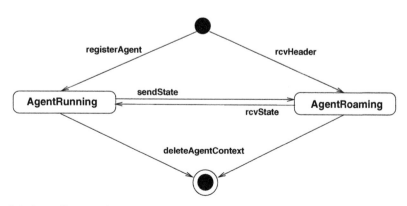

Figure 6.3 State diagram for an agent context.

6.3.2 Agencies

An agency is the place where agents are executed. Kalong does not specify how an agency is further structured (e.g., using the concept of logical *places*); this must be done within the agent-manager component.

Each agency must have at least one address in the form of a URL, for example: *tcp://tatjana.cs.uni-jena.de:4155/whyte/penthouse*, where *tcp* is the protocol name, the number 4155 is the port number on which the agency can receive agents using this protocol, and *whyte/penthouse* is the name of the place to which the migration is directed. Kalong does not specify any format of this URL, but it requires that it consists at least of a protocol name, a host name, and a port number. These are the only parts of a URL Kalong considers.

Addresses are obtained by the underlying network adapter component, which manages a set of different network protocols and defines a server for each protocol listening to a specific port. Therefore, agencies can be accessed using many different URLs. For example, the same agency can be accessed using *tcp://tatjana.cs.uni-jena.de:4155* and *ssl://tatjana.cs.uni-jena.de:4156*. The first address must be used to communicate to this agency over a plain TCP connection, whereas the second URL must be used to have a secure connection using the SSL protocol. Before an agency may be accessed, Kalong must verify that its address meets Kalong's requirements. The addresses of an agency may only differ in the protocol and the port number; all other URL elements must be equal.

Kalong distinguishes the following roles for agencies from the view of a single agent instance. This role information is transparent for the agent manager and only used within Kalong, thus, it might be a little bit confusing that we speak of *agency roles* where we really mean *Kalong roles*.

1. The agency on which the agent was started automatically becomes the *home* agency. An agent must have only one home agency, and an agent's home agency must not be redefined. The home agency does not delete any information about the agent except the agent's object state, which it deletes after the agent has migrated out.

2. A *remote* agency is every agency that an agent visits while executing an itinerary. Usually, a remote agency drops all information about an agent after the agent has left it.

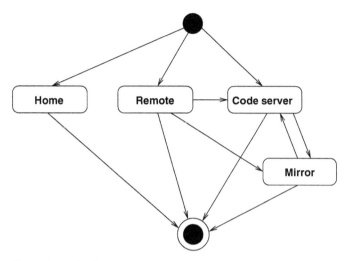

Figure 6.4 The four agency types in Kalong and how agency types can change during an agency's lifetime.

3. A *code server* agency is able to store code units even after the agent has left the agency. Thus, code can be downloaded from this agency later. There can be multiple code server agencies in parallel.

4. The *mirror* agency is able to keep information about code unit and data items even after the agent has left the agency. The mirror is a complete copy of all information stored about an agent at the home agency. There is never more than one mirror agency at any time.

The role of an agency with regard to a specific agent instance might change during its lifetime, as can be seen in Figure 6.4. An agency becomes a home or remote agency by starting or receiving an agent. A home agency releases its role when the agent terminates or the agent manager deletes the corresponding agent context object. A remote agency releases its role when the agent leaves it and migrates to another one or when the agent defines this agency to become a code server or mirror agency. Code server and mirror agencies release their roles only by an agent's order. A mirror agency can be defined to become a code server later. We show how an agent can define a code server or mirror agency in the next section. Table 6.1 compares the agency types with regard to their ability to keep information about agents.

Table 6.1 *Comparison of the four agency types*

Agency type	Data items	Code units	Cardinality
Home	✓	✓	1
Remote			1
Code server		✓	0..n
Mirror	✓	✓	0..1

6.4 Application Programming Interfaces

6.4.1 Interface *IKalong*

Interface *IKalong* defines the main functions of the Kalong component. It is used by the agent manager to access an agent's context and to define a migration strategy. The protocol definition is given as a set of methods with arguments and results in Java syntax. A description of the function of each method should provide enough information to allow its implementation.

The agent manager at the sender agency communicates with Kalong in two phases. First, it registers an agent with Kalong so that Kalong can verify that all used classes are available for transmission and the agent as well as all its components are serializable. Second, it uses the services of this interface to conduct the migration process.

We divide the methods of *IKalong* in four groups:

1. Methods to start and stop transactions.

2. Methods to register agents and define code units.

3. Methods to modify a local agent context.

4. Methods to transfer agent information via the network.

Almost all methods receive an agent name as a parameter to identify the agent context. All methods of interface *IKalong* are assumed to work synchronously.

Throughout this book the term *current agency* always refers to the agency on which the commands are executed.

Manage Transactions

A migration strategy might include several transfers. As it must be an atomic command that is executed either with all its transfers or none at all, Kalong provides a common technique for transaction management, called *two-phase-commit* (2PC) protocol.

The idea of the 2PC protocol is as follows: All commands that modify the agent context information, either locally at the current agency or remotely at any of the destination agencies, must be bracketed by the following transaction management commands. To start a transaction, the following method must be used.

```
public void startTransaction( String agentName ) throws KalongException
```
Starts a transaction. Throws an exception if a transaction is already running.

After this method has been called, no other thread can start a transaction using this agent until the transaction terminates.

To explain the 2PC protocol, we assume that several connections have been opened to different remote agencies. After all messages have been sent, the agent manager must send a *prepare* message (first phase) using the following method.

```
public boolean prepare( String agentName )
```
Sends a prepare message to all receiver agencies. The reply informs about success.

Kalong maintains a list of all connections that were opened since the last call of method *startTransaction*. Method *prepare* sends a *prepare* message to all receiver agencies. Each receiver answers, whether the last transfer was successful or not. Method *prepare* collects these reply messages and returns *true* if all receiver agencies have accepted the transfer and *false* if at least one agency has not accepted the transfer.

The agent manager must now send either a *commit* or *rollback* message to all receiver agencies (second phase) with regard to the result of the previous method. Both methods close all network connections and terminate the transaction.

```
public void commit( String agentName )
```
Sends a commit message to all receiver agencies.

A *commit* message applies all changes made during the last transfer. This might result in an agent being started at a remote agency.

```
public void rollback( String agentName )
```
Sends a rollback message to all receiver agencies.

A *rollback* message recovers the last stable state before the last transfer was started at the receiver agency. Of course, the last three methods require that a transaction has already been started. If no transfer has occurred since the last start of a transaction, method *prepare* will return *true*.

Information about Agencies and Defining Agent Contexts

As already described, agency addresses are defined by the network adapter component. Because this information is all that must be available at the agent manger about the network layer, Kalong must pass on this information.

All addresses of this agency can be requested using the following method.

```
public java.net.URL[] getURLs()
```
Returns an array of URLs of the current agency or returns **null** if this agency has no addresses yet.

This method simply uses the corresponding method of *INetwork* to obtain this information (see Section 6.4.3).

Before agents can migrate, they must be registered with Kalong. If this method is successful, a new agent context exists in Kalong that can be accessed using the given *agentName*. If the method fails for any reason, no agent context is created and an exception is thrown.

```
public void registerAgent( String agentName, StringagentOwner,
    Serializable agent )throws KalongException
```
Registers an agent with name *agentName* and object state *agent* with Kalong.

This method first checks whether an agent context with the given name *agentName* already exists and throws an exception if it does. It also throws an exception if no address of the current agency can be determined. The current agency becomes the home agency for this agent. All classes of the class closure are determined by analyzing object *agent*.

After context creation, the code units for this agent must be defined before any migration can happen.[3] The main method of defining code units is as follows:

```
public int defineUnit( String agentName, String[] classNames )
Defines a new unit with classes classNames. Returns the code unit identifier.
```

All classes with names given in the array *className* are bundled into a single code unit. Parameter *classNames* must not be null or an empty array. Kalong must assign a unique identifier to this unit that it will return to the caller. The definition of code units cannot be changed or modified afterward. The agent manager is responsible for making sure all necessary classes of the class closure are distributed on code units. Classes that are not part of any code unit cannot be transferred to remote agencies, neither by pushing nor by pulling. The agent manager can request the classes of the class closure with the following method:

```
public String[] getClassNames( String agentName )
Returns an array of strings containing the names of all the classes that the current agent uses.
```

The class closure determined by Kalong contains all the classes that are used by the agent, even common Java classes, as for example *java.lang.String*. It is the task of the agent manager to implement a filter function for ubiquitous classes (see Chapter 3) and not to add these to any code unit. In contrast, classes may be added to code units that were not part of the class closure. This might be important in rare cases in which a class is used, but the class name is not part of the agent's Java byte code. Consider the following example:

```
1 public class TestAgent implements Serializable
2 {
3   public void run()
4   {
5     Class aClass = Class.forName( "OtherClass" );
6     SomeInterface object = aClass.newInstance();
7   }
8 }
```

---

3. In rare cases when all classes of the agent can be assumed to already exist at any destination agency, unit definition may be skipped.

In this example, class *OtherClass* is assumed to implement interface *SomeInterface*. The class is defined by using method *Class.forName*, which gets a *String* object as the parameter containing the name of the class. A new instance of this class is created by using method *newInstance* and assigned to a variable of the super type. As a consequence, the byte code of class *TestAgent* does not contain the full class name for class *OtherClass* except as a *String* representation, and this cannot be distinguished from other *String* objects without a semantic analysis of the byte code. To make class *OtherClass* able to migrate, it must be added to some code unit manually.

There is another method by which the agent manager can obtain a list of all classes for which at least one object exists in the serialized agent.

```
public String[] getClassesInUse( String agentName )
```
Returns an array of class names. Each class is used in the serialized agent.

The agent manager can also request the size of a class's byte code.

```
public int getClassSize( String agentName, String className )
```
Returns the size of the given class.

Modifying Agent Context

The following methods are mostly used for retrieving information about the agent context and the agent itself. They must be used within a transaction.

First, to request the address of an agent's home agency, the following method must be used:

```
public String[] getHomeAgency( String agentName )
```
Returns the addresses of the agent's home agency.

Data Items

The following methods are used to access the data items of the external state and to define the object state.

```
public String[] getDataItems( String agentName )
```
Returns an array containing the names of all data items.

The returned array contains all data items, without regard to their current state (defined or undefined). If the agent has no data items in the external state, the return value is an empty array. If only undefined data items are to be requested, then the following method can be used.

```
public String[] getUndefinedDataItems( String agentName )
```
Returns an array containing the names of all undefined data items.

If no undefined data items exist, the return value is an empty array. If only defined data items are to be requested, then the following method can be used.

```
public String[] getDefinedDataItems( String agentName )
```
Returns an array containing the names of all defined data items.

To define and retrieve the value of a data item, the following two methods can be used.

```
public void setData( String agentName, String name,
  Serializable object ) throws KalongException
```
Sets the data item with name *name* to the value given as *object*.

This method throws an exception if the data item is currently undefined and, therefore, cannot be overwritten. For a data item to be deleted permanently, it must be set to the null value.

```
public Serializable getData( String agentName, String name )
throws KalongException
```
Returns the value of the data item with name *name*.

The method throws an exception if the data item does not exist or is currently undefined. To check whether a data item is accessible, its state can be requested using this method:

```
public byte getDataItemState( String agentName, String name )
  throws KalongException
```
Returns the current state of the data item with name *name*.

The return value is 0 if the data item is defined, and 1 if it is undefined. If the data item does not exist, an exception is thrown. In some cases it might be necessary to know the size of a serialized data item in order to decide if it should migrate to the next destination or remain at the current one.

```
public int getDataSize( String agentName, String name )
  throws KalongException
```
Returns the size of the serialized data item with name *name*. Throws an exception if the requested data item does not exist.

The last method must be used to define the object state of an agent.

```
public void setObjectState( String agentName, Serializable state )
```
Defines the agent's object state.

This method must be used before a migration is started.

Code Units

The following methods are used to retrieve information about code units.

```
public int[] getUnits( String agentName ) throws KalongException
```
Returns an array with the identifiers of all units.

If no units were defined yet, the return value is an empty array.

```
public String[] getClassesInUnit( String agentName, int id )
  throws KalongException
```
Returns an array with the names of all classes that are connected with the given unit identifier.

If the given unit identifier is invalid, an exception is thrown. The return value is never null or an empty array. The next method is used when a specific class is to be downloaded.

```
public int[] getUnitForClassName( String agentName, String className )
```
Returns the identifiers of all units that contain the given class name.

If the given class name is not member of any unit, an empty array is returned.

Defining Code Server Agencies

To mark a unit to remain at the current agency after a migration, the addresses of the current agency must be added to the unit's code base.

```
public void addCodeBases( String agentName, int id,
  String[] url ) throws KalongException
```
Adds the given URLs as new code bases for the given unit. Throws an exception if the given identifier is invalid.

The new code bases must be appended to the existing list, because the order of the code base addresses must not be changed. With the following method, the current code bases can be requested.

```
public String[] getCodeBases( String agentName, int id )
  throws KalongException
```
Returns all code bases of the given unit. Throws an exception if the given identifier is invalid.

With the last method, agency addresses can be deleted from a unit's list of code bases.

```
public void deleteCodeBases( String agentName, int id,
  String[] url ) throws KalongException
```
Deletes the given URLs from the code bases for the given unit. Throws an exception if the given identifier is invalid.

Defining Mirror Agencies

The last three methods are to define and delete mirror agencies. It is important to understand that these methods have only a local effect and changing a remote agency to a mirror agency means more than just calling method *setMirrorAgency*. All data items and code units from the current mirror or home agency must already be loaded.

```
public String[] getMirrorAgency( String agentName )
```
Returns the addresses of the current mirror agency if they are defined. Otherwise return null.

```
public void setMirrorAgency( String agentName,
  String[] mirror ) throws KalongException
```
Defines the current mirror agency. Throws an exception if a mirror is defined already.

```
public void deleteMirrorAgency()
```
Deletes the currently defined mirror agency.

The last method has only a local effect and does not send a message to the current mirror agency to release its role.

Sending Messages to Receiver Agencies

The following are methods to transfer messages to a single receiver agency. Multiple connections may not be opened to the same receiver agency during the same transaction. All transfer messages must be part of a transaction.

To start a transfer, the following method must be called:

```
public Object startTransfer( String agentName, URL receiver )
   throws KalongException
```
Opens a connection to the receiver agency whose address is given as a parameter. Returns a handler object for this connection.

Note that the address of the receiver agency must be given as a single URL. The agent manager is responsible for selecting the correct address from the list of all known URLs for the destination. The return value of this method is a *handler* object, which is used to identify this transfer. This specification does not define how this handler object is determined, but it must be unique for all transfers during the same transaction. A transfer cannot be explicitly stopped, because network connections are closed by using the two methods *commit* and *rollback*.

All other methods process according to the following pattern:

1. The agent's context is accessed to obtain further information.

2. This information is sent as an SATP request message to the receiver agency, which must always send a reply message. The type of request depends on the method (Table 6.2).

3. The reply message is analyzed and the result is stored in the agent's context if necessary.

We will now focus on the semantics of each function. The structure of each message is defined in Section 6.5.

There are few constraints in sending messages, because not all messages must be sent as part of a single transfer. We describe these rules by using a finite state machine, the graphical representation of which can be found in Figure 6.5. In the figure, states are named from the viewpoint of the receiver agency, so that, for example, a state named *ADB Rcv*, expresses that the agent

Table 6.2 *Mapping of interface methods to message types*

Interface method	Request message	Reply message
ping	Ping	Ping
sendHeader	Header	Ok/Nok
sendADB	ADB	ADBReply
sendUnits	Unit	Ok/Nok
sendUnitRequest	Unit Request	Unit
sendState	State	Ok/Nok
sendDataUpload	Data Item	Data Item Key
sendDataRequest	Data Request	Data Item
prepare	Prepare	Ok/Nok
commit	Commit	none
rollback	Rollback	none

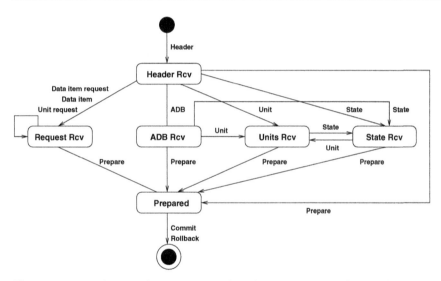

Figure 6.5 State diagram for a SATP transfer. The Ping message that can be sent or received at each state has been omitted, because it does not change the state.

definition block (ADB) was received successfully. For the sender side, states should be renamed accordingly.

```
public boolean ping( Object handler, byte[] data )
```
Sends the given byte sequence **data** to the receiver agency.

This method can be used to check the availability of the remote agency or to check connection quality. The receiver is supposed to send back the byte array *data* unchanged. The method returns true if the same byte sequence was received, if not, it returns `false`. Ping messages may be sent at any point during a transfer and may be sent multiple times.

The following methods do not have a return value but throw an exception if there is an error.

`public void` *sendHeader(Object handler,* `byte` *command)* throws *KalongException*
Sends the header to the receiver agency. Throws an exception if the receiver agency does not accept the header.

The header message contains information about the agent and its home agency. The receiver agency must answer, whether it accepts further messages for this agent or not. The sender should terminate the transfer if the receiver did not accept the header. If the header was not accepted, the receiver must reject any further messages except a ping message.

The header message must be sent prior to all other messages during a transfer, except a ping message. It must not be sent more than once during the same transfer. A header message may be followed by any other message and can be sent between all agency types.

At the receiver agency the agent's name given in the header is used to select the agent context. If no agent with the given name exists, it must be decided whether the transfer should be accepted, perhaps by using the addresses of the home or sender agency. Kalong must ask the agent manager as part of this decision, using method *verifyAgent* of interface *IAgentManager*. The reply code is set accordingly.

The *command* parameter contains the code of a process that should be executed *after* transfer is completed.

No operation (noop) (value 0) This command is sent in most cases, and usually has the effect that code units and/or agent state information are accepted at the remote agency. If an agent's state is sent as part of this transmission, the agent is started.

Release code server agency (value 1) This command is sent to a code server agency to instruct it to release its role and delete all code units.

Release mirror agency (value 2) This command is sent to a mirror agency to instruct it to release its role and delete all data items and code units. If there are *defined* data items left at the mirror agency, the header must be rejected.

Start code server (value 3) Using this command, it is possible to create a code server remotely (i.e., without migrating to it). All code units sent afterwards are immediately copied at the receiver agency.

Release mirror agency to code server (value 4) This command is sent to a mirror agency in order to instruct it to release its role and become a code server agency. The effect is that all data items are deleted, but code units are still available at this agency. If there are *defined* data items left at the mirror agency, the header must be rejected.

`public void `*`sendADB( Object handler,`*` boolean `*`classCache`*`) throws `*`KalongException`*
Sends the agent definition block (ADB) to the receiver agency.

This message is used to transmit information about code units and classes without the code itself. The parameter *classCache* defines whether the receiver should answer with information about class availability.

The header must have been sent before an ADB message. An ADB message may be sent multiple times to the same agency, because it is possible that code bases have changed. After an ADB message is sent, no request messages may be sent to the receiver agency.

`public void `*`sendUnits( Object handler,`*` int[] `*`ids`*` ) throws `*`KalongException`*
Sends code units with the given identifiers to the receiver agency.

This message is used to transmit a set of code units to the receiver agency. The receiver replies whether or not it accepts the transmission.

A header message must have been sent before a unit message can be sent. An agent definition block must be available at the receiver agency before a unit can be accepted. If many code units are to be transmitted they should be sent as one message. After a unit message, unit-request or data-request messages may not be sent, because it does not make sense to request units or data items from an agency to which units or data items were just sent.

`public void `*`sendUnitRequest( Object handler,`*` int[] `*`ids`*` ) throws `*`KalongException`*
Sends a request to download units with the given identifiers to the receiver agency.

This message is used to request units from a home agency, code server agency, or mirror agency. The receiver replies with the requested units, unless one of the following is true.

1. The receiver is not a home agency, code server agency, or mirror agency for this agent.

2. Any of the sent unit identifiers is invalid.

A header message must have been sent before this message is sent. Messages of type ADB, unit, or state may not have been sent before or after this message. If many data code units are to be requested, their identifiers should be bundled into a single message of this type.

```
public void sendState( Object handler, String[] names )
  throws KalongException
Sends the state to the receiver agency.
```

This message is used to transmit an agent's object state and some data items to the receiver agency. The names of the data items to transmit along with the state are given as parameter *names*. This parameter can be null. The receiver answers whether it accepts this message or not.

The effect of this method is that the names of all data items are sent to the destination agency, but some of them are sent without their values. The reason for this is that data items can only be distributed between two types of agencies: the current one and the home (or a mirror) agency. Even if a data item is to remain at the home agency, the agent must have knowledge about this data item if only to prevent the creation of a new data item with the same name, which would cause conflicts when the agent migrates back to its home agency.

Therefore, the state contains the names of all data items. All data items given as parameter *names* are sent with state *defined* and their current value. The state is locally set to *undefined*. All other data items are sent with state *undefined* and without their value.

If the sender agency is not allowed to store data items (i.e., it is a remote agency or code server agency), all data items are transferred with their value to the destination agency without regard to the value of parameter *names*.

A header message must have been sent before a state message may be sent. An agent definition block must be available at the receiver agency before a state message can be received. It is not necessary for the ADB to have been sent during the same transfer. A state message must not be sent to an agency where an agent is currently being executed. After a state message, no unit-request or data-request messages may be sent.

After a transaction in which a state message has been sent, some, or even all, agent related information has to be dropped at the sender agency. If the sender was a remote agency and the agent has copied some code units, the agency becomes a code server. If the agent has not copied code units, all agent related information is deleted. If the sender was a home or mirror agency, there is no change.

```
public void sendDataUpload( Object handler, String[] names )
   throws KalongException
```
Send data items whose names are given as a parameter to the receiver agency.

This message is used to upload data items from the current agency to a home or mirror agency. It must not be sent to the home agency if there is a mirror agency. The receiver answers whether or not the new data values are accepted. The receiver will reject a data item upload if one of the following is true:

1. The receiver is not a home agency or a mirror agency.

2. An uploaded data item is already *defined* at the receiver agency.

A header message must have been sent before this message type is sent. Messages of type ADB, unit, or state may not have been sent before nor may they be sent after this message. If many data items are to be transmitted, they should be bundled into a single message.

Only data items that are *defined* at the current agency can be uploaded. At the receiver agency, these uploaded data items must be *undefined* at first, and set to *defined* after they are received. After a successful transmission, sent data items must be set to *undefined* locally.

```
public void sendDataRequest( Object handler, String[] names )
   throws KalongException
```
Sends a request to download data items with the given names to the receiver agency.

This message is used to request data items from an agent's home or mirror agency. It does not need to be sent to the home agency if there is a mirror agency. The receiver must reply with the requested data items. The receiver may reject the message if either of the following is true:

1. The receiver is not a home agency or a mirror agency for this agent.

2. Any of the data items is *undefined* or does not exist at the receiver agency.

A header message must have been sent before this message is sent. Messages of type ADB, unit, or state may not have been sent before nor may they be sent after this message. If many data items are to be requested, their names should be bundled into a single message.

6.4.2 Interface IAgentManager

This interface is used by Kalong to communicate to the agent manager. It is used during an in-migration of an agent to check whether reception of the agent is allowed. The agent manager could, for example, reject any migration that comes from a host suspected of being malicious. Therefore, it should use the information about the *lastAgency* given in the following method.

```
public boolean verifyAgent( String agentName,
URL[] homeAgency, URL[] lastAgency )
Checks whether an agent with the given name and addresses is allowed to migrate to
this agency.
```

After Kalong has received an agent's state, the agent manager is asked to start agent execution. For this task, the following method is used:

```
public void startAgent( String agentName, Serializable object )
Starts the given agent.
```

The parameter *object* contains the deserialized agent object. All classes not already available at the current agency must already have been downloaded.

6.4.3 Interface INetwork

The third interface defines methods to access the network adapter. The first method is used to get all addresses under which the network adapter is accessible.

```
public URL[] getURLs()
Returns the URLs for all network protocols, or null if no addresses are defined.
```

The next three methods are to handle network connections. The first method is used to open a communication channel to a remote agency.

```
public Object openTransfer( URL receiver ) throws KalongException
Opens a network connection to the given receiver agency and returns an object to identify this transfer. Throws an
exception if the connection cannot be opened.
```

The second method is used to send a message to the destination agency. The return value contains the reply message, which must be processed immediately.

```
public byte[] send( Object handle, byte[] data )throws KalongException
```
Sends the given byte sequence to the receiver, waits for a reply, and returns it. Throws an exception if the method cannot be sent.

Finally, at the end of a transfer, the network connection must be closed again.

```
public void closeTransfer( Object handle )
```
Closes a network connection.

6.4.4 Interface IServer

The last interface defines methods that must be used by the network component to access Kalong. Kalong must provide an implementation of this interface.

These methods are the counterparts of the ones described in the previous section. For example, if method *send* of interface *INetwork* is called at the sender, method *receive* of this interface is called at the receiver.

```
public Object openTransfer()throws KalongException
```
Opens a network connection, returns an object to identify this transfer.

The method returns null if the connection cannot be opened.

```
public byte[] receive( Object handle, byte[] data )throws KalongException
```
Receives the given byte sequence, waits for a reply, and returns it.

```
public void closeTransfer( Object handle )
```
Closes a network connection.

6.5 The SATP Migration Protocol

This section defines the SATP migration protocol, version 1.0.

6.5.1 Introduction

Each method of interface *IKalong* to transfer agent information uses one of the message types defined in this section. Although it might be clear from the names which method uses which message, Table 6.2 gives an overview. A reply message named *Ok/Nok* stands for a reply that only contains the information of whether the receiver has accepted the request.

To describe the message format, we use the Extended Backus-Naur Form as introduced in Chapter 3. First of all, we define the following nonterminal symbols: ⟨Byte⟩ represents a single byte with value range from 0 to 255; ⟨Short⟩ is used for numbers and is two bytes long; ⟨Integer⟩ is also used for numbers and is four bytes long. To code ⟨Short⟩ and ⟨Integer⟩ symbols, we use the big-endian format, where the highest byte is stored first, at the lowest storage address. For example, a 4-byte integer is stored in the following order:

Byte3	Byte2	Byte1	Byte0
0	1	2	3

The first line shows the sequence of bytes in memory, the second line shows the byte offset.

In this section, it will sometimes be necessary to express a byte literal. In this case, we will use hexadecimal numbers (e.g., "0x15" to express the decimal number 21). In addition to the meta symbols introduced above, we define n{⟨A⟩}m as a repetition of symbol ⟨A⟩ between n and m times, where $0 \leq n \leq m$. Mostly, we will use this new meta symbol when we have to define a repetition of exactly n times, so that we write n{⟨A⟩}n.

Sometimes it is necessary to refer to a value of a ⟨Byte⟩, ⟨Short⟩, or ⟨Integer⟩ symbol. In this case, we will write ⟨A_n⟩ to express that symbol ⟨A⟩ contains the value n.

For example, the following ⟨Message⟩ is comprised of $n + 5$ bytes, where the number n is described by symbol ⟨A⟩.

1. ⟨Message⟩ ::= ⟨A_n⟩ + ⟨B⟩ + ⟨C⟩

2. ⟨A⟩ ::= ⟨Byte⟩

3. ⟨B⟩ ::= n{⟨Byte⟩}n

4. ⟨C⟩ ::= ⟨Integer⟩

6.5.2 The SATP Request and Reply Messages Scheme

The normal operation of the SATP protocol is for a sender to transmit a request to the receiver, which answers with a reply message. A request always has the following format:

1. $\langle Request \rangle$ ::= $\langle RequestCode \rangle$ + $\langle Length_n \rangle$ + $\langle RequestParameter \rangle$

2. $\langle RequestCode \rangle$ ::= [$\langle RcPing \rangle$ | $\langle RcHeader \rangle$ | $\langle RcUnit \rangle$ | $\langle RcUnitReq \rangle$ | $\langle RcData \rangle$ | $\langle RcDataReq \rangle$ | $\langle RcADB \rangle$ | $\langle RcState \rangle$ | $\langle RcPrepare \rangle$ | $\langle RcCommit \rangle$ | $\langle RcRollback \rangle$]

3. $\langle Length \rangle$ ::= 1{$\langle Byte \rangle$}4

4. $\langle RequestParameter \rangle$ ::= n{Byte}n

A request starts with a command byte, which is followed by a sequence of 1 to 4 bytes, in which a number of bytes is coded as described below. The format of a $\langle RequestParameter \rangle$ depends on the message type and is defined later for each type.

To transmit a sequence of bytes, we use a byte-count–oriented technique, in which we send the number of the following bytes prior to the raw byte sequence. The advantage of this technique is that the receiver can read data from the network very quickly, especially in Java. Every *String* or byte array is transmitted as such a byte sequence in SATP. Usually, coding a value of type int would result in a sequence of 4 bytes, but up to 3 of them might be wasted, because the number to be coded is less than 2^8, 2^{16} or 2^{24}. To optimize space in these cases, we propose to code a byte length in a new way. We name the original number of bytes the *length*, and the resulting sequence of bytes which contains this number, the *code*. The idea is to use the two highest bits in the first byte of the code to contain the code length. A value of 0 means that the code is only 1 byte long (0 bytes following), a value of 3 means that the code is 4 bytes long (3 bytes following). So, for example, the following code stands for the number 33.

00100001
0

With 1 byte it is only possible to code numbers from 0 to 63. The following 2 bytes are the code for the number 257.

01000001	00000001
0	1

Therefore, in our approach, the highest value for a length is $2^{30} - 1$, which will be sufficient for all cases in SATP.

The format of a reply message depends on whether the request was successful.

5. `<Reply> ::= [ <ReplyOk> | <ReplyNok> ]`

6. `<ReplyOk> ::= "0x6F" + <ReplyParameter>`

7. `<ReplyParameter> ::= <Length`$_n$`> + n{<Byte>}n`

8. `<ReplyNok> ::= "0x70" + <ErrorCode> + <ErrorText>`

9. `<ErrorCode> ::= <Short>`

10. `<ErrorText> ::= <String>`

11. `<String> ::= <Length`$_m$`> + m{<Byte>}m`

If the request message was accepted, then a `<ReplyOk>` answer is sent. It is comprised of a single byte, which must have the value `0x6F`, and a byte sequence that contains the reply parameter. For example, if a unit request was sent, then this byte sequence will contain the units. If the request message was not accepted or the message format was not accepted, then a `<ReplyNok>` answer is sent. The `<ErrorCode>` and the `<ErrorText>` contain a detailed error description.

6.5.3 Specification of All SATP Messages

Ping

The ping message sends a sequence of bytes to the receiver agency, which is supposed to reply with a `<ReplyOk>` message with the unchanged byte sequence as the parameter.

12. `<RcPing> ::= "0x76"`

13. `<PingParameter> ::= n{<Byte>}n`

The parameter is a sequence of arbitrary bytes. The receiver must send back this byte sequence as a `<ReplyOk>` message without any modification, but answers with a `<ReplyNok>` message if it does not accept this ping message.

It may terminate a transfer if, for example, the sender tries to flood the receiver with ping messages.

Header

The header message contains information about the agent and its home agency. The receiver agency must answer whether it accepts (`<ReplyOk>` without any parameters) further messages for this agent or not (`<ReplyNok>` with an error message).

14. `<RcHeader>` ::= "0x66"

15. `<HeaderParameter>` ::= `<Vendor>` + `<Major>` + `<Minor>` + `<AgentName>` + `<HomeAgency>` + `<SenderAgency>` + `<Command>`

16. `<Vendor>` ::= `<String>`

17. `<Major>` ::= `<Byte>`

18. `<Minor>` ::= `<Byte>`

19. `<AgentName>` ::= `<String>`

20. `<HomeAgency>` ::= `<PackedURLArray>`

21. `<SenderAgency>` ::= `<PackedURLArray>`

22. `<Command>` ::= [`<Noop>` | `<ReleaseCodeServer>` | `<ReleaseMirror>` | `<ReleaseMirrorToCodeServer>`]

23. `<Noop>` ::= "0x00"

24. `<ReleaseCodeServer>` ::= "0x01"

25. `<ReleaseMirror>` ::= "0x02"

26. `<StartCodeServer>` ::= "0x03"

27. `<ReleaseMirrorToCodeServer>` ::= "0x04"

The first part of the header is the SATP protocol version number. To ensure that two agencies are able to exchange messages correctly, both need to have the same version of the SATP protocol. The sender declares its version number as part of the header. The receiver should only accept a transfer if its version number is equal to or higher than the sender's. If the receiver rejects a transmission, the agent at the sender agency will receive an error notification.

We use a major–minor scheme to describe the version of the protocol. The minor number is incremented when changes are made to the protocol that do not apply to the general message format (e.g., if the semantics are changed). The major number is incremented if substantial modifications are made with regard to the message format. Both values are coded in a byte each. For example, version 0.1 is earlier than 0.11, which is earlier than 1.0.

The third part of the header is the agent's name. The next two parts contain addresses of the agent's home agency and of the sender agency. A complete URL (e.g., `tcp://tatjana.cs.uni-jena.de:4567/fortknox/gold#abc`, consists of the following parts: protocol (`tcp`), host name (`tatjana.cs.uni-jena.de`), port number (`4567`), path to the resource (`fortknox`), file name of the resource (`gold`), and reference within the resource (`abc`). Because Kalong does not define the structure of a URL, all parts of a valid URL must be transmitted. We can assume that all addresses of the same agency have the same host name, path name, file name and reference, so we only store these parts once. The first element of a `<PackedURLArray>` is the number of URLs following. We name this number n.

28. `<PackedURLArray> ::= <NumberOfURLs`$_n$`> + <URLHostName> + <URLPath> + <URLFile> + <URLRef> + n{ <URLProtocol> + <URLPortNumber> }n`

29. `<NumberOfURLs> ::= <Short>`

30. `<URLHostName> ::= <String>`

31. `<URLPath> ::= <String>`

32. `<URLFile> ::= <String>`

33. `<URLRef> ::= <String>`

34. `<URLProtocol> ::= <String>`

35. `<URLPortNumber> ::= <Short>`

ADB

An ADB message is used to transmit information about code units and classes without the code itself. The receiver should answer with a `<ReplyOk>` message and information about which classes are already available at the receiver's class cache. The receiver should not answer with a `<ReplyNok>` message, except if the ADB message has the wrong format.

36. `<RcADB> ::= "0x67"`

37. `<ADBParameter> ::= <NumberOfUnits`$_n$`> + <CacheUsage>` `+ <UnitDescriptions>`

38. `<NumberOfUnits> ::= <Short>`

39. `<CacheUsage> ::= [ <UseCache> | <DoNotUseCache> ]`

40. `<UseCache> ::= "0x00"`

41. `<DoNotUseCache> ::= "0x01"`

42. `<UnitDescriptions> ::= n{<UnitDescription>}n`

The ADB contains the number of units and information about each code unit. The part `<CacheUsage>` defines whether the receiver agency should check all class descriptions against the local code cache and return information about class availability. In the last rule, n is the number of units (`<NumberOfUnits>`).

Each unit and each class of an agent has a unique identifier, which is assigned during agent creation at the agent's home agency and never changed. Unit identifiers are used for downloading units, and class identifiers are used in the reply to an ADB message to give information about class availability. Each unit description has the following format:

43. `<UnitDescription> ::= <UnitId> + <ClassesDescription>` `+ <CodeBases>`

44. `<UnitId> ::= <Short>`

45. `<ClassesDescription> ::=` `<NumberOfClasses`$_n$`> + n{<ClassDescription>}n`

46. `<NumberOfClasses> ::= <Short>`

47. `<ClassDescription> ::= <ClassId> + <ClassName> + ( <Digest> )`

48. `<ClassId> ::= <Short>`

49. `<ClassName> ::= <String>`

50. `<Digest> ::= <Length`$_d$`> + d{<Byte>}d`

51. `<CodeBases> ::= <NumberOfCodeBases`$_c$`> + c{<CodeBase>}c`

52. `<NumberOfCodeBases> ::= <Short>`

53. `<CodeBase> ::= <NumberOfURLs`$_u$`> + u{<URL>}u`

54. `<URL> ::= <String>`

Each unit description consists of the identifier, the number of classes in the unit, and a list of code bases for the unit. For each class, the class identifier, the class name, and a digest (if the cache is activated) are sent. To code the list of URLs in a code base, we do not use the packed form for URLs as described above, because a list of code bases will mostly contain different addresses for which compression is not worthwhile.

If the receiver agency checks classes against its local cache, the class name and digest are used. If there is already a class with the given name for which the local digest is the same as the given digest, then it is assumed that the identical class is already available.

The ADB reply object contains the identifier for all classes that are already available at the destination agency.

55. `<ADBReplyParameter> ::= <NumberOfClasses`$_n$`> + n{ <ClassId> }n`

Unit

The unit message is used to transmit a set of code units to the receiver agency. The receiver replies whether it accepts the transmission or not. The receiver should only reject unit transmission if the message cannot be parsed because of a format error.

56. `<RcUnit> ::= "0x68"`

57. `<UnitsParameter> ::= <NumberOfUnits`$_n$`> + n{<Unit>}n`

58. `<Unit> ::= <UnitId> + <NumberOfClasses`$_c$`> + c{<Class>}c`

59. `<Class> ::= <ClassName> + <ClassCode>`

60. `<ClassCode> ::= <Length`$_m$`> + m{<Byte>}m`

A unit message contains at least one unit, and each unit is uniquely identified by a number. Each unit contains the code of at least one class. The set of classes that is transmitted for a specific unit depends on the reply of the ADB message. If the receiver already has the code for a specific class and transmits this information to the sender agency, then the sender should not send this class. As a consequence, the set of classes that is transmitted as a unit may be a subset of the classes that belong to this unit.

State

A state message is used to transmit an agent's state to the receiver agency. It consists of URLs and the serialized agent, and can include some data items. The receiver answers whether it accepts this message or not.

61. ⟨RcState⟩ ::= "0x6C"

62. ⟨StateParameter⟩ ::= ⟨MirrorAgencies⟩ + ⟨DestinationAgency⟩ + SerializedAgent + ⟨DataItems⟩ + ⟨DataItemKey⟩

63. ⟨MirrorAgencies⟩ ::= ⟨PackedURLArray⟩

64. ⟨DestinationAgency⟩ ::= ⟨String⟩

65. ⟨SerializedAgent⟩ ::= ⟨Length$_n$⟩ + n{⟨Byte⟩}n

66. ⟨DataItems⟩ ::= ⟨NumberOfDataItems$_m$⟩ + m{⟨DataItem⟩}m

67. ⟨DataItem⟩ ::= ⟨DataItemName⟩ + ⟨DataItemState⟩ + (⟨SerializedDataItem⟩)

68. ⟨NumberOfDataItems⟩ ::= ⟨Short⟩

69. ⟨DataItemName⟩ ::= ⟨String⟩

70. ⟨DataItemState⟩ ::= [⟨Defined⟩ | ⟨Undefined⟩]

71. ⟨Defined⟩ ::= "0x10"

72. ⟨Undefined⟩ ::= "0x11"

73. ⟨SerializedDataItem⟩ ::= ⟨Length$_l$⟩ + l{⟨Byte⟩}l

The part ⟨MirrorAgencies⟩ is a list of addresses of the mirror agency, if there is one. Otherwise, the number of URLs in the ⟨PackedURLArray⟩ is 0. The second part contains the address of the agency to which the transfer is directed. This address is important at the receiver agency if, for example, the agency consists of more than one place, and the name of the destination place is part of the URL. The third part is the serialized agent, which is a sequence of bytes. The last part contains data items of the external state. Each data item has a name, a state, and (optionally) the serialized object as a byte sequence. Symbol `<DataItemKey>` is defined in rule 78.

Unit Request

A unit request message is used to request units from a home, code server, or mirror agency. The receiver answers with a `<ReplyOk>` message and the requested units as a parameter. The receiver must answer with `<ReplyNok>` if there is an error.

74. `<RcUnitReq> ::= "0x69"`

75. `<UnitRequest> ::= <NumberOfUnits`$_n$`> + n{<UnitId>}n`

Symbol `<UnitId>` was already defined in rule 44. The reply message has the format defined in rule 57.

Data Item

A data item message is used to upload data items from the current agency to a home or mirror agency. The receiver answers with a `<ReplyOk>` message if the new data values are accepted, otherwise it answers with a `<ReplyNok>` message.

76. `<RcData> ::= "0x6A"`

77. `<DataParameter> ::= <DataItems> + <DataItemKey>`

78. `<DataItemKey> ::= <Length`$_n$`> + n{<Byte>}n`

Symbol `<DataItems>` was defined previously. Symbol `<DataItemKey>` is a byte sequence that contains a key necessary to upload data items.

Data Request

A data request message is used to request data items from an agent's home or mirror agency. The receiver answers with a `<ReplyOk>` message and

the requested data items as a parameter. The receiver must answer with a
⟨ReplyNok⟩ message if there is an error.

79. ⟨RcDataReq⟩ ::= "0x6B"

80. ⟨DataReqParameter⟩ ::= ⟨NumberOfDataItems$_n$⟩ + n{⟨DataItemName⟩}n

Symbol ⟨DataItemName⟩ was defined above in rule 69.

Prepare

The prepare message is sent to a receiver agency to check whether any error
has been occurred during the current transfer. The receiver agency must
answer with a ⟨ReplyOk⟩ message without parameters if it accepts the whole
transfer, and a ⟨ReplyNok⟩ message with an appropriate error message if
there is an error.

81. ⟨RcPrepare⟩ ::= "0x64"

Commit

The commit message is used to tell the receiver agency to commit all changes
made during the current transfer. The last stable state of the agent's context
can then be dropped.

82. ⟨RcCommit⟩ ::= "0x65"

The commit message is not supposed to send a valid reply message.

Rollback

The rollback message is used to tell the receiver agency to release all changes
made during the current transfer and to restore the last stable state.

83. ⟨RcRollback⟩ ::= "0x6D"

The rollback message is not supposed to send a valid reply message.

Chapter 7

Using Kalong

This chapter describes the implementation of the Kalong mobility model as the Kalong software component, which is the reference implementation of the Kalong specification. We also present some examples of program migration strategies using the Kalong software component. Finally, we show how Kalong can be extended by its own implementations, for example, by implementing mobile agent security techniques.

Contents

7.1 Introduction

We start with a brief introduction to two very important aspects of Kalong as a software component. First, Kalong in itself is not a complete mobile agent toolkit but is designed to be an independent software component for agent migration to be used with (almost) any existing mobile-agent–server architecture. Second, Kalong is designed to work as a virtual machine for the task of agent migration. Therefore, it defines a minimal set of commands or functions, which, combined, can control the entire process of agent migration as defined in the Kalong mobility model.

7.1.1 Kalong as a Software Component

As we already noted, Kalong was developed to be independent of any mobile agent toolkit. It was our target to base Kalong on very few assumptions about the environment (i.e., the mobile agent toolkit) in which Kalong can be used. Therefore, it should be usable in almost all mobile agent software architectures and has already been successfully adapted to work with the Tracy2 architecture. We plan to integrate Kalong into other toolkits, such as Jade and Semoa, in the near future.

Kalong defines four interfaces (see Fig. 7.1). On the left side of Kalong, there are two interfaces used to communicate with the agent manager. Interfaces on the right side are designed to communicate with the network adapter. Interface *IKalong* defines the functions of Kalong, whereas interface *IAgentManager* defines functions of the agent manager object used by Kalong. On the other side, interface *INetwork* defines functions of the network adapter used by Kalong, and interface *INetworkServer* defines the functions of Kalong that can be used by the network server component to be called when messages are received from the network.

Kalong can be easily adapted to any mobile agent toolkit because it is the result of reducing all requirements on a migration component to a common denominator. For example, Kalong's only requirement for mobile agents is that they be Java objects of type *Serializable*, which is at least necessary in any mobile agent toolkit to marshal an object's state.

In addition to the pure functional advantages of Kalong, its flexible migration technique, and its ability to define fine-grained migration strategies, we see a major advantage in its migration component, which provides the ability to make two different mobile agent toolkits interoperable. This usually has two distinct challenges. First, mobile agent toolkits must be able to communicate; that is, they must understand the same migration protocol. Second, mobile agents of one system must be executable at another system. The first challenge is taken on by Kalong. The second challenge must be resolved by the designer of the mobile agent toolkit. The first promising results have been reported by the Semoa research group at Fraunhofer Society in Darmstadt,

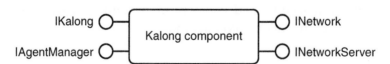

Figure 7.1 The Kalong software component and its interfaces.

Germany, who were able to adapt their toolkit to run Tracy agents [Pinsdorf and Roth, 2002].

7.1.2 Kalong as a Virtual Machine

The second aspect we want to mention here is the basic idea of Kalong as a *virtual machine* or *engine*[1] for agent migration.

Kalong provides a basic set of functions to describe the migration of a mobile agent. For example, it includes commands to define which units should be transferred, and which data items will be part of the state; it also contains commands to load code units or data items. In addition, it offers additional services, such as transaction management, security, and persistence.

With this concept of a virtual machine, it now becomes obvious how to define a *migration strategy* in detail. In the previous chapters we have always used this term to describe the effect of an agent migration, without going into a detailed definition. For example, a push strategy was defined as the action of transmitting all code units of an agent to the destination agency, together with the agent's state and all data items currently defined at the source agency. Using the commands defined in interface *IKalong* in Chapter 6, we can now provide a first impression of how a migration strategy may look.

```
 1 void sendAgent( String agentName, URL destination )
 2 {
 3   Object handle = null;
 4   String[] allDataItems = kalong.getDataItems( agentName );
 5   int[] allUnits = kalong.getUnits( agentName );
 6
 7   kalong.startTransaction( agentName );
 8   handle = kalong.openTransfer( agentName, destination );
 9   kalong.sendHeader( handle, IKalong.NOOP );
10   kalong.sendADB( handle, true );
11   kalong.sendUnits( handle, allUnits );
12   kalong.sendState( handle, allDataItems );
13   kalong.prepare( agentName );
14   kalong.commit( agentName );
15 }
```

---

1. We prefer the term *virtual machine*, although we run the risk of the Kalong virtual machine being confused with the Java virtual machine. In the following chapters, we will always refer to the Kalong virtual machine unless otherwise specified.

The migration commands of Kalong are very low level, of course. To make programming of migration strategies easier, the mobile agent toolkit can define new levels of abstraction on top of Kalong, for example, to bundle often used sequences of commands into new commands so that programming of migration strategies becomes more comfortable for the programmer. We will show the Tracy2 approach for this in Chapter 10.

7.2 Using the Kalong Component

In this chapter we give an introduction to the use of Kalong as a software component and to program migration strategies. This chapter does not contain the full documentation of all classes of the Kalong component. Some deeper introduction into the main classes and the overall design of Kalong can be found in the following section. The full documentation of all classes can be found online at *www.mobile-agents.org*.

7.2.1 Starting and Configuring Kalong

The main class of the Kalong software component is class *Kalong* in package `de.fsuj.kalong`. It has the following two constructors:

`public` *Kalong()*
Creates a new Kalong component.

`public` *Kalong(INetwork network)*
Creates a new Kalong component that uses the given *network* component.

To embed Kalong in an existing mobile agent toolkit, it must be connected to the agent manager and the network (as long as it was not done with the constructor already).

`public void` *registerNetwork(INetwork network)*
Registers a network component with this instance of Kalong.

`public void` *registerListener(IAgentManager listener)*
Registers an agent manager with this instance of Kalong.

Finally the network component must be able to inform Kalong about incoming messages. For this task, Kalong offers the interface

INetworkServer, for which Kalong already provides an implementation.
This implementation can be requested using the following method:

```
public INetworkServer getNetworkServerInterface()
```
Returns an implementation of interface *INetworkServer*.

The following method is to check whether an agent context already exists.

```
public boolean existsAgentContext( String agentName )
```
Returns **true** if an agent context with the given name already exists.

The last method is used to delete an agent context.

```
public void deleteAgentContext( String agentName )
```
Deletes an agent context locally.

When an agent context is deleted, all information about data items, object
state, and code units are removed from the current agency. Calling this
method does not kill an agent currently roaming the agent system. However, this agent can no longer use this agency for downloading data items or
code units, which might cause unexpected behavior or might even crash the
agent.

In the following example, we show how to start and configure a Kalong
instance.

```
1 package test;
2
3 import de.fsuj.kalong.Kalong;
4 import de.fsuj.kalong.IKalong;
5 import de.fsuj.kalong.Network;
6 import de.fsuj.kalong.ProtocolEngine;
7 import de.fsuj.kalong.tcp.TCPEngine;
8
9 public class StartKalong
10 {
11   public static void main( String[] args )
12   {
13     Kalong kalong = null;
14     IKalong iKalong = null;
15     Network network = null;
16     ProtocolEngine tcpProtocol = null;
17
18     kalong = new Kalong();
```

An example for a network component is also part of the Web site. The main class of this component is *Network*, which works as a manager for several network transmission protocols. Each transmission protocol must be implemented by extending class *ProtocolEngine*.

```
19    network = new Network();
20    tcpProtocol = new TCPEngine();
21    network.registerProtocolEngine( tcpProtocol );
22    tcpProtocol.startServer( 5555 );
```

Each protocol engine defines a protocol name that can be used to define URLs. For example, class *TCPEngine* defines the protocol with name "tcp". In line 22 a new thread is started that will accept incoming messages on port 5555.

Now Kalong must be connected to the network component. Because the network component is an independent software component, rather than implementing the interfaces of Kalong, it provides interfaces on its own. To allow communication between these two interfaces, we implement adapter classes. For example, for Kalong we create an adapter that implements the Kalong interface *INetwork* and accesses the network component transparently. For the other communication direction, we need another adapter class that implements an interface of the network components and directs all method invocations to Kalong. We do not print the source code of both classes here; the source code can be found on the Web site.

```
23    NetworkAdapter nAdapter = new NetworkAdapter( network );
24    KalongAdapter kAdapter = new KalongAdapter
          ( kalong.getNetworkServerInterface());
25    kalong.registerNetwork( nAdapter );
26    network.registerListener( kAdapter );
27    kalong.registerListener( new KalongListener() );
28  }
29 }
```

In line 27 we register a listener object with Kalong, which will be informed in case of received agents. This listener must implement interface *IAgentManager*; we will show an example of this listener in Section 7.2.3.

The last method of class *Kalong* is used by the agent manager to request an implementation of interface *IKalong*, which contains all functions to access an agent context and program migration strategies.

public *IKalong getKalongInterface(String agent)*throws *KalongException*
Returns an implementation of interface *IKalong*.

This interface has some minor differences compared with the one presented in the specification (Chapter 6), so we will present its definition in the following section.

7.2.2 Interface IKalong

The difference between this interface and the one defined in Chapter 6 is that it is personalized to a single agent. Whereas in the Chapter 6, almost all functions required a parameter *agentName* of type *String*, we now give the agent's name only once when obtaining the interface.

```
1  public interface IKalong
2  {
3      public static final byte NOOP = 0x00;
4      public static final byte REL_CODESERVER = 0x01;
5      public static final byte REL_MIRROR = 0x02;
6      public static final byte START_CODESERVER = 0x03;
7      public static final byte REL_MIRROR_TO_CODESERVER = 0x04;
8
9      public static final byte DATA_DEF = 0x00;
10     public static final byte DATA_UNDEF = 0x01;
11
12     // transaction management
13     public void startTransaction() throws KalongException;
14     public boolean prepare();
15     public void commit();
16     public void rollback();
17
18     // registering agents
19     public [] getHomeAgency() throws KalongException;
20     public [] getURLs() throws KalongException;
21     public void registerAgent( Serializable agentObject String agentOwner ) throws KalongException;
22     public int defineUnit( String[] classNames ) throws KalongException;
23     public String[] getClassNames() throws KalongException;
24     public String[] getClassesInUse() throws KalongException;
25     public int getClassSize( String className ) throws KalongException;
```

```
26    public String[] getLastAgency() throws KalongException;
27
28    // data items
29    public String[] getDataItems() throws KalongException;
30    public String[] getDefinedDataItems() throws KalongException;
31    public String[] getUndefinedDataItems() throws KalongException;
32    public byte getDataItemState( String dataItem ) throws KalongException;
33    public void setDataItem( String dataItem, Serializable dataObject ) throws KalongException;
34    public Serializable getDataItem( String dataItem ) throws KalongException;
35    public int getDataSize( String dataItem ) throws KalongException;
36    public void setObjectState( Serializable agentObject ) throws KalongException;
37
38    // code units and code servers
39    public int[] getUnits() throws KalongException;
40    public String[] getClassesInUnit( int id ) throws KalongException;
41    public int[] getUnitForClassName( String className ) throws KalongException;
42    public void copyUnit( int id ) throws KalongException;
43    public String[] getCodeBases( int id ) throws KalongException;
44    public void addCodeBases( int id, String[] url ) throws KalongException;
45    public void deleteCodeBase( int id, String[] url ) throws KalongException;
46    public byte[] getByteCode( String className ) throws KalongException;
47
48    // mirrors
49    public String[] getMirrorAgency() throws KalongException;
50    public void setMirrorAgency( String[] mirror ) throws KalongException;
51    public void deleteMirrorAgency() throws KalongException;
52
53    // transfers
54    public Object startTransfer( URL destination ) throws KalongException;
55    public boolean ping( Object handle, byte[] data ) throws KalongException;
56    public void sendHeader( Object handle, byte command ) throws KalongException;
57    public void sendADB( Object handle, boolean classCache ) throws KalongException;
58    public void sendUnits( Object handle, int[] unitIds ) throws KalongException;
59    public void sendUnitRequest( Object handle, int[] unitIds ) throws KalongException;
60    public void sendState( Object handle, String[] dataItems ) throws KalongException;
61    public void sendDataUpload( Object handle, String[] dataItems ) throws KalongException;
62    public void sendDataRequest( Object handle, String[] dataItems ) throws KalongException;
63 }
```

In lines 3 through 7, all valid header commands are defined, which can be used in method *sendHeader* to release a code server or mirror agency.

In lines 9 and 10 all valid states for data items are defined. A description of each method can be found in the documentation on the Web site.

7.2.3 Interface IAgentManager

During the process of receiving an agent from the network, Kalong communicates to the agent manager using interface *IAgentManager*.

```
1 public interface IAgentManager
2 {
3    public Object startInMigration();
4    public boolean receivedInMigration( Object handle, String agentName,
         String agentOwner, String [] homeAgency, String[] lastAgency );
5    public ProtectionDomain getProtectionDomain( Object handle );
6    public void startAgent( Object handle, Serializable agent,
         URL destination );
7    // ...
8 }
```

The first method is called before an SATP header is received to initialize the connection. The second method, *receivedInMigration*, is called after an SATP header is received. The agent manager now has the chance to verify whether this transfer should be accepted. It can make this decision based on the given parameters, the agent's name, the agent's home agency, and the addresses of the sender agency. If the agent manager returns a null value, the sender is informed about header rejection. Otherwise, the return value is an object, which the agent manager can use to identify this transfer in the future.

The third method, *getProtectionDomain*, is called by Kalong before the received agent is deserialized. The return value must be an object of type *ProtectionDomain*, which is a Java class from package *java.security*. A protection domain is a grouping of a code source and permissions granted to all code from this code source. Protection domains are used to specify the permissions of an agent on the current agency. It is given to the class loader, which will then assign this protection domain to all classes of the agent.

The following method creates a protection domain, which grants permission to read all files in the user's home directory.

```
1  public ProtectionDomain getProtectionDomain(Object handle)
2  {
3  // ...
4  PermissionCollection coll = new PermissionCollection();
5  coll.add( new FilePermission("${user.home}/-", "read") );
6  CodeSource cs = new CodeSource( handle.homeAgency[0], null );
7  ProtectionDomain pd = new ProtectionDomain( cs, coll );
8  return pd;
9  }
```

Finally, the fourth method, *startAgent*, is called by Kalong after the agent has been initialized. The second parameter, *agent*, contains a reference to the deserialized agent object, and the third parameter contains the URL of the migration destination. The agent manager might need this URL to dispatch the incoming agent to a specific place, whose name is stored in the URL.

In Section 7.3.3 we show other methods of this interface that can be used to sign and encrypt messages.

7.2.4 Examples to Use Interface `IKalong`

We now show how to use the Kalong component in some typical use cases.

Registering an Agent

Before an agent can migrate or use any other function of Kalong, it must be registered with the component. This is done using method *registerAgent*. The agent object must have already been initialized.

```
1 package test;
2
3 // ...
4
5 public class TestKalong
6 {
7  public static void main( String[] args )
8  {
9    Kalong kalong = new Kalong();
10   IKalong iKalong = null;
11   Runnable agent = new Agent();
```

```
12     agent.run();
13
14     // connection Kalong and the other components
15
16     try
17     {
18       iKalong = kalong.getKalongInterface( "Scaramanga" );
19       iKalong.startTransaction();
20       iKalong.registerAgent( agent );
21
22       String[] allClasses = ikalong.getClassNames();
23       String[] filterClasses = new String[] { "java.*", "javax.*", "org.xml.*" }
24       String[] agentClasses = ArrayUtils.filter( allClasses, filterClasses );
25       iKalong.defineUnit( agentClasses );
26
27     } catch( KalongException e ) {
28       e.printStackTrace();
29     }
30   }
31 }
32
```

```
1 package test;
2
3 public class Agent implements Serializable, Runnable
4 {
5   private Integer value = new Integer(100);
6
7   public void run()
8   {
9     // ...
10  }
11 }
```

As can be seen, an agent can be any object of a class that implements, at a minimum, interface *Serializable*. In this example, class *Agent* also implements interface *Runnable*; therefore, it must provide a method with name *run*. In line 18 the Kalong interface for an agent with name *Scaramanga* is requested, and in line 20 the initialized agent object is registered with Kalong. After it is registered, the given agent object is accessible under the name *Scaramanga*. Note that for sake of readability, we chose short and human-readable agent names in all examples. A real implementation must guarantee that agent names are unique in the entire agent system.

Registration allows Kalong to read the agent's class file and determine the class closure of the agent's main class. This list of class names can be requested using method *getClassNames* of the Kalong interface. In the previous example, this class list would consist of classes *test.Agent*, *java.lang.Object*, *java.lang.Integer*, *java.io.Serializable*, and *java.lang.Runnable*.

Now we must define the agent's code units. As already stated, the user of Kalong is responsible for filtering classes that are ubiquitous and that therefore do not need to migrate to other agencies. The utilities package *de.fsuj.tracy2.util* contains a class *ArrayUtils*, which provides a method for filtering class names.

> *String[] ArrayUtils.filter(String[] source, String[] pattern)*
> Returns the source parameter without Strings that match any of the given pattern.

To describe *pattern*, regular expression can be used. In lines 22 through 24 we use this method to filter out all base Java classes from the list of all agents' classes. In line 25 a single unit that contains all agent's classes is defined.

Accessing Data Items

Kalong provides functions to store data items in the agent's context. To store a data item, method *setDataItem* must be used. After a new data item is stored, it has the state *DATA_DEF*, which is a constant defined in interface *IKalong*. To retrieve a data item, method *getDataItem* must be used. A data item can be any object that is serializable.

```
1    try
2    {
3      iKalong.setDataItem( "firstDataItem", new Integer( 100 ) );
4      assert( iKalong.getDataItemState( "firstDataItem" ) == IKalong.DATA_DEF );
5
6      Integer anInteger = (Integer)iKalong.getDataItem( "firstDataItem" );
7
8      iKalong.getDataItem( "secondDataItem" );
9
10   }
11   catch( KalongException e )
12   {
13     e.printStackTrace();
14   }
```

In line 8 a data item that does not exist is requested. An exception is therefore thrown. The Kalong interface provides other methods to retrieve an array of all data item names or to determine the size of a single serialized data item. The latter can be important when deciding which data items will migrate.

Simple Migration

We now present the implementation of a simple migration. It is in fact the one that we have referred to as *push-all-to-next*, which transmits all of an agent's code and all its data to the next destination.

For the following, we assume that the agent was registered and that code units were already defined. The agent might also have stored some data items in its context. Variable *iKalong* contains a reference to the agent's Kalong interface.

```
1   try
2   {
3     URL destination = new URL( "tcp://tatjana.cs.uni-jena.de:5555" );
4     int[] unitIds = iKalong.getUnits();
5     String[] dataItems = iKalong.getDataItems();
```

Variable *destination* contains the address of the destination agency. The array of integer values with name *unitIds* contains all identifiers of the agent's code units, and the array of Strings with name *dataItems* contains the names of all data items the agent owns.

```
6     iKalong.setObjectState( agent );
7     iKalong.startTransaction();
```

In line 6 the agent object state is stored in the agent's context; the next statement starts the transaction.

```
8     Object handle = iKalong.startTransfer( destination );
9     iKalong.sendHeader( handle, IKalong.NOOP );
10    iKalong.sendADB( handle, true ); // true means to use cache
11    iKalong.sendUnits( handle, unitIds );
12    iKalong.sendState( handle, dataItems );
13  }
14  catch( Exception e )
15  {
```

```
16        e.printStackTrace();
17      }
18    finally
19    {
20      if( iKalong.prepare() )
21      {
22        iKalong.commit();
23      } else
24      {
25        iKalong.rollback();
26      }
27    }
```

This migration strategy consists of a single transfer. The connection to the destination agency is opened using method *startTransfer*. The return value is an object that is used to identify this transfer when sending additional messages. The first message that is sent now must be an SATP header, which transmits the agent's name and some other important information about the agent to the destination agency. The second parameter of this method is the *header command,* which specifies which process will be executed at the end of this transfer at the destination agency. In this case, *NOOP* stands for no operation.

In the following the agent definition block is sent. The second parameter of method *sendADB* defines whether the remote agency should check for classes that are already available and reply this information. Then all units and the state, as well as all data items, are sent. Finally, the entire transaction is prepared and then committed or rolled back.

7.2.5 Push Agent Class and Load Other Classes

The migration strategy of pushing main agent classes and loading other classes assumes that a single code unit was defined for each class and that only the main agent class is transmitted to the next destination, whereas all other classes are loaded dynamically during runtime from the agent's home server.

```
1    try
2    {
3      URL destination = new URL( "tcp://tatjana.cs.uni-jena.de:5555" );
4      String[] dataItems = iKalong.getDefinedDataItems();
```

```
 5
 6          iKalong.setObjectState( agent );
 7          iKalong.startTransaction();
 8
 9          String agentClassName = agent.getClass().getName();
10          int[] unitIds = iKalong.getUnitForClassName(agentClassName);
11
12          Object handle = iKalong.startTransfer( destination );
13          iKalong.sendHeader( handle, IKalong.NOOP );
14          iKalong.sendADB( handle, true ); // true means to use cache
15          iKalong.sendUnits( handle, new int [] { unitIds[0] } );
16          iKalong.sendState( handle, dataItems );
17        }
18    catch( Exception e )
19    {
20        e.printStackTrace();
21    }
22    finally
23    {
24        if( iKalong.prepare() )
25        {
26         iKalong.commit();
27        } else
28        {
29         iKalong.rollback();
30        }
31    }
```

In line 9 the class name of the agent's main class is determined, and in the following line the corresponding code unit that contains this class is requested. This implementation must be extended if the agent itself extends other classes or interfaces. In line 12 the migration process is started and the first unit that contains the agent's base class is selected for transmission.

Loading Data Items from the Home Agency

The following example shows how to download a single data item from the agent's home agency.

```
1    try
2    {
3        URL homeAgency = new URL(iKalong.getHomeAgency()[0]);
```

```
4        String[] dataItemsToLoad = new String[] { "secondDataItem" };
5
6        iKalong.startTransaction();
7
8        Object handle = iKalong.startTransfer( homeAgency );
9        iKalong.sendHeader( handle, IKalong.NOOP );
10       iKalong.sendDataRequest( handle, dataItemsToLoad );
11
12       Integer second = (Integer)iKalong.getDataItem( "secondDataItem" );
13     }
14   catch( Exception e )
15   {
16     e.printStackTrace();
17   }
18   finally
19   {
20     if( iKalong.prepare() )
21     {
22       iKalong.commit();
23     } else
24     {
25       iKalong.rollback();
26     }
27   }
```

The addresses of the agent's home agency can be obtained by calling method *getHomeAgency*. If the home agency is accessible through different network protocols, the returned array contains more than one URL. As a simplification, we chose the first address by default. The name of the data item to load is defined in line 4, and the request to load a data item is sent in line 10. Immediately after this method terminates, the data item is available using method *getDataItem*.

When a data item is loaded, its state is set to *DATA_UNDEF* at the agent's home agency and to *DATA_DEF* at the current agency. If the same data item were to be loaded again from the home agency, the transfer would not be successful and an exception would be thrown locally.

Uploading a Data Item and Migrating to the Next Destination

The next example shows how to handle more than one transfer during a single transaction. The task is to migrate to agency *tatjana.cs.uni-jena.de* but not carry the data item with the name *firstDataItem*. Instead, it is uploaded to the agent's home agency beforehand.

```
1    try
2    {
3      URL destination = new URL( "tcp://tatjana.cs.uni-jena.de:5555" );
4      URL homeAgency = new URL(iKalong.getHomeAgency()[0]);
5      String[] dataItemsToUpload = new String[] { "firstDataItem" };
6
7      iKalong.startTransaction();
8
9      Object handleHome = iKalong.startTransfer( homeAgency );
10     iKalong.sendHeader( handleHome, IKalong.NOOP );
11     iKalong.sendDataUpload( handleHome, dataItemsToUpload );
12
13     Object handleDest = iKalong.startTransfer( destination );
14     iKalong.sendHeader( handleDest, IKalong.NOOP );
15     iKalong.sendADB( handleDest, true ); // true means to use cache
16     iKalong.sendState( handleDest, null );
17   }
18   catch( Exception e )
19   {
20     e.printStackTrace();
21   }
22   finally
23   {
24     if( iKalong.prepare() )
25     {
26       iKalong.commit();
27     } else
28     {
29       iKalong.rollback();
30     }
31   }
```

The type of migration used to transmit the agent to the destination agency is comparable to a *pull* strategy, because no code units are sent.

Defining Code Servers and a Mirror Agency

The next example shows how to make the current agency become a code server agency. The goal is that after the next migration, all code units will remain at the current agency and be downloadable from this agency later.

```
1      try
2      {
3        int[] unitIds = iKalong.getUnits();
4
5        for( int i=0; i<unitIds.length; i++ )
6        {
7          iKalong.copyUnit( unitIds[i] );
8        }
9      }
10     catch( Exception e )
11     {
12       e.printStackTrace();
13     }
```

The important statement is in line 7, where the unit with the given identifier is marked not to be deleted after the next migration. With this method, the addresses of the current agency are added to the list of code bases of the unit.

To define a mirror agency is only slightly more complicated. A mirror agency, by definition, must hold all data items and all code units. Therefore, before a mirror agency can be activated, the agent manager must load all missing data items and code units. Kalong does not provide a method for this.

We assume a situation in which no mirror agency is currently defined. If this is not the case, it would be necessary to release the current mirror agency first.

```
1      try
2      {
3        URL homeAgency = new URL(iKalong.getHomeAgency()[0]);
4        String[] dataItemsToLoad = iKalong.getUndefinedDataItems();
5        int[] unitsToLoad = iKalong.getUndefinedUnits();
6
7        iKalong.startTransaction();
8        Object handleHome = iKalong.startTransfer( homeAgency );
9        iKalong.sendHeader( handleHome, IKalong.NOOP );
10       iKalong.sendDataRequest( handleHome, dataItemsToLoad );
11       iKalong.sendUnitRequest( handleHome, unitsToLoad );
12     }
13     catch( Exception e )
14     {
15       e.printStackTrace();
16     }
```

```
17    finally
18    {
19      if( iKalong.prepare() )
20      {
21        iKalong.commit();
22      } else
23      {
24        iKalong.rollback();
25      }
26    }
27
28  iKalong.setMirrorAgency();
```

In line 28 the current agency is defined to be a mirror agency from this point on.

Release a Code Server or Mirror Agency

Now we can show an example of how to release a remote code server or mirror agency by sending a header command. Releasing code servers is an important task for freeing resources at the other agencies that currently hold a copy of the agent's code. Releasing mirror agencies is necessary for defining a new mirror, as mentioned previously.

Following is an example of how to release a code server.

```
1   try
2   {
3     URL codeServerToRelease = new URL("tcp://tatjana.cs.uni-jena.de:5555");
4
5     iKalong.startTransaction();
6
7     Object handle = iKalong.startTransfer( codeServerToRelease );
8     iKalong.sendHeader( handle, IKalong.REL_CODESERVER );
9
10    int[] allUnits = iKalong.getUnits();
11    String[] deleteCodeBase = new String[].toString()} codeServerToRelease {;
12    for( int i=0; i<allUnits.length; i++ )
13    {
14      iKalong.deleteCodeBase( allUnits[i], deleteCodeBase );
15    }
16  }
17  catch( Exception e )
```

```
18        {
19          e.printStackTrace();
20        }
21        finally
22        {
23          if( iKalong.prepare() )
24          {
25            iKalong.commit();
26          } else
27          {
28            iKalong.rollback();
29          }
30        }
```

To simplify the code, we assume that we know the address of the code server that should be released. This address must be obtained from the agent's context using, for example, method *getCodeBases*, which returns all known code bases for a given unit. To release a code server is defined as a header command in line 8. No additional messages need to be sent to the destination in this case. After the transfer, the code server must be deleted from the list of code bases of all units. This is done in lines 10 through 15.

If a mirror agency is to be released, the header command must be changed to *REL_MIRROR* and finally method *deleteMirrorAgency* must be called.

7.3 Extending Kalong

In the previous sections we presented the basic Kalong migration protocol and its reference implementation as a Kalong software component. The main advantage of Kalong is that it provides a new optimized migration technique, which allows the programmer of mobile agents to describe a migration strategy in a very fine-grained way. We gave examples to illustrate how migration strategies can be implemented. In Chapter 8, we will present results of several real-world performance measurements.

As we have mentioned several times, Kalong was designed to work with many, if not all, mobile agent toolkits. We introduced the Kalong migration component as a virtual machine for agent migration. It provides a minimal set of functions or commands to describe a migration strategy. Because the focus of Kalong is on migration optimization, it does not, for example, provide any means for the problem of mobile agent security.

Therefore, we present a technique to extend the basic Kalong protocol. We show that the Kalong specification defines only the common portions of a protocol family and that the Kalong software component offers a way to define new migration protocols on the basis of Kalong. With this technique, it is possible to add security to Kalong in a very modular way.

In this section we present a technique to extend the basic Kalong migration protocol as defined in Chapter 6. The extension mechanism is a powerful technique to complement Kalong with other services related to agent migration. For example, the extension mechanism allows for compression of each SATP message before Kalong sends it to the destination agency or inspection of each incoming class code to detect malicious agents[2]. The extension mechanism defines some selected points where a user of a Kalong component can modify the structure of each SATP message. It is *not* possible to define *new* SATP message types, but each SATP message can be modified before it is sent to the destination and immediately after it is received at the destination platform. We now describe the interface of the extension mechanism. We then present some examples of how this technique can be used to supplement Kalong and provide solutions for some selected security problems of mobile agents.

7.3.1 The Kalong Extension Interface

The extension mechanism of Kalong consists of a single interface, *IAgentManager*, defined in package *de.fsuj.kalong*. It defines methods that are called by Kalong during the process of an in- or out-migration. For the following we denote the central component of an agency that controls agent execution as the *agent manager*. An instance of interface *IAgentManager* is part of the agent manager and must be registered after starting the Kalong component using method *registerListener*, as described in Section 7.2.1. Without this listener, Kalong does not accept in-migrations and cannot start any out-migration.

By registering a listener object, the agent manager is able to modify the structure of each SATP message. To distinguish such a new migration protocol from the basic Kalong migration protocol, each listener must define a *vendor*

---

2. A malicious agent is one that tries to pilfer information from its host environment or tries to damage its host through so-called denial-of-service attacks. We give further of examples of malicious agents in Chapter 5.

name and a *version* in the form of a *major* and *minor* number. As already defined, a migration can be successful only if both the sender and receiver agency support the same protocol.

The following methods must be implemented by the agent manager to define the new migration protocol version information.

```
public String getProtocolName()
```
Returns the name of the protocol.

```
public String getVendorName()
```
Returns the protocol vendor name.

```
public byte getMajorVersion()
```
Returns the protocol major version number.

```
public byte getMinorVersion()
```
Returns the protocol minor version number.

The general communication protocol between Kalong and its listener is that Kalong first informs the listener about the beginning of a migration process (either in- or out-migration). The listener must return a so-called handle object to identify this migration process later. This handle object must be given as the first parameter in all other methods.

```
public Object startOutMigration( String agentName,
  URL destination )
```
An out-migration has been started. The method must return an object by which this transfer can be identified later.

At a destination agency, Kalong calls the following method immediately after it has accepted a network connection from a sender agency.

```
public Object startInMigration()
```
An in-migration has been started. The method must return an object by which this transfer can be identified later.

Methods *codeMessage* and *decodeMessage* are used to code and decode messages or parts of messages. Note that a listener must always implement both variants. If it provides a method to *code* a message, for example, there must also be an analogous method to later *decode* it.

The following method is called whenever Kalong is going to send an SATP message to the destination agency. This is not only the case during out-migrations, because all reply messages are coded using this method as well. Thus, for example, if a sender agency has requested a unit for downloading, the destination agency calls this method to code the real unit transfer. The listener can modify this message, for example, by compressing it or signing it digitally. During this process the listener might need more information about the agent, so a parameter *context* is given, which provides the listener with access to some important methods of the agent's context object.

```
public byte[] codeMessage( Object handle, byte messageType,
byte[] message, IContext context ) throws KalongException
```
Codes an SATP message that is given in parameter *message* and returns it.

The corresponding method that is called after receiving an SATP message is:

```
public byte[] decodeMessage( Object handle, byte messageType,
byte[] coded, IContext context ) throws KalongException
```
Decodes a received message that is given as parameter *coded*.

The type of message is given as parameter *messageType*. Interface *IContext* defines constant values for all SATP message types.

The next pair of methods is called to code and decode class codes. Parameter *classCode* contains the original byte code of the class with name *className*.

```
public byte[] codeClassCode( Object handle, String className,
byte[] classCode ) throws KalongException
```
Codes the given class that is given as Java byte code.

The corresponding method to decode a class is as follows:

```
public byte[] decodeClassCode( Object handle, String className,
byte[] codedClass ) throws KalongException
```
Decodes the given class code and returns a valid Java byte code.

This method must return the original byte code of the class with name *className* so that it can be loaded and defined by a Java class loader object.

The next two methods are used to code and decode the serialized object state of an agent.

```
public byte[] codeObjectState( Object handle, byte[] state )
throws KalongException
```
Codes the agent's object state.

```
public byte[] decodeObjectState( Object handle, byte[]
codedstate ) throws KalongException
```
Decodes the agent's object state.

The last method must return a byte sequence that can be deserialized using the standard Java deserialization mechanism.

The next three methods are called only during an in-migration. The first one is called by Kalong after a *Header* message is received. The purpose of this method is to decide whether the migration request should be accepted. The listener can use all information that was received along the *Header* message.

```
public boolean receivedInMigration( Object handle, String
agentName, String[] homeAgency, String[] lastAgency )
```
Decides whether an in-migration for this agent is allowed.

The method must return true if the migration request is accepted; otherwise, it returns false. In many cases the given information about the agent's home agency and the agency from which the agent came is not sufficient to make a qualified decision. However, this is the only information that is sent as part of an SATP header. If more information is needed (e.g., certificates of the agent's owner), these must be added to the SATP header message using methods *codeMessage* and *decodeMessage*.

The purpose of the last two methods was already explained in Section 7.2.3.

```
public ProtectionDomain getProtectionDomain( Object handle )
```
This method is called when Kalong deserializes a received agent. The returned protection domain defines the permissions of this agent.

```
public void startAgent( Object handle, Serializable agent,
URL destination )
```
The given agent was successfully deserialized and must now be started by the agent manager.

7.3.2 A First Example: Compression of All SATP Messages

To give an impression of the range of application of Kalong's extension mechanism, we present an example in which each SATP message is compressed before it is sent to the remote agency.

The following example shows parts of the source code of class *ZIPAgentManager* that implements message compression using standard Java techniques provided by classes *GZIPInputStream* and *GZIPOutputStream*, defined in package *java.util.zip*. Implementing message compression is very easy, because the listener must implement only two methods to code and decode SATP messages: *codeMessage* and *decodeMessage*. All other methods to code and decode object states or Java classes immediately return the given information unchanged.

```
1  public class ZIPAgentManager implements IAgentManager
2  {
3      public String getVendorName()
4      {
5          return "TRACYZIP";
6      }
7
8      public byte getMajorVersion()
9      {
10         return 0x01;
11     }
12
13     public byte getMinorVersion()
14     {
15         return 0x00;
16     }
17
18     public byte[] codeMessage(Object handle, byte messageType, byte[] raw,
           IContext context) throws KalongException
19     {
20         try
21         {
22             ByteBuffer bb = new ByteBufferList();
23             bb.putInt( raw.length );
24
25             ByteArrayOutputStream baos = new ByteArrayOutputStream();
26             GZIPOutputStream zos = new GZIPOutputStream( baos );
27             zos.write( raw, 0, raw.length );
28             zos.close();
29
30             bb.putBytesWithLength( baos.toByteArray() );
31             return bb.toByteArray();
32
33         } catch( Exception e )
34         {
```

```
35                throw new KalongException( e );
36            }
37        }
38
39    public byte[] decodeMessage(Object handle, byte messageType, byte[] coded,
          IContext context) throws KalongException
40    {
41        try
42        {
43            ByteBuffer bb = new ByteBufferList( coded );
44            int length = bb.getInt();
45
46            byte[] zipped = bb.getBytesWithLength();
47            byte[] unzipped = new byte[ length ];
48
49            ByteArrayInputStream bais = new ByteArrayInputStream( zipped );
50            GZIPInputStream zis = new GZIPInputStream( bais );
51
52            int pos = 0;
53            do
54            {
55                pos += zis.read( unzipped, pos, length-pos );
56            } while( pos < length );
57            zis.close();
58
59            return unzipped;
60        } catch( Exception e )
61        {
62            throw new KalongException( e );
63        }
64    }
65
66    public byte[] codeObjectState(Object handle, byte[] state) throws
          KalongException
67    {
68        return state;
69    }
70
71    public byte[] decodeObjectState(Object handle, byte[] codedstate)
          throws KalongException
72    {
73        return codedstate;
74    }
75
```

```
76    public byte[] codeClassCode(Object handle, String name,
          byte[] classCode) throws KalongException
77    {
78        return classCode;
79    }
80
81    public byte[] decodeClassCode(Object handle, String name,
          byte[] codedClass) throws KalongException
82    {
83        return codedClass;
84    }
85
86    // some methods are missing
87 }
```

Both methods work regardless of the message type all SATP messages will be compressed. The original message is written to an instance of class *GZIPOutputStream*, which itself uses an instance of class *ByteArrayOutputStream* to store the compressed data. The format of the compressed message consists of a four-byte integer that contains the length of the original message, followed by a byte array that contains the compressed message. To create this message format, we use class *ByteBuffer*, which is part of the Tracy project and defined in package *de.fsuj.tracy.util*. It provides several methods to code Java's primitive data types into flat byte arrays. Decoding a compressed message is very straightforward. The message is given to an instance of class *GZIPInputStream*, from which the inflated data is read until all bytes are received. Finally, the original message is returned to Kalong.

Because this example gives only a first impression of how to use this interface, we do not show the implementation used to verify an incoming agent or to start one.

7.3.3 How to Implement Security Solutions with Kalong

In this section we show how Kalong's extension mechanism can be used to implement some simple security solutions.

Class Code Filtering

Code filtering is used to inspect incoming classes and to check whether they implement code fragments considered malicious. An example for this was presented earlier. When an agent implements method *finalize*, it might attack the garbage collector thread.

Class code filtering can be implemented using the Kalong extension mechanism. Whenever Kalong receives a code unit, it calls method *decodeClass* of the Kalong listener object for each class. This method gets the class name and the class byte code, as it was received from the network, as parameters. It must return a valid Java byte code for this class. For the following we assume that no other class coding is implemented, meaning that parameter *codedClass* already contains valid Java byte code, which is inspected only within this method.

```
1  public class FilterAgentManager implements IAgentManager
2
3  // ...
4
5  public byte[] decodeClass(String name, byte[] codedClass) throws
       KalongException
6  {
7    filterClass( name, codedClass );
8    return codedClass;
9  }
10
11 void filterClass(String name, byte[] bytecode) throws KalongException
12 {
13   try
14   {
15     ClassFileStructure cfs = new ClassFileParser(new
           BycalDataInputStream(new ByteArrayInputStream(bytecode)))
           .parseClassFile();
16     ClassStructure cs = new ClassStructure(cfs);
17     Method fin = cs.getMethod("finalize()");
18
19     if(fin != null)
20     {
21       throw new KalongException("class has a finalize method");
22     }
23   } catch(IOException e)
24   {
25     throw new KalongException("class code cannot be analyzed and is,
           therefore, not accepted");
26   } catch(AccessFlags_Exception f)
27   {
```

```
28      throw new KalongException("class code cannot be analyzed and is,
           therefore, not accepted");
29    }
30  }
31 }
```

Method *decodeClass* calls method *filterCode* and returns the byte code as it was received if the byte code filter did not find any malicious code. Otherwise, this method throws an exception with an appropriate error message, which is sent back to the sender agency.

Method *filterClass* uses the ByCAl tool, which was developed as part of the Tracy project to analyze Java classes on the level of byte code. The class file is read using class *ClassFileStructure* and analyzed using class *ClassStructure*. The latter class provides a method to check whether a method with a given name exists (*getMethod*). If a method with name *finalize* is found, it throws an exception; otherwise, it returns silently.

Agent Authentication

Agent authentication can be done by verifying a digital signature of the agent's owner or the last agency the agent came from. Digitally signing with the agent's owner private key can be done only at the agent's home agency. Therefore, only the immutable or static part of an agent can be digitally signed. All mutable data, such as the agent's object state or data items of the external state, cannot be signed with the owner's key.

We show an example in which the static parts of an SATP header message, which consist of the agent's name and its home agency, are digitally signed at the agent's home agency. At each host the agent visits, this signature is verified against the owner's public key.

Signing a header message can be implemented using method *codeMessage* of interface *IAgentManager*. This method is called by Kalong whenever an SATP message is to be sent to a destination agency. The message type is given as parameter *messageType*. The header as it was created by Kalong is given as a parameter *message*.

```
1 public class SigningAgentManager implements IAgentManager
2 {
3   // ...
4
```

```
5  public byte[] codeMessage(byte messageType, byte[] message,
       IContext context) throws KalongException
6  {
7    if(messageType == IContext.HEADER)
8    {
9      if(agentCertificate != null)
10     {
11       try
12       {
13         byte[] codedAgentCertificate = agentCertificate.getEncoded();
14
15         ByteBuffer bb = new ByteBufferList();
16         bb.putBytesWithLength(codedAgentCertificate);
17         bb.putBytesWithLength(message);
18
19         if(agentNameSignature == null)
20         {
21           ByteBuffer buffer4sig = new ByteBufferList();
22           buffer4sig.putString(context.getAgentName()).putURLArray(context.
                 getHomeAgency());
23           agentNameSignature = signBytes(signEngine, agentPrivateKey,
                 buffer4sig.toByteArray());
24         }
25
26         bb.putBytesWithLength(agentNameSignature);
27         return bb.toByteArray();
28
29       } catch(Exception f)
30       {
31         f.printStackTrace();
32         return null;
33       }
34     } else
35     {
36       return null;
37     }
38   } else
39   {
40     return message;
41   }
42 }
43 }
```

This code excerpt does not show how to obtain certificates or private keys from a local *keystore* file, because this is done using fundamental Java security mechanisms. We assume that variable *agentCertificate* contains the agent owner's certificate and that *agentPrivateKey* already contains the private key of the agent's owner. For the sake of simplicity, we send the agent owner's certificate as part of the header message too. In real applications, only the distinguished name of this certificate would be part of the header, and the destination agency would have to load the certificate from a public key server.

This method creates a new header message that consists of three parts: (1) the owner's certificate (line 16), (2) the original header message (line 17), and (3) the digital signature (line 26). The conditional in line 19 decides whether the agent's signature must be created (because the current agency is the home agency) or can be reused. In the latter case, variable *agentNameSignature* already contains the agent's signature. Otherwise, the agent's name and its home agency URLs are signed in line 23. To verify a signature, the destination agency must implement method *decodeMessage* of interface *IAgentManager*, as shown in the following excerpt.

```
1   public byte[] decodeMessage(byte messageType, byte[] message,
       IContext context) throws KalongException
2   {
3     if(messageType == IContext.HEADER)
4     {
5       ByteBuffer bb = new ByteBufferList(message);
6       byte[] codedAgentCertificate = bb.getBytesWithLength();
7       byte[] msg = bb.getBytesWithLength();
8       agentNameSignature = bb.getBytesWithLength();
9
10      try
11      {
12        CertificateFactory cf = CertificateFactory.getInstance("X509");
13        ByteArrayInputStream bais1 = new ByteArrayInputStream
              (codedAgentCertificate);
14        agentCertificate = (X509Certificate) cf.generateCertificate(bais1);
15        agentPublicKey = agentCertificate.getPublicKey();
16
17      } catch(Exception e)
18      {
19        agentCertificate = null;
20        agentPublicKey = null;
21        remoteAgencyCertificate = null;
22        remoteAgencyPublicKey = null;
23      }
24
```

```
25      return msg;
26   } else
27   {
28      return message;
29   }
30 }
```

First, the header message is split into the three components: certificate, original header message, and digital signature (lines 6 through 8). The owner's certificate is then initialized, and the owner's public key is requested (lines 12 through 15).

The process of verifying the digital signature is done in another method, when the header message is checked to decide whether an agent will be accepted.

```
1  public boolean validateHeader(String agentName, URL[] homeAgency, URL[]
        lastAgency)
2  {
3    try
4    {
5      if( keystore.getCertificateAlias(agentCertificate) == null )
6      {
7        return false;
8      } else
9      {
10         ByteBuffer buffer4sig = new ByteBufferList();
11         buffer4sig.putString(agentName).putURLArray(homeAgency);
12         return verifySignature(signEngine, agentPublicKey,
               buffer4sig.toByteArray(), agentNameSignature);
13       }
14   } catch(Exception e)
15   {
16     e.printStackTrace();
17     return false;
18   }
19 }
```

First, it is checked for whether the owner's certificate is trusted (line 5); next (line 12), the signature is verified. Using the same technique, it is possible to sign all classes using the owner's public key and to verify their integrity.

Read-Only Data Items

The next two examples focus on protecting data items against illegal modifications or illegal access. This service can also be implemented using the extension mechanism of Kalong, but we provide a version that implements an adapter to access the main Kalong interface. This adapter is called MDL, and it allows agents to access data items of their external state and some of the other information provided by Kalong. The general concept is that agents can use not only the two methods *setDataItem* and *getDataItem* as defined in interface *IKalong*, but also two new methods, *setReadOnlyDataItem* and *setEncryptedDataItem*.

Following is the code to sign a data item. We assume that the agent has already defined the keystore alias of its owner in variable *alias* and the keystore password in variable *password*.

```
1  public void setReadOnlyDataItem(String name, Serializable value) throws MDLException
2  {
3    String alias = null;
4    char[] password = null;
5    SignedObject signedObject = null;
6
7    // request of owner's alias and password is not shown here
8
9    try
10   {
11     priKey = (PrivateKey) keystore.getKey( alias, password );
12     signedObject = new SignedObject( value, priKey, signEngine );
13   } catch( Exception e )
14   {
15     throw new MDLException( e );
16   }
17
18   setDataItem( name, signedObject );
19 }
```

The owner's private key is read from the keystore file in line 11, and the data item is encapsulated together with its signature by an object of class *SignedObject*, which automatically signs the data item in line 18.

When the data item is accessed using method *getDataItem*, it must be checked for what type the data item is. If the data item is an object that is an instance of *SignedObject*, then the signature is verified and the data value returned to the caller. The following source code shows how to access Kalong to read a data item with name *name* (line 13). In line 23 it is determined whether the data item is of type *SignedObject*. We assume that variable *pubKey* is defined outside this method and already contains the public key of the agent's owner. Finally, in line 29 the object is verified and the original data item returned to the caller in line 42.

```
1   public Serializable getDataItem(String name) throws MDLException
2   {
3     Serializable dataValue = null;
4     SignedObject signedObject = null;
5     boolean dataVerified = false;
6
7     /*
8      * Read the data item from the external state.
9      */
10    try
11    {
12      kalongInterface.startTransaction();
13      dataValue = kalongInterface.getDataItem(name);
14    } catch(Exception e)
15    {
16      throw new MDLException(e.getMessage());
17    } finally
18    {
19      kalongInterface.prepare();
20      kalongInterface.commit();
21    }
22
23    if( dataValue instanceof SignedObject )
24    {
25      signedObject = (SignedObject)dataValue;
26
27      try
28      {
29        dataVerified = signedObject.verify( pubKey, signEngine );
30      } catch( Exception e )
31      {
32        throw new MDLException( "signed data item cannot be verified due to:
               " + e.getMessage() );
33      }
34
35      if( ! dataVerified )
```

```
36        {
37            throw new MDLException( "signed data item was tampered with" );
38        }
39
40        try
41        {
42            return (Serializable)signedObject.getObject();
43        } catch( Exception e )
44        {
45            throw new MDLException( e );
46        }
47    }
48
49    // ...
50  }
```

Protect Data Items for a Target Agency

Finally, we present the code to encrypt a data item so that it can be read only at a single target agency. The agent calls this method to store a data item under the given name, which is encrypted with the public key of the agency whose local keystore alias is given in parameter *targetAlias*.

Data encryption is done in Java using objects of class *Cipher*, and we assume that an object with name *rsaCipher* has been initialized to use asymmetric RSA encryption. In line 9 the cipher is initialized for *encryption* using the public key of the target agency, which is obtained from the local keystore file. Data encryption works using the same technique as described for a signed object. We use an object of type *SealedObject*, which serializes the data item and encrypts it using the given cipher object (line 10). Finally, this object is stored in the agent's external data state (line 17).

```
1  public void setEncryptedDataItem(String name, Serializable value,
       String targetAlias) throws MDLException
2  {
3    SealedObject sealedObject = null;
4    PublicKey targetPublicKey = null;
5
6    try
7    {
8      targetPublicKey = keystore.getCertificate( targetAlias ).getPublicKey();
9      rsaCipher.init( Cipher.ENCRYPT_MODE, targetPublicKey );
10     sealedObject = new SealedObject( value, rsaCipher );
11   } catch( Exception e )
```

```
12   {
13     e.printStackTrace();
14     throw new MDLException( e );
15   }
16
17   setDataItem( name, sealedObject );
18 }
```

Data decryption is implemented in method *getDataItem*. In addition to the source code presented earlier, we show here what must be done when the data item is of type *SealedObject*.

```
1  public Serializable getDataItem(String name) throws
       MDLException
2  {
3
4    // ...
5
6    } else if( dataValue instanceof SealedObject )
7    {
8      try
9      {
10       rsaCipher.init( Cipher.DECRYPT_MODE, agencyPrivateKey );
11       return (Serializable)((SealedObject)dataValue).getObject( rsaCipher );
12     } catch( Exception e )
13     {
14       throw new MDLException( "data item cannot be decrypted
             due to: " + e.getMessage() );
15     }
16   } else
17
18   // ...
19
20 }
```

In line 10 the cipher object is initialized for *decryption* using the private key of the current agency. Finally, in line 11 the object is decrypted and returned to the caller.

Summary

In this chapter we introduced the Kalong software component, which is the reference implementation of the Kalong mobility model. The main advantages of the Kalong software component are:

- Kalong can be seen as a virtual machine for agent migration. It provides generalized low-level functions that can be used to control the migration process of a mobile agent in a very fine-grained way.

- The Kalong software component is independent of any mobile agent toolkit. It does not rely on specific design issues made by the mobile agent toolkit and should therefore be usable in almost any mobile agent toolkit.

- The Kalong software component is extendable in as much as it defines several points in the migration process where the agent manager is called to modify or extend the structure of each SATP message. We have shown how basic security protocols can be implemented using the extension mechanism of Kalong.

We have presented a few examples to give an impression of how migration strategies can be implemented. For a complete overview of all migration strategies, refer to Section 10.5.5.

Chapter 8

Evaluation

In this chapter we examine several series of measurements to demonstrate the performance of our new migration component, Kalong. Our goal is to give some impression how fast (or slow) migration can be in Java-based mobile agent toolkits, and how different parameters (e.g., code size, network quality, code compression, and security enhancements) influence the migration performance. Finally, we show the effect of the new features of Kalong, which provide the ability to send data items back to the agent's home agency, load code from a code server instead of from the home agency, and the effect of mirror agencies.

Contents

Our performance experiments are a first step toward a comprehensive performance analysis of the migration process of mobile agents as a whole. Because of some restrictions in the availability of network nodes and the variation in network qualities, we had to limit our experiments in the following aspects:

- We only recognize the Kalong migration component as part of a very simple mobile agent toolkit, which is not as complex as Tracy. We do not compare our results to other mobile agent toolkits, because there is not yet a benchmark suite for mobile agents (e.g., in the form of several mobile agents that perform specific migrations). Therefore, we developed our own mobile agents tailored to show the specific advantages of Kalong.

- We only measure the performance of mobile agents and do not compare it to the client-server approach. Kalong only provides a framework to attack the performance bottleneck problem of mobile agents, so it does not make sense to compare client-server approaches with Kalong at this early stage. We are currently working on approaches for sophisticated migration strategies to solve this problem.

- We only measure migration times and do not assess the performance of an entire agent system. The agents that we used in the experiments do not produce load on each visited agency.

- We only measure the time for a single mobile agent. We have no data to predict how Kalong's performance will change with a higher number of agents that migrate in parallel.

- We only have a few network nodes available, especially in the wide-area network, so we could not study how migration times increase in real-world applications.

8.1 Related Work

8.1.1 Performance Evaluation of Existing Mobile Agent Toolkits

As far as we know, only two toolkits have ever been explored concerning migration performance. First, Gray [1997b] proposes some performance evaluations in his thesis on the AgentTCL toolkit (which was later renamed in D'Agents). The AgentTCL toolkit provides some basic functions for a flexible and secure mobile agent toolkit. Gray's results for migration times show long delays because of the slow TCL script interpreter and the migration protocol overhead.

Second, the Tacoma toolkit was evaluated by Johansen et al. [1997]. Tacoma is also a non-Java–based mobile agent toolkit. The authors give values for the migration time of one agent from its current server to a remote server, including time for serializing and deserializing, creating and initiating, as well as sending an acknowledgement message.

We are not aware of any broad analysis of performance aspects of a Java-based mobile agent toolkit. For a discussion of the scalability of the Jade toolkit, see Korba and Song [2002].

8.1.2 Performance Comparison of Mobile Agent Toolkits

Some work has been done to compare existing mobile agent toolkits. Dikaiakos and Samaras [2000] define some *micro-benchmarks* to assess a mobile agent toolkit (e.g., one to capture the overhead of local agent creation or one to capture the overhead of point-to-point messaging). Silva et al. [2000] compare eight mobile agent toolkits using twelve experiments. Their results show the influence of several factors (e.g., the number of agent servers to visit on one tour, the influence of the agent's size, and the influence of class caching) on the performance of mobile agents. In our opinion, different mobile agent toolkits cannot be compared without taking some fundamental design issues of each system into account. Unfortunately, Silva et al. did not consider the different security strategies, different migration and transmission strategies, and other differences in each toolkit's implementation.

8.2 Methodology

8.2.1 Experiments and Measurements

We conducted eight different experiments; for each experiment the migration time for a specific mobile agent in a specific environment was measured. Each experiment consisted of several measurements for which the same agent was started several times. Agents used in different measurements varied (e.g., in code size or in the number of servers to be visited).

To conduct these experiments, we developed a simple mobile agent toolkit. The main function of this agency is to start agents, to measure the migration time for each agent, to compute statistical information (mean value and confidence interval) for a measurement, and to generate a file that contains all the results of the experiment.

In each experiment we distinguish two roles for the computers involved. The computer on which all agents are started is the *master*, all computers that are only visited by the agents are called *clients*.

For each experiment the Java virtual machine must be restarted. When the agency is started it is parameterized with the name of the experiment to start. It then starts all the measurements sequentially. As already stated, the only information we are interested in is the time an agent needs for a migration.

To measure the time for a single migration of a mobile agent, we have to consider the period of time from the initiation of the migration process (go-statement) to the point when the agent is restarted at the destination server. Because of the lack of a global time in a distributed system, we cannot simply compare time stamps originating from different computer systems. Therefore, we always consider at least two migrations: the first one to the destination server and the second one back to the origin—we call this a *ping-pong migration*. Therefore, printed times are never those for a single migration but always for a complete round trip, which usually consists of only two computers, but in some cases includes as many as seven computers. As a consequence, the measured migration times not only consist of the pure network transmission time but also the time for serializing the agent at the sender agency and deserializing it at the receiver agency for each migration. We also consider the time necessary to link the agent's code, which involves verifying and preparing class code. The process of serializing an agent takes, according to our measurements less than 2 milliseconds (ms). The process of deserializing the agent's state and the linking agent's code takes on average between 1 and 5 ms, and is linear with respect to state size and class size.

Each agent migration is repeated between 200 and 1000 times; we only report mean values and the 95% significance interval. The longest 5% of the values were dropped, because we want to disregard times lengthened by the Java garbage-collector task.[1] To illustrate our results we always used line graphs, although in some experiments box charts would have been the correct diagramming technique, because intermediate values cannot be interpolated. However, in our opinion, line graphs make our results more obvious to the reader.

8.2.2 Programming Agents for the Measurements

The common behavior of the agents used in the experiments is defined in class *BaseAgent* in package *examples.agent*, which states that an agent executes the itinerary given in a configuration file and then migrates back to its home agency.

In general there is a single agent class for each measurement. This class extends class *BaseAgent* and defines special functions as necessary in the concrete measurement, (e.g., sending data items back to the agent's home agency).

---

1. The Java garbage collector is started whenever there is not enough memory to create new objects. Freeing memory takes between 300 and 900 ms in our experiments.

In some cases it is necessary to artificially increase the size of the agent's code, for example, to show how migration time depends on code size. We use static String objects for this purpose, which become part of the agent's code and are not part of the agent's object state.

When we refer to migration strategies in the remainder of this chapter, we use the name of the Java class that implements this strategy in Kalong, rather than the name we introduced in Chapter 3. Thus, the strategy that pushes all code to the next destination is now named PushToNext (rather than push-all-to-next), the strategy that loads code per class on demand is named PullPerClass (rather than pull-per-unit), and the strategy that loads all classes at once is named PullAllClasses (rather than pull-all-units).

8.2.3 Test Environment

To obtain our measurements, we used seven computers placed at the University of Jena (Germany), one placed at the University of Weimar (Germany),[2] one placed at the Fraunhofer Society Darmstadt (Germany),[3] and one at the University of Irvine (California, USA). More information about the computers used can be found in Table 8.1. All the computers used the latest version of the Java virtual machine (build 1.4.1_01-b01).[4] The Java virtual machine was initialized to use an initial heap size of 80 MB and a

Table 8.1 *Some parameters of the computer systems used in our experiments*

Name	Location	Processor	MHz	RAM	OS
tiffany	Jena	Athlon	900	512	Linux 2.4.18
honey	Jena	Athlon	1400	512	Linux 2.4.18
tanya	Jena	Athlon	900	256	Linux 2.4.18
patricia	Jena	Athlon	900	256	Linux 2.4.18
solitaire	Jena	Athlon	900	256	Linux 2.4.18
melina	Jena	Athlon	800	256	Linux 2.4.18
inga	Jena	Athlon	1400	256	Linux 2.4.18
natalja	Weimar	Pentium 3	800	1024	Linux 2.4.0
semoaext	Darmstadt	Pentium 2	450	512	SunOS 5.8
anna	Irvine (USA)	Pentium 4	1700	896	Linux 2.4.18

2. The city of Weimar is located about 20 km from Jena.

3. The city of Darmstadt is located about 300 km from Jena.

4. Measurements were done in January 2003.

maximum heap size of 200 MB. The stack size was set to 512 KB. All of the computers were fully dedicated during the experiments, as were all of the computer systems.

For most measurements we used the local-area network (LAN) in our department at the University of Jena, which is a Fast-Ethernet network with a bandwidth of 100 Mbit/sec where computers are connected via a single router. Some measurements were done using a fully dedicated Ethernet network with a bandwidth of 100 Mbit/sec and 10 Mbit/sec connected via a switch.

Measurements of migration times to the computers in Weimar, Darmstadt, and Irvine were done using our standard Internet connection, which is a 155 Mbit/sec uplink to the German GigaBit Research Network (G-Win), which has a theoretical bandwidth of 2.5 Gbit/sec. The University of Weimar is also connected to G-Win using a 155 Mbit/sec uplink. The quality of the network connections at Darmstadt and Irvine could not be determined.

8.3 Results of the Basic Experiments

8.3.1 Transmission Time with Regard to Code Size and Network Quality

In the first experiment we examined the time for a ping-pong migration of a single agent with different sizes, through different networks. The agent was created on tiffany and had to migrate to and from one other agency. We compared the migration time for the following code sizes: 1685, 4185, 6685, 11,685, 22,685, and 51,685 bytes. The agent's state is negligible in this experiment, because it was smaller than 100 bytes. The agent was transmitted using the PushToNext strategy without enabling the code cache. All migrations were repeated 1000 times.

Figure 8.1 shows the migration times for all high-bandwidth connections. The destination agency was started on melina. The graph also shows a measurement when the sender agency as well as the receiver agency were located on the same computer (tiffany) and the agent migrated using the local loop without using the network.

The best migration performance was achieved using the 100 Mbit/sec network via a switch, where the smallest agent (1685 byte) only needed 23 ms for a single migration. The migration time only increased slightly, to 34 ms, for the largest agent (51,685 bytes). Migration using the 100 Mbit/sec network via a router was only a few milliseconds slower: 25 ms for the smallest agent and

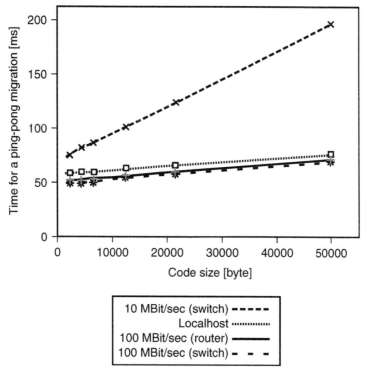

Figure 8.1 Time for a ping-pong migration between computers tiffany and melina, using different high-bandwidth networks. The localhost measurement was done on computer tiffany.

35.5 ms for the largest agent. The measurement using the internal network loop of the operating system was, surprisingly, slower than both measurements using a 100 Mbit/sec network. Here, one migration takes 28 ms for the smallest agent and 38 ms for the largest agent. The only explanation we have found for this so far is that the higher computational load of executing two parallel agencies on a single computer. Migrating agents using a 10 Mbit/sec network is noticeably slower than the other network types. The smallest agent needs about 37 ms for a single migration, and the largest agent needs about 98 ms.

As can be seen from Figure 8.1, migration time is positively correlated with the code size of the agent, and the 95% confidence intervals show that, measured migration times are not significantly different when transmitting small agents (fewer than 11,685 bytes) using fast networks. This gives hints for the construction of an optimization strategy: It is not always worthwhile to reduce a 10 KB agent to 5 KB, because the difference generally cannot be measured in fast networks. Using the 10 Mbit/sec network, all results are significantly different.

Comparing our results to the theoretical possible migration times, we found that real migration time is about eight times slower than theoretical migration time using a 100 Mbit/sec network. In a 10 Mbit/sec network, measured migration times are only twice as high as possible. In other words, we have achieved a network throughput of about 13 Mbit/sec in the 100 Mbit/sec network and a throughput of almost 5 Mbit/sec in the 10 Mbit/sec network. The reason for these quite slow values is the fixed overhead of the Java programming language and the Java virtual machine, which is known to have slower performance for network operations than native code implementations.

Figure 8.2 shows the migration times in a network with a bandwidth of 64 Kbit/sec, which is the quality of a dial-up ISDN connection. This type of network is simulated using the traffic shaper technique of the Linux operating system, which artificially decreases throughput of a network device. The destination agency was started on computer melina. Although migration times are very slow, we achieved a throughput that was only slightly below the theoretical optimum. For example, a single migration of the 51,685-byte agent takes 7220 ms, which results in a throughput of about 56 Kbit/sec. It is questionable whether this high throughput can be achieved in a real

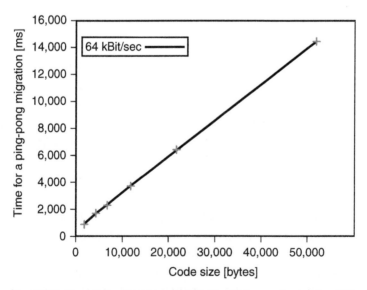

Figure 8.2 Time for a ping-pong migration between computers tiffany and melina using a ISDN network connection (64 Kbit/sec).

network environment, but we were unfortunately unable to test it in that environment.

Finally, Figure 8.3 shows the results of a ping-pong migration using a wide-area network. A migration of the smallest agent to the University of Weimar

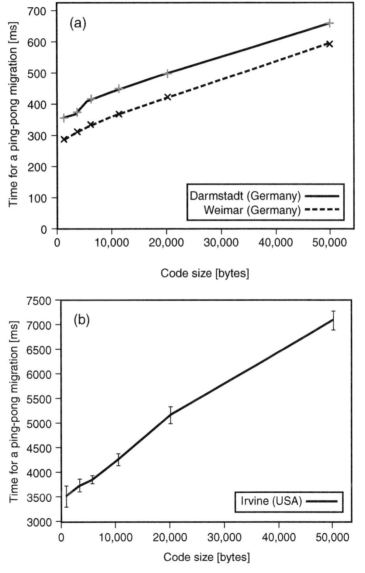

Figure 8.3 Time for a ping-pong migration in different wide-area networks. (a) Migrations between computer tiffany and computer natalja (Weimar), and between computer tiffany and computer semoaext (Darmstadt). (b) Migration between computer tiffany and computer anna (Irvine).

(natalja) takes about 135 ms and the largest agent takes about 300 ms. A migration to the Fraunhofer Society Darmstadt (semoaext) is only about 13% slower than the migration to Weimar. The reason for this is probably that the agent is transmitted to natalja over a 155 Mbit/sec network connection, whereas it is transferred to semoaext using a GigaBit network. The migration to anna at the University of Irvine takes the longest, as expected. The time for a single migration ranges from 1800 ms for the smallest agent and 3562 ms for the largest agent.

8.3.2 Transmission Time with Regard to Data Compression

In the second experiment we examined the effect of data compression on network load and transmission time. We used the same agents as in the previous experiment, and measured the time for a single ping-pong migration between agencies at tiffany and melina. If the agent is sent in a compressed form, all SATP messages are compressed using the technique described in Section 7.3.2. The agent is transmitted using the PushToNext migration strategy without activating the code cache. All measurements were repeated 1000 times.

We compare the effect of data compression in two network environments: a 100 Mbit/sec network connected via a router (Fig. 8.4(a)) and a 10 Mbit/sec network connected via a switch (Fig. 8.4(b)). As can be seen from the graphs, data compression has a negative effect on the migration performance for all code sizes in a high-bandwidth network. A migration is on average 40% slower than without data compression. This is a result of two drawbacks of compressed data.

1. Compressing small amounts of data sometimes increases the size of a message. For example, a SATP ADB message consists in our experiment on an average of 79 bytes in the uncompressed and 93 bytes in the compressed form.

2. Although a class of length 11,685 bytes is reduced to 2176 bytes, migration time is longer, because it takes 12 ms to achieve this compression.

The consequence is that, although less data has to be transmitted, the overall migration time is longer, because the time necessary for compression exceeds the time saved by the smaller network load. Therefore, in the high-bandwidth network, migration times with enabling data compression will almost always

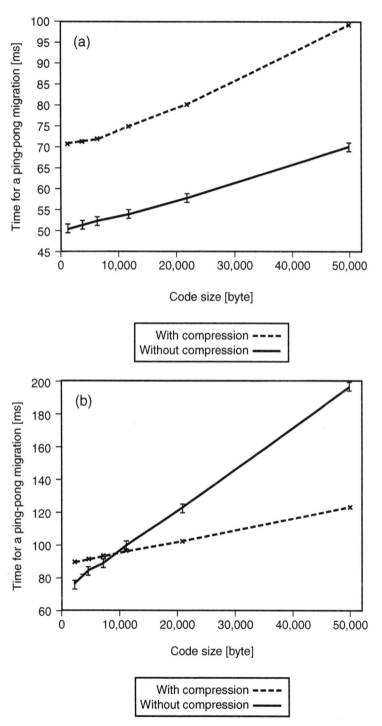

Figure 8.4 Time for a ping-pong migration with regard to compression. (a) Using a 100 Mbit/sec network via a router. (b) Using a 10 Mbit/sec network via a hub.

be longer than those without compression. Only for very large agents might this technique lead to a reduction of migration time. Such agents were out of the scope of our measurements.

In contrast, using the same computers in the low-bandwidth network, data compression has a positive effect for agents larger than approximately 10,000 bytes. For smaller agents, we see the same effect as in the high-bandwidth network: more time is lost computing the compressed SATP message than is gained by transmitting smaller messages. For larger agents, we can now observe the expected effect. Sending the agent with compressed SATP messages leads to shorter migration times. Now the time saved by sending the smaller messages over the network exceeds the time needed to compress the messages.

As a consequence, we can conclude that the break-even point, where both curves intersect, depends on the network type. The lower the bandwidth of the underlying network, the smaller the agent may be to make the effort for data compression pay off. We can assume that in wide-area networks, data compression is worthwhile even for the smallest agent used in our experiments.

To further improve the effect of data compression, we address two possibilities. First, the process of compressing data can be done *before* the agent migrates. In the current implementation, data compression is done during the migration process. However, for the static parts of the agent, especially the agent's code, compression could be done earlier, for example, while the agent is being executed. On remote agencies, compressed code units should be saved and reused rather than dropped and recomputed during the next migration. Because the agent's code is usually the largest part of the agent, this should improve the migration time dramatically. Second, we could use sophisticated compression algorithms for Java byte code, such as those described by Pugh [1999] and Bradley et al. [1998], which will reduce the size for Java classes more than the *gzip* algorithm that we have used in our implementation. Both optimizations will be subject to further investigation.

8.3.3 Transmission Time with Regard to Security

In the next experiment we examined the cost of techniques that improve the security of a migrating agent. The goal was to show how migration times change when agents migrate using the SSL network transmission protocol instead of TCP and the security extension we described in Section 7.3.3.

The secure SSL network transmission protocol was configured to use server authentication and not to reuse sessions. The security extension we use includes digital signatures for SATP headers, state, and code messages. We used the same agents with the same code sizes as in the previous experiments. The agents are transmitted using the PushToNext strategy without enabling the code cache. All migrations were repeated 1000 times.

We conducted the experiment in two network environments. The first graph (Fig. 8.5(a)) shows the migration times between tiffany and melina connected by a 100 Mbit/sec network (router), whereas the second graph (Fig. 8.5(b)) shows migration times between tiffany and natalja.

The first graph shows that SSL transmission is between 2.5 times and 3 times more costly than using TCP; it takes 73.5 ms for the smallest agent and 88 ms for the largest agent to migrate. The difference between the two transmission types is approximately 52 ms in the fast network. The reason for the longer time is the time-consuming handshaking protocol between sender and receiver to authenticate the server and to exchange encryption keys, which increases the network load. This cost does not depend on the agent's size, which means that migration time slows more drastically for small agents. In addition, all data sent over the network must be encrypted and decrypted, which increases the network load only slightly but slows down migration times because of the high computational effort.

If we activate, in addition to SSL transmission, all the security extensions described in Section 7.3.3 (i.e., signing of the SATP header, state, and all class files and inspecting classes at the destination to filter out malicious code), we can see in Figure 8.5(a) that migration times increase again. The migration time is now 231 ms for the smallest agent and 253 ms for the largest agent, which is approximately 7 to 10 times longer than migrating the agent without the security extension and with TCP. The total difference between the two types of migration is approximately 215 ms. The reason for this could seem to be a higher network load, because for each SATP message a digest must be sent over the network. However, because we use the MD5 algorithms, each digest is only 16 bytes long, and during an agent migration in our experiments, only about 3 to 5 digests are transmitted, which should not have any effect on the migration time. Therefore, the longer migration times must be the result of the time to compute message digests. For example, we found out that it takes 150 ms to determine the digest for a class of length 11,685 bytes.

The most interesting result of these two measurements is that all security extensions increase network load only slightly, but increase migration times considerably because the high computational effort for signing and

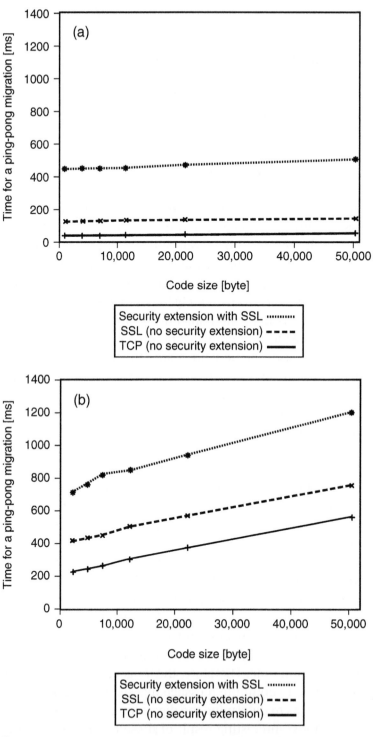

Figure 8.5 Time for a ping-pong migration with regard to different transmission protocols and security extensions. (a) Using a 100 Mbit/sec network via a router. (b) Using a wide-area network to natalja.

encryption. As can be seen from the graphs, the difference between the SSL curve and the *Security extension* curve is constantly about 300 ms for two migrations and does not depend on the network type. Notwithstanding, if we compare the SSL curve with the TCP curve, we can see that the difference between both is higher in the wide-area network than in the local-area network, because SSL increases the network load of the whole connection and is, therefore, dependent on the network type.

We can state that the migration overhead caused by security techniques can be expected to decrease (measured as a percentage) if the bandwidth of the underlying network is decreasing. As in a low-bandwidth network, if migration times are higher, the constant overhead for security will not be of great weight. For example, we can expect migration times to increase by less than 10% when migrating between Jena and Irvine.

This result has a great practical advantage. Improving the security of mobile agents can only be achieved with much effort, which results in a slowdown of migration times. Because the quality of the security techniques implemented for these experiments must be classified as basic, we can imagine that more sophisticated techniques will increase migration times even more. In specific application domains or in networks where these security techniques are not necessary, Kalong's possibility to *switch off* this extension can be of great benefit. On the other hand, in wide-area networks where security of agent migration might be required, security has only a small effect on the already long migration time.

8.3.4 Effect of Migration Strategies

In this section we evaluate the influence of different migration strategies on migration performance. We conducted this experiment in a 100 Mbit/sec network with all computers located in Jena. The agents were transmitted using the TCP transmission protocol. Measurements were repeated 1000 times.

The goal of this experiment was to show that the difference between known migration strategies can be measured in a real-world network. This effect was forecasted in our mathematical model in Section 3.4.3. It was not our goal to determine whether any migration strategy was faster than the others, because, as we have already discussed, which migration strategies should be chosen is dependent on the concrete application scenario—and this decision is affected by several parameters, for example, the agent's code size, the network type, and the probability for code execution to name a few.

To perform our experiment, we simulated a typical application from the information retrieval domain. The agent visits several network nodes where each platform has a database with documents of different types, for example, simple text files, structured text files in XML or HTML, or images. Each document was characterized by a set of keywords. The agent had to visit each platform. First, it filtered all documents according to a given set of keywords. The result was a set of *interesting* documents. Second, all these documents were examined in detail, which resulted in the set of all *significant* documents, which the agent makes a copy of before migrating to the next platform. For an interesting document to be examined, a specific class file for the given document type is necessary. Therefore, an agent consists of one class file for the agent itself, which contains the code necessary to perform the first step and all auxiliary tasks such as communication and route managing. There are also five other class files, one for each document type, which contain special code for the second step. If the agent finds a document of a specific type, the corresponding class file must be downloaded dynamically if it is not already available on the current platform.

The experimental setup consists of a cluster of seven agencies on computer systems tiffany, honey, melina, inga, tanya, patricia, and solitaire. On each platform we can change the number of document types that the agent will find interesting. By doing this, we can directly influence the number of classes that will be downloaded.

The agent class is 2012 bytes, whereas all auxiliary classes are each 10,000 bytes. In Figure 8.6 the graph shows various numbers of document types found interesting, the number of classes needed at runtime, and various migration strategies. Note that in our experiments the agent does not take any data with it when it migrates to the next server. Therefore, our results show only the time of migrating code and initial data (which is again fewer than 100 bytes).

It can be seen that strategies PushToNext, PullAllClasses, and the strategy in which no code is transmitted (because it is assumed that code is already available at all destinations, perhaps as a result of activating the code cache) are not dependent on the number of classes to load. This is clear, because the first two migration strategies always transmit all code without regard to its necessity. Obviously transmitting no code is faster than all other migration strategies, because the network loader is smallest. If the agent must load all classes (PullAllClasses) it is on average 1.4 times slower than pushing the code to the next destination, because pulling all classes needs an additional network transmission on each agency.

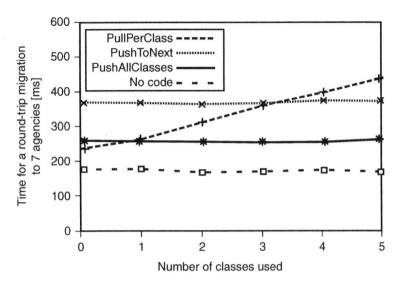

Figure 8.6 Times for a migration to seven agencies using different migration strategies.

Strategy PullPerClass is dependent on the number of classes to be downloaded dynamically, because only classes that are needed for agent execution are loaded. It is faster than all other methods (except transmitting no code at all) if there are no interesting documents, because then only the agent class itself must be transmitted. If only one additional class file must be loaded (of size 10,000 bytes) strategy PullPerClass is as fast as the PushToNext strategy which transmits 50,000 bytes of code. When increasing the number of document types, the PullPerClass strategy is more than 70% slower than the PushToNext strategy and about 20% slower than the PullAllClasses strategy. This performance difference only results from the fact that code must be downloaded dynamically in the PullPerClass strategy.

This experiment confirms the results of our mathematical model. The different amounts of data sent over the network in each migration strategy can be measured in the form of different migration times. The number of classes at which PushToNext and PullPerClass intersect depends on the class size and the network type. For larger classes, this point can be expected to be higher, because the difference between sending all classes and sending only some classes becomes greater. In networks with lower bandwidth, it is more expensive not only to transmit data but also to open a network connection, therefore the differences among all of the migration strategies can be expected to be greater. For example, it can be expected that the PullPerClass

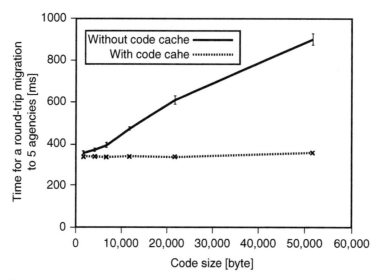

Figure 8.7 Time for a migration to five agencies in a wide-area network with regard to the code cache.

migration strategy will be slower than the PushToNext strategy even for a small number of classes. However, as already explained, it was not the goal of this experiment to quantitatively compare migration strategies to find the *fastest*, because it is not possible for one to be universally the fastest. Our results show that it is worthwhile to consider different migration strategies and to choose a suitable one with regard to the application, the network environment, the agent's size, and many other parameters. Kalong's ability to program such migration strategies dynamically and to react in a very flexible and fine-grained way to these parameters is a necessary feature.

8.3.5 Effect of Caching

In this experiment we want to analyze the effect of the Kalong's code cache. As already described in Chapter 3, the Kalong protocol can check whether an agent's code is already available at the destination agency before it sends the code. In this experiment we compare migration times of a single agent migrating to five agencies. The agent is started at natalja (Weimar), then migrates to four agencies in Jena (tiffany, honey, melina, inga), and returns back to natalja. The agent uses the PushToNext migration strategy, once with and once without enabling the code cache. All measurements were repeated 200 times.

The solid line in Figure 8.7 shows the migration time for different code sizes if the agent does not enable the code cache. It shows that migration time depends on the code size, as expected. The dashed line shows the migration time if the agent activates the code cache and if all of the agent's code is already available at the destination agency. Migration times are no longer dependent on the code size, because no code is transmitted at all in this case. The migration time is the time necessary to transfer the agent's state and data items.

The effect of the code cache depends directly on code size, of course. For small pieces of code (1685 bytes) the difference is only 15 ms for the round trip. For the largest piece of code (51,685 bytes) the complete migration time without using the cache is 2.5 times higher than with the code cache enabled.

Of course, the code cache can only have a positive effect if at least one class of the agent is already available at the destination agency. Figure 8.7 can also be interpreted so that the solid line shows the time for the first migration, whereas the dashed line shows the migration time for all following migrations for the same agent (data is the same for both this interpretation and that described in the figure legend). An interesting question that we have not examined so far is how the code cache increases migration performance if many agents of the same type (i.e., using the same classes) migrate to the same agencies.

Another interesting question concerns the overhead of the cache protocol. Unfortunately we were not able to measure this overhead, but we can speculate about the increase on network load that it causes. If we assume that an agent consists of five classes and each class name is 20 characters long, then the ADB message is composed of $5 \times (20 + 16)$ bytes, because the digest for each class is 16 bytes long. The answer message of type ADBReply consists of only one byte for each class. This means 185 bytes must be exchanged between the sender agency and the receiver agency in order to prevent the transmission of an agent's code.

8.3.6 Effect of Data Uploading

In the next experiment we examined the performance benefit of sending data items back to the agent's home server instead of taking them to all other agencies as part of the agent's state. We compared the migration time for a complete round trip to seven and five agencies for different data items in a local 100 Mbit/sec network and a wide-area network. The agent migrated using the PushToNext migration strategy and without using the code cache.

The size of the agent was 2443 bytes. The measurements were repeated 1000 times.

The first graph (Fig. 8.8(a)) shows the result for the local network. The agent starts at tiffany and first migrates to honey. There, the agent gets a new data item of a given size (5,000, 10,000, 20,000, or 60,000 bytes). Then, the agent migrates to five other agencies (melina, inga, tanya, patricia, and solitaire) before returning to its home agency. The dashed line shows the result if the agent takes the new data item to all other agencies as part of its state. The migration time depends on the size of the data item, as expected. The solid line shows the result if the agent sends the new data item back to its home agency before it leaves honey. Here, the migration time does not depend on the data item size, because the agent does not carry the data item. The migration time only depends on the code size and the constant size of the state. Figure 8.8(a) shows that for small data items it is slower to send them back. In these cases, the time to open an additional network connection to the home agency and to send a small data item is greater than the time that is needed to carry this data to all other agencies. For data items larger than about 11,000 bytes, sending the data item back is faster. For example, in the case of a 60,000 byte data item, sending the data item home is 1.6 times faster than taking it along.

The second graph (Fig. 8.8(b)) shows the result for the wide-area network, where the agent is started at tiffany (Jena) and then migrates to four other agencies in Weimar and Jena (natalja, inga, natalja, inga) before migrating back home. It is now faster for all data items to send the data item back than to carry it along. The solid line shows the time for carrying the data item to all agencies, which increases with the size of the data item. In contrast to the first graph, sending the data item back is now also dependent on the data size, which can be explained by the time required to send the data item back to the home server from Weimar to Jena using a low-bandwidth network connection. However, in the wide-area network the difference is greater; sending the data item home is twice as fast as carrying it as part of the state. It is obvious that the performance benefit depends on the number of agencies to which the data item will not need to be carried and the bandwidth of the underlying network. If the number of servers is higher or the network slower, the performance increase is greater.

8.3.7 Effect of Code Servers

In this experiment we were interested in the performance gain that could be achieved by using code servers instead of home servers for dynamic

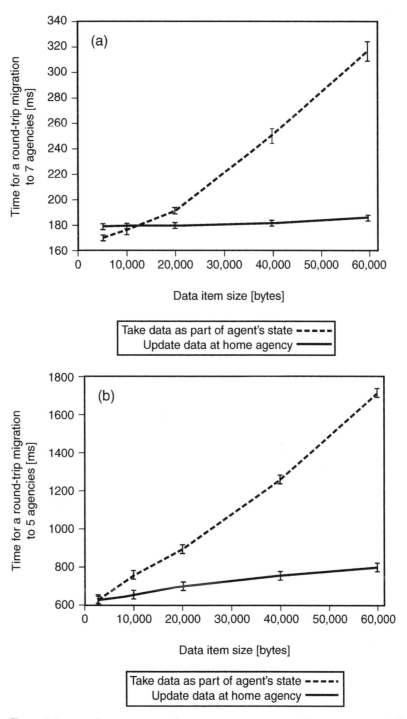

Figure 8.8 Time for migration of one agent to seven and five agencies in different networks. The agent creates a data item with a given size and takes it as part of its state or sends it back to its home agency.

code loading. An agent can initialize a code server dynamically during run-time at any agency that it is currently visiting. The effect is that some or all code units remain at the code server even if the agent migrates to another agency. In future migrations, the agent can download classes from this code server, for example, if it is nearer to the current agency than the home agency.

We compared the time for a complete round trip to four agencies to the size of the classes that had to be loaded. The agent base class was 2176 bytes and needed one other class of 2,500, 5,000, 10,000, 20,000, or 50,000 bytes. Both classes were loaded dynamically during runtime. All measurements were repeated 200 times.

Our scenario consisted of four agencies: natalja, honey, tiffany, and inga. The agent started on natalja (Weimar) and migrated using the PullAllClasses migration strategy. In the first case, the code was loaded from the agent's home server; in the other case, all code was loaded from a code server that the agent initialized on agency honey. In the second case migration times included the time to release the code server at the end.

Figure 8.9 shows the results of our measurement. The dashed line shows the migration times for an agent that always loads classes from its home agency. The time depends on the code size and increases steadily with the size of the code that must be downloaded over the wide-area network. If only a small class must be loaded, the agent needs about 676 ms for the complete

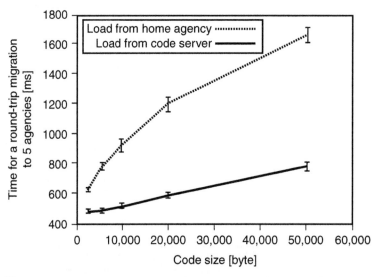

Figure 8.9 Time for a migration to four agencies using the Pull strategy with regard to different locations of the code server.

tour; when loading the largest code, it needs about 1453 ms. The solid line shows the results if the agent loads classes from a code server that is located in the local network (on agency honey). Migration time depends on the code size, of course, but the increase is not so steep. Even for the smallest agent, this type of migration only needs 494 ms, which is an improvement of 17% compared to the first migration type. For the largest agent, the improvement is even greater. The agent needs 717 ms, which is an improvement of more than 50%.

The experiment shows that it is worthwhile to use code servers to improve the performance of loading code. If a code server could be placed at a node that is accessible by a faster network than the home server, a code server makes sense. Using code servers has no drawback, because there is no time lost in activating a code server and it takes very little time to release a code server after the agent has terminated. In our measurements, sending the SATP message to release the code server took less than 10 ms.

8.3.8 Effect of Mirrors

The last experiment considered the effect of a mirror server to reduce costs for loading and updating data items. The scenario in this experiment consisted of five agencies on computers natalja, honey, tiffany, melina, and inga. The agent was 3095 bytes of code and migrated using the PushToNext migration strategy without enabling the code cache. All measurements were repeated 200 times.

The agent started at natalja and then migrated to honey, where it created a data item with 1,000, 5,000, 10,000, or 20,000 bytes. In the first case, the data item was sent to the agent's home server, while in the other case, the agent initialized a mirror server at honey. The agent then migrated to the other agencies, where it loaded the data item from the home server or the mirror server, modified it, and uploaded it again. Finally, if a mirror agency exists, the data item is loaded from the mirror agency to the home agency. Therefore, a data item is transmitted seven times among the agency, the mirror server, and the home agency.

The solid line in Figure 8.10 shows the migration time for the first case, when data items were updated at the home agency. The migration time has a positive correlation with the data size and grows from 946 ms for the smallest data item to 1582 ms for the largest data item. The dashed line shows the time for the second case, when data items were uploaded at the mirror agency.

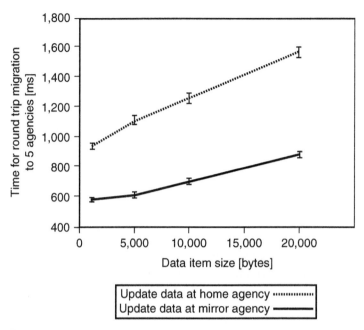

Figure 8.10 Time for a migration to five agencies, where the agent uploads data items either on its home server or on a near mirror server.

The complete round trip only took 584 ms for the smallest data item, which is about 38% faster than the first scenario, and took only 887 ms for the largest data item, which is an increase of about 44%. The reason for the faster time is obviously the fact that the mirror server was accessible over a high-bandwidth connection and six of the seven data transmissions used this type of network. Without the mirror server, all data transmission was done using the low-bandwidth connection between Jena and Weimar. We can conclude that it makes sense to activate a mirror agency for data uploading and downloading if this mirror agency can be accessed using a faster network type than the home agency uses. The higher the network load for data transmissions between an agency and the mirror the greater the benefit of the mirror.

Summary

To conclude Part III, we present some ideas we are currently working on for more sophisticated migration strategies. Although it might be best for most application domains to delegate the decision about the migration strategy to the agent programmer, it is undoubtedly more convenient in our case to let Kalong determine the migration strategy itself. We call a migration strategy that decides on the next migration strategy in an autonomous fashion an *automated migration strategy*. In some situations, for example, if the agent roams the Internet without a fixed itinerary but decides at each agency to which host the next migration should be directed to, there is no alternative to an automated migration strategy if migration should be optimized, because the user has no knowledge about the route that the agent will take.

We have shown that the performance of agent migration depends on several factors, including network quality, execution probability of each code unit, the size of each code unit, and so forth. We now have to face two problems. First, all these parameters must be determined. We will present some techniques that we have developed to gather information about the network quality later. Currently we are working toward a technique to analyze an agent's code to determine the execution probability of each code class by static or dynamic code analysis. Second, we have to find algorithms to decide, on the basis of these parameters, how the next migrations should be processed.

Let's start with the second step, because it turns out to be simpler. Our goal is to decide which classes should be pushed from the sender to the destination agency right away and which classes should be loaded from the agent's home server later. We first disregard all other Kalong features that complicate this decision (e.g., code servers and mirror servers). Because each class transmission is independent of any other class, we must simply compare the migration times for each class.

If the mobile agent consists of u code units, where each code unit comprises of exactly a single class, the size of code unit k equals $B_c^k, k = 1, \ldots, u$. The network is modeled using delay δ and throughput τ, each assumed to be available for all pairs of network nodes. The time to transmit code unit k from the sender agency L_i to the destination agency L_{i+1} equals

$$T_{push}^k = \frac{B_c^k}{\tau(L_i, L_{i+1})}$$

We do not factor in the agent's data and state size $B_d + B_s$ and the network delay $\delta(L_i, L_{i+1})$, because these costs arise in both cases. The alternative to pushing the code unit is to impose on the destination agency to load missing code units on demand from the agent's home server L_0 instead of transmitting it from the sender agency. We have to consider the execution

```
1   public Set findClasses( int[] code, float [] exProb, float throughput1,
2                              float throughput2, float delay2, int request )
3   {
4       float pushCase, pullCase;
5       Set result = new HashSet();
6
7       for( int i=0; i<code.length; i++ )
8       {
9           pushCase = ((float)code[i] / throughput1 );
10          pullCase = exProb[i] * ( delay2 + ((float)code[i] + (float)request ) / throughput2
                  );
11
12          if( pushCase < pullCase )
13          {
14              result.add( new Integer(i) );
15          }
16      }
17
18      return result;
19  }
```

Figure 8.11 Method to determine which classes to push to the next destination.

probability $P_{L_{i+1}}^k$ that code unit k is really needed at destination L_{i+1}, so the cost amounts to

$$T_{pull}^k = P_{L_{i+1}}^k \left(\delta(L_{i+1}, L_0) + \frac{(B_c^k + B_r)}{\tau(L_{i+1}, L_0)} \right)$$

The cost to request a code unit equals B_r. Here we have to include the delay to open a network connection, because each code unit is loaded using a new connection. We are aware of the fact that both equations are based on the simple mathematical model of network load and transmission time developed in Chapter 3 which has to be improved and refined to serve as a real forecast instrument.

For each code unit k we compare speed and choose the technique that has the shorter time. Figure 8.11 shows the source code of a method that implements this decision process. Parameter *code* contains the size of all code units and *exProb* contains the execution probability for all code units on agency L_{i+1}. The network parameters are given by *throughput1* for the connection between L_i and L_{i+1} and *throughput2* for the connection between L_{i+1} and L_0. Network delay is given for only the home connection, and parameter *request* contains the cost for a code request.

For example, an agent consists of two code units, where $B_c^1 = 20$ KB and $B_c^2 = 10$ KB. The execution probabilities are $P_{L_{i+1}}^1 = 0.8$ and $P_{L_{i+1}}^2 = 0.2$. The network connection to the destination agency has throughput $\tau(L_i, L_{i+1}) = 800$ Kbit/sec and the one between destination agency and home server has throughput $\tau(L_{i+1}, L_0) = 240$ Kbit/sec. Delay is 15 ms and the cost of a code unit request is 100 bytes. It turns out that it does cost 200 ms to push the first code unit, whereas it takes 548 ms to load it later. Therefore, the first code unit is pushed to the destination agency. For the second code unit, the cost for pushing is 100 ms, whereas loading it later on demand only takes 70 ms—so this code unit is not pushed. If we decrease throughput between the destination agency and the home agency, the result changes so that now all code units should be pushed, because it is more costly to load missing units later.

The decision process is more difficult if not only the next migration but several migrations need to be planned. Not only must the network parameters be known for all agencies to be visited, but the execution probability for all code units at all destinations must also be known. At this point we might regard this as a limitation of this kind of automated migration strategies, because it can be extremely expensive to bring together network information about all future agencies at the current agency.

In principle, even the decision to initialize a code server or mirror agency can be made using the same technique as described above. The question whether a code server should be initialized at the current agency can be answered by comparing transmission time for the next migrations if all code must be loaded from the home server with transmission time if some code may be loaded from the code server. If migration time can be reduced, a code server should be initialized.

We are not currently able to determine all necessary information about network quality and execution probability. Therefore, we were not able to verify our technique in a real-world environment. However, we are currently working on extensions of Kalong, for which we now present the current state of implementation.

Network Analysis

We have developed a tool to monitor network performance and have integrated it in the Tracy mobile agent system. On each agency, this component gathers information about network quality by testing network connections to neighbor agencies. Two agencies are neighbors if they are members of the same *domain*, which is never more than a subnetwork, as defined by the Tracy domain manager concept (see Chapter 10 for more information). Time measurements are done using *ping* messages sent periodically between two agencies, from which network throughput and latency are deduced. The monitor component provides an application programming interface so that other components or agents can use the results. In the second step, monitor components located at different agencies communicate to exchange network information using mobile agents. Using this technique, it is also possible to use information about throughput and latency of a remote agency, which is necessary to implement such automated migration strategies as previously described. Steffen Schreiber implemented this network monitoring tool as part of his diploma thesis [Schreiber, 2002].

Agent Profiling

To determine the execution probability of classes in a Java-based mobile agent, we plan to use *profiling* techniques used in compiler construction, which are usually used to predict the probability of executing specific code portions.

A first approach to determine a profile is to instrument the agent's source code and to count how often a basic block is executed. This type of profiling is called *dynamic*, because the agent must be executed to obtain profile information. The advantage of dynamic profiling is that it provides very accurate information. However, because the profile depends on the agent instance and not only on the type of agent, different input data, for example, a different user task, might lead to a completely different profile. Therefore, such a profile is undoubtedly valuable if a single agent is reused many times for comparable tasks, but it is questionable whether dynamic profile information can be transferred to other instances, even if they are of the same agent type. Another drawback of dynamic profiling is that it increases not only the code by adding new statements for counting, but also the data, because the information must be part of the agent's state and so must be carried through the network.

Another approach works *statically* and uses source code analysis to estimate profiles. It uses techniques such as branch prediction or analysis of method invocation frequencies to forecast how often specific pieces of code will be used. The advantage is that it is done before executing the agent and, therefore, will neither increase the code nor the agent's data. Static profiling will never be as accurate as dynamic profiling, but it works for all agents of the same type and can, therefore, be used several times.

Class Splitting

As an extension of the last technique, we consider the idea of *class splitting* to reduce network traffic for mobile agents. So far, all migration strategies load agents' code as complete Java class files. If there is at least one method of a class file necessary for agent execution, then the entire class file is transmitted. We have named the level of code transmission the *code granularity*. It can be assumed that invocation frequency is not the same for all methods of the same class. Therefore, it makes sense to increase the granularity of code and to split a class into two or more new classes and distribute methods according to their execution probability. Groups of methods that are used with the same probability, because they call each other, should be members of the same class, whereas other methods with lower execution probability should form another class. If a method is called that is not implemented in the main class, then class that contains the code is loaded. The effect of class splitting is that the resulting classes, and especially the main class, are smaller than the single original class, which will, in turn, reduce network transmission time.

Chris Fensch implemented a software component for class splitting as part of his diploma thesis [Fensch, 2001]. It provides a simple interface where the user can define to split a class into *n* other classes and specify which class should contain which methods. Classes are split on the level of Java byte code. The result of splitting code is completely transparent to the programmer. This set of new classes can be used as if it were still only a single class, because all of the fragments are linked together.

Figure 8.12 shows an example of the class splitting technique. Part(a) shows the original agent. Using profiling technique, we found that method *startAgent*, which is only called once in Tracy (when the agent is started), is never used on visited agencies, and, therefore, should not be part of the main agent. Part(b) shows the result of two classes, *AnAgent*, which only contains a stub for method *startAgent*, and class *Split*, which contains the code for this method. Method *startAgent* of class *AnAgent* creates an instance of class *Split*, if one does not already exist, and forwards the method invocation to this object. The figure also shows how the split class

```
 1  package My Agent;
 2
 3  class AnAgent extends MobileAgent
 4  {
 5    private Vector route;
 6
 7    //...
 8
 9    public void start Agent()
10    {
11      //...
12      route = new Vector();
13      //...
14    }
15  }
```

(a)

```
 1  package My Agents;
 2
 3  class AnAgent extens MobileAgent
 4  {
 5    private Vector route;
 6    private transient Split I1;
 7
 8    public void startAgent()
 9    {
10      if( I1 == null )
11      {
12        I1 = new Split( this );
13      }
14      I1.startAgent();
15    }
16
17    void access$123( Vector x)
18    {
19      route = x;
20    }
21  }
```

```
 1  package My Agents;
 2
 3  class Split
 4  {
 5    private AnAgent this$0;
 6
 7    Split (AnAgent x)
 8    {
 9      this$0 = x ;
10    }
11
12    public void startAgent()
13    {
14      //...
15      this $0.access$123(new Vector ());
16      //...
17    }
18  }
```

(b)

Figure 8.12 Example for the class splitting technique. We picture Java source code, although class splitting works on the level of Java byte code. (a) Original agent. (b) The splitted agent consists of two classes.

can access private variables of the original agent using an auxiliary method that was introduced by the splitting algorithm.

The idea of class splitting was proposed in the area of Java applets already [Krintz et al., 1999]. We are currently working on experiments to verify the effect of class splitting for real-world agents [Braun et al., 2004].

Part IV

The Tracy Mobile Agent Toolkit

Chapter 9

Running a Tracy Agency

In the last part of this book we introduce you to an existing mobile agent toolkit named Tracy and the applied programming of stationary and mobile software agents.

We begin in this chapter with a brief introduction to the architecture of Tracy; first the basic conceptual model, which actually consists of *software agents*, *services* that agents can use in order to fulfill their task, and the basic Tracy *agency* software that provides these services as well as hosts software agents; then details of configuring and starting an agency and the main user interface with which agents can be started and maintained.

Contents

9.1 Welcome to Tracy

We have already stated that dozens of mobile agent toolkits have been developed over the last few years. Although this number reflects an enormous research output by different groups all over the world, it also reveals the premature status of research and the lack of coordination between projects. Today's mobile agent toolkits are almost all stand-alone software systems unable to communicate with each other, and sometimes not more than prototypes tailored to a specific research issue.

Current Status of Mobile Agent Toolkits

This is a result of the lack of any reference architecture for agencies for mobile agents as well as the absence of an open and extendable implementation. Therefore, each research group has to develop its own prototype. Because of the complexity of developing a prototype and limited resources of the research groups, this prototype is more a proof-of-concept implementation focusing on a single research issue and leaving out the elementary functional components necessary for a full mobile agent toolkit. The research community has to admit that such a reference architecture has been developed in the area of distributed artificial intelligence in the form of the FIPA standard [O'Brien and Nicol, 1998], for which a widely used implementation exists as the Jade toolkit [Bellifimine et al., 2003].

We also face disparate perceptions of basic concepts of mobile agents, for example:

■ What should a mobile agent be from the programmer's point of view: an object of a specific type, which defines several basic functions for mobile agents like communication and migration, or just any serializable object?

■ What level of communication is necessary: a simple one between agents residing at the same agency or a complex one which also allows for remote communication?

■ What level of security is necessary: one that protects hosts against only malicious agents, or is it necessary to protect agents against malicious agencies too?

■ What kind of mobility is necessary?

The disadvantageous consequence of these isolated islands of research is that findings cannot be transferred between projects in the form of definite implementations (e.g., software components that could be installed in other mobile agent toolkits). Sometimes even the general research idea cannot be adapted to another mobile agent toolkit because of the differences in basic concepts, as previously described. Another deficit is the number of different migration protocols that currently exist. Except for two toolkits (i.e., Aglets and Grasshopper) that support the MASIF migration protocol proposed as OMG standard in 1998, it is virtually impossible to make two toolkits interoperable.

Although the MASIF standard provides a common migration protocol, because of its complexity (which makes it difficult to implement the complete standard) and the lack of an independent software component for MASIF, only a few research groups use it.[1]

In contrast to the large number of prototype implementations, few systems have been developed as full-featured mobile agent toolkits that can be used in industrial-strength applications. These offer techniques for all important issues of agent programming, such as migration, communication, security, management, and so forth. However, even these systems are not willingly used, because of their complexity and size. They are built as monolithic systems with many features, and are not easy to configure and handle. It is almost always impossible to extend these systems by adding the features necessary or to tailor them to fit certain application scenarios by removing unwanted elements.

Some people see this as the biggest problem hampering the spread and acceptance of mobile agents.[2] If a system is not adaptable to real-world requirements, potential users are not willing to use this mobile agent toolkit or any form of mobile agents.

The Tracy Architecture—Kernel, Agency, and Plugins

To amend this situation, one of the most important challenges of our Tracy project was to develop a new model and a reference architecture for mobile agent toolkits. It was naturally not our goal to develop the nth mobile agent toolkit specialized to a specific research issue; we aspired to build a toolkit that could be used for the development of industrial-strength real-world applications. Tracy is a modular, component-oriented, extendable software system that executes stationary and mobile software agents written in the Java programming language. Tracy uses the standard Java execution environment without any modifications in the virtual machine or within any of the core Java APIs. We made a considerable effort to provide services for agent communication, security of mobile agents, an easy-to-use graphical user interface, and several other features that we firmly believe that distinguish Tracy from all other existing mobile agent toolkits.

We added to previous work done by the Tracy team in designing the first Tracy architecture and benefitted from experiences learned when porting it

---

1. There has been one attempt to provide a light version of MASIF in Java named *Simple MASIF implementation* (SMI) [Dillenseger, 2000]. However, even SMI has not become widely used, which might have to do with its close relation to CORBA. For more information, go to *mobilitools.objectweb.org/*

2. Compare, for example, *dsonline.computer.org/0208/f/kot.htm.*

to mobile platforms and investigating the feasibility of using Tracy within an existing electronic commerce application [Kowalczyk et al., 2002].

One of our main design goals for Tracy was to build an extendable mobile agent toolkit that could be adapted to various application domains and runtime environments. Therefore, Tracy is designed as a microkernel [Buschmann et al., 1996] that provides basic services to execute agents and control their life-cycles. Agents can be any Java class that implements the interface *java.lang.Runnable*, which is actually a major difference from other existing mobile agent toolkits, for example Aglets or Grasshopper, for which an agent class must extend the predefined class *MobileAgent*.

In addition to the microkernel, there is an *agency* component that uses an *agent directory* to manage all agents currently residing on this host, whether they are currently running or waiting. The agency provides basic functions for agents to understand their environment, for example to find other agents on this host. The agency offers functions to start and stop agents and uses the microkernel for these tasks. Each agent is registered with the agency when it is started. It makes no difference whether the agent is started locally or has migrated to this agency. The agent directory entry exists for the entire lifetime on the local host and is deleted when the agent leaves the server by migration or when the agent is killed.

Additionally, an agency has the task to manage *plugins*, which is our method of providing high-level services within Tracy. A *plugin* is a software component that provides a *service* that is not mandatory to run an agency, but extends its functionality. Plugins can be added dynamically to a running agency, they can be stopped (e.g., in case of a fault) and restarted later. In fact, the basic version of Tracy only consists of the microkernel and the agency. All other services, such as inter-agent communication, blackboard, migration, persistency, partial solutions of mobile agent security challenges, user management, and permission management, are all implemented as plugins. Tracy already provides many plugins, some of which we will introduce in Chapter 10.

Such an open architecture has many advantages. Because the mobile agent toolkit has a very small imperative core as a basis for many plugins to be added on, it is very modular. The main advantage of this type of architecture is that the user can extend and improve Tracy simply by developing your own plugins. We believe that it will be possible to enable the exchange of research results on the basis of such software components in the future.

Second, Tracy can be readily adapted to various application domains and runtime environments. You can configure your Tracy system according to your requirements and hardware prerequisites. If you do not need a specific plugin as part of your application domain, you can just remove it and, thereby reduce the memory footprint of an agency.

The Tracy architecture makes it very easy to port a mobile agent toolkit to other devices, because services no longer needed can simply be removed. If a plugin is too heavy for a resource-limited mobile device for example, it can be replaced by a smaller component with fewer services. Code reuse is also supported, because the architecture guarantees that software components are usable at any mobile agent toolkit built on this architecture.

Currently, Tracy comes with the following plugins:

AgencyShell to communicate to an agency via a textual user interface.

AgentLauncher to start agents automatically during the start-up process of Tracy.

DomainManager to create a logical agency network, where agents can ask for surrounding agencies.

Message for inter-agent communication.

Migration for agent mobility (using the Kalong component).

Place for agents to understand their environment.

Survival for waking up agents at a particular time.

The following plugins are also already available, but will not be introduced in this book and are not part of the Tracy version available for public download from our Web site.

AgentPolicy to assign permissions to agents dynamically, using rules comparable to today's firewall configuration.

Blackboard a persistent data store for agents to leave any kind of information for other agents. A blackboard just provides another means of communication between agents.

Email to send message via SMTP, to the agent owner, for example.

Key to load certificates and keys from local keystore files and public LDAP directories. This plugin is also needed if you want to use code signing and other mobile agent security-related techniques.

Persistence to save agents on a persistence data store to achieve fail-over in error situations.

Taas (Tracy Authentication and Authorization Service) to provide user management, which includes granting permissions to users dynamically.

WebService to provide the capability for other plugins to deploy Web services using SOAP interfaces.

Tracy can be used as a stand-alone application and controlled via a textual user interface (provided by the *AgencyShell* plugin) or can be used by other applications using a SOAP interface (provided by the *Web-Service* plugin).

Let us summarize the most important terms introduced in this section:

Agency is a software component that is an addition to a Tracy microkernel and provides basic services to running agents, for example, it maintains an agent directory and mediates between plugins and agents.

Agent must be implemented as a Java class that implements interface `java.lang.Runnable`.

Host is the computer system on which a Tracy agency is running.

Micro kernel is a software component that is an addition to a Java virtual machine and is responsible for running software agents.

Plugin is a software component that implements or provides a service. Plugins can be dynamically started and stopped at runtime.

Service is an API that can be used by agents; a service is identified by a name.

System is a set of Tracy agencies that belong to the same application domain.

9.2 Installation of Tracy

In this section we explain how to install and configure a Tracy agency.

9.2.1 Before You Start the Installation

Before you start the installation process, you should make sure that your system fulfills the hardware and software requirements to run Tracy.

Because Tracy is written entirely in Java, it should be able to run on every platform for which a Java runtime environment (JRE) in version 1.4 is available. We recommend using version 1.4.2. We have successfully tested Tracy on Microsoft Windows, SUN Solaris, HP Tru64, and several Linux operating systems. If you want to program your own agents, you will need the Java software development kit (SDK) or any other Java compiler (e.g., Jikes). Your system should have at least 128 MB of main memory, although we prefer at least 256 MB main memory. Tracy needs about 10 MB disk space for the core classes, all plugins, and the complete documentation.

9.2.2 Installation

Install the Tracy Agency

We now start with the installation process of Tracy in a minimal version, which only consists of the agency and some of the most important plugins. We assume that you have already installed the Java runtime environment and the Java software development kit on your system.

The installation process is very easy, because Tracy is distributed as a single archive file that contains all the files necessary to start a Tracy agency as well as the complete online documentation of the Tracy API. Create a directory where Tracy should be installed, for example */usr/local/tracy* on a Unix system or *C: Tracy* on a Windows system. This directory will be named TRACY_HOME in the following.

The Tracy archive can be downloaded from our Web site *www.mobile-agents.org*. You can choose between two archive files; the first is named *tracy2.tar.gz* and the second is named *tracy2.zip*. They differ only in the file format, not in the set of files. Copy one of these files into the directory TRACY_HOME and unpack it by typing:

- `$> tar xzf tracy2.tar.gz` on Linux or Unix
- `$> unzip tracy2.zip` on Windows

If unpacking of the archive was successful, then you should have the following directory structure in TRACY_HOME:

- *bin* contains Unix scripts and Windows batch files to start an agency.
- *doc* contains the Tracy API documentation.
- *conf* contains exemplary configuration files for Tracy and all plugins.
- *lib* contains Java class files of the micro kernel and the agency, bundled in several Java archives (JARs).
- *plugins* contains several Tracy plugins as JAR files.

In fact, you can store configuration files in any directory you want; *conf* is simply the default directory where the Tracy start script looks for configuration files.

Installing Tracy Plugins

If you want to install other plugins later, just copy the JAR file of the plugin into the *plugins* directory and the appropriate configuration file in the *conf* directory or any other directory where configuration files are stored.

When Tracy is launched, all JAR files in the *plugins* directory are expected to contain a Tracy plugin. Each Tracy plugin must include a manifest file that contains mandatory information about the plugin. Because it is not in the scope of this book to explain how to program your own plugins, we do not go into details here. More information can be found in the Tracy programming guide, which is part of Tracy's online documentation.

9.2.3 Configuration

In this section we describe how to configure a minimal version of Tracy. To configure Tracy you must have at least the following five files:

- *kernel.conf* to configure the Tracy kernel
- *agency.conf* to configure a Tracy agency
- *tracy.policy* to configure the static permissions of Tracy
- *jaas.login* to configure the JAAS login module
- *jaas.policy* to configure user permissions

All these files are necessary to configure the Java virtual machine and the Tracy kernel. There should also be a configuration directory for each agency that is started in addition to a kernel. This directory contains a configuration file for each plugin that should be started. All configuration files should be stored in a single directory so that they can be found by Tracy. It is good practice to create a separate directory for each configuration.

Configuration files are plain text files that consist of several key-value pairs—one pair per line. Key and value are separated by an equals sign.

Configure the Tracy Kernel

The configuration of the Tracy kernel is confined to defining the kind of logging that should be used for the microkernel component. For example, the following configuration file:

```
1 logger.class = "de.fsuj.tracy2.logging.SimpleLogger"
2 logger.level = 4
```

defines which Java class should be used for logging messages and defines the number of logging messages that should be produced. In detail, the keys have the following meaning:

logger.class Tracy uses its own logging mechanism. This variable defines the class that should be used for logging. You can choose between a simple logger (class *de.fsuj.tracy2.logging.SimpleLogger*) that prints all messages to the console and the built-in Java logging technique (class *de.fsuj.tracy2.logging.JavaLogger*). If you want to use the built-in Java logging you should also create a file named *javalog.properties* that contains some configuration information for the Java logging mechanism. For more information about the latter configuration file, see Java's online documentation.

logger.level Defines the number of logging messages to be produced. Allowed values are between 0 and 6. With value 0 very fine-grained logging messages are produced, whereas with value 6 only severe errors are logged. To start, this value should be set to 4.

Configure a Tracy Agency

To configure the agency that should be started on top of the Tracy kernel, file *agency.conf* is used. Here is an example of this file.

```
1 name = "MainAgency"
2 class = "de.fsuj.tracy2.agency.Agency"
3 url = "file:${user.dir}/lib/agency.jar"
4 classloader = "de.fsuj.tracy2.kernel.AgencyClassLoader"
5 logger.level = 4
```

The keys have the following meaning:

name defines the logical name of the agency, which must be a sequence of characters beginning with a letter, and which may not contain any white spaces. The *full agency name* is the concatenation of the logical name and the full qualified domain name of the host, for example, *MainAgency.tatjana.cs.uni-jena.de.*

class defines the name of the main class of this agency; the value defined in line 2 is the default value that is used when this key is missing.

url defines the URL where the code for this agency can be found; the value defined in line 3 is the default value that is used when this key is missing.

classloader defines the class loader used to load each agency (whereas the Tracy kernel is loaded using the system class loader); usually remains unchanged; the value defined in line 4 is the default value that is used when this key is missing.

logger.class and logger.level define the logging mechanism for the Tracy agency in the same way as the kernel does.

Configure Plugins

For each plugin that exists in the *plugins* directory, there must exist a configuration file with the same name as the plugin. For example, if there is a plugin named *AgencyShell.jar* then there also must exist a configuration file named *AgencyShell.conf* in the configuration directory. Configuration files must always end with the suffix *.conf.* Please note that some operating systems might not distinguish between upper- and lowercase letters. Examples of plugin configuration files will be presented in Section 9.4.

Configure the Tracy Policy file

The Tracy policy file defines the static permissions of all code components of a Tracy agency. The file must have the name *tracy.policy*, should contain a single entry for each JAR file, should by default grant all permissions to the component. It is not essential to grant all permissions to the microkernel and the agency, but it simplifies the configuration process.

```
1 grant codeBase "file:${user.dir}/lib/kernel.jar" {
2       permission java.security.AllPermission;
```

```
 3 };
 4
 5 grant codeBase "file:${user.dir}/lib/agency.jar" {
 6         permission java.security.AllPermission;
 7 };
 8
 9 grant codeBase "file:${user.dir}/plugins/-" {
10         permission java.security.AllPermission;
11 };
```

For sake of simplicity, we also inserted a grant entry for *all* plugins here and grant each of them *all* permissions. You can adapt this configuration to your own preferences (see the plugin documentation to learn which permission each plugin needs).

This file can also be used to grant permissions to agents in a static way, that is, you cannot revoke these permissions after they have been granted, which is sufficient in many application scenarios. The way to grant permissions to agents is comparable to the examples above. You have to define the code base from where all agent's code is loaded, for example, a JAR file, and grant permissions to it. Whenever an agent is started from this code base it will receive these permissions. Another way to grant permissions to agents is via the agent owner, which is explained in the following section.

9.2.4 Configure JAAS

Finally, you have to configure JAAS, that is used within Tracy to authenticate users and grant permissions to them. For a detailed introduction into the concepts of JAAS, we refer to the book by Oaks [2001].

A detailed introduction to the security concepts provided by Tracy will follow in Chapter 10. Here, we describe only the meaning of the two files necessary to configure JAAS. The first one is named *jaas.login* and defines *how* a user must authenticate to use the AgencyShell plugin. Therefore, you only need to modify this file if you want to use this plugin later. The second file is named *jaas.policy* and defines which permissions each user should have. At first glance, you might say that this is also important only when using the AgencyShell plugin, because it defines what a user is allowed to do with a Tracy agency. However, in Tracy an agent inherits all permissions of its owner when running on its home agency, therefore, this file is just another means to grant permissions to agents and supplements the configuration file *tracy.policy*.

The first file must contain the name of a *login module* that is used by JAAS to identify a user. On a Windows operating system, the *NTLoginModule* must be chosen.

```
1 Tracy {
2     com.sun.security.auth.module.NTLoginModule required;
3 };
```

The name of the login module must be *Tracy*, because the AgencyShell plugin looks for exactly this login module. On a Unix operating system, the *UnixLoginModule* must be chosen.

```
1 Tracy {
2     com.sun.security.auth.module.UnixLoginModule required;
3 };
```

The effect of both login modules is that a user is identified with his or her login name as defined by the underlying operating system and does not have to type in a password. If you want a Tracy user to authenticate with a password too, then you have to develop your own login module and register it using this file. For more details on how login module should be developed, see Java's online documentation.

Finally, we have to define which permissions a user should have, which is done using a file similar to that used to define static permissions of code components.

```
1 grant
2   Principal com.sun.security.auth.UnixPrincipal "braun" {
3     permission java.util.PropertyPermission "*", "read";
4     permission de.fsuj.tracy2.kernel.AgencyPermission "MainAgency",
          "shutdown";
5     permission de.fsuj.tracy2.agency.AgentPermission "MainAgency",
          "listAgents,startAgent,stopAgent";
6     permission de.fsuj.tracy2.agency.PluginPermission "MainAgency",
          "listPlugins,startPlugin,stopPlugin";
7 };
```

The file consists of several *grant* entries (the example shows only one), where each entry defines the permissions of a single user. The user is identified by his or her login name. The example defines that user *braun* has the permission to read all Java properties and also has the right to start and stop agents and plugins and to shut down the agency. We will give a detailed introduction into the Tracy specific permissions in the online documentation.

9.3 Starting and Stopping a Tracy Agency

After you have completed the installation and configuration process of Tracy, you can launch a Tracy agency. For the following, we assume that you are in directory TRACY_HOME. To start a Tracy agency, you should use one of the following script or batch files, which can be found in directory *bin*.

- ■ for Unix: *tracy.sh*
- ■ for Windows: *tracy.bat*

If all Tracy configuration files are stored in directory *conf*, then you can simply type in the following command (on a Unix/Linux system):

```
$> ./bin/tracy.sh run
```

Tracy is now started in the same window where you typed in the command. If you want to start Tracy as a background process, you have to use the following command:

```
$> ./bin/tracy.sh start
```

Dependent on the logging mechanism and the logging level, you might see the following messages:

```
 1 Tracy2 Loader V1.0
 2 (Mon Oct 13 18:35:04 CET 2003) [INFO] de.fsuj.tracy2.kernel: Starting Tracy2 Version 1.0
 3 (Mon Oct 13 18:35:04 CET 2003) [INFO] de.fsuj.tracy2.kernel: Java Version 1.4.2
 4 (Mon Oct 13 18:35:04 CET 2003) [INFO] de.fsuj.tracy2.kernel: Tracy home directory /usr/local/tracy
 5 (Mon Oct 13 18:35:04 CET 2003) [INFO] de.fsuj.tracy2.kernel: User home directory /home/braun
 6 (Mon Oct 13 18:35:04 CET 2003) [INFO] de.fsuj.tracy2.kernel: starting micro kernel
 7 (Mon Oct 13 18:35:04 CET 2003) [INFO] de.fsuj.tracy2.kernel: thread pool started (20/50/100)
 8 (Mon Oct 13 18:35:04 CET 2003) [INFO] de.fsuj.tracy2.kernel: micro kernel started successfully
 9 (Mon Oct 13 18:35:04 CET 2003) [INFO] de.fsuj.tracy2.agency: agency "MainAgency" starting
10 (Mon Oct 13 18:35:06 CET 2003) [INFO] de.fsuj.tracy2.agency: no plugins found
11 (Mon Oct 13 18:35:06 CET 2003) [INFO] de.fsuj.tracy2.agency: agency "MainAgency" started
```

Because there are no plugins, you unfortunately cannot do anything sensible with this agency except stopping it. If you have started Tracy as a background process, you should use the following command to halt the agency:

```
$> ./bin/tracy.sh stop
```

Otherwise, you can just abort Tracy by hitting Ctrl-C. This shuts down Tracy agency properly and results in the following logging messages:

```
1 (Mon Oct 13 18:36:58 CET 2003) [INFO] de.fsuj.tracy2.kernel: micro kernel shutting down
2 (Mon Oct 13 18:36:58 CET 2003) [INFO] de.fsuj.tracy2.agency: agency "MainAgency" shutting down
3 (Mon Oct 13 18:36:58 CET 2003) [INFO] de.fsuj.tracy2.agency: agency "MainAgency" shut down
4 (Mon Oct 13 18:36:58 CET 2003) [INFO] de.fsuj.tracy2.kernel: all agent threads terminated
5 (Mon Oct 13 18:36:58 CET 2003) [INFO] de.fsuj.tracy2.kernel: thread pool shutting down
6 (Mon Oct 13 18:36:58 CET 2003) [INFO] de.fsuj.tracy2.kernel: thread pool shut down
7 (Mon Oct 13 18:36:58 CET 2003) [INFO] de.fsuj.tracy2.kernel: micro kernel shut down
```

Both start scripts accept the following options:

run Start a Tracy agency within this process.

start Start a Tracy agency as background process.

stop Stop a Tracy agency.

--help Prints help information.

--ini Defines the directory where all configuration files can be found. If you omit this option, the Tracy loader will use directory *conf*.

All options that start only with a single dash are passed to the Java virtual machine.

Thus, under the assumption that you have placed all configuration files in directory *conf/minimal*, you can use the following command to start a Tracy agency on a Unix system:

```
$> ./bin/tracy.sh start --ini conf/minimal -Xms128m -Xmx256m
```

This example also shows how to define options that are passed to the Java virtual machine.

9.4 Installation and Usage of Basic Plugins

In this section we will describe how to install and configure two very important plugins: *AgencyShell* and *AgentLauncher*. The AgencyShell plugin provides a textual user interface (console) to administrate a running agency. The AgentLauncher plugin starts agents while launching the agency.

9.4.1 AgencyShell

Introduction

If you store the *AgencyShell* plugin in the *plugins* directory, you can communicate with a running agency using a textual user interface (sometimes also called a shell or console).

Using the textual user interface of Tracy, you can administrate the whole agency, including starting and stopping agents, listing all agents currently residing on this agency, and so forth. You can also start and stop plugins and administrate them if they provide their own commands for the shell.

When the AgencyShell plugin is started, it uses the Java authentication and authorization system to log in users (i.e., file *jaas.login* is read to select the login module which defines how users have to authenticate). The login module that was mentioned previously identifies the user as the one who is actually starting Tracy. Other login modules, especially the one that comes with the *Taas* plugin requires the user to authenticate with a user name and a password, which are verified against a Tracy user management database.

After the user has logged in, AgencyShell provides a simple textual user interface comparable to a Unix shell or a DOS command prompt. In general, the console provides two focus points. The first is that of the agency, which is actually the one that you enter after logging in. In this focus you can only administrate the agency. The second focus is that of a plugin. To change focus from the agency to one of the plugins, you must enter command `cf` (change focus), which will be explained below. The following set of commands can be used in the agency focus as well as in a plugin focus.

`author [--help]` Prints the author of a component according to the current focus.

`docs [--help]` Prints a URL where documentation can be found for this component according to the current focus.

`exit [--help]` Exits the shell without closing the agency. Note that this command can only be used at the agency focus.

`echo []`

`echo [--help | STRING | ${NAME}]` Outputs the given arguments followed by a new line. If `NAME` is a valid variable name, its value is displayed. The `STRING` argument could be every character sequence except those used for variable definition.

`gc [--help]` Starts the Java VM garbage collector.

`help [--help]` Outputs a summary of commands that are provided by this component according to the current focus.

`info [--help]` Prints basic information about this component according to the current focus.

`memory [--help]` Prints information about system memory usage.

`set []`

`set [--help | NAME = VALUE]` Without options, name and value of each environment variable is displayed. The output is sorted in ascending order. When a key-value pair is specified, a new environment variable is defined or an existing one is redefined.

`shutdown [--help | --delay MILLISEC]` Shuts down the agency. If the option `--delay` is used, the shut down process is delayed for the given time (in milliseconds).

`statistics [--help]` Outputs statistical information about this component according to the current focus.

`unset []`

`unset [--help | VARIABLE_NAME]` Undefines the environment variable with the given name.

`version [--help]` Prints version information about this component according to the current focus.

`who [--help]` Shows all users currently logged in.

`whoami [--help]` Shows the current username.

To conclude this subsection, we present an example to show how environment variables can be defined and read.

```
[1]> set
kernel.logging.level = 4
```

```
kernel.logging.class = de.fsuj.tracy2.logging.SimpleLogger
agency.name = MainAgency
agency.class = de.fsuj.tracy2.agency.Agency
agency.url = file:/usr/local/tracy/lib/agency.jar
agency.classloader = de.fsuj.tracy2.kernel.AgencyClassLoader
agency.logging.level = 4
agency.logging.class = de.fsuj.tracy2.logging.SimpleLogger

[2]> set my.agent.url = "file:/${user.dir}/examples/"

[3]> echo ${my.agent.url}
file:/usr/local/tracy/examples

[4]> unset my.agent.url

[5]> echo ${my.agent.url}
```

The last command does not produce any output, because the environment variable with name *my.agent.url* no longer exists.

Agency Commands to Start and Stop Agents

The following commands are only available in the agency focus and are used to start and stop agents.

agents [PREFIX] [-a] [-u NAME] [-l] [-n] [-d] [-o] [-r] Lists all agents running on this agency by name. If a PREFIX is given, then only agents whose names start with this prefix are displayed. Option -a displays not only the user's agents but all agents currently residing at this agency. With the -u you can select whose agents should be displayed. With -n only the agents' nicknames are displayed and with -l information about the start time is printed. The following options are to modify sorting of the output: with -d, agent names are displayed in ascending order of their start time, with -o, agent names are displayed in ascending order by their owner's names, and with -r, the order can be reversed.

runagent AGENTNAME Reruns an already existing agent that bears name AGENTNAME.

startagent -n NICKNAME -c CLASSNAME -u CODEBASE Starts a new agent. The given nickname is used as an easy-to-read name for the agent. The agency then generates a unique *full agent name* that consist of the given nickname and an implicit name (represented as hex value). The nickname is not necessarily unique, but it is guaranteed that no two agents bear the same full name. The `CLASSNAME` parameter must contain the complete name of the agent's main class. The `CODEBASE` parameter must contain a valid URL where the agent's code can be found.

`stopagent AGENTNAME` Stops agent with name `AGENTNAME` and removes it from this agency. Note that you need to enter the full agent name as the agent's name.

Finally, we present an example of how to start an agent.

First, we start an agent with nickname *Bond*:

```
[1]> startagent -n Bond -c examples.agents.TimerAgent
-u file:${user.dir}/agents/
agent with name "Bond" was started
```

Then, we prove that the agent has really been started:

```
[2]> agents
Bond.2BB5BC41A09766AF@MainAgency.tatjana.cs.uni-jena.de
```

Now, we start the `agents` command with two options:

```
[3]> agents -ln
Bond tracyadmin Mon Oct 13 19:23:00 CET 2003 Mon Oct 13 19:23:15 CET 2003
```

Because we used option `-n`, only the agent's nickname is displayed and because we used option `-l` (as you can see, you can shorten these two options), the first date represents the time at which the agent was started and the second date is when the agent was last executed.

Finally, we stop the agent:

```
[4]> stopagent Bond.2BB5BC41A09766AF@MainAgency.tatjana.cs.uni-jena.de
agent with name "Bond.2BB5BC41A09766AF@MainAgency.tatjana.cs.uni-jena.de"
was stopped.
```

Agency Commands to Work With Plugins

When you administrate an agency, you can start and stop plugins and change the focus of existing plugins. Here is a list of all commands:

`back` Change focus back to the agency.

cf PLUGINNAME Change focus to plugin with name PLUGINNAME.

plugins [SERVICENAME] Lists all running plugins. If parameter SERVICENAME is set, then all plugins that provide this service are displayed.

startplugin CODEBASE Starts a new plugin. Only the URL to the plugin's JAR file must be provided. The name of the plugin is defined by the name of the JAR file, the plugin's service name is obtained from the manifest file included in the archive.

services [PLUGINNAME] Without options, all available services are displayed. If parameter PLUGINNAME is set, only the service that is provided by the plugin with the given name is printed.

stopplugin PLUGINNAME Stops the plugin with name PLUGINNAME.

Now we present two examples of how to work with plugins. For this purpose we use the message plugin. The first examples demonstrate how to start a new plugin. We assume a situation in which there are already several plugins running:

```
[1]> plugins
AgencyShell, Survival, Agency
```

We now start a new plugin:

```
[2]> startplugin file:${user.dir}/plugins/Message.jar
plugin with name "Message" was started

[2]> plugins
AgencyShell, Survival, Agency, Message

[3]> stopplugin Message
plugin with name "Message" was stopped

[4]> plugins
AgencyShell, Survival, Agency
```

In the second example we look for plugins which provide the "survival" service. If such a plugin exists, we change the focus to this plugin and ask for some help. Finally we move back to the agency focus.

```
[1]> plugins survival
Survival

[2]> cf Survival

[3]> help
author      Prints the author of this component
back        Change focus to the agency.
docs        Prints a URL where documentation for this component
            can be found.
echo        Prints the given parameter.
gc          Starts the Java VM garbage collector.
help        Prints this help screen.
info        Prints some basic information about this component.
locale      Usage: locale [-a|--all] [-l|--language LANGUAGE
            -c|--country COUNTRY]. Shows current locale, list
            all available locales and sets the current locale.
memory      Prints information about memory usage.
set         Usage: set KEY = VALUE. Defines an environment
            variable. KEY must be a word, VALUE can be
            a word, a variable (which is resolved) or a
            number.
statistics  Prints some statistical information about this
            component.
unset       Undefines an environment variable.
version     Prints information about the version of this
            component.

[4]> back
```

After the last command, you are back in the agency focus.

Telnet

In addition to the console that starts when launching an agency, Tracy offers another way to administrate an agency, a Telnet session. The basic console has some severe drawbacks that are a result of the Java programming language, which cannot read arbitrary characters from the keyboard. Therefore, Tracy provides a Telnet server to which you can connect using any Telnet client software.

The Tracy Telnet server is also part of the AgencyShell plugin if you enabled the Telnet server by defining variable `remoteshell` as to be `true` as shown in the following excerpt of the AgencyShell configuration file.

```
1 remoteshell.enable = true
2 remoteshell.port = 4444
```

remoteshell.enable defines whether the remote shell via Telnet should be activated. Allowed values are `true` and `false`.

remoteshell.port defines the port where the remote shell waits for connections.

The advantage of a Telnet session as compared to the basic console is mainly that of an improved level of convenience:

■ A history of commands.

■ Editing of command lines using arrow keys.

■ Automatic completion of commands, agent names, plugin names, file names, and variable names.

The following table gives an overview of all allowed short-cuts and their purposes.

Shortcut	Purpose
Backspace	Delete character before cursor
Left	Move cursor left one character
Right	Move cursor right one character
Pos1	Move cursor to beginning of line
End	Move cursor to end of line
Next	Display next history line
Prev	Display previous history line
Del	Delete character under cursor
Ins	Toggles insert–overwrite mode
Alt-Left Alt-b	Move cursor left one word
Alt-Right Alt-f	Move cursor right one word
Tab	Complete commands and file or path names (path names if word under cursor starts with file:)

(cont'd)

Shortcut	Purpose
Ctrl-a	Complete agent names
Ctrl-f	Complete plugin names
Ctrl-s	Complete service names
Ctrl-k	Kill text until end of line
Ctrl-y	Yank (insert) last killed text
Ctrl-l	Clear telnet screen
Ctrl-d	Logout

9.4.2 AgentLauncher

The task of the AgentLauncher plugin is to start agents automatically during the launch of an agency. This plugin cannot be administrated at runtime and does not provide any new shell commands, because its only purpose is to start agents at the end of the start-up process of a Tracy agency. The AgentLauncher plugin is always started after all other plugins have been started. This is because agents might immediately use services provided by other plugins.

The associated configuration file for this plugin contains entries describing the agent's nickname, its owner, its class name, and a URL where the class for the agent can be found for each agent to be started. Here is an example:

```
1 agent.0.owner = "tracyadmin"
2 agent.0.nickname = "Bond"
3 agent.0.class = "de.fsuj.tracy2.agents.test.Agent"
4 agent.0.url = "file:${user.dir}/agents/"
```

Each agent must have a unique ID, and the agents are started in ascending order according to this ID. The keys have the following meaning:

agent.<id>.owner defines the agent's owner. Tracy grants permissions to agents according to the user that started them. It can be said that an agent inherits all permissions of its owner. Therefore, it is important to define who should be the owner of an agent. If the given user does not exist, then the agent will have no permissions, unless other plugins grant permission to this agent.

agent.<id>.nickname defines the agent's nickname. Each agent has a nickname that is used as a human-readable name to complement the implicit name given by the agency. The nickname is not necessarily unique, so it is possible for several agents to bear the same nickname but different full names.

agent.<id>.class defines the class name for the agent to start. The given value must contain the fully qualified class name (i.e., including the package name).

agent.<id>.url defines the URL where the agent's classes can be found.

Summary

In this chapter we described the development of another mobile agent toolkit and how Tracy is different from all other mobile agent toolkits currently available. The main idea behind Tracy is to have an extendable agent toolkit, which consists chiefly of a kernel that provides only basic services to execute agents. All services such as agent migration, agent communication, agent persistency, parts of agent security, and so forth, are provided by so-called plugins.

You have learned how to:

- install and configure a Tracy agency,

- start and stop a Tracy agency using script files,

- install and use basic plugins, for example, to start agents after launching an agency, and

- administrate a Tracy agency using the shell plugin and a Telnet console.

In the next chapter we will show how to program mobile and stationary agents in Tracy.

Chapter 10

Programming Agents with Tracy

In this chapter we describe how to program mobile and stationary agents with Tracy. We explain the agent's life-cycle and how agents communicate to their owners. After that we discuss how agents communicate to services in general, the following plugins, and the services that they provide:

- Survival—to let an agent be restarted from time to time
- Place—to let agents be informed about themselves and other agents
- Messaging—to communicate to other agents on the same agency
- Migration—to let agents migrate to other agencies
- DomainManager—to let agents *see* their network environment

Contents

10.1 The First Agent

In this section we present first examples of very simple Tracy agents. The goal is to show which interfaces a Tracy agent must implement and which methods an agent must provide in order to be executed by a Tracy agency. We also show how agents can use services that are provided by plugins, and teach along the way about the life-cycle of agents and some details on how agents are executed within a Tracy agency. The examples presented in this section use the following two plugins:

- Survival—used by an agent to schedule its own execution.

- AgencyShell—used by an agent to write messages to its owner.

For the following chapter, we assume that both plugins have been installed correctly (i.e., their JAR files have been stored in the *plugins* directory and the AgencyShell plugin has been configured as shown in Chapter 9). The Survival plugin does not need to be configured.

10.1.1 Creating a Tracy Agent

Tracy agents need to implement interface *java.lang.Runnable*, which is a core JDK interface that defines only a single method, run, without any parameters and without a return value. This is the only interface that any kind of *stationary* software agent must implement—in Tracy we do not distinguish between different types or classes of agents, as is done in other mobile agent toolkits. Tracy does not define a common superclass for software agents that provides methods to access services or to obtain any information about the agent itself. If you want to program *mobile* agents, the agent class must also implement interface *java.io.Serializable*, which ensures that the agent's object can be transferred into a flat byte stream.

```
1 package examples.agents;
2
3 public class MyFirstAgent implements java.lang.Runnable
4 {
5   public void run()
6   {
7     System.out.println( "Hello World!" );
8   }
9 }
```

As always, when introducing a new programming language or programming environment, the first example should be the simplest—it only prints a *Hello World!* message to the console. Place this file in a directory named *examples/agents*—in this example we assume all paths to be relative to your home directory (which might be */home/user*). Compile this class as usual with the Java compiler. We assume that the resulting class is stored in the same directory as the Java source file, thus, there should be a Java class file named *examples/agents/MyFirstAgent.class*.

Starting the Agent

Now, start a Tracy agency, which should be configured as shown in Chapter 9. At the command prompt, you should type in the following command:

```
[1]> startagent -n MyAgent -c examples.agents.MyFirstAgent -u file:/home/user/
```

If there is any error, for example, if the given class cannot be found at the given URL, an appropriate error message will be shown. Otherwise the agent's class is instantiated and the agency calls agent's *run* method. You should immediately see the message Hello World! on your screen.

Let's now go into some details of starting an agent. After the agent class has been instantiated, agent execution is started by method *run*. As software agents are active and autonomously acting objects, each agent is assigned control of its own thread from a thread pool. Note the slight difference: An agent is neither on the same level as to a thread nor owns the same thread for its whole lifetime, but an agent is executed by a thread while it is active (i.e., in state *Running*). After the agent's *run* method has terminated, the agent might die or switch to state Tracy calls Waiting.

The Agent's Life Cycle

The two states and how they may change are some of the most important things to know about the agent's lifecycle. After the agent's *run* method has terminated, the agency must decide whether the agent should be switched to state Waiting or killed and removed from the agency. The rule for this is very simple: If the agent has registered with a service, then the agent is switched to state Waiting, otherwise it is terminated immediately.

When the agent is in state Waiting, it is only a passive object that is waiting to become active again. Because it does not need an active thread of control in this state, the thread is returned to the thread pool and can be re-used to execute other agents. The reason to employ thread pools is performance, because creating a new thread is still one of the most expensive operations within a Java runtime environment.

As you can see from the previous example, method *run* is the only mandatory method that an agent class must implement. It defines the behavior of the agent, that is the complete control flow that is performed inside the agent's thread. As a consequence, this method is the only possible starting point for an agent. In Tracy, agents are usually started several times during their lifetimes. This is very different from other mobile agent toolkits, where the agent's main method (named *live* or *startAgent*) is called only once. In Tracy, an agent frequently switches between states *Running* and *Waiting*. For example, assume a scenario in which agents send messages to each other. After agent α has sent a message to agent β, it should switch to state *Waiting* until agent β has answered. It is poor programming practice to wait actively for the answer, which would waste computing power. Therefore, when agent β has released its answer, agent α will be restarted by the agency. It is up to the agent to distinguish why it has been started and what has to be done now, for example, it might need to react to the answer and send further messages. As you will learn from the examples in the remainder of this chapter, it is common to program agents as finite state machines, which is a good means to control their complexity.

The immediate reason for this type of programming is, of course, the asynchronous message passing that is used in this example. If we had used a synchronous communication protocol, agent α would have waited (actively) for the answer of agent β. Thus, what we learn from this example is that an agent's main method *run* might be started several times instead of only once as in this example. However, whether it is in fact started several times depends on the overall task of the agent.

Agents Can Die

Let's come back to our first example. If you type in the command to see the list of all agents currently running on this agency, you will not see agent *MyAgent*. The reason for this should be obvious by now. Because the agent has not used or registered with any service, there is nothing to prevent the agent from being terminated and removed.

Before we show how to use services and how to make agents switch to state *Waiting*, we mention some basic features of Tracy concerning the security of software agents. In Tracy, each agent has its own class loader, which means that agents are unable to refer to each other in terms of object references. Even two agents of the same type (i.e., the same Java class), are not allowed to hold references to each other, because their classes are not visible. Additionally, each thread that executes an agent belongs to an own thread group. This prevents threads from accessing each other, which would make it possible to stop or otherwise attack them. To protect the agency and the underlying host against malicious agents, we use the Java sandbox technique. Permissions are granted to agents as described in Chapter 9. If an agent violates its rights, it will usually be terminated.

10.1.2 How to Use Services

As already mentioned, Tracy agents are not derived from any existing super-class for software agents (unlike the Aglets or Grasshopper toolkits). In these systems there is a class, *MobileAgent*, that already defines several methods that access services, for example, to send a message or to start the migration process. Therefore, Tracy agents must use another technique to access services; we use the concept of *context objects* for this. An agent must request a context object from a service using a static method *getContext* which is defined in class *de.fsuj.tracy2.kernel.Context*. Such a context object defines several methods that agents can use to communicate to a service and we call this the service API.

We now show a first example of an agent that uses the *shell* service to send a message on its owner's console. This service is provided by the AgencyShell plugin. The drawback of the first example above is that the "Hello World!" message is printed using the *System.out* stream that is shown on the console from which the Tracy agency was started. If the user is logged in using a Telnet session, he or she is not able to see this message. Therefore, we modify the first example:

```
1 package examples.agents;
2
3 import de.fsuj.tracy2.kernel.Context;
4 import de.fsuj.tracy2.plugins.shell.interfaces.IAgentShellContext;
5
6 public class MyFirstAgent implements java.lang.Runnable
7 {
8   public void run()
```

```
 9  {
10    IAgentShellContext cxt;
11
12    if( (cxt = (IAgentShellContext)Context.getContext( "shell" )) != null )
13    {
14      cxt.writeToUser( "Hello World!" );
15    }
16  }
17 }
```

This example requires some explanation. In line 4 we import the agent context interface of the *shell* service. In line 12 we request a context object using method *getContext* with the name of the service as a parameter. If a service with the given name cannot be found, then method *getContext* returns *null*. Finally, in line 14 we print the message to the user.

Method *getContext* determines the agent calling it by determining its current thread and asking which agent is currently executed by this thread. Then the task is delegated to the agency, which has a directory of all services, and checks whether the requested service is available. In the last step, the agency requests an agent context interface from the plugin that provides the needed service. The plugin must guarantee that there is only a single context object for each agent, for example, by maintaining a map of all agents currently holding a context interface.

Actually, we face two problems with this first example. First, if the current agency does not provide a service under the given name, class *IAgentShellContext* does not exist. Second, the service registered under the given name *shell* might return a context object which is incompatible with the expected type *IAgentShellContext*.

The first problem can be solved with Java's dynamic class-loading concept. The class of type *IAgentShellContext* is not loaded until it is accessed, which, in the previous example, is not until the typecast. If the agent first verifies that a service with the given name exists, this problem can be solved. The second problem can be solved by comparing class names. The following example shows the resulting code sequence:

```
1 package examples.agents;
2
3 import de.fsuj.tracy2.kernel.Context;
4 import de.fsuj.tracy2.plugins.shell.interfaces.IAgentShellContext;
5
6 public class MyFirstAgent implements java.lang.Runnable
```

```
 7 {
 8  public void run()
 9  {
10     IAgentShellContext cxt;
11
12     if( Context.existsContext("shell",
13                 "de.fsuj.tracy2.plugins.shell.interfaces.IAgentShellContext"))
14     {
15       cxt = (IAgentShellContext)Context.getContext("shell");
16       ...
17     }
18  }
19 }
```

If you start this agent, the agent's message will now be printed in the user's console, even if the user has logged in via Telnet. If the user is logged in more than once, the message will be printed on each console. If the user is currently not logged in, the message will not get lost, but will be printed to the user's console the next time he or she logs in. However, we do not know a technique to start an agent without being logged in, so you cannot experience this yet.

However, this agent will terminate as quickly as the agent in the previous example. This is because the agent uses a service with which it has not registered.

10.1.3 How to Register with a Service

Whether an agent can register with a service depends on the service. In the last example, the agent has requested a context object of the *shell* service, but has not registered with it (actually, agents cannot register with the *shell* service).

We now present the first example of a service, with which agents can register. It is the *survival* service. We begin with a simple example.

```
1 package examples.agents;
2
3 import de.fsuj.tracy2.kernel.Context;
4 import de.fsuj.tracy2.plugins.shell.interfaces.IAgentShellContext;
5 import de.fsuj.tracy2.plugins.survival.interfaces.IAgentSurvivalContext;
6
7 public class MyFirstAgent implements java.lang.Runnable
```

```
 8 {
 9  public void run()
10  {
11    IAgentShellContext cxt;
12
13    Context.getContext( "survival" );
14
15    if( (cxt = (IAgentShellContext)Context.getContext( "shell" )) != null )
16    {
17      cxt.writeToUser( "Hello World!" );
18    }
19  }
20 }
```

This agent first requests a context object of the *survival* service and implicitly registers with it in line 13. The difference between simply using a service and registering with it depends on the type of service and cannot be deduced from the agent's source code. The effect is that this agent will survive thread termination, that is, after method *run* has terminated, the agent will continue to live. You can prove this by typing in the command to print the list of all agents. We say that the agent is now in state *Waiting*, where it exists as a passive object without a control thread.

If you type in the *ls* command to display the names of all agents currently residing at this agency, you will see something like the following:

```
[2]> ls
MyAgent.A567CB123A766AF7@MainAgency.tatjana.cs.uni-jena.de
```

What you see here is the *full agent name* of your agent. It consists of the nickname that you have defined, a sequence of characters that represent a number in hexadecimal format, followed by a "@" and the name of the agency on which the agent was started. The hexadecimal number is named *uuid* which stands for *universal unique identifier*. It is a number that is computed by the agency to make each agent name unique. Combined with the full agency name, this makes the full agent name globally (i.e., within a Tracy system) unique. Neither the name nor the agent's home agency change after the agent has been initialized.

Thus, what you have learned from this example is that an agent must register with a service in order to survive termination of its main method. If the agent has not registered with a service, it will be disposed by the agency as soon as its *run* method has terminated. Otherwise, the agent remains alive, but in state *Waiting* until the user, the agency, or any other plugin restarts it. In this example it can only be activated by an external event. Later, when we use asynchronous messaging, the agent may be awakened by a message from another agent or from its owner. To restart an agent, type in the `runagent` command, followed by the agent's full name. However, the agent still does not do anything sensible except print *Hello World* messages to its owner. Every time you start the agent, a new message will be printed. To eventually delete the agent manually, you have to use the `stopagent` command, followed by the agent's name. An agent can also release the connection to the *Survival* service if it wants to die.

In the following sections, we will introduce all the basic services that are shipped with the Tracy agency, beginning with the *Survival* plugin.

10.2 Survival

The most important job of the *Survival* plugin is to prevent an agent from being disposed after its *run* method has terminated. It can also be used to schedule future agent execution. For example, an agent can define that it wants to be started once at a specific time or time interval. An agent can also define that it wants to be started periodically.

The complete API of the *Survival* service consists of the following methods:

`public void` *schedule(Date date)*
Starts the agent once at the given *date*.

`public void` *schedule(Date firstDate, long period)*
Starts the agent at the given *firstDate* and then every *period* milliseconds.

`public void` *schedule(long delay)*
Starts the agent once after the given *delay* in milliseconds.

`public void` *schedule(long delay, long period)*
Starts the agent after the given *delay* in milliseconds and then every *period* milliseconds.

`public void` *cancel()*
Deregisters from this service. Stops every previously defined timer.

The following example shows an agent that registers with the *survival* service to be started every five seconds.

```
1 package examples.agents;
2
3 import de.fsuj.tracy2.kernel.Context;
4 import de.fsuj.tracy2.plugins.survival.interfaces.IAgentSurvivalContext;
5 import de.fsuj.tracy2.plugins.shell.interfaces.IAgentShellContext;
6
7 public class MyFirstAgent implements java.lang.Runnable
8 {
9  private int state = 0;
10
11  public void run()
12  {
13     IAgentSurvivalContext survivalCxt;
14     IAgentShellContext shellCxt;
15
16     switch( state )
17     {
18       case 0:
19         if( (survivalCxt = Context.getContext( "survival" )) != null );
20         {
21           survivalCxt.schedule( 1000, 5000 );
22         }
23         state = 1;
24         break;
25       case 1:
26         if( (shellCxt = (IAgentShellContext)Context.getContext( "shell" )) != null );
27         {
28           shellCxt.writeToUser( "Hello World!" );
29         }
30         break;
31     }
32  }
33 }
```

This example shows an agent that uses a finite state machine. When the agent is first started, it is in state 0, where it registers with the *survival* service. In line 21, the agent defines that it wants to be restarted every 5 seconds after a first initial delay of 1 second. After that it switches to state 1 and terminates. As previously mentioned the agent is not disposed of because it is registered with at least one service. The plugin that provides the *survival* services restarts the agent after the defined period of time. Now, the agent is in state 1 which causes a "Hello World!" message to be printed at the user's console. Because the agent remains in this state, the agent is restarted every 5 seconds and always prints the same message.

10.3 Place

The *Place* plugin provides the *place* service, which agents can use to retrieve information about their environment. As we have mentioned before, an agent is not able to communicate to the hosting agency directly; the only way to do so is to use a plugin that provides a service for this task. The most important service of this plugin is to provide agents a means to obtain their own names and the names of other agents currently residing at the same agency. The *Place* plugin does not need to be configured.

The complete API of the *place* service consists of the following methods. The first four methods can be used by an agent to obtain information about itself.

```
public String getNickname()
```
Returns the agent's nickname.

```
public String getFullAgentName()
```
Returns agent's full name.

```
public String getHomeAgencyName()
```
Returns the name of the agent's home agency, that is, the agency on which the agent was started.

```
public String getOwnerName()
```
Returns the name of the agent's owner.

The following method can be used to retrieve the name of this agency.

```
public String getAgencyName()
```
Returns the name of the current agency.

The following methods can be used to get the names of other agents currently residing at this agency.

```
public String[] getAgentNames()
```
Returns the name of all agents currently residing at this agency.

> `public` *String[] getAgentNamesByNickname(String nickName)*
> Returns the name of all agents with the given *nickName.*

The following methods can be used to get information about installed plugins and services.

> `public` *String[] getPluginNames()*
> Returns the names of all plugins currently running at this agency.

> `public` *String[] getServiceNames()*
> Returns the names of all services that are provided by plugins currently running at this agency.

> `public` *String[] getPluginNamesForService(String serviceName)*
> Returns the names of all plugins that provide the service with the given *serviceName.*

> `public` *String getServiceOfPlugin(String pluginName)*
> Returns the name of the service that is provided by the plugin with the given *pluginName.*

Finally, the following method can be used to start new agents.

`public` *String startAgent(String className, URL codeBase, String nickName)*
Starts an agent with the given *nickName*. The agent's main class is given by *className* and the agent's classes can be found under the URL given by *codeBase*. The method returns the agent's full name.

As an example, we show an agent that requests the name of its owner and writes a greeting message to the owner.

```
1 package examples.agents;
2
3 import de.fsuj.tracy2.kernel.Context;
4 import de.fsuj.tracy2.plugins.place.interfaces.IAgentPlaceContext;
5 import de.fsuj.tracy2.plugins.shell.interfaces.IAgentShellContext;
6
7 public class MyAgencyAgent implements Runnable
8 {
9     public void run()
10    {
11        IAgentPlaceContext agencyCxt;
12        IAgentShellContext shellCxt;
13
14        if( (agencyCxt = (IAgentPlaceContext)Context.getContext("place")) != null )
```

```
15            {
16                if( (shellCxt = (IAgentShellContext)Context.getContext("shell")) != null )
17                {
18                    shellCxt.writeToUser( "Hello " + agencyCxt.getOwnerName() + "!" );
19                    shellCxt.writeToUser( "This agency: " + agencyCxt.getAgencyName() );
20                }
21            }
22        }
23    }
```

In line 14 the agent requests a context object of the *place* service. In line 18 the name of the agent's owner is requested and a message is sent to the owner including the owner's name and, in the following line, the name of the agency.

10.4 Messaging

10.4.1 Introduction

An important function of any mobile agent toolkit is to provide some kind of communication model so that agents can *talk* to each other and exchange information. As you might already have guessed, communication is also provided as a plugin. In the following section we will introduce a straight-forward communication model and show how Tracy agents can exchange messages.

The principal way for Tracy agents to communicate to each other using this plugin is by asynchronous message passing. We have deliberately not included any kind of direct communication that allows agents to invoke methods of other agents either by a direct reference or any kind of proxy object. This restriction is necessary for security reasons. Any kind of direct reference would affect agents in a direct way, which is a contradiction to the concept of agent autonomy.

If agents want to send messages to other agents, they have to know the name of the recipient, which is usually the full name of the agent. Every agent has a message queue in which new messages are stored. The agent can decide on its own how to handle these messages. It can decide whether to accept messages by closing its message queue (temporarily), which preserves the autonomy of the agent.

You might have the impression that we also provide a kind of remote communication, that is, the ability to send messages to agents that are currently located at other agencies. However, this plugin does not support any kind of remote communication. Even if both agencies were located on the same host, sending messages between them would not be possible. This restriction is a result from our interpretation of mobile agents: An agent must move to the destination platform if it wants to communicate to other agents there.

10.4.2 The Message Plugin API

When an agent wants to send or receive messages, the first thing it has to do is, of course, register with the `Message` plugin, that is, to request a context object from it. This context object provides the `Message` plugin API, which we explain in detail in this section.

Sending Messages

After an agent has requested this context object, it can immediately start sending messages to other agents using one of the following methods:

`public void` *sendMessage(String recipient, String subject)*
Sends a message to the given *recipient* with the given *subject* and empty message body.

`public void` *sendMessage(String recipient, String subject, String body)*
Sends a message to the given *recipient* with the given *subject* and *body*.

As you can deduce from these methods, a message is comparable to an email and consists of the following parts:

■ recipient—the full name of an agent

■ subject—a String object that contains a description of the kind of message

■ body—a String object that contains the actual message content

■ time stamp—the time at which the message was created

We start here with an example in which an agent sends a welcome message to all agents whose nicknames are *Bond*. For the sake of simplicity, we do not verify whether the requested plugins are available.

```
1 package examples.agents;
2
3 import de.fsuj.tracy2.kernel.Context;
4 import de.fsuj.tracy2.plugins.message.interfaces.IAgentMessageContext;
5 import de.fsuj.tracy2.plugins.place.interfaces.IAgentPlaceContext;
6
7 public class MyMessageAgent implements Runnable
8 {
9     protected IAgentMessageContext amc;
10    protected IAgentPlaceContext aac;
11
12    public void run()
13    {
14        aac = (IAgentPlaceContext)Context.getContext( "place" );
15        amc = (IAgentMessageContext)Context.getContext( "message" );
16        Context.getContext( "survival" );
17
18        String myName = aac.getMyName();
19        String[] agentNames = aac.getAgentNamesByNickName( "Bond" );
20
21        for( int i=0; i<agentNames.length; i++ )
22        {
23            amc.sendMessage( agentNames[i], "Hello", "My name is: " + myName );
24        }
25    }
26 }
```

We have to face two possible error situations when sending messages. The first one occurs when the given name of the recipient is wrong. In this case, method *sendMessage* throws an *IllegalArgumentException*. In the previous example we do not catch this exception, which might terminate the agent if any of the agents with nickname *Bond* have died or migrated between requesting all agent names and sending a message to this agent. The same exception is thrown by method *sendMessage* if the given recipient exists but has not registered with the Message plugin yet. Another possible error situation occurs when the recipient has, for example, temporarily closed its message queue. Before we explain this in detail, we show how to receive messages in general.

Receiving Messages

To receive messages, an agent must have registered with the Message plugin already, that is, it must have a context object, and it must have enabled reception of messages using the following method:

```
public void enableMessaging()
```
Activates reception of messages.

Calling this method is comparable to opening a queue in which incoming messages are stored. As we have already mentioned, an agent cannot receive messages without having registered with this plugin. If an agent has already registered but has not activated its message queue, then the sender will receive a *IllegalStateException*. This exception indicates that the receiver (temporarily) refuses to receive the message.

To close the message queue, an agent can use the following method:

```
public IMessage [] disableMessaging()
```
Prevents reception of messages and returns all messages still pending in the message queue.

This method returns all messages that are pending in the message queue, so that the message queue is always empty before it is closed. If there are no messages in the message queue, this method returns an empty array.

Finally, the current status of the message queue can be requested by the following method:

```
public boolean isMessagingEnabled()
```
Returns the current status of the message queue.

To fetch a message from the message queue is a process that must be initiated by the agent itself. Because of the general model of Tracy agents, we cannot use a technique where the message plugin delivers messages by invoking a specific method of an agent. However, there must be some kind of signal sent to an agent to notify it about new messages. The only type of signal that can be sent to agents by plugins is to *restart*, which invokes method *run*. As a consequence, agents should be programmed to always actively check first if there are any new and undelivered messages, using the following method:

```
public boolean hasMoreMessages()
```
Returns **true** immediately, if the message queue is not empty. Otherwise returns **false**.

If there are new messages in the queue, then the agent should go on to the second step—fetching the next message of the queue using the following method:

> public *IMessage getNextMessage()*
> Fetches the next message out of the message queue.

If this method is called when no message is available, an *Illegal-StateException* is thrown. It is guaranteed that the order in which messages will be fetched out of the message queue is the same in which they were added to it. The return value of method *getNextMessage* is an object of class *IMessage*. This class provides the following methods to retrieve the elements of a message:

> public *String getSender()*
> Returns the originator of the message, which is usually the full name of an agent.

> public *String getSubject()*
> Returns the subject of this message.

> public *String getBody()*
> Returns the message text body.

The last two methods might return null values or empty String objects. Finally, with the last method, the time of creation can be requested:

> public *Date getTimeStamp()*
> Returns the time when this message was created.

This time is approximately the time when the message was sent.

Finally, we present an example of an agent that is able to receive messages and immediately sends back every message to the originator.

```
1 package examples.agents;
2
3 import de.fsuj.tracy2.kernel.Context;
4 import de.fsuj.tracy2.plugins.message.interfaces.IAgentMessageContext;
5 import de.fsuj.tracy2.plugins.message.interfaces.IMessage;
6
7 public class MyMessageAgent implements Runnable
8 {
9    protected IAgentMessageContext amc;
```

```
10
11    public void run()
12    {
13        IMessage msg;
14
15        amc = (IAgentMessageContext)Context.getContext( "message" );
16        amc.enableMessaging();
17
18        while( amc.hasMoreMessages() )
19        {
20          msg = amc.getNextMessage();
21          amc.sendMessage( msg.getSender(), "Rcvd: " + msg.getSubject(),
                 msg.getBody() );
22        }
23    }
24 }
```

10.5 Migration

10.5.1 Introduction

Migration of software agents between different agencies is, of course, one of the most important tasks in a *mobile* agent toolkit. Many existing toolkits, therefore, see the migration service as a core component of the agency that is implemented in lower layers of their software architectures. In Tracy migration is a service on the same level as inter-agent communication or user management. If a migration service is not necessary for a specific application domain, you can simply omit it. Otherwise, Tracy allows you to use multiple migration plugins, all of which provide a migration service. For example, the first plugin could provide the Kalong mobility model and the second could provide the Aglets mobility model, which implements the MASIF migration protocol. Then an agent can decide which migration service it wants to use for the next migration.

The migration plugin that we introduce in this section is named MDL and uses, of course, the Kalong software component as described in Chapters 6 and 7 and the network component that was mentioned in Section 6.4.3. However, MDL enhances the usage and functionality of Kalong to a certain extent and provides an easy-to-use interface to conduct migration strategies.

The main drawback of Kalong is that the main interface used to configure a migration strategy (interface *IKalong*) is fairly low-level and offers a large set of decision capabilities. Thus, it is difficult to master it in full detail, and even experienced programmers will experience a learning curve when using this interface to program agent mobility. Another problem is that placing commands to conduct a migration process within the business logic of an agent leads to a more complex source code. It is, therefore, advisable to split these two aspects of mobile agent programming into separate classes.

Based on this insight, we introduce a new layer of abstraction. The description of migration strategies is moved to separate Java classes and an agent defines which strategy should be used for the next migration by selecting an appropriate one by name. This technique can be compared to the *Strategy* pattern, described by Gamma et al. [1995]. Introducing migration strategies as separate Java classes simplifies programming of mobile agents and makes the agent's source code clear and well structured. It also makes agents more adaptable to specific application domains, as it is now easy to adopt a different migration strategy if the application makes it necessary.

The MDL plugin already comes with several migration strategies, including those mentioned in earlier chapters. An overview of these migration strategies is given at the end of this section, where we introduce the programming of proprietory migration strategies.

Another benefit of MDL as compared to other mobility models is the way destination agencies are addressed. In almost all other mobile agent toolkits, the programmer and the agent have to know the host name and a port number where the destination agency will accept SATP connections using a specific network transmission protocol, for example SSL. Because port numbers of agencies might change during the lifetime of an agent, it is advisable to use only the logical agency name, which does not change. As a consequence, each agency must be able to resolve a logical agency name and to retrieve information about network protocol and corresponding port numbers of destination agencies. This feature is provided as a plugin named *Tracy Naming Service* (TNS). A short example that describes the functionality of TNS is given in Section 10.5.3.

Finally, MDL uses and even extends the mechanism of Kalong to adapt the SATP protocol. We already introduced this basic concept of Kalong in Chapter 7, where we presented examples of Kalong extensions that inspect class codes or compress SATP messages.

The technique used in MDL is called *SATP pipelining*, and it is an enhancement of Kalong's extension mechanism. With Kalong it was only possible to register a single listener object that is called at certain points during the migration process. With SATP pipelining not only one but many *pipeline steps* can be linked together. This makes it possible for a first pipeline step to inspect an agent's class code, the second pipeline step signs all static information of an agent (static part of the header, code, etc.), and the third step compresses each SATP message before sending it to the destination.

Information about used pipeline steps is sent as part of the SATP header. When the destination agency receives the header, it can verify that it knows all pipeline steps that were processed at the sender agency and has the correct version of them. If the destination agency will not be able to process all requested pipeline steps, it will reject the agent. Otherwise, the pipeline steps are processed in reversed order for all SATP messages. With regard to pipeline steps, a major benefit of MDL is that the set of pipeline steps to be processed can be modified at runtime by the agent. Besides some mandatory pipeline steps that must be processed for each migration (without regard to whether it is an incoming or outgoing migration or defined by the Tracy administrator), an agent can also select other pipeline steps.

10.5.2 Installation

MDL is very flexible and can be configured like other Tracy plugins. Usually, the following aspects of MDL should be configured:

- Network transmission protocols
- Kalong scripts (which is a superset of all migration strategies)
- Pipeline steps that should be processed during a migration

Network Transmission Protocols

First it should be defined which network transmission protocols can be used to transfer agents to destination agencies. To register a network protocol, the following four entries should be defined in file *MDL.conf*:

protocol.\<number\>.name defines the protocol name, under which this network component is to be registered. This protocol name can then be used in URLs that address destination agencies.

protocol.<number>.class defines the name of the class in which this network component is implemented.

protocol.<number>.url defines the URL from where the code of this network component can be loaded. This entry can be omitted if the corresponding class is part of the plugin JAR file.

protocol.<number>.port defines the port on which the network component is accepting incoming migration requests.

For example, in the following we register the network protocol that is implemented in class *TCPEngine* under the protocol name *tcp*.

```
1 protocol.0.name = "tcp"
2 protocol.0.class = "de.fsuj.tracy2.network.tcp.TCPEngine"
3 protocol.0.port = 31000
```

For a detailed introduction on how to develop additional network transmission protocols, see the Tracy online documentation.

Kalong Scripts and Migration Strategies

The more general form of migration strategies are *Kalong scripts.* Such a script is implemented as a Java class and provides methods to access all features of Kalong. The difference between Kalong scripts and migration strategies is that only the latter one can be used to transfer agent objects, that is, to send the state of an agent.

Kalong scripts are an essential part of the MDL plugin, because several basic functions, for example, loading a data item from the agent's home agency, are actually implemented as such scripts. Therefore, it is necessary for a small set of Kalong scripts to always be registered with MDL. Otherwise, specific features of MDL cannot be used.

Migration strategies are also registered as Kalong scripts. Every script must have a unique name. To register a script, the following entries must be defined:

script.<number>.name defines the name of the Kalong script as it should be used by agents.

script.<number>.class defines the name of the class of this Kalong script.

script.<number>.url defines the URL where the class can be found. If this entry is missing, the class must be available in the plugin JAR file.

For example, in the following we register a Kalong script, under name *pushAgent*, whose class is part of the migration plugin JAR. Actually, this class implements a migration strategy, in which an agent is transmitted with all data and code to the next destination agency. We use this migration strategy in the examples presented in the rest of this section.

```
1 script.0.name = "pushAgent"
2 script.0.class = "de.fsuj.tracy2.plugins.migration.scripts.PushAgent"
```

The following Kalong scripts must be registered and their entries should not be deleted from the configuration file delivered with the MDL plugin, because they are used by MDL to perform some basic operations.

LoadDataItem is used when a data item has to be loaded from an agent's home or mirror agency.

ReleaseCodeServer can be used to release all code server agencies that an agent has initialized during its itinerary. This script is used by MDL when an agent is going to die, so that code server agencies will not become orphans. However, it can also be used by agents.

ReleaseMirror can be used to release a mirror agency. The script loads all data items that might be defined on the mirror agency before releasing it. This script is used by MDL when an agent is going to die, but can also be used by agents.

UploadDataItem is used to send a data item back to an agent's home or mirror agency.

Pipeline Steps

Finally, all pipeline steps that should be used to modify SATP messages must be registered using the following entries:

pipelinestep.<number>.name defines the name of the pipeline step as it can be used by MDL or by agents.

pipelinestep.<number>.class defines the name of the class in which this pipeline step is implemented.

pipelinestep.<number>.url defines the URL from where the code of this pipeline step can be loaded. If this entry is missing, the corresponding class must be available in the plugin JAR file.

For example, in the following we register a pipeline step that compresses all SATP messages before they are sent to the destination agency.

```
1 pipelinestep.0.name = "zip"
2 pipelinestep.0.class = "de.fsuj.tracy2.plugins.migration.pipesteps.ZipPipelineStep"
```

The current version of MDL already comes with the following five pipeline steps that are all part of the MDL archive file. File *MDL.conf* already contains entries to register all these pipeline steps.

Cipher encrypts all SATP messages with the public key of the destination agency.

FilterFinalize inspects incoming Java classes and rejects those classes that implement method *finalize*.

PathHistory adds the agency name to the list of visited agencies and signs this list. Incoming agents are checked according to the path history. If the agent has visited an agency listed on a user-defined blacklist, the agent is rejected.

Signer signs the SATP header and all other static parts of an agent, for example, its code with the private key of the agent owner. At a destination agency, the signature is verified.

Zip compresses all SATP messages.

Further, we can define that specific pipeline steps must be executed for all agents, without regard to whether the agent has selected them or not. We name such pipeline steps *mandatory*. For example, the administrator of a Tracy agency might define that each agent that migrates to an agency should be scanned to decide whether its code might be malicious. We already mentioned a case in which an agent implements method *finalize* and the consequences this might have for the agency. Mandatory pipeline steps can be included at the beginning or at the end of the SATP pipeline. To configure mandatory pipeline steps, you have to use the following keys:

pipeline.mandatory.head.<number>.name inserts a pipeline step at the beginning of the pipeline for all SATP connections.

pipeline.mandatory.tail.<number>.name appends a pipeline step at the end of the pipeline for all SATP connections.

The head and the tail of a pipeline must be seen from the perspective of an outgoing SATP connection. For example, if we configure the pipeline to have the $Signer$ step at the beginning (head) and the Zip at the end, then every message sent as part of an outgoing SATP connection will be processed first by the $Signer$ and last by the Zip pipeline step. If we want to add the $FilterFinalize$ pipeline step to be processed at the end of every incoming SATP connection, we have to configure MDL as follows:

```
1 pipeline.mandatory.head.0.name = "filterFinalize"
```

For an incoming SATP connection, the order in which pipeline steps are processed must be inversed. Therefore, a step inserted at the *head* is then processed last. You cannot register a mandatory pipeline step to be processed exclusively for an incoming or an outgoing SATP connection.

10.5.3 Programming Mobile Agents

The mobility model that is provided by MDL is based on the Kalong model that we introduced in Chapter 3. From the programmer's viewpoint we currently offer a weak form of mobility, in which an agent can start a migration simply by defining the name or a URL of the destination agency. After the agent has migrated it is restarted by invoking method run of the agent. The basic mobility model of Tracy does not support the transmission of a method identifier that should be invoked at the destination. However, this can be easily implemented by an agent itself, should this become necessary.

The agent cannot only define *to which* agency it should be transferred to but also *how* this should happen by defining the migration strategy. As already mentioned, MDL supports the concept of migration strategies that are implemented in separate classes and must be registered with the migration plugin. The agent can then select one of the registered migration strategies for the next migration. If the agent does not select any migration strategy, then the migration strategy that was registered first is selected as the default.

In this section we introduce how agents can communicate with the migration service using interface $IAgentMigrationContext$ which is part of package $de.fsuj.tracy2.plugins.migration$.

Simple Migration

We start with an example of a mobile agent.

```
1 package examples.agents;
2
```

```
 3 import java.io.Serializable;
 4 import de.fsuj.tracy2.plugins.migration.interfaces.IAgentMigrationContext;
 5
 6 public class MobileAgent implements Runnable, Serializable
 7 {
 8  public void run()
 9  {
10    IAgentMigrationContext migrationContext =
11        (IAgentMigrationContext)Context.getContext( "migration" );
12
13    try
14    {
15      migrationContext.setDestination( new URL( "tcp://tatjana.cs.uni-jena.de:4040" ) );
16      migrationContext.setMigrationStrategy( "pushAgent" );
17    } catch( Exception e )
18    {
19      e.printStackTrace();
20    }
21  }
22 }
```

The first and most important difference to all other agents that we have presented so far is that a mobile agent not only has to implement interface *java.lang.Runnable* but also interface *java.io.Serializable*. This is necessary, as mobile agents must be serializable in order to be transferred over the network as plain byte array.

After the agent has requested a context of the migration service, it defines the address of the destination agency using method *setDestination*.

public void *setDestination(URL address)*
Defines the address of the destination agency as URL object.

The second method is to define the migration strategy:

public void *setMigrationStrategy(String name)*
Defines the migration strategy that should be used for the next migration.

Only if a destination **and** a valid migration strategy were defined, will the agent migrate. If no migration strategy was defined, the first strategy registered is selected by default. If you select a migration strategy unknown to MDL, a migration error will occur.

The migration context does not provide a method to initialize the migration process directly. This is because the agent alone does not decide directly, as part of its code, whether the migration process can be started. Other plugins might disapprove this action. For example, a communication plugin might not want an agent to migrate if there are still pending messages in the message queue. Therefore, every time method *run* of an agent terminates, the microkernel of Tracy carries out a voting protocol. Each plugin is asked whether this agent should be killed, switched to state *Waiting* (e.g., to wait for new messages), or may migrate. Only if all plugins agree, is the migration plugin asked to initialize the migration process.

The agent presented previously does not do anything sensible. It simply migrates to the destination agency and is restarted there. However, it immediately tries to migrate to the agency where it is currently located. Because this is impossible, the migration feature will produce an error message.

After introducing the two main methods of interface *IAgentMigration-Context*, we now consider the first complete example of a mobile agent that migrates to a remote agency and back to its home agency.

```
1 package examples.agents;
2
3 import java.io.Serializable;
4 import de.fsuj.tracy2.plugins.migration.interfaces.IAgentMigrationContext;
5
6 public class PingPong implements Runnable, Serializable
7 {
8   private static final int ATHOME = 0;
9   private static final int ATREMOTE = 1;
10   private static final int BACKHOME = 2;
11
12   private int state = ATHOME;
13
14   public void run()
15   {
16     IAgentMigrationContext migrationContext =
17             (IAgentMigrationContext)Context.getContext( "migration" );
18
19     if( state == ATHOME )
20     {
21       migrationContext.setDestination( new URL( "tcp://tatjana.cs.uni-jena.de:4040" ));
22       migrationContext.setMigrationStrategy( "pushAgent" );
23
24       state = ATREMOTE;
25
```

```
26        return; // now the migration process starts
27
28    } else if( state == ATREMOTE )
29    {
30        URL home = migrationContext.getHomeAgency( "tcp" );
31
32        migrationContext.setDestination( home );
33        migrationContext.setMigrationStrategy( "pushAgent" );
34
35        state = BACKHOME;
36
37        return; // now the migration process starts
38
39    } else
40    {
41        IAgentShellContext shellContext =
42            (IAgentShellContext)Context.getContext( "shell" );
43
44        shellContext.writeToUser( "I'm back!" );
45
46        return;
47    }
48  }
49 }
```

This examples shows a typical pattern of programming mobile agents using finite state machines. When the agent is started, it is in state *ATHOME*. The agent decides to migrate to an agency that is running on *tatjana.cs.uni-jena.de* and listening on port 4040 for a TCP connection. For sake of simplicity we assume that the migration was successful. After the agent has been received at *tatjana.cs.uni-jena.de*, it is started and is now in state *ATREMOTE*. Because the agent intends to migrate back to its home agency immediately, it requests the address of its home agency in line 30. The agent uses a method of interface *IAgentMigrationContext* to select an agency URL with a specific protocol. We will discuss this issue later. Finally, the agent returns to its home agency and is restarted there with state *BACKHOME*. It finally prints a message to its owner and terminates.

As mentioned before, one drawback we notice in the previous example is the rather complicated way agencies are addressed. Instead of an agency's name, you use the name of the underlying host and a port number. Although this is a common technique used in most other mobile agent toolkits, we find this extremely inconvenient and, therefore, implemented a technique to obtain host names and port numbers dynamically. This feature is named *Tracy Naming Service* (TNS) and is a plugin that is used by the migration plugin.

The only information a programmer has to know to initialize a migration process is the name of an agency, for example `fortknox.-tatjana.cs.uni-jena.de`. The advantage is obvious: Within an agent system, only agency names should be propagated, not port numbers and available network protocol information, which might change during the lifetime of an agent.

To initialize agent migration using the TNS you have to define the destination agency name using the following method:

```
public void setDestination( String agencyName )
Defines the agency name of the next destination.
```

The only difference here is that the parameter must now be an object of type `String` and no longer of type `URL`. You can also define which network protocol should be used for the next migration using the following method:

```
public void setProtocol( String protocol )
Defines the protocol that should be used for the next migration.
```

The default protocol is the first one that was registered in the configuration file.

As already stated, TNS is implemented as a plugin and must be configured accordingly in the agency configuration file. (For an example, see the exemplary configuration file in the distribution archive). If the TNS plugin is not started on both agencies, logical agency names cannot be resolved and an appropriate error message will be returned to the agent.

Migration Errors

Until now, we did not consider errors that might happen during the migration process. Actually, there could be several errors, but the most frequent is for the destination agency to be unavailable. If there is a migration error, the migration process is stopped and the agent is restarted at the current agency, that is, where the migration was started. To indicate an error situation, an error code is set in the migration context. To request the error code, the following method can be used:

```
public int getErrorCode()
```
Returns the error code of the last migration attempt. If no error occurred, value 0 is returned.

A detailed error message that might be given to the agent programmer can be requested by the following method:

```
public String getErrorDescription()
```
Returns an error description, for example, an exception message.

To handle error situations, an agent should request the error code of its migration context and react to it according to the requirements. For example, in a simple scenario, the agent could terminate whenever it determines that the last migration attempt was not successful.

```
1 package examples.agents;
2
3 import java.io.Serializable;
4 import de.fsuj.tracy2.plugins.migration.interfaces.IAgentMigrationContext;
5
6 public class PingPong implements Runnable, Serializable
7 {
8   private static final int ATHOME = 0;
9   private static final int ATREMOTE = 1;
10   private static final int BACKHOME = 2;
11
12   private int state = ATHOME;
13
14   public void run()
15   {
16     IAgentMigrationContext migrationContext =
17             (IAgentMigrationContext)Context.getContext( "migration" );
18
19     if( migrationContext.getErrorCode() != 0 )
20     {
21       migrationContext.reset();
22       return;
23     }
24
25     if( state == ATHOME )
```

```
26    {
27      migrationContext.setDestination(tatjana.cs.uni-jena.de);
28      migrationContext.setMigrationStrategy( "pushAgent" );
29
30      return;
31  ...
```

If the first migration fails, then this agent is restarted at its home agency. The migration context is the same as before. Now the agent checks the error code and notices the error situation. In this case, the agent must use method *reset* to delete the destination information, and finally terminates with the return statement. If the agent does not delete the destination address, it would continually try to migrate to the given agency. All possible error codes are defined in interface *IAgentMigrationContext*. For sake of simplicity we only present the most frequent error codes here.

Error code 0xB0 The selected network transmission protocol is not supported at this agency.

Error code 0xB1 The selected network transmission protocol is not supported at the destination agency.

Error code 0xB3 The selected migration strategy does not exist.

Error code 0xB7 The connection is rejected by the destination agency, that is, the agency is not listening on the given port number.

Data Items

As you know, Kalong provides the ability to define data items that are part of the agent's *external state*. These data items are usually transferred as part of the agent's state, but the agent can define that certain data items should remain at the home agency. Furthermore, the agent can load data items from the home agency and send data items back to it later.

The general concept was already introduced in Chapter 7 and we will, therefore, only present a small example here. First, we show how an agent can store data items in the external state. The method to store data items is:

> **public void** *setDataItem(String name, Serializable value)*
> Stores the given *value* under the given *name* in the external state.

Note, that the object to store must implement interface *java.io.Serializable*.

Whether the external state will be migrated along with the agent depends on the migration strategy. For example, using the *pushAgent* strategy, all data items are transferred to the destination agency, so that the agent can there access the data item again:

```
public Serializable getDataItem( String name )
Returns the data item of the external state with the given name.
```

If the data item is not available at the current agency, an exception is thrown. If you are not sure whether a data item is already available locally or must be loaded from the agent's home agency, you should use the following method:

```
public Serializable getDataItem( String name, boolean load )
Returns the data item with the given name. If the data item is not available and load
equals true, then it is loaded from the agent's home agency or mirror agency.
```

You can also explicitly load a data item from the agent's home agency or the mirror agency if it is defined but not yet loaded:

```
public boolean loadDataItem( String[] names )
Loads the given data items from the agent's home or mirror agency. Returns true if all
given data items could be loaded.
```

If you want to send data items back to the agent's home or current mirror agency, then you can use the following method:

```
public boolean uploadDataItem( String[] names )
Sends all given data items back to the agent's home or mirror agency. Returns true if
uploading was successful.
```

Until now, we always stressed that code classes that are not available at the current agency can be downloaded from the agent's home agency, code server agency, or mirror agency automatically on demand. The MDL plugin provides a new technique, so that the programmer can start the process of code downloading manually, as soon as it is obvious that a specific class will be used in the future. This technique, called *code prefetching*, provides the advantage that code can be downloaded in parallel with agent execution, a feature that might improve the performance of mobile agents considerably.

Consider the following source code:

```
1 package examples.agents;
2
```

```
 3 import java.io.Serializable;
 4 import de.fsuj.tracy2.plugins.migration.interfaces.IAgentMigrationContext;
 5 import de.fsuj.tracy2.plugins.migration.interfaces.IMonitor;
 6
 7 public class SampleAgent implements Runnable, Serializable
 8 {
 9   public void run()
10   {
11     try
12     {
13       IAgentMigrationContext migContext = (IAgentMigrationContext)
                                          Context.getContext("migration");
14
15       // ...
16
17       if( /* ... */ )
18       {
19           // assume that it is known now that class A is used in future
20           IMonitor monitor = migContext.loadClassNonBlocking( "examples.agents.A" );
21
22           // ...
23
24           monitor.waitForTermination(); // synchronize
25
26           A a = new A();
27
28           // ...
29
30       }
31     } catch( Exception e )
32     {
33       e.printStackTrace();
34     }
35   }
36 }
```

We assume that in line 20 it is already known that class *A* will be used in the future. In this line, the process of asynchronous class loading is started. The method invocation returns immediately and a new thread has been started that processes class loading in parallel. Later, when agent execution reaches line 24, the agent's thread and the class loading thread synchronize and in line 26 class *A* is instantiated. Data items can be loaded asynchronously too, using *loadDataItemNonBlocking* instead of method *loadDataItem* that was introduced in Chapter 7.

10.5.4 Programming Kalong Scripts

The interface *IAgentMigrationContext* that was introduced earlier only provides some very high-level methods for agents to access the Kalong mobility model. For this, MDL provides a new abstraction in the form of class *KalongScript*. Once a Kalong script is registered, agents can start it using the name under which the script was registered.

> **public boolean** *executeScript(String name)*
> Starts execution of the Kalong script that was registered under the given name.

Because an agent cannot start a migration process, a Kalong script does not provide access to any method that can be used to define and send an agent's serialized object. Method *executeScript* does not accept parameters other than the name of the script. However, sometimes it might be necessary to pass parameters to a script, which can be done using *properties* for Kalong scripts:

> **public void** *setProperty(String key, Object value)*
> Defines a property of the migration context with the given *name* and *value*.

With this method, you can define a key-value pair in the migration context of an agent. A Kalong script can access these key-value pairs as we show in the following example of the *LoadDataItem* script:

```
1 package de.fsuj.tracy2.plugins.migration.scripts;
2
3 import de.fsuj.tracy2.plugins.migration.KalongScript;
4 import de.fsuj.tracy2.kalong.IKalong;
5 import de.fsuj.tracy2.kalong.KalongException;
6
7 import java.net.URL;
8
9 public class LoadDataItem extends KalongScript
10 {
11     public void run() throws KalongException
12     {
13         URL destination = null;
14         final String[] dataItemNames;
15
16         if( containsProperty( "data.items.name" ))
```

```
17              {
18                  dataItemNames = (String[])getProperty( "data.items.name" );
19              } else
20              {
21                  return;
21              }
23
24          try
25          {
26              startTransaction();
27
28              final String protocol = getLastProtocolUsed();
29
30              if ( isMirrorAgencyDefined() )
31              {
32                  destination = getMirrorAgencyAsURL( protocol );
33              } else
34              {
35                  destination = getHomeAgencyAsURL( protocol );
36              }
37
38              final Object handle = startTransfer( destination );
39              sendHeader(handle, IKalong.NOOP);
40              sendDataRequest(handle, dataItemNames );
41
42          } finally
43          {
44              if (prepare())
45              {
46                  commit();
47              } else
48              {
49                  rollback();
50              }
51          }
52      }
53 }
```

The main method of a Kalong script is *run*, which is invoked when the script
is started. The script just presented expects the agent's migration context to
contain a property named *data.items.name*, which must contain an array
of String objects where each object contains the name of a data item that
should be loaded. If such a property does not exist, the script immediately

terminates. Most methods used in this example should already be well-known from Chapter 7. In line 26, a transaction is started. In line 28 the name of the protocol that was used for the last migration of this agent is selected. In line 32 and line 35 the address of the destination agency is determined, and in line 38 the connection is opened. Finally, in line 40 the data-item request is sent to the destination agency.

For a complete overview of all methods provided by class *KalongScript*, see the Tracy online documentation.

10.5.5 Programming Migration Strategies

Finally, in this section we introduce the programming of migration strategies. Migration strategies are a special form of Kalong scripts and provide methods for the definition and sending of an agent's serialized object. The base class of all migration strategies is *MigrationStrategy* in package *de.fsuj.tracy2.plugins.migration*. Migration strategies cannot be started by agents using method *executeScript* but can only be selected by name for the next migration process.

To pass parameters to migration strategies, the same technique is used as for Kalong scripts. Following is a list of property keys that are recognized by all migration strategies:

- `mdl.destination` The corresponding value must be a URL that contains the destination address or a String that contains a logical agency name.

- `mdl.ubiclasses` The corresponding value must contain an array of String objects that are regular expressions to be matched by fully qualified Java class names, which should not migrate. This key-value pair is optional. A default value is defined as constant *SYSTEMCLASSES* in class *MigrationStrategy*.

- `mdl.usecache` If the migration properties contain an entry with this key, the Kalong code cache is activated for the next migration regardless of the default value of the migration strategy.

- `mdl.notusecache` If the migration properties contain an entry with this key, the Kalong code cache is disabled for the next migration regardless of the default value of the migration strategy.

We now have two ways to define the address of the destination agency: using method *setDestination* of interface *IAgentMigrationContext* (remember that this method is overloaded) and using method *setProperty* of the same interface with key *mdl.destination*.

Class *MigrationStrategy* also defines some convenient methods to access property values, define code units, or start the migration process:

```
protected URL destination()
```
Returns the URL of the destination agency.

If the address of the next migration destination was defined as a URL object, then this method returns that value. If an agent has been defined as a logical agency name, then this method actually translates the agency name into a URL by communicating to the TNS plugin. You should always use this method, if you want to access the destination address instead of reading migration property *mdl.destination* yourself.

```
protected boolean useCache()
```
Returns **true** if the class cache should be activated for the next migration.

Again, this method is preferred to reading property values *mdl.usecache* and *mdl.notusecache* manually. The following methods provide two frequently used ways to define code units:

```
protected void defineUnitForEachClass()
```
Defines a single code unit for each class of the agent.

```
protected void defineUnitforAllClasses()
```
Defines a single unit for all classes of the agent.

The following source code defines method *migrate*, that can be used by derived migration strategies to start the migration process in a very flexible way.

```
protected void migrate( URL destination, int[] codeUnits,
    String[] dataItems, boolean useCache )
```
Starts a migration process to the given *destination*, transferring the given code units and the given data items. The last parameter indicates whether the class cache should be used.

This method opens a new network transfer and sends the *Agent Definition Block* (ADB) as well as all units and data items, as specified in the parameters. Here is the source code of this method:

```
1  protected final void migrate(final URL destination, final int[] units,
2              final String[] dataItems, final boolean useCache) throws MDLException
3  {
4      final Object handle;
5
6      if (destination == null)
7      {
8          throw new MDLException( ERROR_NO_DESTINATION );
9      }
10
11     try
12     {
13         handle = kalong.startTransfer(destination);
14         kalong.sendHeader(handle, IKalong.NOOP);
15         kalong.sendADB(handle, useCache);
16
17         if (units != null && units.length != 0)
18         {
19             kalong.sendUnits(handle, units);
20         }
21
22         kalong.sendState(handle, dataItems);
23
24     } catch (KalongException e)
25     {
26         throw new MDLException(e);
27     }
28 }
```

The most convenient way to implement a migration strategy is to extend class *MigrationStrategy* and implement the following two methods that are defined as *abstract* in this class.

protected abstract void *defineUnits()*
Defines the way code units are defined for agent classes.

protected abstract void *migrateAgent()*
Defines how the agent should be transferred to the next destination.

Both methods are called by *MigrationStrategy*'s method *run*. This method starts a transaction, defines the agent object state, and then calls method *defineUnits* if code units have not already been defined. Finally, it invokes method *migrateAgent* to start the migration process and commits (or rolls back) the transaction.

In the rest of this section we present three examples of migration strategies that are already part of the MDL plugin.

Push all classes This migration strategy implements one of the most used migration techniques in mobile agent toolkits. It combines all agent classes into a single code unit and transfers this unit together with all data items and the agent's state to the next destination.

Pull each class This strategy defines a separate code unit for each agent class. It then transfers the agent with all data items and the agent's state. However, no code units are transferred.

Push agent class This strategy defines a separate code unit for each class. It then transfers the agent with all data items and the agent's state, together with the agent's main class. The agent's main class is the only code unit transferred. All other classes must be loaded on demand.

The first migration strategy is implemented as class *PushAgent* in package *de.fsuj.tracy2.plugins.migration.scripts*.

```
1  package de.fsuj.tracy2.plugins.migration.scripts;
2
3  import de.fsuj.tracy2.kalong.KalongException;
4  import de.fsuj.tracy2.plugins.migration.MigrationStrategy;
5
6  public class PushAgent extends MigrationStrategy
7  {
8      protected void defineUnits() throws KalongException
9      {
10         defineUnitForAllClasses();
11     }
12
13     protected void migrateAgent() throws KalongException
14     {
15         final int[] unitIds;
16         final String[] definedDataItems;
17
18         unitIds = getUnits();
19         definedDataItems = getDefinedDataItems();
```

```
20
21          migrate(destination(), unitIds, definedDataItems, useCache() );
21     }
23 }
```

In line 18 all code units, and in line 19 all data items, that are currently defined are requested. In line 21 the migration process is started.

The second migration strategy is implemented in class *PullPerClass*. It does not transmit any code units, it only transmits the migrating agent's current object state. It defines a single code unit for each class. In line 15 the migration process is started and the two null values indicate that no code units or data items will be transmitted per the default setting.

```
 1 package de.fsuj.tracy2.plugins.migration.scripts;
 2
 3 import de.fsuj.tracy2.kalong.KalongException;
 4 import de.fsuj.tracy2.plugins.migration.MigrationStrategy;
 5
 6 public class PullPerClass extends MigrationStrategy
 7 {
 8     protected void defineUnits() throws KalongException
 9     {
10         defineUnitForEachClass();
11     }
12
13     protected void migrateAgent() throws KalongException
14     {
15         migrate( destination(), null, null, useCache() );
16     }
17 }
```

The last migration strategy is implemented in class *PushAgentLoadOther*. It defines a single code unit for each class and only transmits the main agent class to the next destination, while all other classes are loaded dynamically during runtime from the agent's home server.

```
1 package de.fsuj.tracy2.plugins.migration.scripts;
2
3 import de.fsuj.tracy2.kalong.KalongException;
4 import de.fsuj.tracy2.plugins.migration.MigrationStrategy;
5
6 public final class PushAgentLoadOther extends MigrationStrategy
7 {
```

```
 8    protected void defineUnits() throws KalongException
 9    {
10        defineUnitForEachClass();
11    }
12
13    protected void migrateAgent() throws KalongException
14    {
15      final String agentClassName = getAgent().getClass().getName();
16      final int[] units = getUnitForClassName(agentClassName);
17      final String[] definedDataItems = getDefinedDataItems();
18
19      migrate(destination(), new int[] {units[0]}, definedDataItems, useCache());
20    }
21  }
```

In line 15 the class name of the agent's main class is determined and in the following line the corresponding code unit that contains this class is requested. This implementation must be extended if the agent itself extends other classes or interfaces. In line 19 the migration process is started and the first unit that contains the agent's base class is selected for transmission.

Finally, here is a list of all other migration strategies already provided by the MDL plugin. All migration strategies are located in package *de.fsuj.tracy2.plugins.migration.scripts*.

PushAgentWithoutCache works as the *PushAgent* strategy but disables the code cache by default.

PushClassesInUse defines a separate code unit for each class and transmits all data items, the agent's state and all code, but only for classes where an object exists in the serialized agent's state and in the external state.

PushToAll defines a separate code unit for all classes. This migration strategy accepts a property named *all.destinations*, which must contain an array of URLs. It transfers all code units to all these addresses and then starts the migration to the first destination.

PullPerClassWithoutCache works like PushToAll, but disables the code cache by default.

PullAllClasses defines one code unit for all classes and does not transfer any code units along with the agent's data items and state.

PullAllClassesWithoutCache works like PushAllClasses, but disables the code cache by default.

MirrorAndPush does not define a mapping of classes to code units, and, therefore, cannot be used for the initial migration of an agent. It first loads code units and data items from the agent's home agency or last mirror agency that are still missing and not defined at the current agency. If there is already a mirror agency, it is released and the current agency becomes the new mirror agency.

MirrorAndPushWithoutCache works like MirrorAndPush, but disables the code cache by default.

Worm works like a worm that roams the network and initializes each agency that it visits to become a code server. It does not transmit any code along with its state transmission, but always loads necessary classes from the last agency it has visited before. It defines a single common code unit for all classes.

WormWithoutCache works like Worm, but disables the code cache by default.

10.6 Managing Logical–Agency Networks

10.6.1 Introduction

The Tracy Domain Manager Service is an approach to construct and evolve a network of agencies. It is indispensable if mobile agents are to move through the network automatically.

The basic concept we employ is that of a *logical-agency network*. We define a logical network as an undirected graph in which vertices represent agencies and an edge exists between a pair of vertices if there is the possibility of transmitting mobile agents between the corresponding agencies. Not all agencies are able to exchange mobile agents because of different transmission protocols, firewalls, or private subnetworks that are only reachable via a gateway server. A logical-network view is a necessary prerequisite for a mobile agent to be able to move through the network in an autonomous fashion. On each agency an agent can ask for this service for the neighboring agencies and decide which agency to migrate to next.

Without such a network service, the agent's programmer has to code the agent's itinerary into its business logic. Although this is sufficient in many applications and in small networks, it is not reasonable to define an agent's route in a wide-area network or in a dynamic environment (e.g., where agencies move in and out of the visible network). In such a scenario, a mobile agent must be able to find a suitable itinerary on its own, that is, it extends its autonomy to the task of initial-route planning. In addition, it must be in a position to react to the ever-changing environment of connections and agencies. Therefore, the agent can modify and refine the initial itinerary while it is traveling the network.

Our approach has a two-level structure, where agencies within a subnetwork are combined into a domain. All agencies within a single domain enlist at a central server, which is called a *domain manager* (Fig. 10.1). Each domain manager registers itself with a unique central server named *master*. Domains can be connected to each other so that mobile agents can also reach agencies in other domains. Connecting and disconnecting of agencies to the network is fully automatic and dynamic. Our approach is multi-agent based, that is, several stationary and mobile agents communicate with each other to build and evolve the logical network view.

The main characteristics of this approach are its robustness in failure situations and its high performance [Braun et al., 2001a]. This approach can guarantee that at all times there is a domain manager for each domain. If a domain manager crashes (because its hosting agency crashes) all remaining agencies vote for the new domain manager. If the original domain manager is relaunched, it can reclaim this role.

A logical-agency network is the foundation for more sophisticated services of this kind, which all need information about neighboring agencies, or even all agencies currently reachable. One research topic is to develop

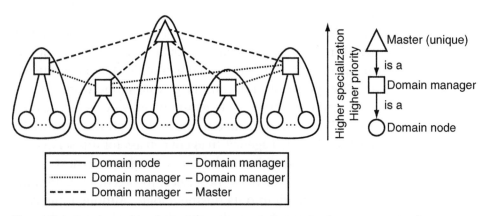

Figure 10.1 Topology of our logical-agency network. An edge between a pair of vertices indicates that the corresponding agencies know each other.

algorithms to plan (semi-) optimal routes for mobile agents with regard to application capabilities (data, user-level services) offered on agencies and network quality information. We are currently developing a network-performance–measuring component for the Tracy toolkit. This component measures transmission time to other agencies periodically and provides this information to mobile agents to support the planning of an optimal route through the network. It uses the logical-agency–network view to define a set of servers where network quality should be tested. On an even higher level of abstraction the logical-agency network can be used to propagate information about applications offered on one agency to others in the network. A mobile agent can use this service-oriented information to plan its route, optimizing it with regard to its application context and according to the original specifications of its owner.

For a introduction of the implementation and the protocols of the Tracy domain management, see Braun et al. [2001a] and the Tracy online documentation. In the following section we confine our discussion to the interface that this plugin provides for agents.

10.6.2 Installing the DomainManager plugin

As described in the last section, each agency plays a specific role in the logical-agency network: domain node, domain-manager node, and master node. In the following we describe how an agency takes on one of these roles during the startup process of this plugin and we will show how this process can be influenced by configuring the plugin. When we use the term agency in this section, we mean the *DomainManager* plugin unless otherwise noted.

The determination of the agency's role is done semi-automatically when launching the agency. First, the agency takes the role of a domain node, assuming that there is another agency that already holds the role of the domain-manager node. To find this domain-manager node and, later, register on it, the new agency sends out a UDP multicast message to all computer systems in the same subnetwork. Therefore, the most important entry in the configuration file is the following:

```
1 udp.port = 42024
```

This entry defines the port number on which this agency is listening to incoming UDP multicast messages. Obviously, this port number must be the same on all agencies that want to join the same logical-agency network.

If there is a domain-manager node in this subnetwork, it receives the multicast message and answers with a single UDP package containing its URL. Migrations can be addressed to this URL. In the second step, the new agency now checks with the same transmission protocol whether it can send mobile agents to the domain manager. In the third step, the new agency sends a mobile agent to the domain-manager node to register the new domain node there. The mobile agent returns to indicate that the registration process was successful. This process is fully automatic and because it uses UDP messages and very small mobile agents, the whole registration process concludes in less than 40 ms, on average, in a 100 Mbit/s network.

If no domain manager agency has answered the UDP multicast message or if the domain manager and the new agency do not share at least one transmission protocol, the new agency takes on the role of a domain manager node. It is possible for two domains to exist in one subnetwork at the same time for the following three reasons: (1) if the new agency sends out the UDP multicast message to a UDP port other than the one the domain-manager plugin receives messages on, the registration process will not start; (2) if the two agencies do not share at least one transmission protocol; (3) because UDP is an unreliable communication channel (the multicast message as well as the answer package may get lost which will cause the registration process to fail). Actually, in our implementation, the UDP multicast is resent three times to compensate for UDP's unreliability.

If you want to skip the first step of this process, you can define the address of an agency that is expected to already be in the role of a domain manager. If such an address is defined, no UDP multicast messages are sent, and the new agency immediately tries to send a mobile agent to the agency whose address is given in the following entry of the configuration file:

```
1 manager = "tcp://192.168.1.41:42024"
```

If the whole registration process fails for any reason, a new domain is created within a subnetwork. Agencies within this subnetwork can now be registered at two separate domain manager nodes. In the current implementation the choice of domain-manager nodes is driven by the first-come-first-served principle, that is, the domain manager node that answers the UDP multicast first is chosen. When the new agency is in the role of the domain-manager node, it should connect to other domain-manager nodes nearby. The only drawback of having two domains in one subnetwork results from slightly increased migration times to agencies in the other domain inside the same subnetwork. The agent must search for the agencies it wants to visit by first migrating via two domain-manager nodes instead of reading the information locally at its current agency.

The highest level role an agency may assume is that of the master node. Whereas the preceding process is fully automatic, the decision on the master node is made manually by the administrator of the agency that should become master node, using the following entry in the configuration file:

```
1 master = "tcp://192.168.1.42:42024"
```

If the new agency becomes a domain-manager node, it will use this URL to address the master node and register with it.

To define an agency as a master node, the line just stated should contain the address of this agency. A master node has the same function as a domain-manager node but it keeps its role over its whole lifetime. The address of the master node should be passed to all domain-manager nodes in the agency network so that they can register with the master node and retrieve information about other domain-manager nodes to which they can connect.

With the simple concepts introduced so far, some problems arise in realistic application situations. As can be deduced from the definition of roles within the logical network, the lifetime and the quality of each type is different. We assume that a domain manager node has a longer lifetime and is more reliable than a domain node, which could be a mobile device using a wireless connection. The master's lifetime and reliability are assumed to be even higher than those of a domain-manager node. However, this assumption has not been made in the approaches presented so far.

One shortcoming results from the selection process that starts when a domain manager node is shutting down. Instead of choosing an arbitrary node, this selection process can only prevent a short-living or unreliable (e.g., on a mobile host) node from becoming domain manager for a short time. The other drawback is strongly related to this; if the domain-manager node is restarted, it should be able to take back the role of domain-manager node from the present one. Two agencies accidentally starting at the same time would thus cause a collision problem.

We now introduce a concept of priorities to influence the role of an agency within the logical network. The priority of a domain-information plugin is modeled as a value between -128 and $+127$. This priority is defined by the administrator before the domain-manager plugin is started. The priority value should result from the reliability and long life of this agency. The higher this value, the more important the role that this agency may assume within the network (see Fig. 10.1). The default value of an agency equals 0. To define the priority, the following entry in the configuration file can be used:

```
1 priority = 10
```

With the concept of priorities, the launching process of the plugin changes slightly. When a new node receives the UDP packages containing the URL and priority information of found domain manager nodes (remember that several domain managers might exist in a single subnetwork), it now compares the priorities of theses nodes with its own. If its own priority is higher, the new node becomes the domain manager. Otherwise, it tries to register at one of these nodes, starting with the one with highest priority.

If a new node becomes domain manager, a process of changing roles is started: A mobile agent is started to visit all domain manager nodes, and notifies each node to release its role and fall back to the role of a domain node. Each node is informed about the new domain-manager node, so no new registration process is necessary.

When a domain-manager node is shutting down, it selects the next domain manager from the list of all known domain nodes, according to their priority. To inform the new domain manager and all connected domain nodes about the new situation, the process just described starts.

To prevent two agencies starting at the same time from becoming domain-manager nodes, the priorities and the agency's names can be used. When receiving the UDP package containing the URL and priority of another domain-manager node, the new node can determine which node is going to take the role of domain manager by comparing the priorities of both nodes. If both priorities are equal, the node is chosen alphabetically by its URL.

10.6.3 The DomainManager API

In this section we give an overview of the DomainManager API, by which an agent can obtain information about other agencies in its environment.

The first method is used to retrieve the current role of this agency.

```
public int getRole()
```
Returns the current role of this domain node.

The returned value is one of the following constants defined in interface *IAgentDomainContext* which is located in package *de.fsuj.tracy2.-plugins.domainservice.interfaces*:

- ROLE_NODE—the agency is a simple domain node
- ROLE_MANAGER—the agency is a domain manager
- ROLE_MASTER—the agency is a master-domain manager

If the current role of the agency cannot be determined because of a running voting process where it is not yet clear which role the agency will take in the future, value ROLE_BUSY will be returned.

The next method can be used by agents to retrieve the addresses of domain nodes.

```
public IAgencyURL[] getDomainNodes()
Returns the addresses of all agencies that are currently registered as domain nodes.
```

This method returns an array of objects of type *IAgencyURL*, which is defined in package *de.fsuj.tracy2.plugins.domainservice.interfaces.-IAgencyURL*. This class defines a collection of several URLs that can be used to address an agency. The differences between these URLs are, therefore, only the protocol names and the port numbers. For an overview of all methods provided by this class, see the Tracy online documentation.

The information about domain nodes is only available at a domain-manager node or a master node. Therefore, an agent has to migrate to such a manager node before requesting the list of all known domain nodes. If this method is called at a domain node, null will be returned.

The next method can be used to retrieve information about domain manager nodes.

```
public IAgencyURL[] getDomainManagers()
Returns the addresses of all domain managers that are known at this agency.
```

If this method is called at a domain node, the address of the unique domain manager is returned. If this method is called at a domain manager, the addresses of all other known domain managers are returned, not including the current agency. If this method is called on a master node, the addresses of all known domain managers are returned.

Finally, at all domain-manager nodes in the logical agency network, the following method can be used to obtain the address of the unique-master node.

public *IAgencyURL getMasterDomainManager( )*
Returns the address of the master-domain manager.

At domain nodes, this information might not be available. Therefore, agents have to migrate to domain-manager nodes to obtain this information. If no master-domain manager is available, this method returns null.

In the following example, an agent retrieves the addresses of all known domain nodes while it is residing at a domain-manager node. If such addresses are found, it prints them on its owner's console.

```
1 package examples.agents;
2
3 import de.fsuj.tracy2.kernel.Context;
4 import de.fsuj.tracy2.plugins.domainservice.interfaces.IAgentDomainContext;
5 import de.fsuj.tracy2.plugins.domainservice.interfaces.IAgentShellContext;
6
7 import java.net.URL;
8
9 public class MyDomainServiceAgent implements Runnable
10 {
11     public void run()
12     {
13         IAgentDomainContext domainCxt;
14         IAgentShellContext shellCxt;
15         IAgencyURL[] domainNodes;
16
17         if((domainCxt = (IAgentDomainContext)Context.getContext("domainservice")) != null
18         && (shellCxt = (IAgentShellContext)Context.getContext("shell")) != null )
19         {
20             if( domainCxt.getRole() == IAgentDomainContext.ROLE_MANAGER )
21             {
22                 domainNodes = domainCxt.getDomainNodes();
23                 shellCxt.writeToUser( "Current system runs in domain manager role!" );
24
25                 if( domainNodes != null )
26                 {
27                     shellCxt.writeToUser( "Known domain nodes are:" );
28                     for( i=0; i < domainNodes.length; i++)
29                     {
```

```
30                    shellCxt.writeToUser( domainNode[i].toString() );
31                }
32              }
33            }
34          }
35        }
36 }
```

Summary

In this chapter we have shown how to program mobile and stationary software agents using the Tracy toolkit. We pointed out that software agents in Tracy are only Java objects of type *Runnable*, which is a very important difference from other mobile agent toolkits. We defined the agent life-cycle and stressed that agents in Tracy should be programmed as finite-state-machines, especially when they implement some kind of communication protocol. We admit that programming of agents is somewhat different from most programming experience (and may be more complex than writing *normal* software components), which mainly is the result of the asynchronous message transfer scheme that is used in most agent toolkits—not only in Tracy. This is an open issue in current research and we are working on techniques to make programming of mobile and communicative agents more easy in the future.

We introduced some very important plugins, for example, to let agents communicate with each other and get information about their environments. As mentioned before, you will be able to find more interesting plugins on our Web site *www.mobile-agents.org*, along with some documentation to develop your own plugins for Tracy and more examples of mobile agents.

We see the extendability of Tracy as its major advantage over other mobile agent toolkits available today. We would like to encourage all research groups working on topics related to mobile agents to implement their research results in Tracy. There are many open issues in mobile agent research, some which have been discussed in this book. A lot of work as already been done on paper, but has not yet been implemented. We hope that many people will find Tracy useful and helpful for their work and will help to create a large user community.

Bibliography

Anurag Acharya, Mudumbai Ranganathan, and Joel Saltz. Sumatra: A language for resource-aware mobile programs. In Jan Vitek and Christian F. Tschudin, editors, *Mobile Object Systems: Towards the Programmable Internet (MOS '96), Linz (Austria), July 1996 (Selected Presentations and Invited Papers)*, volume 1222 of *Lecture Notes in Computer Science*, pages 111–130. Springer-Verlag, 1997.

Adobe Systems, Inc. *PostScript® Language Reference*. Addison-Wesley, 3rd edition, 1999.

Alfred V. Aho, Ravi Sethi, and Jeffrey D. Ullman. *Compilers: Principles, Techniques, and Tools*. Addison-Wesley, 1986.

Joan Ametller, Sergi Robles, and Joan Borrell. Agent Migration over FIPA ACL Messages. In Eric Horlait, Thomas Magedanz, and Roch H. Glitho, editors, *Proceedings of 5th International Workshop on Mobile Agents for Telecommunication Applications (MATA 2003), Marakech (Morocco), October 2003*, volume 2881 of *Lecture Notes in Computer Science*, pages 210–219. Springer-Verlag, 2003.

Wolfram Amme, Niall Dalton, Michael Franz, and Jeffery von Ronne. SafeTSA: A Type Safe and Referentially Secure Mobile-Code Representation Based on Static Single Assignment Form. *ACM SIGPLAN Notices*, 36(5):137–147, 2001.

David Anderson. Seti@home. In Oram [2001], pages 67–76.

Ken Arnold, James Gosling, and David Holmes. *The Java^{TM} Programming Language*. The Java Series. Addison-Wesley, 3rd edition, 2000.

Marco Avvenuti and Alessio Vecchio. MobileRMI: a toolkit for enhancing Java Remote Method Invocation with mobility. In *6th ECOOP Workshop on Mobile Object Systems: Operating System Support, Security and Programming Languages, Sophia Antipolis (France), June 2000*, 2000. Paper is only available online at `cui.unige.ch/~ecoopws/ws00`.

László Babai, Lance Fortnow, Leonid A. Levin, and Mario Szegedy. Checking computations in polylogarithmic time. In *Proceedings of the Twenty Third Annual ACM Symposium on Theory of Computing (STOC 1991), New Orleans (USA), May 1991*, pages 21–32. ACM Press, 1991.

Mario Baldi, Silvano Gai, and Gian Pietro Picco. Exploiting code mobility in decentralized and flexible network management. In Kurt Rothermel and Radu Popescu-Zeletin, editors, *Proceedings of the First International Workshop on Mobile Agents (MA '97), Berlin (Germany), April 1997*, volume 1219 of *Lecture Notes in Computer Science*, pages 13–26. Springer-Verlag, 1997.

Mario Baldi and Gian Pietro Picco. Evaluating the tradeoffs of mobile code design paradigms in network management applications. In Koji Torii, Kokichi Futatsugi, and Richard A. Kemmerer, editors, *Proceedings of the 20th International Conference on Software Engineering (ICSE '98), Kyoto (Japan), April 1998*, pages 146–155. IEEE Computer Society Press, 1998.

Michel Barbeau. Modeling and comparison of bandwidth usage of three migration strategies of mobile agents. In Ahmed Karmouch and Roger Impey, editors, *Mobile Agents for Telecommunication Applications, Proceedings of the First International Workshop (MATA 1999), Ottawa (Canada), October 1999*, pages 197–210. World Scientific Pub., 1999.

Joachim Baumann. Mobile agents: A Triptychon of Problems. In *1st ECOOP Workshop on Mobile Object Systems: Objects and Agents: Love at First Sight or Shotgun Wedding?, Aarhus (Denmark), August 1995*, 1995.

Joachim Baumann. *Mobile Agents: Control Algorithms*, volume 1658 of *Lecture Notes in Computer Science*. Springer-Verlag, 2000.

Joachim Baumann, Fritz Hohl, Nikolaos Radouniklis, Kurt Rothermel, and Markus Straßer. Communication concepts for mobile agent systems. In Kurt Rothermel and Radu Popescu-Zeletin, editors, *Proceedings of the First International Workshop on Mobile Agents (MA '97), Berlin (Germany), April 1997*, volume 1219 of *Lecture Notes in Computer Science*, pages 123–135. Springer-Verlag, 1997.

Joachim Baumann, Fritz Hohl, Kurt Rothermel, Markus Schwehm, and Markus Straßer. Mole 3.0: A Middleware for Java-Based Mobile Software Agents. In Nigel Davie, Kerry Raymond, and Jochen Seitz, editors, *Middleware '98: IFIP International Conference on Distributed Systems Platforms and Open Distributed Processing*, pages 355–372. Springer-Verlag, 1998.

Christoph Bäumer, Markus Breugst, Sang Choy, and Thomas Magedanz. Grasshopper—A universal agent platform based on OMG MASIF and FIPA standards. In Ahmed Karmouch and Roger Impey, editors, *Mobile Agents for Telecommunication Applications, Proceedings of the First International Workshop (MATA 1999), Ottawa (Canada), October 1999*, pages 1–18. World Scientific Pub., 1999.

Werner Van Belle and Theo D'Hondt. Agent Mobility and Reification of Computational State: An Experiment in Migration. In Thomas Wagner and Omer F. Rana, editors, *Agents Workshop on Infrastructure for Multi-Agent Systems*, volume 1887 of *Lecture Notes in Computer Science*, pages 166–173. Springer-Verlag, 2001.

Fabio Bellifimine, Giovanni Caire, Agostino Poggi, and Giovanni Rimassa. Jade—A White Paper. *EXP in search of innovation*, 3(3):6–19, 2003.

Shimshon Berkovits, Joshua D. Guttman, and Vipin Swarup. Authentication for mobile agents. In Giovanni Vigna, editor, *Mobile Agents and Securtiy*, volume 1419 of *Lecture Notes in Computer Science*, pages 114–136. Springer-Verlag, 1998.

Lorenzo Bettini and Rocco De Nicola. Translating strong mobility into weak mobility. In Gian Pietro Picco, editor, *Mobile Agents, Proceedings of the 5th International Conference (MA 2001), Atlanta (USA), December 2001*, volume 2240 of *Lecture Notes in Computer Science*, pages 182–197. Springer-Verlag, 2001.

Walter Binder and Volker Roth. Secure mobile agent systems using Java: where are we heading? In Gary B. Lamont, Hisham Haddad, George Papadopoulos, and Brajendra Panda, editors, *Proceedings of the 2002 ACM Symposium on Applied Computing (SAC), Madrid (Spain), March 2002*, pages 115–119. ACM Press, 2002.

Andrew Birrell and Bruce Nelson. Implementing remote procedure calls. *ACM Transactions on Computer Systems*, 2(1):39–59, 1984.

J. K. Boggs. IBM Remote Job Entry Facility: Generalize Subsystem Remote Job Entry Facility. Technical Report 752, IBM Technical Disclosure Bulletin, August 1973.

Quetzalcoatl Bradley, R. Nigel Horspool, and Jan Vitek. JAZZ: An Efficient Compressed Format for Java Archive Files. In *Proceedings of the 1998 Conference of the IBM Center for Advanced Studies on Collaborative Research (CASCON '98), Toronto (Canada), December 1998*, page 7. IBM Press, 1998.

Jeffrey Bradshaw, editor. *Software Agents*. The MIT Press, Menlo Park, CA, 1996.

Peter Braun, Jan Eismann, and Wilhelm Rossak. Managing Tracy Agent Server Networks. Technical Report 12/01, Friedrich-Schiller-Universität Jena, Institut für Informatik, 2001a.

Peter Braun, Christian Erfurth, and Wilhelm Rossak. Performance Evaluation of Various Migration Strategies for Mobile Agents. In Ulrich Killat and Winfried Lamersdorf, editors, *Fachtagung Kommunikation in verteilten Systemen (KiVS 2001), Hamburg (Germany), February 2001*, Informatik aktuell, pages 315–324. Springer-Verlag, 2001b.

Peter Braun, Steffen Kern, Christian Fensch, and Wilhelm Rossak. Class splitting as a method to reduce the migration overhead of mobile agents. In *Proceedings of the International Symposium on Distributed Objects and Applications (DOA 2004), Larnaca (Cyprus), October 2004*, Lecture Notes in Computer Science. Springer-Verlag, 2004.

Frank Buschmann, Regine Meunier, Hans Rohnert, Peter Sommerlad, and Michael Stal. *Pattern-oriented Software Architecture: A System of Pattern*. John Wiley and Sons, 1996.

Giacomo Cabri, Letizia Leonardi, and Franco Zambonelli. Mobile agent technology: Current trends and perspectives. In *Congresso annuale AICA '98, Napoli (Italy), November 1998*, 1998a.

Giacomo Cabri, Letizia Leonardi, and Franco Zambonelli. Reactive tuple spaces for mobile agent coordination. In Kurt Rothermel and Fritz Hohl, editors, *Proceedings of the Second International Workshop on Mobile Agents (MA '98), Stuttgart (Germany), September 1998*, volume 1477 of *Lecture Notes in Computer Science*, pages 237–248. Springer-Verlag, 1998b.

Giacomo Cabri, Letizia Leonardi, and Franco Zambonelli. Weak and strong mobility in mobile agent applications. In *Proceedings of the 2nd International Conference and Exhibition on The Practical Application of Java (PA JAVA 2000), Manchester (UK), April 2000*, 2000. The paper is only available online at `polaris.ing.unimo.it/MOON/papers/`.

Jiannong Cao, Xinyu Feng, Jian Lu, and Sajal K. Das. Mailbox-based scheme for designing mobile agent communication protocols. *Computer*, 35(9):54–60, 2002.

Nicholas Carriero and David Gelernter. How to write parallel programs: A guide for the perplexed. *ACM Computing Surveys*, 21(3):323–357, 1989.

Antonio Carzaniga, Gian Pietro Picco, and Giovanni Vigna. Designing distributed applications with mobile code paradigms. In *Proceedings of the 19th International Conference on Software Engineering (ICSE '97), Boston (USA), April 1997*, pages 22–32. ACM Press, 1997.

Arjav J. Chakravarti, Xiaojin Wang, Jason Hallstrom, and Gerald Baumgartner. Implementation of strong mobility for multi-threaded agents in java. In *Proceedings of the 32nd International Conference on Parallel Processing (ICPP 2003), Kaohsiung (Taiwan), October 2003*, pages 321–332. IEEE Computer Society Press, 2003.

David M. Chess, Benjamin Grosof, Colin G. Harrison, David Levine, Colin Paris, and Gene Tsudik. Itinerant agents for mobile computing. In Huhns and Singh [1997], pages 267–282.

David M. Chess, Colin G. Harrison, and Aaron Kershenbaum. Mobile agents: Are they a good idea? In Jan Vitek and Christian F. Tschudin, editors, *Mobile Object Systems: Towards the Programmable Internet (MOS '96), Linz (Austria), July 1996 (Selected Presentations and Invited Papers)*, volume 1222 of *Lecture Notes in Computer Science*, pages 25–45. Springer-Verlag, 1997b.

Dimitris N. Chorafas. *Agent Technology Handbook*. McGraw-Hill, 1997.

Paolo Ciancarini, Andrea Omicini, and Franco Zambonelli. Coordination technologies for internet agents. *Nordic Journal of Computing*, 6(3):215–240, 1999.

William R. Cockayne and Michael Zyda, editors. *Mobile Agents: Explanations and Examples*. Manning Publications, 1997.

Gianpaolo Cugola, Carlo Ghezzi, Gian Pietro Picco, and Giovanni Vigna. Analyzing mobile code languages. In Jan Vitek and Christian F. Tschudin, editors, *Mobile Object Systems: Towards the Programmable Internet (MOS '96), Linz (Austria), July 1996 (Selected Presentations and Invited Papers)*, volume 1222 of *Lecture Notes in Computer Science*, pages 93–110. Springer-Verlag, 1997a.

Gianpaolo Cugola, Carlo Ghezzi, Gian Pietro Picco, and Giovanni Vigna. A characterization of mobility and state distribution in mobile code languages. In Max Mühlhäuser, editor, *Special Issues in Object-Oriented Programming: Workshop Reader of the 10th European Conference on Object-Oriented Programming (ECOOP '96), Linz (Austria), July 1996*, pages 309–318. dpunkt Verlag, 1997b.

Grzegorz Czajkowski and Thorsten von Eicken. JRes: A resource accounting interface for Java. *ACM SIGPLAN Notices*, 33(10):21–35, 1998.

Jocelyn Desbiens, Francis Renaud, and Martin Lavoie. Communication and tracking infrastructure of a mobile agent system. In *Proceedings of the 31st Annual Hawaii International Conference on System Science (HICSS), Hawaii (USA), January 1998*, volume 7, pages 54–63. IEEE Computer Society Press, 1998.

Marios D. Dikaiakos and George Samaras. Qualtitative performance analysis of mobile agent systems: A hierachical approach. Technical Report TR-2000-2, University of Cyprus, Department of Computer Science, June 2000.

Bruno Dillenseger. MobiliTools: An OMG Standards-based Toolbox for Agent Mobility and Interoperability. In Harmen R. van As, editor, *Telecommunication Network Intelligence, 6th IFIP Conference on Intelligence in Networks (SMARTNET 2000), Vienna (Austria), September 2000*, volume 178, pages 353–366. Kluwer Academic Publishers, 2000.

Fred Douglis and John K. Ousterhout. Transparent Process Migration: Design Alternatives and the Sprite Implementation. *Software—Practice and Experience*, 21 (8):757–785, 1991.

F. Brent Dubach, Robert M. Rutherford, and Charles M. Shub. Process-originated migration in a heterogeneous environment. In *Seventeenth Annual ACM Computer Science Conference, Louisville (USA), February 1989*, pages 98–102. ACM Press, 1989.

Guy Edjlali, Anurag Acharya, and Vipin Chaudhary. History-based access control for mobile code. In *Proceedings of the Fifth ACM Conference on Computer and Communications Security (CCS '98), San Francisco (USA), November 1998*, pages 38–48. ACM Press, 1998.

Guy Edjlali, Anurag Acharya, and Vipin Chaudhary. History-based access control for mobile code. In Jan Vitek and Christian D. Jensen, editors, *Internet Programming—Security Issues for Mobile and Distributed Objects*, volume 1603 of *Lecture Notes in Computer Science*, pages 413–432. Springer-Verlag, 1999.

Christian Erfurth, Peter Braun, and Wilhelm Rossak. Migration Intelligence for Mobile Agents. In *Artificial Intelligence and the Simulation of Behaviour (AISB) Symposium on Software mobility and adaptive behaviour. University of York (United Kingdom), March 2001*, pages 81–88, 2001a.

Christian Erfurth, Peter Braun, and Wilhelm Rossak. Some thoughts on migration intelligence for mobile agents. Technical Report 09/01, Friedrich-Schiller-Universität Jena, Institut für Informatik, April 2001b.

Joseph R. Falcone. A programmable interface language for heterogeneous distributed sytems. *ACM Transactions on Computer Systems*, 5(4):330–351, July 1987.

William M. Farmer, Joshua D. Guttman, and Vipin Swarup. Security for mobile agents: Authentication and state appraisal. In Elisa Bertino, Helmut Kurth, Giancarlo Martella, and Emilio Montolivo, editors, *Proceedings of the Fourth European Symposium on Research in Computer Security (ESORICS 1996), Rome (Italy), September 1996*, volume 1146 of *Lecture Notes in Computer Science*, pages 118–130. Springer-Verlag, 1996a.

William M. Farmer, Joshua D. Guttman, and Vipin Swarup. Security for mobile agents: Issues and requirements. In *Proceedings of the 19th National Information Systems Security Conference (NISSC), Baltimore (USA), October 1996*, pages 591–597, 1996b.

Christian Fensch. Class Splitting as a Method to Reduce Network Traffic in a Mobile Agent System. Diplomarbeit, Friedrich-Schiller-Universität Jena, Institut für Informatik, 2001.

Jacques Ferber. *Multi-Agent Systems: An Introduction to Distributed Artificial Intelligence*. Addison-Wesley, 1999.

Timothy W. Finin, Richard Fritzson, Don McKay, and Robin McEntire. KQML as an Agent Communication Language. In Nabil R. Adam, Bharat K. Bhargava, and Yelena Yesha, editors, *Proceedings of the 3rd International Conference on Information and Knowledge Management (CIKM '94), Gaithersburg (USA), November/December 1994*, pages 456–463. ACM Press, 1994.

Leonard N. Foner. Entertaining Agents—A Sociological Case Study. In W. Lewis Johnson, editor, *Proceedings of the First International Conference on Autonomous Agents, Marina del Rey (USA), Februar 1997*, pages 122–129. ACM Press, 1997.

Stan Franklin and Art Graesser. Is it an agent, or just a program?: A taxonomy for autonomous agents. In Jörg P. Müller, Michael Wooldridge, and Nicholoas R. Jennings, editors, *Proceedings of the 3rd ECAI Workshop on Agent Theories, Architectures, and Languages (ATAL 1996), Intelligent Agents III, Budapest (Hungary), August 1996*, volume 1193 of *Lecture Notes in Computer Science*, pages 21–35, 1997.

Richard Fritzson, Timothy W. Finin, Don McKay, and Robin McEntire. KQML—A language and protocol for knowledge and information exchange. In *Proceedings of the Thirteenth International Workshop on Distributed Artificial Intelligence*, pages 126–136, 1994.

Alfonso Fuggetta, Gian Pietro Picco, and Giovanni Vigna. Understanding code mobility. *IEEE Transactions on Software Engineering*, 24(5):342–361, 1998.

Munehiro Fukuda, Lubomir F. Bic, Michael B. Dillencourt, and Fehmina Merchant. Intra- and inter-object coordination with MESSENGERS. In Paolo Ciancarini and Chris Hankin, editors, *Proceedings of the First International Conference on Coordination Languages and Models (COORDINATION '96), Cesena (Italy), April 1996*, volume 1061 of *Lecture Notes in Computer Science*, pages 179–196. Springer-Verlag, 1996.

Munehiro Fukuda, Yuichiro Tanaka, Naoya Suzuki, Lubomir Bic, and Shinya Kobayashi. A Mobile-Agent PC Grid. In *Proceedings of the 5th Annual International Workshop on Active Middleware Services (AMS 2003), Autonomic Computing Workshop, Seattle (USA), June 2003*, pages 142–150. IEEE Computer Society Press, 2003.

Stefan Fünfrocken. Transparent migration of Java-based mobile agents. In Kurt Rothermel and Fritz Hohl, editors, *Proceedings of the Second International Workshop on Mobile Agents (MA '98), Stuttgart (Germany), September 1998*, volume 1477 of *Lecture Notes in Computer Science*, pages 26–37. Springer-Verlag, 1999.

Erich Gamma, Richard Helm, Ralph Johnson, and John Vlissides. *Design Patterns: Elements of Reusable Object-Oriented Software*. Addison-Wesley, 1995.

Norbert Glaser. *Conceptual Modelling of Multi-Agent Systems: The Comomas Engineering Environment (Multiagent Systems, Artificial Societies, and Simulated Orga)*. Kluwer Academic Publishers, 2002.

Robert S. Gray. Agent Tcl: A flexible and secure mobile agent system. In *Proceedings of the Fourth Annual Tcl/Tk Workshop, Monterey (USA), July 1996*, pages 9–23. USENIX Association, 1996.

Robert S. Gray. *Agent Tcl: A flexible and secure mobile-agent system*. PhD thesis, Dartmouth College, Computer Science, 1997.

Robert S. Gray. Mobile agents: Overcoming early hype and a bad name (panel). In Anupam Joshi and Hui Lei, editors, *IEEE International Conference on Mobile Data Management (MDM '04), Berkeley (USA), January 2004*, pages 302–303. IEEE Computer Society Press, 2004.

Robert S. Gray, George Cybenko, David Kotz, Ronald A. Peterson, and Daniela Rus. D'Agents: Applications and performance of a mobile-agent system. *Software—Practice and Experience*, 32(6):543–573, 2002.

Robert S. Gray, George Cybenko, David Kotz, and Daniela Rus. Agent Tcl. In Cockayne and Zyda [1997].

Robert S. Gray, David Kotz, Ronald A. Peterson, Joyce Barton, Daria A. Chacón, Peter Gerken, Martin O. Hofmann, Jeffrey Bradshaw, Maggie R. Breedy, Renia Jeffers, and Niranjan Suri. Mobile-agent versus client/server performance: Scalability in an information-retrieval task. In Gian Pietro Picco, editor, *Mobile Agents, Proceedings of the 5th International Conference (MA 2001), Atlanta (USA), December 2001*, volume 2240 of *Lecture Notes in Computer Science*, pages 229–243. Springer-Verlag, 2001.

Shaw Green, Leon Hurst, Brenda Nangle, Padraig Cunningham, Fergal Somers, and Richard Evans. Software agents: A review. Technical Report TCD-CS-1997-06, Intelligent Agent Group, Trinity College (Ireland), 1997.

Arne Grimstrup, Robert S. Gray, David Kotz, Maggie R. Breedy, Marco M. Carvalho, Thomas B. Cowin, Daria A. Chacon, Joyce Barton, Chris Garrett, and Martin Hoffmann. Toward Interoperability of Mobile-Agent Systems. In Niranjan Suri, editor, *Proceedings of the 6th International Conference on Mobile Agents (MA 2002), Barcelona (Spain), October 2002*, volume 2535 of *Lecture Notes in Computer Science*, pages 106–120. Springer-Verlag, 2002.

Object Management Group. The Common Object Request Broker: Architecture and Specification, Rev. 3, 2002.

Thomas Gschwind. Comparing Object Oriented Mobile Agent Systems. In *6th ECOOP Workshop on Mobile Object Systems: Operating System Support, Security and Programming Languages, Sophia Antipolis (France), June 2000*, 2000. Paper is only available online at `cui.unige.ch/~ecoopws/ws00`.

Dieter K. Hammer and Ad T. M. Aerts. Mobile Agent Architectures: What are the Design Issues? In *Proceedings International Conference and Workshop on*

Engineering of Computer-Based Systems (ECBS '98), Maale Hachamisha (Israel), March/April 1998, pages 272–280. IEEE Computer Society Press, 1998.

Colin G. Harrison, David M. Chess, and Aaron Kershenbaum. Mobile agents: Are they a good idea? Research Report RC 19887, IBM Research Division, 1995.

Carl E. Hewitt. Viewing control structures as patterns of passing messages. *Journal of Artificial Intelligence*, 8(3):323–364, 1977.

Fritz Hohl. A model of attacks of malicious hosts against mobile agents. In Serge Demeyer and Jan Bosch, editors, *Proceedings of the 4th ECOOP Workshop on Mobile Object Systems: Secure Internet Mobile Computation, Brussels (Belgium), July 1998*, volume 1543 of *Lecture Notes in Computer Science*, page 299. Springer-Verlag, 1998a.

Fritz Hohl. Protecting mobile agents from malicious hosts. In Giovanni Vigna, editor, *Mobile Agents and Securtiy*, volume 1419 of *Lecture Notes in Computer Science*, pages 90—111. Springer-Verlag, 1998b.

Fritz Hohl, Peter Klar, and Joachim Baumann. Efficient code migration for modular mobile agents. In *3rd ECOOP Workshop on Mobile Object Systems: Operating System support for Mobile Object Systems, Jyvälskylä (Finland), June 1997*, 1997.

Fritz Hohl and Kurt Rothermel. A protocol preventing blackbox tests of mobile agents. In *ITG/VDE Fachtagung Kommunikation in Verteilten Systemen (KiVS '99), Darmstadt (Germany), March 1999*, pages 170–181. Springer-Verlag, 1999.

Michael N. Huhns and Munindar P. Singh, editors. *Readings in Agents*. Morgan Kaufmann Publishers, 1997.

IEEE IC-Online. The Future of Software Agents, Internet Computing Online Virtual Roundtable with Mani Chandy, Danny Lange, Pattie Maes, John Ousterhout, Jeff Rosenschein, Sankar Virdhagriswaran, James E. White. `http://www.computer.org/internet/v1n4/round.htm`, July/August 1997.

IKV. *Grasshopper Programmer's Guide, Release 2.2*. IKV++ GmbH, Berlin, March 2001a.

IKV. *Grasshopper User's Guide, Release 2.2*. IKV++ GmbH, Berlin, March 2001b.

Torsten Illmann, Tilman Krüger, Frank Kargl, and Michael Weber. Transparent Migration of Mobile Agents Using the Java Platform Debugger Architecture. In Gian Pietro Picco, editor, *Mobile Agents, Proceedings of the 5th International Conference (MA 2001), Atlanta (USA), December 2001*, volume 2240 of *Lecture Notes in Computer Science*, pages 198–212. Springer-Verlag, 2001.

Ashraf Iqbal, Joachim Baumann, and Markus Straßer. Efficient algorithms to find optimal agent migration strategies. Technical Report 1998/05, Universität Stuttgart, Fakultät für Informatik, April 1998.

Leila Ismail and Daniel Hagimont. A performance evaluation of the mobile agent paradigm. *ACM SIGPLAN Notices*, 34(10):306–313, 1999.

Ravi Jain, Farooq Anjum, and Amjad Umar. A comparison of mobile agent and client-server paradigms for information retrieval tasks in virtual enterprises. In *Proceedings of the Academia/Industry Working Conference on Research Challenges (AIWORC '00), Buffalo, NY (USA), April 2000*, pages 209–214. IEEE Computer Society Press, 2000.

Wayne A. Jansen. Countermeasures for mobile agent security. *Computer Communications: Special Issue on Advances in Research and Application of Network Security*, 23(17):1667–1676, 2000.

Dag Johansen. Mobile agent applicability. In Kurt Rothermel and Fritz Hohl, editors, *Proceedings of the Second International Workshop on Mobile Agents (MA '98), Stuttgart (Germany), September 1998*, volume 1477 of *Lecture Notes in Computer Science*, pages 80–98. Springer-Verlag, 1999.

Dag Johansen, Nils P. Sudmann, and Robbert van Renesse. Performance issues in TACOMA. In *3rd ECOOP Workshop on Mobile Object Systems: Operating System support for Mobile Object Systems, Jyväslkylä (Finland), June 1997*, 1997.

Dag Johansen, Robbert van Renesse, and Fred B. Schneider. Operating system support for mobile agents. In *Proceedings of the 5th IEEE Workshop on Hot Topics in Operating Systems (HotOS-V), Orcas Island (USA), May 1995*, pages 42–45. IEEE Computer Society Press, 1995.

Neeran M. Karnik. *Security in Mobile Agent Systems*. PhD thesis, Univeristy of Minnesota, Department of Computer Science, 1998.

Neeran M. Karnik and Anand R. Tripathi. Design Issues in Mobile Agent Programming Systems. *IEEE Concurrency*, 6(6):52–61, 1998.

Neeran M. Karnik and Anand R. Tripathi. Security in the Ajanta Mobile Agent Programming System. *Software—Practice and Experience*, 31(4):301–329, April 2001.

Joe Kilian. A note on efficient zero-knowledge proofs and arguments. In *Proceedings of the Twenty Fourth Annual ACM Symposium on Theory of Computing, Victoria (Canada), May 1992*, pages 723–732. ACM Press, 1992.

Joseph Kiniry and Daniel Zimmerman. A Hands-On Look at Java Mobile Agents. *IEEE Internet Computing*, 1(4):21–30, July/August 1997.

Frederick C. Knabe. *Language Support for Mobile Agents*. PhD thesis, Carnegie Mellon University, Pittsburgh, Pa. (USA), December 1995.

Frederick C. Knabe. An overview of mobile agent programming. In Mads Dam, editor, *Proceedings of the 5th LOMAPS Workshop on Analysis and Verification of Multiple-Agent Languages, Stockholm (Sweden), Juni 1996*, volume 1192 of *Lecture Notes in Computer Science*, pages 100–115. Springer-Verlag, 1997a. Invited paper.

Frederick C. Knabe. Performance-oriented implementation strategies for a mobile agent language. In Jan Vitek and Christian F. Tschudin, editors, *Mobile Object Systems: Towards the Programmable Internet (MOS '96), Linz (Austria), July 1996 (Selected Presentations and Invited Papers)*, volume 1222 of *Lecture Notes in Computer Science*, pages 229–244. Springer-Verlag, 1997b.

Pål Knudsen. Comparing two distributed computing paradigms—a performance case study. Master's thesis, University of Tromsø (Norway), August 1995.

Reuven Koblick. Concordia. *Communications of the ACM*, 42(3):96–97, 1999.

Larry Korba and Ronggong Song. Modeling and simulating the scalability of a multi-agent application system. Technical Report NRC/ERB-1097, National Research Council Canada, Institute for Information Technology, August 2002.

David Kotz and Robert S. Gray. Mobile Agents and the Future of the Internet. *ACM Operating Systems Review*, 33(3):7–13, 1999.

Ryszard Kowalczyk, Peter Braun, Jan Eismann, Bogdan Franczyk, Wilhelm Rossak, and Andreas Speck. InterMarket: Towards Intelligent Mobile Agent-based e-Marketplaces. In *Proceedings of the 9th Annual Conference and Workshop on the Engineering of Computerbased Systems (ECBS-2002), Lund (Sweden), April 2002*, pages 268–275. IEEE Computer Society Press, 2002.

Natasha Kravtsova and Andre Meyer. Searching for music with agents. In Eric Horlait, editor, *Mobile Agents for Telecommunication Applications, Proceedings of the Second International Workshop (MATA 2000), Paris (France), September 2000*, volume 1931 of *Lecture Notes in Computer Science*, pages 195–203. Springer-Verlag, 2000.

Chandra Krintz, Brad Calder, and Urs Hölzle. Reducing transfer delay using java class file splitting and prefetching. *ACM Sigplan Notices*, 34(10):276–291, 1999.

Danny B. Lange and Mitsuru Oshima. *Programming and Deploying Java Mobile Agents with Aglets*. Addison-Wesley, 1998.

Adam Langley. Freenet. In Oram [2001], pages 123–132.

Sashi Lazar and Deepinder Sidhu. Discovery: A Mobile Agent Framework for Distributed Applications. Technical report, Maryland Center for Telecommunications Research, Department of Computer Science and Electrical Engineering, University of Maryland Baltimore County, 1998.

Tim Lindholm and Frank Yellin. *The Java Virtual Machine Specification*. Addison-Wesley, 2nd edition, 1999.

Catherine Meadows. Detecting attacks on mobile agents. In *DARPA Workshop on Foundations for Secure Mobile Code, Monterey (USA), March 1997*, 1997. Position Paper.

Jim Melton. *Understanding SQL's Stored Procedures: A Complete Guide to SQL/PSM*. Morgan Kaufmann Publishers, 1998.

Silvio Micali. CS proofs. In *Proceedings of the 35th IEEE Symposium on Foundations of Computer Science, Santa Fe (USA), November 1994*, pages 436–453. IEEE Computer Society Press, 1994.

Dejan S. Milojicic, Markus Breugst, Ingo Busse, John Campbell, Stefan Covaci, Barry Friedman, Kazuya Kosaka, Danny Lange, Kouichi Ono, Mitsuru Oshima, Cynthia Tham, Sankar Virdhagriswaran, and Jim White. MASIF: The OMG Mobile Agent System Interoperability Facility. In Kurt Rothermel and Fritz Hohl, editors, *Proceedings of the Second International Workshop on Mobile Agents (MA '98), Stuttgart (Germany), September 1998*, volume 1477 of *Lecture Notes in Computer Science*, pages 50–67. Springer-Verlag, 1999.

Katsuhiro Moizumi and George Cybenko. The travelling agent problem. *Mathematics of Control, Signals and Systems*, 14(3):213–232, 2001.

Luc Moreau. Distributed Directory Service and Message Router for Mobile Agents. Technical Report ECSTR M99/3, University of Southampton (UK), 1999.

Luc Moreau. A Fault-Tolerant Directory Service for Mobile Agents based on Forwarding Pointers. In *The 17th ACM Symposium on Applied Computing (SAC '2002)—Track on Agents, Interactions, Mobility and Systems, Madrid (Spain), March 2002*, pages 93–100, 2002.

Luc Moreau and Daniel Ribbens. Mobile Objects in Java. *Scientific Programming*, 10(3):91–100, 2002.

Luc Moreau, Victor Tan, and Nicholas Gibbins. Transparent migration of mobile agents. In *IEE Seminar: Mobile Agents—Where are They Going?*, pages 2/1–2/11, Savoy Place, London, April 2001. IEE.

Amy L. Murphy and Gian Pietro Picco. Reliable communication for highly mobile agents. *Autonomous Agents and Multi-Agent Systems*, 5(1):81–100, 2002.

George C. Necula. Proof-carrying code. In *Proceedings of the 24th ACM Symposium on Principles of Programming Languages (POPL '97), Paris (France), January 1997*, pages 106–119. ACM Press, January 1997.

George C. Necula and Peter Lee. Proof-carrying code. Technical Report CMU-CS-96-165, School of Computer Science, Carnegie Mellon University, Pittsburgh, Pa., November 1996.

George C. Necula and Peter Lee. Safe, untrusted agents using proof-carrying code. In G. Vigna, editor, *Mobile Agents and Security*, volume 1419 of *Lecture Notes in Computer Science*, pages 61–91. Springer-Verlag, 1998.

Bruce J. Nelson. *Remote procedure call*. PhD thesis, Carnegie-Mellon University, Pittsburgh, Pa. (USA), 1981.

Eric Newcomer. *Understanding Web Services*. Addison-Wesley, 2002.

Scott Oaks. *Java Security*. O'Reilly, 2001.

ObjectSpace. *Voyager Core Package Technical Overview: The Agent ORB for Java*, 1997.

ObjectSpace. *Voyager Core Package Version 2.0: Technical Overview*, 1998.

Paul O'Brien and Richard Nicol. FIPA—towards a standard for software agents. *BT Technology Journal*, 16(3):51–59, 1998.

Andrea Omicini and Franco Zambonelli. Coordination of mobile information agents in TuCSoN. *Internet Research: Electronic Networking Applications and Policy*, 8 (5):400–413, 1998.

Andrea Omicini, Franco Zambonelli, Matthias Klusch, and Robert Tolksdorf, editors. *Coordination of Internet Agents: Models, Technologies, and Applications*. Springer-Verlag, 2001.

Andy Oram, editor. *Peer-to-Peer: Harnessing the Power of Disruptive Technologies*. O'Reilly, 2001.

Joann J. Ordille. When agents roam, who can you trust? In *Proceedings of the First Conference on Emerging Technologies and Applications in Communications, Portland, Oregon (USA), May 1996*, 1996.

A. Outtagarts, M. Kadoch, and S. Soulhi. Client-Server and Mobile Agent: Performances Comparative Study in the Management of MIBs. In Ahmed

Karmouch and Roger Impey, editors, *Mobile Agents for Telecommunication Applications, Proceedings of the First International Workshop (MATA 1999), Ottawa (Canada), October 1999*, pages 69–81. World Scientific Pub., 1999.

Stavros Papastavrou, George Samaras, and Evaggelia Pitoura. Mobile agents for WWW distributed database access. In *Proceedings of the 15th International Conference on Data Engineering, Sydney (Australia), March 1999*, pages 228–237. IEEE Computer Society Press, 1999.

Holger Peine. An introduction to mobile agent programming and the Ara system. Technical Report ZRI-Report 1/97, Department of Computer Science, University of Kaiserslautern, Germany, 1997.

Holger Peine and Torsten Stolpmann. The architecture of the Ara platform for mobile agents. In Kurt Rothermel and Radu Popescu-Zeletin, editors, *Proceedings of the First International Workshop on Mobile Agents (MA '97), Berlin (Germany), April 1997*, volume 1219 of *Lecture Notes in Computer Science*, pages 50–61, Berlin, Germany, 1997. Springer-Verlag.

Charles Perkins. RFC 2002, 1996. `http://www.rfc-editor.org`.

Larry L. Peterson and Bruce S. Davie. *Computer Networks—A Systems Approach*. Morgan Kaufmann Publishers, 3rd edition, 2003.

Michael Philippsen and Matthias Zenger. JavaParty—Transparent Remote Objects in Java. *Concurrency: Practice and Experience*, 9(11):1225–1242, 1997.

Gian Pietro Picco. *Understanding, Evaluating, Formalizing, and Exploiting Code Mobility*. PhD thesis, Politecnico di Torino (Italy), 1998.

Gian Pietro Picco. μCODE: A Lightweight and Flexible Mobile Code Toolkit. In Kurt Rothermel and Fritz Hohl, editors, *Proceedings of the Second International Workshop on Mobile Agents (MA '98), Stuttgart (Germany), September 1998*, volume 1477 of *Lecture Notes in Computer Science*, pages 160–171. Springer-Verlag, 1999.

Gian Pietro Picco, Amy L. Murphy, and Gruia-Catalin Roman. LIME: Linda meets mobility. In *Proceedings of the 1999 International Conference on Software Engineering (ICSE), Los Angeles (USA), May 1999*, pages 368–377. ACM Press, 1999.

Ulrich Pinsdorf and Volker Roth. Mobile agent interoperability patterns and practice. In *Proceedings of the 9th Annual Conference and Workshop on the Engineering of Computer-based Systems (ECBS-2002), Lund (Sweden), April 2002*, pages 238–244. IEEE Computer Society Press, 2002.

Evaggelia Pitoura and George Samaras. Locating objects in mobile computing. *IEEE Transaction on Knowledge Data Engineering*, 13(4):571–592, 2001.

Valentina Plekhanova, editor. *Intelligent Agent Software Engineering*. Idea Group Publishing, 2002.

William Pugh. Compressing Java class files. *ACM SIGPLAN Notices*, 34(5):247–258, 1999.

Antonio Puliafito, Salvatore Riccobene, and Marco Scarpa. An Analytical Comparison of the Client-Server, Remote Evaluation and Mobile Agents Protocols. In Dejan S. Milojicic, editor, *Proceedings of the First International Symposium on Agent Systems and Applications (ASA '99)/Third International Symposium on Mobile Agents (MA '99), Palm Springs (USA), October 1999*, pages 278–292. IEEE Computer Society Press, 1999.

Antonio Puliafito, Salvatore Riccobene, and Marco Scarpa. Which paradigm should I use? An analytical comparison of the client-server, remote evaluation and mobile agent paradigms. *Concurrency and Computation: Practice and Experience*, 13(1):71–94, 2001.

Lars Rasmusson, Andreas Rasmusson, and Sverker Janson. Using agents to secure the internet marketplace – reactive security and social control. In *Practical Applications of Agents and Multi-Agent Systems (PAAM '97), London (UK), April 1997*, 1997.

James Riordan and Bruce Schneier. Environmental key generation towards clueless agents. In Giovanni Vigna, editor, *Mobile Agents and Securtiy*, volume 1419 of *Lecture Notes in Computer Science*, pages 15–24. Springer-Verlag, 1998.

Ronald L. Rivest. The MD5 Message-Digest Algorithm. RFC 1321, 1992.

Volker Roth. Secure recording of itineraries through cooperating agents. In Serge Demeyer and Jan Bosch, editors, *Proceedings of the 4th ECOOP Workshop on Mobile Object Systems: Secure Internet Mobile Computation, Brussels (Belgium), July 1998*, volume 1543 of *Lecture Notes in Computer Science*, pages 297–298. Springer-Verlag, 1998.

Volker Roth. Distributed image indexing and retrieval with mobile agents. In *IEE European Workshop on Distributed Imaging*, pages 14/1–14/5, 1999.

Volker Roth. On the robustness of some cryptographic protocols for mobile agent protection. In Gian Pietro Picco, editor, *Mobile Agents, Proceedings of the 5th International Conference (MA 2001), Atlanta (USA), December 2001*, volume 2240 of *Lecture Notes in Computer Science*, pages 1–14. Springer-Verlag, 2001.

Volker Roth. Obstacles to the adoption of mobile agents (panel). In Anupam Joshi and Hui Lei, editors, *IEEE International Conference on Mobile Data Management (MDM '04), Berkeley (USA), January 2004*. IEEE Computer Society Press, 2004.

Volker Roth and Vania Conan. Encrypting Java Archives and its application to mobile agent security. In Frank Dignum and Carles Sierra, editors, *Agent Mediated Electronic Commerce: A European AgentLink Perspective*, volume 1991 of *Lecture Notes in Computer Science*, pages 229–239. Springer-Verlag, 2001.

Volker Roth and Mehrdad Jalali. Concepts and architecture of a security-centric mobile agent server. In *Proceedings of the Fifth International Symposium on Autonomous Decentralized Systems (ISADS 2001), Dallas, (USA), March 2001*, pages 435–442. IEEE Computer Society Press, 2001.

Volker Roth and Jan Peters. A scalable and secure global tracking service for mobile agents. In Gian Pietro Picco, editor, *Mobile Agents, Proceedings of the 5th International Conference (MA 2001), Atlanta (USA), December 2001*, volume 2240 of *Lecture Notes in Computer Science*, pages 169–181. Springer-Verlag, 2001.

Antony Rowstron. Wcl: A co-ordination language for geographically distributed agents. *World Wide Web Journal*, 1(3):167–179, 1998.

Marcelo Gonçalves Rubinstein and Otto Carlos Muniz Bandeira Duarte. Evaluating tradeoffs of mobile agents in network management. *Networking and Information Systems Journal*, 2(2):237–252, 1999.

Marcelo Gonçalves Rubinstein, Otto Carlos Muniz Bandeira Duarte, and Guy Pujolle. Evaluating the performance of a network management application based on mobile agents. In Enrico Gregori, Marco Conti, Andrew T. Campbell, Cambyse Guy Omidyar, and Moshe Zukerman, editors, *Proceedings of the Second International IFIP-TC6 Networking Conference: Networking Technologies, Services, and Protocols, Performance of Computer and Communication Networks and Mobile and Wireless Communications (Networking 2002), Pisa (Italy), May 2002*, volume 2345 of *Lecture Notes in Computer Science*, pages 515–526. Springer-Verlag, 2002.

Marcelo Gonçalves Rubinstein, Otto Carlos Muniz Bandeira Duarte, and Guy Pujolle. Scalability of a network management application based on mobile agents. *Journal of Communication and Networks, IEEE/Korean Institute of Communications Science (KICS)*, 5(3):240–248, 2003.

Jeff Rulifson. RFC 5: The Decode-Encode Language, 1969. Avaliable online at `www.faqs.org/rfcs/rfc5.html`.

George Samaras, Marios D. Dikaiakos, Constantinos Spyrou, and Andreas Liverdos. Mobile Agent Platforms for Web-Databases: A Qualitative and Quantitative Assessment. In Dejan S. Milojicic, editor, *Proceedings of the First International Symposium on Agent Systems and Applications (ASA '99)/Third International Symposium on Mobile Agents (MA '99), Palm Springs (USA), October 1999*, pages 50–64. IEEE Computer Society Press, 1999.

Tomas Sander and Christian F. Tschudin. On software protection via function hiding. In David Aucsmith, editor, *Proceedings of the Second International Workshop on Information Hiding*, volume 1525 of *Lecture Notes in Computer Science*, pages 111–123. Springer-Verlag, April 1998a.

Tomas Sander and Christian F. Tschudin. Protecting mobile agents against malicious hosts. In Giovanni Vigna, editor, *Mobile Agents and Security*, volume 1419 of *Lecture Notes in Computer Science*, pages 44–59. Springer-Verlag, 1998b.

Ichiro Satoh. Adaptive Protocols for Agent Migration. In *Proceedings of 21st IEEE International Conference on Distributed Computing Systems (ICDCS '2001), Mesa (USA), April 2001*, pages 711–714. IEEE Computer Society Press, 2001.

Ichiro Satoh. Dynamic Configuration of Agent Migration Protocols for the Internet. In *Proceedings of the 2002 International Symposium on Applications and the Internet (SAINT '2002), Nara City (Japan), January/February 2002*, pages 119–126. IEEE Computer Society Press, 2002.

Fred B. Schneider. Towards fault-tolerant and secure agentry. In Marios Mavronicolas and Philippas Tsigas, editors, *Proceedings of the 11th International Workshop on Distributed Algorithms (WDAG '97), Saarbrücken (Germany), September 1997*, volume 1320 of *Lecture Notes in Computer Science*, pages 1–14. Springer-Verlag, 1997. Invited paper.

Bruce Schneier. *Secrets and Lies—Digital Security in a Networked World*. John Wiley and Sons, 2000.

Steffen Schreiber. Beschreibung und Analyse von dynamischen Netzen für Agentensysteme. Diplomarbeit, Friedrich-Schiller-Universität Jena, Institut für Informatik, July 2002.

Tatsurou Sekiguchi, Hidehiko Masuhara, and Akinori Yonezawa. A Simple Extension of Java Language for Controllable Transparent Migration and its Portable Implementation. In P. Ciancarini and A. L. Wolf, editors, *Proceedings of the Third International Conference on Coordination Models and Languages (Coordination '99), Amsterdam (The Netherlands), April 1999*, volume 1594 of *Lecture Notes in Computer Science*, pages 211–226. Springer-Verlag, 1999.

Clay Shirky. Listening to Napster. In Oram [2001], pages 21–37.

John Shoch and Jon Hupp. The 'worm' programs—early experience with a distributed computation. *Communications of the ACM*, 25(3):172–180, 1982.

Charles M. Shub. Native code process-originated migration in a heterogeneous environment. In *Eighteenth Annual ACM Computer Science Conference, Washingtion DC (USA), February 1990*, pages 266–270. ACM Press, 1990.

Louis Moura Silva, Guilherme Soares, Paulo Martins, Victor Batista, and Luís Santos. Comparing the performance of mobile agent systems. *Journal of Computer Communications, Special Issue on Mobile Software Agents for Telecommunications*, 23(8):769–778, 2000.

Guilherme Soares and Louis Moura Silva. Optimizing the migration of mobile agents. In Ahmed Karmouch and Roger Impey, editors, *Mobile Agents for Telecommunication Applications, Proceedings of the First International Workshop (MATA 1999), Ottawa (Canada), October 1999*, pages 270–271. World Scientific Pub., 1999.

Tammo Spalink, John H. Hartman, and Garth A. Gibson. A mobile agent's effects on file service. *IEEE Concurrency*, 8(2):62–69, 2000.

Constantinos Spyrou, George Samaras, Paraskevas Evripidou, and Evaggelia Pitoura. Wireless Computational Models: Mobile Agents to the Rescue. In *Proceedings of the 10th International Workshop on Database & Expert Systems Applications (DEXA-1999), Florence (Italy), September 1999*, pages 127–133. IEEE Computer Society Press, 2000.

James W. Stamos. *Remote Evaluation*. PhD thesis, Massachusetts Institute of Technology, Cambridge, MA (USA), 1986.

Bjarne Steensgaard and Eric Jul. Object and native code thread mobility among heterogeneous computers. In *Proceedings of the 15th ACM Symposium on Operating Systems Principles, Copper Mountain (USA), December 1995*, pages 68–78. ACM Press, 1995.

Luk Stoops, Tom Mens, and Theo D'Hondt. Fine-grained interlaced code loading for mobile systems. In Niranjan Suri, editor, *Proceedings of the 6th International Conference on Mobile Agents (MA 2002), Barcelona (Spain), October 2002*, volume 2535 of *Lecture Notes in Computer Science*, pages 78–92. Springer-Verlag, 2002.

Markus Straßer, Joachim Baumann, and Fritz Hohl. Mole—a Java based mobile agent system. In Max Mühlhäuser, editor, *Special Issues in Object-Oriented Programming: Workshop Reader of the 10th European Conference on Object-Oriented Programming (ECOOP '96), Linz (Austria), July 1996*, pages 301–308. dpunkt Verlag, 1997.

Markus Straßer and Markus Schwehm. A performance model for mobile agent systems. In H. R. Arabnia, editor, *Proceedings of the International Conference on Parallel and Distributed Processing Techniques and Applications (PDPTA '97), Las Vegas (USA)*, volume 2, pages 1132–1140. CSREA Press, 1997.

Nils P. Sudmann and Dag Johansen. Software deployment using mobile agents. In Judy M. Bishop, editor, *Proceedings of IFIP/ACM Working Conference on Component Deployment (CD 2002), Berlin (Germany), June 2002*, volume 2370 of *Lecture Notes in Computer Science*, pages 97–107. Springer-Verlag, 2002.

Java Object Serialization Specification. Sun Microsystems Inc., July 1999. `http://java.sun.com/j2se/1.3/docs/guide/serialization/spec/serial-title.doc.html`.

Java Remote Method Invocation: Distributed Computing for Java. Sun Microsystems Inc., July 2002. `http://java.sun.com/marketing/collateral/javarmi.html`.

Niranjan Suri, Jeffrey M. Bradshaw, Maggie R. Breedy, Paul T. Groth, Gregory A. Hill, Renia Jeffers, and Timothy S. Mitrovich. An Overview of the NOMADS Mobile Agent Systems. In *6th ECOOP Workshop on Mobile Object Systems: Operating System Support, Security and Programming Languages, Sophia Antipolis (France), June 2000*, 2000. Paper is only available online at `cui.unige.ch/~ecoopws/ws00`.

Hock Kim Tan and Luc Moreau. Extending Execution Tracing for Mobile Code Security. In Klaus Fischer and Dieter Hutter, editors, *Second International Workshop on Security of Mobile MultiAgent Systems (SEMAS '2002), Bologna (Italy), June 2002*, DFKI Research Report, RR-02-03, pages 51–59. DFKI Saarbrucken, 2002. URL `http://www.ecs.soton.ac.uk/~lavm/papers/semas02.ps.gz`.

Andrew S. Tanenbaum. *Modern Operating Systems*. Prentice-Hall, 2nd edition, 2001.

Éric Tanter, Michael Vernaillen, and José Piquer. Towards transparent adaption of migration policies. In *8th ECOOP Workshop on Mobile Object Systems: Agent Applications and New Frontiers, Malaga (Spain), June 2002*, 2002. Paper is only available online at `cui.unige.ch/~ecoopws/ws02/`.

Joseph Tardo and Luis Valente. Mobile agent security and Telescript. In *Proceedings of 41st IEEE International Computer Conference (COMPCON '96): Technologies for the Information Highway, Santa Clara CA (USA), February 1996*, pages 58–63. IEEE Computer Society Press, 1996.

Prasannaa Thati, Po-Hao Chang, and Gul Agha. Crawlets: Agents for high performance web search engine. In Gian Pietro Picco, editor, *Mobile Agents, Proceedings of the 5th International Conference (MA 2001), Atlanta (USA), December 2001*, volume 2240 of *Lecture Notes in Computer Science*, pages 119–134. Springer-Verlag, 2001.

Wolfgang Theilmann and Kurt Rothermel. Disseminating mobile agents for distributed information filtering. In Dejan S. Milojicic, editor, *Proceedings of the First International Symposium on Agent Systems and Applications (ASA '99)/Third International Symposium on Mobile Agents (MA '99), Palm Springs (USA), October 1999*, pages 152–161. IEEE Computer Society Press, 1999.

Tommy Thorn. Programming languages for mobile code. *ACM Computing Surveys*, 29(3):213–239, 1997.

Takeshi Umezawa, Ichiro Satoh, and Yuichiro Anzai. A mobile agent-based frameworld for configurable sensor networks. In Ahmed Karmouch, Thomas Magedanz, and Jaime Delgado, editors, *Proceedings of the 4th International Workshop on Mobile Agents for Telecommunication Applications (MATA 2002), Barcelona (Spain), October 2002*, volume 2521 of *Lecture Notes in Computer Science*, pages 128–139. Springer-Verlag, 2002.

Giovanni Vigna. *Mobile Code Technologies, Paradigms, and Applications*. PhD thesis, Politecnico di Milano (Italy), February 1998.

Alex Villazon and Walter Binder. Portable Resource Reification in Java-Based Mobile Agent Systems. In Gian Pietro Picco, editor, *Mobile Agents, Proceedings of the 5th International Conference (MA 2001), Atlanta (USA), December 2001*, volume 2240 of *Lecture Notes in Computer Science*, pages 213–228. Springer-Verlag, 2001.

Larry Wall, Tom Christiansen, and Jon Orwant. *Programming Perl*. O'Reilly Associates, Inc., 3rd edition, 2000.

Tim Walsh, Paddy Nixon, and Simon Dobson. As strong as possible mobility: An architecture for stateful object migration on the Internet. In *6th ECOOP Workshop on Mobile Object Systems: Operating System Support, Security and Programming Languages, Sophia Antipolis (France), June 2000*, 2000. Paper is only available online at `cui.unige.ch/~ecoopws/ws00`.

Xiaojin Wang, Jason Hallstrom, and Gerald Baumgartner. Reliability Through Strong Mobility. In *7th ECOOP Workshop on Mobile Object Systems: Development of Robust and High Confidence Agent Applications, Budapest (Hungary), June 2001*, 2001. Paper is only available online `http://cui.unige.ch/~ecoopws`.

Gerhard Weiss, editor. *Multiagent Systems: A Modern Approach to Distributed Artifical Intelligence*. MIT Press, 2000.

James E. White. Mobile agents. In Bradshaw [1996], pages 437–472.

James E. White, C. S. Helgeson, and D. A. Steedman. System and method for distributed computation based upon the movement, execution, and interaction of processes in a network. US Patent 5.603.031, 1997.

Uwe G. Wilhelm, Levente Buttyán, and Sebastian Staamann. Protecting the itinerary of mobile agents. In Serge Demeyer and Jan Bosch, editors, *Proceedings of the 4th ECOOP Workshop on Mobile Object Systems: Secure Internet Mobile Computation, Brussels (Belgium), July 1998*, volume 1543 of *Lecture Notes in Computer Science*, page 301. Springer-Verlag, 1998.

Pawel Wojciechowski. Algorithms for location-independent communication between mobile agents. Technical report, Département Systèmes de Communication, Ecole Polytechnique Fédérale de Lausanne, 2001.

Pawel Wojciechowski and Peter Sewell. Nomadic Pict: Language and Infrastructure Design for Mobile Agents. In Dejan S. Milojicic, editor, *Proceedings of the First International Symposium on Agent Systems and Applications (ASA '99)/Third International Symposium on Mobile Agents (MA '99), Palm Springs (USA), October 1999,* pages 2–12. IEEE Computer Society Press, 1999.

Pawel Wojciechowski and Peter Sewell. Nomadic Pict: Language and Infrastructure Design for Mobile Agents. *IEEE Concurrency,* 8(2):42–52, 2000.

David Wong, Noemi Paciorek, and Dana Moore. Java-based Mobile Agents. *Communications of the ACM,* 42(3):92–105, March 1998.

Michael Wooldridge and Nicholas R. Jennings. Agent theories, architectures, and languages: A survey. In Michael J. Wooldridge and Nicholas R. Jennings, editors, *Intelligent Agents: ECAI-94 Workshop on Agent Theories, Architectures, and Languages, Amsterdam (The Netherlands), August 1994,* volume 890 of *Lecture Notes in Computer Science,* pages 1–39. Springer-Verlag, 1995a.

Michael Wooldridge and Nicholas R. Jennings. Intelligent agents: Theory and practice. *The Knowledge Engineering Review,* 10(2):115–152, 1995b.

Bennet S. Yee. A sanctuary for mobile agents. In Jan Vitek and Christian D. Jensen, editors, *Internet Programming—Security Issues for Mobile and Distributed Objects,* volume 1603 of *Lecture Notes in Computer Science,* pages 261–274. Springer-Verlag, 1999.

Adam Young and Moti Yung. Sliding encryption: A cryptographic tool for mobile agents. In Eli Biham, editor, *Proceedings of the 4th International Workshop on Fast Software Encryption (FSE '97), Haifa (Israel), January 1997,* volume 1267 of *Lecture Notes in Computer Science,* pages 230–241. Springer-Verlag, 1997.

J. Zander and R. Forchheimer. Softnet—an approach to high level packet communication. In *Proceedings of the Second ARRL Amateur Radio Computer Networking Conference, San Francisco (USA), March 1983,* 1983.

Michael Zapf and Kurt Geihs. What Type Is It? A Type System For Mobile Agents. In Robert Trappl, editor, *Proceedings of Second International Symposium* From Agent Theory to Agent Implementation *(AT2AI-2) at the 15th European Meeting on Cybernetics and Systems Research (EMCSR 2000), Vienna (Austria), April 2000.* Austrian Society for Cybernetic Studies, 2000.

Index

Printed and bound by CPI Group (UK) Ltd, Croydon, CR0 4YY

03/10/2024

01040339-0010